# Object-Oriented Analysis, Design and Implementation

*An Integrated Approach*

**Third Edition**

**Brahma Dathan**
Professor Emeritus,
Computer Science Department,
Metropolitan State University, Minnesota, USA

**Sarnath Ramnath**
Professor,
Computer Science and Information Technology Department,
St. Cloud State University, Minnesota, USA

All rights reserved. No part of this book may be (i) modified, reproduced or utilised in any form, or by any means, electronic or mechanical, including photocopying, recording or by any information storage and retrieval system, in any form of binding or cover other than in which it is published, without permission in writing from the publisher; or (ii) used or reproduced in any manner for the purpose of training, development or operation of artificial intelligence (AI) technologies and systems, including generative AI technologies, without permission in writing from the copyright holder.

**OBJECT-ORIENTED ANALYSIS, DESIGN AND IMPLEMENTATION: AN INTEGRATED APPROACH, THIRD EDITION**

**UNIVERSITIES PRESS (INDIA) PRIVATE LIMITED**

*Registered Office*
3-6-747/1/A & 3-6-754/1, Himayatnagar, Hyderabad 500 029, Telangana, India
info@universitiespress.com; www.universitiespress.com

*Distributed by*
Orient Blackswan Private Limited

*Registered Office*
3-6-752 Himayatnagar, Hyderabad 500 029, Telangana, India

*Other Offices*
Bengaluru / Chennai / Guwahati / Hyderabad
Kolkata / Mumbai / New Delhi / Noida / Patna

© Universities Press (India) Private Limited 2010, 2014, 2025
First Edition published 2010
Reprinted 2012
Second Edition published 2014
Reprinted 2016, 2018 (twice) and 2022
Third Edition published 2025
Reprinted 2026

*Cover and book design*
© Universities Press (India) Private Limited 2010, 2014, 2025

ISBN: 978-93-93330-76-5

This edition is for sale only in India, Pakistan, Bhutan, Bangladesh, Sri Lanka, Nepal, The Maldives, Middle East, Malaysia, Indonesia and Singapore.

Customers from the rest of the world, please order the print book from Springer Nature Switzerland AG. ISBN: 978-3-031-71239-5

502331

*Typeset in* NimbusRom 10 pt by 12 pt *by*
Mohan Boda, Hyderabad

*Printed in India by*
Ashwin Printing Agency

*Published by*
Universities Press (India) Private Limited
3-6-747/1/A & 3-6-754/1, Himayatnagar, Hyderabad 500 029, Telangana, India

Care has been taken to confirm the accuracy of the information presented in this book. The authors and the publisher, however, cannot accept any responsibility for errors or omissions or for consequences from application of the information in this book, and make no warranty, express or implied, with respect to its contents.

# Preface to the Third Edition

Ten years have passed since our last edition, and a lot has changed in this time. Computer science curricula have changed, a new version of Java has become available, new ideas about teaching and learning have been explored, changes have taken place in the way that object-oriented principles are put into practice, and we have got useful feedback from other instructors, and discovered ways of integrating new and relevant concepts into our case studies. The most important change of all, however, is what we have learned from our students through numerous iterations of our course.

The third edition incorporates our response to all these changes, while maintaining the basic structure of using student project experiences. As university curricula and student experiences change, so too does the background of students entering this course. To accommodate this variability, all expected background materials have now been placed in one chapter (Chapter 2).

The goal of all education is to effect a transformation in the learner's perspective. We noticed from earlier offerings of the course that a signficant percentage of students were failing to grasp the importance of the analysis and design phases, and their role in appropriately modeling the software system. Data from research into student learning also indicates that appreciation of abstract concepts is a significant threshold for students. Based on all this, we decided to place a special emphasis on the processes used for creating models. We added a new chapter (Chapter 3) as a comprehensive introduction to modeling, focusing on the role of the UML language in the software construction process. The central role of modeling has been emphasized again through the next two chapters on analysis and design.

The need to embed security at all stages of development of computing systems has become increasingly obvious. Accordingly, securing the software is considered in the design and implementation phases. We are also underscoring the importance of identifying and correcting poor designs at the outset: recognition of bad smells and applying refactoring has been built into the design phase. To highlight the Java language changes with the new version, we have provided both Swing and FX implementations of case studies, where appropriate.

The ability to reuse software is one of the main advantages of the object-oriented approach. To ensure that students recognize this, we have dedicated an entire chapter to presenting the principles involved in software reuse, and also connected these to the SOLID principles of class design. The role of substitutability deserves special attention in this context. We have recognized this as a "threshold" concept, and in accordance with best practices, presented the concept at various levels. The basic ideas are presented in the chapter on reuse, and more advanced concepts have been presented in a later chapter. All of this has been done through examples that make the concept accessible to students.

Choosing the right model for a given set of requirements is something we have seen students struggle with, especially in the context of choosing between finite state machine and use case models. We developed an innovative intermediate stage, where the syntactic struture of well-written requirements would naturally guide students to the right model.

As with the previous editions, our students have been patient partners in the refining of these methods, and we hope that all our efforts will help provide a better experience for students.

**Brahma Dathan**
**Sarnath Ramnath**

# Contents

*To our former students and readers for their feedback and encouragement, and to our future readers, to help them build a solid foundation in the principles of object-oriented development*

# Chapter 1
# Introduction

The object-oriented paradigm is currently the most popular way of analyzing, designing, and developing application systems, especially large ones. To obtain an understanding of this paradigm, we could begin by asking: *What exactly does the phrase "object-oriented" mean?* Looking at it quite literally, labeling something as "object-oriented" implies that objects play a central role, and we elaborate this further as *a perspective that views the elements of a given situation by decomposition into objects and object relationships.* In a broad sense, this idea could apply to any setting, and examples of its application can, in fact, be found in business, chemistry, engineering, and even philosophy. Our business is with creating software and therefore this book concentrates on the object-oriented analysis, design, and implementation of software systems. Our situations are therefore problems that are amenable to software solutions, and the software systems that are created in response to these problems.

Designing is a complex activity in any context, simply because there are competing interests and we have to make critical choices at each step with incomplete information. As a result, decisions are often made using some combination of rules of thumb and past experience. Software design is no exception to this, and in the process of designing a system, there are several points where such decisions have to be made. As a field of study matures, the collective wisdom of its practitioners shapes these thumb rules, and the forces active in the field of software development have slowly but surely been moving us in the direction of object-orientation. Making informed choices in any field of activity often requires an understanding of the underlying philosophy and the forces that have shaped it. It is therefore appropriate to start our study of object-oriented software analysis and design by outlining the philosophy, its development and where things stand at the present time. Throughout the case studies used in this text, the reader will find examples of how our guiding philosophy is helping us make choices at all stages.

This chapter, therefore, intends to give the reader a broad introduction to the complex topic of object-oriented software development. We start by defining the notion of object-orientation, the circumstances that motivated its development, and why it came to be the desired approach for software development. In the course of this discussion, we present the central concepts that characterize the methodology, how this development has influenced our view of software, and some of its pros and cons. We conclude by presenting a brief history of the evolution of object-oriented languages and object-oriented programming.

## 1.1 What is the Object-Oriented Paradigm?

The traditional view of a computer program is that of a process that has been encoded in a form that can be executed by a computer. This view originated from the fact that the first computers were developed mainly to automate a well-defined process (that is, an algorithm) for numerical computation, and dates back to the first stored-program computers. Accordingly, the software creation process was seen as a translation from a description in some "natural" language, to a sequence of operations that could be executed on the computer. This view works well to introduce the concept of programming, but is inadequate when we are faced with the task of constructing a complex piece of software. The way we manage this complexity is to view the software as consisting of several modules.

There are two widely accepted ways of decomposing the software into a collection of modules:

- The "process-centered" approach
- The "data-centered" or the object-oriented approach

The process-centered approach to software development used what is called *top-down functional decomposition.* The first step in such a design was to recognize what the process had to deliver (in terms of input and output of the program) which was followed by decomposition of the process into a *main module* and several *functional sub-modules.* Structures to store data were defined and the computation was carried out by invoking the sub-modules, each of which performed some computation on the stored data elements. It is important to note that the essential primary data components were all defined in a main module, and these were kept separate from the process. Whenever any of the functional sub-modules was invoked, the relevant data modules were passed as parameters.

In the data-centered approach, the important task was to identify the important data abstractions. Instead of thinking about the data elements to be passed as parameters to a sub-process, we think of the principal data abstraction associated with the sub-process. This data abstraction contains the associated data component, and the sub-process then becomes a method invoked on the abstraction. Consequently, the data component is no longer passed as a parameter.

Looking at these two approaches in this way, there does not appear to be much difference between them. The picture changes, as we shall see, when we consider the cost element.

### 1.1.1 What Makes the Object-Oriented Approach Preferable?

As we started using software in many applications, the cost of developing the software became a factor. The only answer seemed to be to create software that could be **reused.** Reuse has two dimensions: **extensibility** and **modifiability**. Extensibility occurs when the system is designed to allow the addition of new functionalities. The idea was apparently first introduced into software development in 1988 by Bertrand Meyer, when he stated the **Open-Closed Principle**:

"Software must be open for extension but closed for implementation."

In his original writing, he suggested that this would take place by direct inheritance, but the idea has since evolved in other ways. Modifiability is a broader concept, which has sometimes been defined as the system's receptiveness to change. If a change involves modifying several modules, then the cost of incorporating the change goes up. When modules are closedly tied to each other, changing one module results in changes to the others, which in turn increases the cost of change. The object-oriented approach, as we shall see, enables **loosely coupled** modules.

Integral to the concept of reuse is the idea of a reusable solution to a commonly occurring problem. The idea of reusing solutions (aka "patterns") in urban architecture was suggested by Christopher Alexander in 1977, and was proposed as an aid to designing cities. In 1987, Kent Beck and Ward Cunningham proposed the idea of applying patterns to enable reuse in object-oriented software. Once these ideas were established, it became apparent that the object-oriented (that is, data-centered) approach to partitioning software into modules was, in fact, superior.

### 1.1.2 Object-Oriented Software Development

The overall philosophy of object-orientation is to define the software system as a collection of objects of various types that interact with each other through well-defined interfaces. A software object can be designed to handle multiple functions and can therefore participate in several processes. A software component is also capable of storing data, which adds another dimension of complexity to the process. The manner in which all of this has departed from the traditional process-oriented view is that instead of implementing an entire process end-to-end and defining the required data structures along the way, we first analyze the entire set of processes and from this identify the necessary software components. Each component represents a data abstraction and is designed to store information along with procedures to manipulate the same. The execution of the original processes is then broken down into several steps, each of which can be logically assigned to one of the software components. The components can also communicate with each other, as needed, to complete the process.

It is interesting to draw some parallels with the process used for designing simple electromechanical systems. For several decades now, it has been fairly easy for people with limited knowledge of engineering principles to design and put together simple systems in their backyards and garages. So much so, it has become a hobby that even a 10-year-old could pursue. The reasons for this success are easy to see: *easily understandable designs, similar (standard) solutions for a host of problems, an easily accessible and well-defined "library" of "building-blocks", interchangeability of components across systems,* and so on. Some of the pioneers in the field of software design began to ask whether we could not also design software using such "off-the-shelf" components. The object-oriented paradigm, one could argue, has really evolved in response to these needs. There are, of course, several differences with the hardware design process (inevitable, because the nature of software is fundamentally different from the nature of hardware), but parallels can be drawn between many of these defining characteristics of hardware design and what today's advocates of good software design recommend. This methodology, as we shall see in the chapters to follow, provides us with a step-by-step process for software design, a language to specify the output from each step of the process so that we can transition smoothly from one stage to the next, the ability to reuse earlier designs, standard solutions that adhere to well-reasoned design principles, and even the ability to incrementally fix a poor design without breaking the system.

## 1.2 Key Concepts of Object-Oriented Design

During the development of this paradigm, as one would expect, several ideas and approaches were tried and discarded. Over the years, the field has stabilized so that we can safely present the key ideas whose soundness has stood the test of time.

**The Central Role of Objects:** Object-orientation, as the name implies, makes objects the centerpiece of software design. The design of earlier systems was centered around processes which were susceptible to change, and when this change came about, very little of the old system was "re-usable". The notion of an object is centered around a piece of data and the operations (or **methods**) that can be used to modify it. This makes possible the creation of an abstraction that is very stable since it is not dependent on the changing requirements of the application. The execution of each process relies heavily on the objects to store the data and provide the necessary operations; with some additional work, the entire system is "assembled" from the objects.

**The Notion of a Class:** Classes allow the software designer to look at the objects as different types of entities. Viewing objects in this way allows us to use the mechanisms of classification to categorize these types, define hierarchies, and engage with the ideas of specialization and generalization of objects.

**Abstract Specification of Functionality:** In the course of the design process, the software engineer specifies the properties of the objects (and by implication, the classes) that are required by the system. This specification is abstract, in that it does not place any restrictions on how the functionality is achieved. This specification, called an **interface** or an **abstract class**, is like a *contract* for the implementer and also facilitates formal verification of the entire system.

**A Language to Define the System:** The **Unified Modeling Language (UML)** has been chosen by consensus as the standard tool for describing the end products of the design activities. The documents generated in this language can be universally understood and are thus analogous to the "blueprints" used in other engineering disciplines.

**Standard Solutions:** The existence of an object structure facilitates the documenting of standard solutions, called **design patterns**. Standard solutions are found at all stages of software development, but design patterns are perhaps the most common form of reuse of solutions.

**An Analysis Process to Model a System:** Object-orientation provides us with a systematic way to translate a functional specification to a *conceptual design*. This design describes the system in terms of *conceptual classes*, from which the subsequent steps of the development process generate the *implementation classes* that constitute the finished software.

**The Notions of Flexibility and Adaptability:** Software has flexibility that is not typically found in hardware, and this allows us to modify existing entities in small ways to create new ones. **Inheritance**, which creates a new *descendant class* that modifies the features of an existing (*ancestor*) class, and

**Composition**, which uses objects belonging to existing classes as elements to constitute a new class, are mechanisms that enable such modifications with classes and objects.

## 1.3 Other Related Concepts

As the object-oriented methodology developed, the science of software design progressed too, and several desirable software properties were identified. Not central enough to be called object-oriented concepts, these ideas are nonetheless closely linked to them and were perhaps better understood because of these developments

### 1.3.1 Modular Design and Encapsulation

**Modularity** refers to the idea of putting together a large system by developing a number of distinct components independently and then integrating these to provide the required functionality. This approach, when used properly, usually makes the individual modules relatively simple and thus easier to understand than the system that is designed as a monolithic structure; in other words, the design must be *modular.* The system's functionality must be provided by a number of well-designed, cooperating modules. Each module must obviously provide certain functionality that is clearly specified by an interface. The interface also defines how other components may interact or communicate with the module.

We would like that a module clearly specify what it does, but not expose its implementation. This separation of concerns gives rise to the notion of **encapsulation**, which means that the module hides details of its implementation from external agents. The **abstract data type (ADT)**, the generalization of primitive data types such as integers and characters, is an example of applying encapsulation. The programmer specifies the collection of operations on the data type and the data structures that are needed for data storage. Users of the ADT perform the operations without concerning themselves with the implementation.

### 1.3.2 Cohesion and Coupling

Each module provides certain functionality; the **cohesion** of a module tells us how well the entities within a module work together to provide this functionality. Cohesion is a measure of how focused the responsibilities of a module are. If the responsibilities of a module are unrelated or varied and use different sets of data, cohesion is reduced. Highly cohesive modules tend to be more reliable, reusable, and understandable than less cohesive ones. To increase cohesion, we would like that all its constituents contribute to some well-defined responsibility of the module. This may be quite a challenging task. In contrast, the worst approach would be to arbitrarily assign entities to modules, resulting in a module whose constituents have no obvious relationship.

**Coupling** refers to how dependent modules are on each other. The very fact that we split a program into multiple modules introduces some coupling into the system. Coupling could result because of several factors: a module may refer to variables defined in another module or it may call the methods of another module and use the return values. The amount of coupling between modules can vary. In general, if modules do not depend on each others' implementation, that is, modules depend only on the published interfaces of other modules and not on their internals, we say that the coupling is *low*. In such cases, changes in one module will not necessitate changes in other modules as long as the interfaces themselves do not change. Low coupling allows us to modify a module without worrying about the ramifications of the changes on the rest of the system. By contrast, *high* coupling means that changes in one module would necessitate changes in other modules, which may have a domino effect and also make it harder to understand the code.

### 1.3.3 Modifiability and Testability

A software component, unlike its hardware counterpart, can be easily modified in small ways. This modification can be carried out to change both *functionality* and *design*. The ability to change the functionality of a component allows for systems to be more **adaptable**; the advances in object-orientation have set higher standards for adaptability. Improving the design through incremental change is accomplished by **refactoring**, again a concept that owes its origin to the development of the object-oriented approach. There is some risk associated with activities of both kinds; and in both cases, the organization of the system in terms of objects and classes has helped develop systematic procedures that mitigate the risk.

The **testability** of a concept, in general, refers to both *falsifiability*, that is, the ease with which we can find counterexamples, and the *practical feasibility* of reproducing such counterexamples. In the context of software systems, it can simply be stated as the ease with which we can find the bugs in our software and the extent to which the structure of the system facilitates the detection of bugs. Several concepts in software testing (for example, the idea of *unit testing*) owe their prominence to concepts that came out of the development of the object-oriented paradigm.

### 1.3.4 Code Security

Computer software pervades a large part of society, and attempts to make a quick profit by exploiting software flaws have become commonplace. Code that may look harmless at first glance could often be exploited by wily hackers to retrieve and/or modify unauthorized information, reduce data availability, etc. Researchers and practitioners have identified some standard sources of such vulnerabilities. Avoiding these vulnerabilities often requires an approach that encompasses sound hardware and software architecture, use of safe programming languages, robust application design, and employment of appropriate programming practices.

In this book, we will identify a number of instances of pitfalls in application design and implementation and discuss ways to avoid them. **Secure coding** is the employment of proper coding practices to minimize or even eliminate software vulnerabilities. Although we discuss secure coding with respect to Java, the approaches in most cases are also applicable to other programming languages.

## 1.4 Benefits of the Paradigm

From a practical standpoint, it is useful to examine how object-oriented methodology has modified the landscape of software development. As with any development, we do have pros and cons. The advantages listed below are largely consequences of the ideas presented in the previous sections.

- Objects often reflect entities in application systems. This makes it easier for a designer to come up with the classes and the design. In a process-oriented design, it is much harder to find such a connection that can simplify the initial design.
- Object-orientation helps increase productivity through reuse of existing software. Inheritance makes it relatively easy to extend and modify the functionality provided by a class. Language designers often supply extensive libraries that users can extend.

- It is easier to accommodate changes. One of the difficulties with application development is changing requirements. With some care taken during design, it is possible to isolate the varying parts of a system into classes.
- The ability to isolate changes, encapsulate data, and employ modularity reduces the risks involved in system development.

## 1.5 Dealing with Drawbacks of the Paradigm

The above advantages do not come without a price tag. Let us examine each of these in turn and understand how they can, or are being, ameliorated.

### 1.5.1 Reduced Performance

Reduced performance is sometimes touted as one casualty of employing the object-oriented paradigm. It is true that modern applications tend to feature a large number of objects that interact with each other in complex ways and at the same time support a visual user interface. For example, a banking application might have numerous accounts or a video game could have a large number of items and characters. Objects also tend to have complex associations, which can result in *non-locality*, leading to poor memory access times. In addition, object creation and destruction are expensive. Most object-oriented systems run on separate virtual machines, a fact that adds a separate overhead. While addressing these issues is beyond the scope of this book, we do note that faster processors, parallelism, and techniques like inlining of method invocations, compiler directives, and suitable run-time optimizations have resulted in improved performance. So, inefficiency is not always a serious concern in modern object-oriented systems.

### 1.5.2 Complexity of the System

Object-oriented systems can easily have hundreds of classes. The ability of a developer to effectively reuse the code to make changes to the software can be handicapped by the complexity of the system. Fortunately, this can be addressed with some effort. Using the right approach, a developer can be taught how to recognize the architecture, the data abstractions, and the various patterns employed. Developers also need to master how to document these aspects of the software, using the most appropriate diagrams from the modeling language. It is also important that this process use the recommended best practices (like the SOLID principles) throughout the construction process.

### 1.5.3 Learning the Object-Oriented Paradigm

Programmers and designers schooled in other paradigms, usually in the imperative paradigm, find it difficult to learn and use object-oriented principles. Fortunately, using the right approach (as we have attempted in this text), it is possible overcome this handicap. The imperative view is that a program is a process. The process can be built using sub-processes, and the data is available on demand to the sub-process executing currently. The object-oriented approach is built on data abstractions, and this distinction needs to be brought home.

For someone new to this paradigm, it is tempting to see a program as a process. This gives rise to a tendency to "write a program" without paying sufficient attention to the question: *what data abstractions do I need to define?* A newcomer might also fail to see the connection between the task of defining the data abstraction and that of constructing a program that performs a certain process.

Our approach is therefore to address this by incorporating appropriate ideas of software analysis and software design, and integrating them into the object-oriented software construction process. This allows us to emphasize the importance of recognizing and defining the data abstractions. We hope that such an integrated experience will give the students more confidence in the paradigm and help them fight the temptation to "code first and think later".

Another challenge a student faces is the large number of library classes that are part of modern object-oriented languages. It is difficult to develop even medium-sized applications in any language without learning a number of library classes. While the availability of such libraries speeds up application construction, a newcomer could easily be intimidated by the challenge of understanding the structure. Online documentation in the form of tutorials, codelabs, and workshops has ameliorated this task.

## 1.6 History

The history of the object-oriented programming approach could be traced to the idea of ADTs and the concept of objects in the Simula 67 programming language, which was developed in the 1960s for performing simulations. The first true object-oriented programming language that appeared before the larger software development community was Smalltalk in 1980, developed at Xerox PARC. Smalltalk used objects and messages as the basis for computation. Classes could be created and modified dynamically. Most of the vocabulary in the object-oriented paradigm originated from this language.

Toward the end of the 1970s, Bjarne Stroustrup, who was doing doctoral work in England, needed a language for creating simulations of distributed systems. He developed a language based on the class concept in Simula 67, but this language was not particularly efficient. However, he persisted in his attempt and developed an object-oriented language at Bell Laboratories as a derivative of C, which would blossom into one of the most successful programming languages, C++. The language was standardized in 1997 by the American National Standards Institute (ANSI).

The 1980s saw the development of several other languages such as Object Lisp, CommonLoops, Common Lisp Object System (CLOS), and Eiffel. The rising popularity of the object-oriented model also propelled changes in the language Ada, originally sponsored by the U.S. Department of Defense in 1983. This resulted in Ada 9X, an extension to Ada 83 with object-oriented concepts including inheritance, polymorphism, and dynamic binding.

The 1990s saw two major events. One was the development of the Java programming language in 1996. Java appeared to be a derivative of C++, but many of the controversial and troublesome concepts in C++ were deleted. Although it was a relatively simple language when it was originally proposed, Java has undergone substantial additions in later versions, making it a moderately difficult language. Java also comes with an impressive collection of libraries (called packages) to support application development. A second watershed event was the publication of the book *Design Patterns* by Gamma et al. in 1994. The book considered specific design questions (23 of them) and provided general approaches to solving them using object-oriented constructs. The book (as also the approach it advocated) was a huge success as both practitioners and academicians soon recognized its significance.

The last few years have seen the acceptance of some dynamic object-oriented languages that were developed in the 1990s. Dynamic languages allow users more flexibility; for example, the ability to dynamically add a method to an object at execution time.

## 1.7 Discussion and Further Reading

In this chapter, we have given an introduction to the object-oriented paradigm. The central object-oriented concepts such as classes, objects, and interfaces will be elaborated in the next chapter. Cohesion and coupling, which are major software design issues, will be recurring themes for most of the text.

The reader would be well-advised to learn or refresh the non–object-oriented concepts of the Java language by reading the Appendix before moving on to the next chapter. It is worthwhile and enjoyable to read a short history of programming languages from a standard text on the subject such as Sebesta [1]. The reader may also find it helpful to get the perspectives of the designers of object-oriented languages (such as the one given on C++ by Stroustrup [2]).

## Projects

1. Download the Java development kit onto your computer and install an IDE. After learning how to use the IDE, write programs in Java to perform the following:

   Read a sequence of strings from the keyboard and store them in an array. Then print the strings in the reverse order they were input.

## Exercises

1. Identify two major players who would have a stake in the software development process. What are some of the concerns of each? How would they benefit from the object-oriented model?
2. Think of some common businesses and examine what characteristics their systems might share at a very broad level.
3. How does the object-oriented model support the notion of ADTs and encapsulation?
4. Consider an application that you are familiar with, such as a university system. Divide the entities of this application into groups, thus identifying the classes. Come up with at least five classes.
5. In Question 4, suppose we put all the code (corresponding to all of the classes) into one single class. What happens to cohesion?
6. What are the benefits of learning design patterns?
7. Consider the following approach to storing information about a set of employees. What are some of the drawbacks? What would you like to do to overcome the drawbacks?

```
int[] employeeId = int[10];
string[] employeeName = string[10];
string[] employeePhone = string[10];
float[] employeeSalary = float[10];
```

## References

1. Sebesta, RW. 2007. *Concepts of Programming Languages, Eighth Edition*. Addison-Wesley Publishing Company: Boston, MA, USA.

2. Stroustrup, B. 1994. *The Design and Evolution of C++*. Addison-Wesley Publishing Company: New York, NY, USA.

# Chapter 2

# Basics of Object-Oriented Programming

In the last chapter, we saw that the fundamental program structure in an object-oriented program is the object. We also outlined the concept of a class, which is used to define a new type, enabling a programmer to create objects of types that are not directly supported by the language.

In this chapter, we describe the basic process of object-oriented programming. We use the programming language Java (as we will do throughout the book). We begin with the basic processes associated with defining classes, and how these classes can be used in an application. Next, we look at how to create relationships between the classes and use them. We are all familiar with data structures and how they are created; in the object-oriented world, data structures are objects. To illustrate this, we create and employ a collection class.

To build reusable programs, it is very important that we have the ability to separate the abstraction from the implementation. Object-oriented programs enable this through interfaces and abstract classes; we discuss and present illustrative examples for these concepts. Run-time errors in object-oriented programs are managed through exceptions, which are defined by classes and used as objects. We then introduce the concept of a hierarchy of classes, related through the idea of inheritance. Closely associated with inheritance are the concepts of polymorphism and dynamic binding, which enable the programmer to exploit the hierarchical class structure defined by inheritance.

The power of any language is enhanced through idioms and metaphors. Design patterns are the idioms of object-oriented design that document standard solutions to commonly arising problems. Each pattern is typically named such that it draws on the English meaning of the word to identify its applicability, thereby serving as a metaphor. In this chapter, we introduce the concept of design patterns through the Iterator pattern, which solves the problem of accessing the items in a data structure without knowledge of the structure, and finds application in creating iterative (looping) code. Object-oriented languages usually provide support for genericity and run-time type identification; we introduce Java language features that enable us to specify generic classes and identify the type of objects at run-time. Finally we look at the role played by Java's `Object` class, which brings all the classes under one big hierarchy.

## 2.1 The Basics

To understand the notion of objects and classes, we start with an analogy. When a car manufacturer decides to build a new car, it has to expend considerable effort before the first car can be rolled out of the assembly lines. For instance:

- The user community that will buy the car has to be identified and the user's needs have to be assessed. For this, the manufacturer may form a team.
- After assessing the requirements, the team may be expanded to include automobile engineers and other specialists who come up with a preliminary design.
- A variety of methods may be used to assess and refine the initial design: the team may have experience in building a similar vehicle; prototypes may be built; and simulations and mathematical analysis may be performed.

Perhaps after months of such activity, the design process is completed. Another step that needs to be performed is the building of the plant where the car will be produced. The assembly line has to be set up, and people need to be hired.

After such steps, the company is ready to produce cars. The design is now reused many times in the manufacturing process. Of course, the design may have to be fine-tuned during the process based on the company's observations and user feedback.

The development of software systems often follows a similar pattern. User needs must be assessed, a design must be completed, and then the product must be built.

From the standpoint of object-oriented systems, a different aspect of the car manufacturing process is important. The design of a certain type of car will call for specific types of engine, transmission, brake system, and so on, and each of these parts in itself has its own design ("blueprint"), production plants, etc. In other words, the company follows the same philosophy in the manufacture of the individual parts as it does in the production of the car. Of course, some parts may be bought from manufacturers, but they in turn follow the same approach. Since the design activity is costly, a manufacturer might reuse or adapt earlier designs, for the car as well as the parts.

The above approach can be compared with the design of object-oriented systems, which are composed of many objects that interact with each other. Often these objects represent real-life players and their interactions represent real-life interactions. Just like the design of a car, the design of an object-oriented system consists of designs of its constituent parts and the design of their interactions.

For instance, a banking system could have a set of objects that represent customers, another set of objects that stand for checking accounts, and a third set of objects that correspond to loans. An object is thus a program entity that often represents a real-life object.

Every object has a set of **properties** or **attributes** attached to it. The attribute or property of an object is a part of an object and it serves to partly describe the object and holds some value that is required in some interaction of the object with the rest of the system. For example, a customer object may have properties or attributes such as name, address, phone number, etc. The values of all the properties of an object constitute the **state** of the object.

For every object, the system maintains a value for each of its attributes, thereby maintaining its state. For example, all customers may have the attributes name, phone number, and address. For a specific customer, the values associated with these attributes may be "Tom", "123-4567", and "1 Main Street". These three values together form the state of the object.

Also associated with an object is its **behavior**, which is the set of actions that can be performed on or by an object. For example, one of the behaviors exhibited by a bank customer may be a deposit she makes to one of her checking accounts. When a customer actually makes a deposit into her checking account in real life, the system acts on the corresponding (software) account object to mimic the deposit in software. Another behavior may be that a customer takes out a loan; a new loan object is created and connected to the customer object. When a payment is made on the loan, the system acts on the corresponding (software) loan object.

The system must provide a way for the programmer to describe the properties and behavior of all objects. The class mechanism provides this support. A **class** is a template definition of the methods and variables needed for a particular kind of object. An object is a particular instance of a class.

Thus from an object-oriented point of view, a banking system should have classes representing customers, loans, and accounts. When a new customer enters the system, we should be able to create a new customer object in software. This software entity, the customer object, should have all of the relevant features of the real-life customer. For example, it should be possible to associate the name and address of the customer with this object; however, customer's attributes that are not relevant to the bank will not be represented in software either. As an example, it is difficult to imagine a bank being interested in whether a customer is right-handed; therefore, the software entity will not have this attribute either.

A class is a design that can be reused any number of times to create objects. For example, consider an object-oriented system for a university. There are student objects, instructor objects, staff member objects, and so on. Before such objects are created, we create classes that serve as templates (or blueprints) for students, instructors, staff members, and courses. The class for students is defined as follows:

```
public class Student {
  // code to implement a single student
}
```

Consider the first line of the above code, `public class Student {`. The first token, `public`, is a keyword that makes the corresponding class available throughout the file system. The second token, `class`, is a keyword that says that we are creating a class and that the following token is the name of the class. The third token, `Student`, is the name of the class.

The left curly bracket (`{`) signifies the beginning of the definition of the class. Following this are placed the details of the class, and the corresponding right curly bracket (`}`) ends the definition.

Proceeding in this fashion, we can create classes `Instructor`, `StaffMember` and `Course`.

```
public class Instructor {
  // code to implement a single instructor
}

public class StaffMember {
  // code to implement a single staff member
}

public class Course {
  // code to implement a single course
}
```

The above definitions are stubs that show how to create four classes, without giving any details. (In the finished system, the comments will be replaced by the details.)

New classes are defined in the above manner. The Java programming language has thousands of classes that are pre-defined, such as the `String` class. One way that a program can use a class is by creating objects that belong to that class. The process of creating an object is also called **instantiation.** Each class introduces a new type name. Thus `Student`, `Instructor`, `StaffMember`, and `Course` are types that we have introduced.

The following code instantiates a new object of type `Student`.

```
new Student();
```

The `new` operator causes the system to allocate an object of type `Student` with enough memory for storing information about one student. The operator returns the address of the location that contains this object. A variable that stores this address and can be used for accessing the object is called a **reference.**

The above statement may be executed when we have a new student admitted to the university.

Once we instantiate a new object, we must store its reference somewhere, so that we can use it later in some appropriate way. For this, we create a variable of type `Student`.

```
Student harry;
```

Notice that the above definition says that `harry` is a reference, a variable that can store addresses of objects of type `Student`. Thus, we can write

```
harry = new Student();
```

We cannot write

```
harry = new Instructor();
```

because `harry` is of type `Student`, which has no relationship (as far as the class declarations are concerned) to `Instructor`, which is the type of the object created on the right-hand side of the assignment.

Whenever we instantiate a new object, we must remember the reference to that object somewhere. When the program runs, it invokes various actions on the instantiated objects. The implementation of a class tell us what kind of actions can be performed by the objects of that class.

## 2.2 Implementing Classes

In this section, we discuss some of the basics of creating classes. Let us focus on the `Student` class that we initially coded as

```
public class Student {
  // code to implement a single student
}
```

We would certainly like the ability to store a name for the student: given a `Student` object, we should be able to specify that the student's name is `"Tom"` or "Jane", or, in general, some piece of text. The name is thus an attribute of Student, and we introduce a variable name of type String to store this attribute and later on access and modify it if and when needed. The code is embellished as follows:

```
public class Student {
   private String name; // field to remember the name
  // code for doing other things
}
```

A **field** is a variable defined directly within a class and which corresponds to an attribute. Every instance of the object will have storage for the field.

Next, we would like to assign a name to a student. The action, such as assigning a name, is an example of a behavior of the object. The Student object responds to the action by assigning the name to itself, that is, storing the name in the field name.

```
public class Student {
  private String name;
  public void setName(String studentName) {
    name = studentName;
  }
}
```

The code that we added is called a **method**. The method's name is setName. A method is like a procedure or function in imperative programming in that it is a unit of code that is not activated until it is invoked. Again, as in the case of procedures and functions, methods accept parameters. Each parameter states the type of the parameter expected. A method may return nothing (as is the case here) or return an object or a value of a primitive type. Here, we have put void in front of the method name, meaning that the method returns nothing. The left and right curly brackets begin and end the code that defines the method.

Unlike functions and procedures, methods are usually invoked through objects. The setName() method is defined within the class Student and is invoked on objects of type Student.

```
Student aStudent = new Student();
aStudent.setName("Ron");
```

The method setName() is invoked on that object referred to by aStudent. Intuitively, the code within that method must store the name somewhere. Remember that every object is allocated its own storage.

Let us examine the code within the method setName(). It takes one parameter, studentName, and assigns the value in that String object to the field name.

It is important to understand how Java uses the `name` field. Every object of type `Student` has a field called `name`. We invoked the method `setName()` on the object referred to by `aStudent`. Since `aStudent` has the field `name` and we invoked the method on `aStudent`, the reference to `name` within the method will act on the `name` field of `aStudent`.

The `setName()` method is an example of a **modifier** or a **setter**, that is, a method that modifies (or sets) the value of a field. If a program wants to access the data stored in a field, it would use an **accessor** or **getter** method. The `getName()` method accesses or gets the contents of the `name` field and returns it.

```
public String getName() {
  return name;
}
```

To illustrate this further, consider two objects of type `Student`.

```
Student student1 = new Student();
Student student2 = new Student();
student1.setName("John");
student2.setName("Mary");
System.out.println(student1.getName());
System.out.println(student2.getName());
```

Members (fields and methods for now) of a class can be accessed by writing

```
<object-reference>.<member-name>
```

The object referred to by `student1` has its `name` field set to `John`, whereas the object referred to by `student2` has its `name` field set to `Mary`. The field `name` in the code

```
name = studentName;
```

refers to different objects in different instantiations and thus different instances of fields.

Let us write a complete program using the above code.

```
public class Student {
   // code
   private String name;
   public void setName(String studentName) {
     name = studentName;
  }
  public String getName() {
    return name;
  }
```

```
  public static void main(String[] s) {
    Student student1 = new Student();
    Student student2 = new Student();
    student1.setName("John");
    student2.setName("Mary");
    System.out.println(student1.getName());
    System.out.println(student2.getName());
  }
}
```

The keyword `public` in front of the method `setName()` makes the method available wherever the object is available. But what about the keyword `private` in front of the field `name`? It signifies that this variable can be accessed only from code within the class `Student`. Since the line

```
name = studentName;
```

is within the class, the compiler allows it. However, if we write

```
Student someStudent = new Student();
someStudent.name = "Mary";
```

outside the class, the compiler will generate a syntax error.

As a general rule, fields are often defined with the `private` access specifier and methods are usually made `public`. The general idea is that fields denote the state of the object and the state can be changed only by interacting through pre-defined methods, which denote the behavior of the object. Usually, this helps preserve data integrity.

In the current example though, it is hard to argue that data integrity plays a role in making `name` private because all that the method `setName()` does is change the `name` field. However, if we wanted to perform some checks before actually changing a student's name (which should not happen that often), this gives us a way to do it.

For a more justified use of `private`, consider the grade point average (GPA) of a student. Clearly, we need to keep track of the GPA and need a field for it. GPA is not something that is changed arbitrarily: it changes when a student gets a grade for a course. So making it public could lead to integrity problems because the field can be inadvertently changed by bad code written outside. Thus, we code as follows:

```
public class Student {
    // fields to store the classes the student has taken
    private String name;
    private double gpa;
    public void setName(String studentName) {
        name = studentName;
```

```
    }
    public void addCourse(Course newCourse) {
       // code to store a ref to newCourse in the Student object.
    }
    private void computeGPA() {
       // code to access the stored courses, compute and set the
          gpa
    }
    public double getGPA() {
       return gpa;
    }
    public void assignGrade(Course aCourse, char newGrade) {
       // code to assign newGrade to aCourse
       computeGPA();
    }
}
```

We now write code to utilize the above idea.

```
Student aStudent = new Student();
Course aCourse = new Course();
aStudent.addCourse(aCourse);
aStudent.assignGrade(aCourse, 'B');
System.out.println(aStudent.getGPA());
```

The above code creates a `Student` object and a `Course` object. It calls the `addCourse()` method on the student, to add the course to the collection of courses taken by the student, and then calls `assignGrade()`. Note the two parameters: `aCourse` and `'B'`. The implied meaning is that the student has completed the course (`aCourse`) with a grade of `'B'`. The code in the method should then compute the new GPA for the student using the information presumably in the course (such as number of credits) and the number of points for a grade of 'B'.

### 2.2.1 Constructors

In the above code, the operation `new Student()` created a new `Student` object with no information. We set the name of the student after creating the object, which is somewhat unnatural. Since every student has a name, when we create a student object, we probably know the student's name as well. It would be convenient to store the student's name in the object as we create the `Student` object.

Java and other object-oriented languages allow the initialization of fields by using what are called **constructors.** A constructor is like a method in that it can have an access specifier (like `public` or `private`), a name, parameters, and executable code. However, constructors have the following differences or special features:

- Constructors cannot have a return type, not even `void`.
- Constructors have the same name as the class in which they are defined.
- Constructors are called when the object is created.

For the class `Student`, we can write the following constructor:

```
public Student(String studentName) {
  name = studentName;
}
```

The syntax is similar to that of methods, but there is no return type. The keyword `public` signifies that the constructor can be invoked from any other program that has access to the `Student` class. The code in the constructor stores the parameter `studentName` in the attribute `name`.

Let us rewrite the `Student` class with this constructor and a few other modifications.

```
public class Student {
  private String name;
  private String address;
  private double gpa;
  public Student(String studentName) {
     name = studentName;
  }
  public void setName(String studentName) {
    name = studentName;
  }
  public void setAddress(String studentAddress) {
    address = studentAddress;
  }
  public String getName() {
    return name;
  }
  public String getAddress() {
    return address;
  }
  public double getGpa() {
    return gpa;
  }
  public void computeGPA(Course newCourse, char grade) {
```

```
    // use the grade and course to update gpa
  }
}
```

We now maintain the address of the student and provide methods to set and get the name and the address. With the above constructor, an object is created as below.

```
Student aStudent = new Student("John");
```

When the above statement is executed, the constructor is called with the given parameter, `John`. This is stored in the `name` field of the object.

In previous versions of the `Student` class, we did not have a constructor. In such cases, where we do not have an explicit constructor, the system inserts a constructor with no arguments. Once we insert our own constructor, the system removes this default, no-argument constructor.

As a result, it is important to note that the following is no longer legal because there is no constructor with no arguments.

```
Student aStudent = new Student();
```

A class can have any number of constructors. Every constructor must have a unique signature, that is, constructors must differ in the way they expect parameters. The following code adds two more constructors to the `Student` class:

```
public class Student {
  private String name;
  private String address;
  private double gpa;
  public Student(String studentName) {
     name = studentName;
  }
  public Student(String studentName, String studentAddress) {
     name = studentName;
     address = studentAddress;
  }
  public Student() {
  }
 //other code deleted
}
```

Notice that all constructors have the same name, which is the name of the class. One of the new constructors accepts the name and address of the student and stores it in the appropriate fields of the object. The other constructor accepts no arguments and does nothing: as a result, the name and address fields of the object are `null`. All of the following are therefore valid ways of instantiating the `student` object `aStudent`:

```
Student aStudent = new Student();
Student aStudent = new Student("John");
Student aStudent = new Student("John", "201 Wall St., New York,
                                        NY")
```

### 2.2.2 Printing an Object

Suppose we want to print an object. We might try

```
System.out.println(student);
```

where `student` is a reference of type `Student`. Unfortunately, when we compile and run the program, we see something like

```
Student@dc8569
```

which is not very meaningful to someone expecting to see the name and address. By default, for all objects, Java prints the name of the class of which the object is an instance, followed by the `@` symbol and a value, which is the unsigned hexadecimal representation of an integer, called the hash code of the object. It does not print the values stored for any of the fields.

To obtain meaningful information, we add a method called `toString()` in the class. This method contains code that tells Java how to convert the object to a `String`.

```
public String toString() {
  // return a string
}
```

Whenever an object is to be represented as a `String`, Java calls the `toString()` method on the object. The method call `System.out.println()` uses the `toString()` method to convert its arguments to the string form.

We can complete the `toString` method for the `Student` class as below.

```
public String toString() {
  return "Name " + name + " Address " + address + " GPA " + gpa;
}
```

It is good practice to put the `toString()` method in every class and return an appropriate string. The author of the class can decide which fields are to be included in the string representation. Sometimes, the method may become slightly more involved than the simple method we have above; for instance, we may wish to print the elements of an array that the object maintains, in which case, a loop might be employed to concatenate the elements.

It is highly recommended that you put the "annotation" `@Override` in front of the method header.

```
@Override
public String toString() {
// return a String object reference
}
```

The annotation makes Java verify the method signature: that it actually conforms to the `toString()` method for returning a text representation of the object. This practice can sometimes avoid subtle bugs.

### 2.2.3 Sharing Data Across All Objects

Sometimes, we need fields that are common to all instances of a class, that is, such a field must have the same value for all the objects of the class. This is ensured by creating only one instance of the field and sharing this instance among all the objects of the class. Such fields are called **static** fields. In contrast, fields maintained separately for each object are called **instance** fields.

Let us turn to an example. Most universities usually have the rule that students not maintaining a certain minimum GPA will be put on academic probation. This minimum standard is the same for all students, but it is conceivable that a university may raise or lower this standard.

We would like to introduce a field for keeping track of this minimum GPA. Since the value has to be the same for all students, it is unnecessary to maintain a separate field for each `Student` object. In fact, it is risky to keep a separate field for each object: since every instance of the field has to be given the same value, special effort will have to be made to update all the copies of the field whenever we decide to change its value. This can give rise to integrity problems and is also quite inefficient.

Suppose we decide to call this new field, `minimumGPA`, and make its type `double`. We define the variable as below.

```
private static double minimumGPA;
```

The specifier `static` means that there will be just one instance of the field `minimumGPA`; the field will be created when the class is initialized by the system. Note that there does not have to be any objects for this field to exist. This instance will be shared by all instances of the class.

Suppose we need to modify this field occasionally and we also want a method that tells us what its value is. We typically write what are called **static methods** to achieve this.

```
public static void setMinimumGPA(double newMinimum) {
   minimumGPA = newMinimum;
}
public static double getMinimumGPA() {
   return minimumGPA;
}
```

The keyword `static` specifies that the method can be executed without using an object. The method is called as below.

```
<class_Name>.<method_name>
```

For example,

```
Student.setMinimumGPA(2.0);
System.out.println("Minimum GPA requirement is "
                   + Student.getMinimumGPA());
```

Methods and fields with the keyword `static` in front of them are usually called **static methods** and **static fields**, respectively. They are also referred to as **class members**.

It is instructive to see in the above case, why we want the two methods to be static. Suppose they were instance methods. Then they need to be called using an object, as in the following example:

```
Student student1 = new Student("John");
student1.setMinimumGPA(2.0);
```

While this is technically correct, it has the following disadvantages:

- It requires that we create an object and use that object to modify a static field. This goes against the spirit of static members; they should be accessible even if there are no objects.
- Someone reading the above fragment may be led to believe that `setMinimumGPA()` is used to modify an instance field.

On the other hand, a static method cannot access any instance fields or methods. This is because a static method may be accessed without using any objects at all; hence there may not be any objects created yet when the static method is in use.

## 2.3 Creating and Working with Related Classes

Most object-oriented applications will have classes that are related. The simplest relationship is when every object of a given class holds a reference to an object of another given class. Consider the university system we introduced earlier in this chapter, where we identified and wrote the skeletons of four classes: `Student`, `Instructor`, `StaffMember`, and `Course`. To understand the nature of their relationships, we take a close look at the structure of each class.

Objects of the `Course` class represent courses that are taught at the university. A course exists in the school catalog, with a name, course ID, brief description, and number of credits. Here is a possible definition of the class.

```
public class Course {
  private String id;
  private String name;
  private int numberofCredits;
  private String description;
  public Course(String courseId, courseName) {
    id = courseId;
    name = courseName;
  }
  public void setNumberOfCredits(int credits) {
    numberOfCredits = credits;
  }
  public void setDescription(String courseDescription) {
    description = courseDescription;
  }
  public String getId() {
    return id;
  }
  public String getName() {
    return name;
  }
  public int getNumberOfCredits() {
    return numberOfCredits;
  }
  public String getDescription() {
    return description;
  }
}
```

A department selects from the catalog a number of courses to offer every semester. A section is a course offered in a certain semester, held in a certain place on certain days at certain times. (We will not worry about the instructor for the class, capacity, etc.) Let us create a class for this.

We will use `String` objects for storing the place, days, time, and semester. Thus, we have three fields named `place`, `daysAndTimes`, and `semester` with the obvious semantics.

Clearly, this seems inadequate: this class does not hold the name and other important details of the course. On the other hand, it is redundant to have fields for these because the information is available in the corresponding `Course` object. What we do, therefore, is to provide a field that remembers the corresponding course. We can do this by having the following field declaration:

```
private Course course;
```

When the `Section` instance is created, this field can be initialized.

```
public class Section {
  private String semester;
  private String place;
  private String daysAndTimes;
  private Course course;
  public Section(Course theCourse, String theSemester,
                 String thePlace, String theDaysAndTimes) {
    course = theCourse;
    place = thePlace;
    daysAndTimes = theDaysAndTimes;
    semester = theSemester;
  }
  public String getPlace() {
    return place;
  }
  public String getDaysAndTimes() {
    return daysAndTimes;
  }
  public String getSemester() {
    return semester;
  }
  public Course getCourse() {
    return course;
  }
  public void setPlace(String newPlace) {
    place = newPlace;
  }
  public void setDaysAndTimes(String newDaysAndTimes) {
    daysAndTimes = newDaysAndTimes;
  }
```

```
}
```

By storing a reference to a `Course` object within each `Section` object, we have created an **association** between the two classes. This association captures the relationship "every section has a course." This association is depicted by having a rectangle each to represent the `Course` and `Section` objects, and then connecting the two rectangles by a line. This is shown in Figure 2.1.

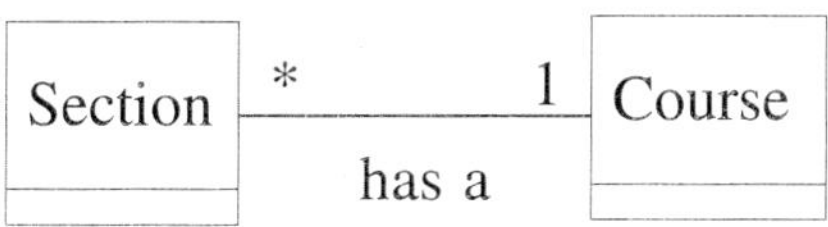


**Fig. 2.1** UML representation for a many-to-one relationship between section and course, that is, many sections can be associated with a single course.

In a typical university, each section would correspond to exactly one course, but a course would have a number of sections associated with it. It is also possible that a course has been defined, but has never been offered, that is, there are zero sections corresponding to a course. This aspect of the association is reflected in the figure by placing an asterisk (`*`) next to `Section` and the numeral 1 next to `Course`. We implement this association by storing a reference to a `Course` object within each `Section` object.

Consider the piece of code to create courses and sections. A course would be created by invoking the constructor. We have a couple of options for how `Section` objects are created. One approach would be to invoke the constructor for `Section` directly.

```
Course cs350 = new Course("CS 350", "Data Structures");
Section cs350Section1 = new Section(cs350, "Fall 2004",
                                     "Lecture Hall 12",
                                     "T H 1-2:15");
Section cs350Section2 = new Section(cs350,"Fall 2004",
                                     "Lecture Hall 25",
                                     "'M W F 10-10:50");
```

A drawback of this approach is we are not verifying that the `Course` object exists. For instance, it would be syntactically correct to write:

```
Course c1 = null;
Section cs350Section1 = new Section(c1, "Fall 2004",
                                     "Lecture Hall 12",
                                     "T H 1-2:15");
Section cs350Section2 = new Section(c1,"Fall 2004",
```

```
                                               "Lecture Hall 25",
                                               "‘M W F 10-10:50");
```

At some later stage in the program, one might try to access the Course object associated with cs350Section1, resulting in an error. An alternative, safer, approach is to create the Section in Course. This would require that we add a new method named createSection() in Course, which accepts the semester, the place, days, and time as parameters and returns an instance of a new Section object for the course. The code using this method is as follows:

```
Course cs350 = new Course("CS 350", "Data Structures");
Section cs350Section1 = cs350.createSection("Fall 2004",
                                               "Lecture Hall 12",
                                               "T H 1-2:15");
Section cs350Section2 = cs350.createSection("Fall 2004",
                                               "Lecture Hall 25",
                                               "‘M W F 10-10:50");
```

Let us get to the task of coding the createSection() method. To invoke the constructor of Section from createSection(), we need a reference to the Course object, and references to the semester, place, and days and times available. References to the semester, place, and days and times available were passed as parameters to createSection(), but we did not pass a reference to the Course object. Although this is not an explicit parameter to the method, the Course object on which the createSection() method is invoked is itself the reference we need. Java provides a way to get hold of this reference. The reference to the object on which the createSection() method was invoked is available through a special keyword called this.

We can code the createSection() method as below.

```
public Section createSection(String semester, String place,
String time) {
  return new Section(this, semester, place, time);
}
```

The keyword this obtains the reference to the Course object and is passed to the constructor of Section. In addition to passing a reference to itself to methods, we can use this to obtain the fields of the object, which comes in handy for resolving conflicts. For example,

```
public class Section {
    private String place;
    public void setPlace(String place) {
        this.place = place;
    }
}
```

The identifier place on the right-hand side of the assignment refers to the formal parameter; on the left-hand side, it is prefixed by this, which makes it a reference to the private field.

## 2.4 Defining and Working with Collections

In the university application, for any given section, a faculty member would like to see the list of students in the section. It makes sense, therefore, to store a list of the registered students within each Section object. One approach for implementing a collection is to define an array within the class. If we used such an approach within our Section class, we would add a field to reference the array as follows:

```
public class Section {
    private Student studentList[];
    private int numStudents;
    //  other code not shown
}
```

An additional field, numberOfStudents, could be used to keep track of the number of registered students. Within the constructor, we would have to instantiate the array object, as shown.

```
public class Section {
  public Section(Course theCourse, String theSemester,
                 String thePlace, String theDaysAndTimes) {
    course = theCourse;
    place = thePlace;
    daysAndTimes = theDaysAndTimes;
    semester = theSemester;
    studentList = new Student[30];
    numberOfStudents = 0;
  }
  //  other code not shown
}
```

Say, we want a method that prints out all the students in the section. Our code would be something like this.

```
  public void printStudents() {
    for (int count = 0; count < numberOfStudents; count++) {
        studentList[count].toString();
    }
  }
```

### Associations between classes

Associations between classes can be of different kinds. As depicted in Figure 2.2, we could have one-to-one, one-to-many, many-to-one, or many-to-many relationships.

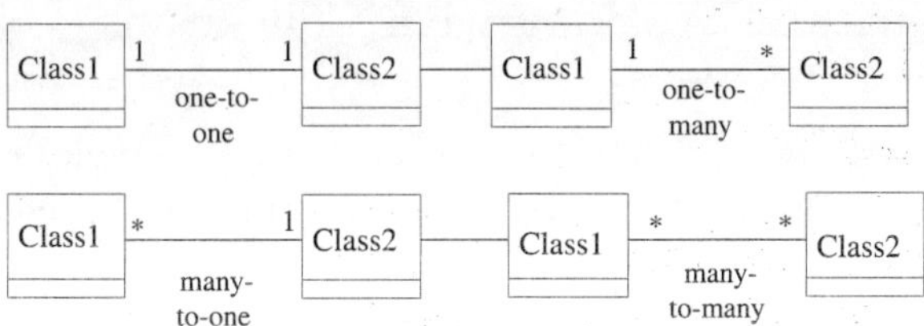


**Fig. 2.2** UML representations for the different kinds of associations based on the arity of the association, that is, the number of instances of `Class1` that are related to the number of instances of `Class2`.

A one-to-one relationship is the simplest situation. An example of this is that of a student and their transcript. Every student has exactly one associated transcript, and no transcript may be associated with more than one student. In such cases, we can easily represent the relationship with a reference field in the two associated classes. For example, we can have a `Transcript` (`Student`) object for each transcript (student). The `Transcript` (`Student`) can then have a field to refer to the corresponding `Student` (`Transcript`) object.

A one-to-many relationship occurs when an object of one class is related to several objects of another class. For instance, a `Course` object can be connected to (containing references to) multiple `Section` objects. The asterisk (*) stands for any value greater than or equal to zero. The many-to-one relationship represents the converse situation, where several objects of one class could be related to the same object of another class. Since there is a one-to-many relationship from `Course` to `Section`, there is a many-to-many relationship from `Section` to `Course`. The above relationship can be implemented with a collection of `Section` references in `Course` and a `Course` reference in `Section`.

A many-to-many relationship is a frequent occurrence. An example would be class sections and students in a university: a student can in general be enrolled in multiple sections, and a section will have multiple students. Such relationships may themselves have associated attributes. Such a relationship is conveniently implemented using a third class and storing references to objects of this relationship. Examples of such implementations will be discussed in later chapters.

A method to add a student to a section would be as follows:

```
public void addStudent(Student student) {
  if (numberOfStudents < 30) {
      studentList[numberOfStudents] = student;
      numberOfStudents++;
  }
}
```

In the above code, the class `Section` uses the class `Student`, but defines its own collection of students, and defines the methods needed for managing the collection. Such an approach is not very desirable for the following reasons:

- *Lack of cohesion*: While implementing a type (in this case, `Section`), we should not be distracted by implementation considerations for a different type, which in this case, is a collection for the type `Student`. Such code is non-cohesive. The author of the type (`Section`) would need to be cognizant of the nuances of various collection implementation strategies.
- *Unnecessary coupling*: Sometimes, we may want to change the kind of collection being used, say, from an array to a linked list. If we employed a solution like the one above, changing the kind of collection would involve making complex changes to various parts of the application.
- *Lack of reuse*: In complex systems, we may have multiple classes accessing the same collection. For instance, in our university system, both the billing sub-system and the registration sub-system may have to access the same list of students. Implementing a list separately in each sub-system is both wasteful and error-prone. Instead, a separate collection class could be implemented and utilized at different places in the application. This also provides an opportunity for employing more sophisticated programming techniques such as generics (discussed later in the book).

Object-oriented systems, therefore, use collection classes to manage collections.

### 2.4.1 Creating a Collection Class

We create a simple collection class for managing a list of students, which provides methods for adding a student, deleting a student, and printing the list of students.

```
public class StudentLinkedList {
  // fields for maintaining a linked list
  public void add(Student student) {
```

```
    // code for adding a student to the list
  }
  public void delete(String name) {
    // code for deleting a student from the list
  }
  public void print() {
    // code for printing the list
  }
  // other methods
}
```

The class Section can now be written to use this collection class as follows:

```
public class Section {
  private  StudentLinkedList studentList;
  private String semester;
  private String place;
  private String daysAndTimes;
  private Course course;
  public Section(Course theCourse, String theSemester,
                 String thePlace, String theDaysAndTimes) {
    course = theCourse;
    place = thePlace;
    daysAndTimes = theDaysAndTimes;
    semester = theSemester;
    studentList = new StudentLinkedList();
  }
  public void addStudent(Student student) {
    studentList.add(student);
  }
  public void deleteStudent(String name) {
    studentList.delete(name);
  }
  public void printStudents() {
    studentList.print();
  }
}
```

Note that methods for adding, deleting, and printing are very much simplified when we leave the management of the list to the collection class. It is instructive to complete the code for StudentLinkedList.

### 2.4.2 Implementation of StudentLinkedList

A linked list consists of nodes, each of which stores the address of the next node. We thus write the following class:

```
public class StudentNode {
  private Student data;
  private StudentNode next;
  public StudentNode(Student student, StudentNode initialLink) {
    this.data = student;
    next = initialLink;
  }
  public Student getData() {
    return data;
  }
  public void setData(Student student) {
    this.data = student;
  }
  public StudentNode getNext() {
    return next;
  }
  public void setNext(StudentNode node) {
    next = node;
  }
}
```

This class will be required in StudentLinkedList only. Therefore, we can use what are called **inner classes** in Java. An inner class is a class enclosed within another class. Thus, we write

```
public class StudentLinkedList implements StudentList {
 private StudentNode head;
 private class StudentNode {
  private Student data;
  private StudentNode next;
  public StudentNode(Student student, StudentNode initialLink) {
    this.data = student;
    next = initialLink;
  }
  public Student getData() {
    return data;
  }
  public void setData(Student student) {
    this.data = student;
  }
```

```
    public StudentNode getNext() {
      return next;
    }
    public void setNext(StudentNode node) {
      next = node;
    }
  }
  public void add(Student student) {
    // code for adding a student to the list
  }
  public void delete(String name) {
    // code for deleting a student from the list
  }
  public void print() {
    // code for printing the list
  }
}
```

The inner class StudentNode is now declared as private, so that it cannot be used from code outside of the class.

Let us code the add method.

```
  public void add(Student student) {
    head = new StudentNode(student, head);
  }
```

The code creates a new StudentNode and puts it at the front of the list.

Next, we code the print() method.

```
  public void print() {
    System.out.print("List: ");
    for (StudentNode temp = head; temp != null; temp =
    temp.getNext()) {
      System.out.print(temp.getData() + " ");
    }
    System.out.println();
  }
```

The code starts at the front of the list, extracts the data in the corresponding node, and prints that data. Printing ends when the node it points to is null; that is, the next node does not exist. Assuming that the Student class has an appropriate toString() method, we will get the name, address, and GPA of each student printed.

Finally, we code the method to delete a student. We will need to look at each Student object and check if the name field matches the given name. How

### How do objects refer to themselves?

In general, assume that we have a class `C` with a method `m()` in it, as shown below. Also shown is another class `C2`, which has a method named `m2()` that requires an object of type `C` as its only parameter.

```
public class C {
  public void m() {
  // this refers to the object on whom m is being invoked
  }
}

public class C2 {
  public void m2(C aC) {
  // code
  }
}
```

Suppose that we create an instance of `C` from the outside and invoke `m()` as below.

```
C c1 = new C(); c1.m();
```

The reference `c1` points to an instance of `C`. Suppose `m()` contained the following code:

```
public void m(){
   C2 c2 = new C2(); c2.m2(this);
}
```

In the above code, **`this`** is a reference that points to the same object as `c1`. Figure 2.3 depicts this relationship between the objects.

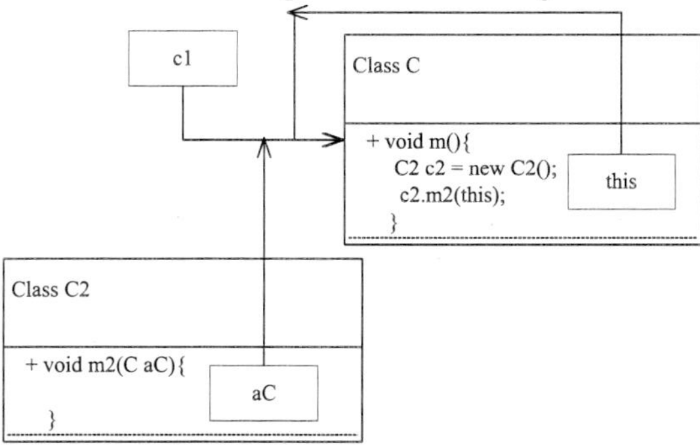


**Fig. 2.3** Class diagram representing an object referring to itself. `c1` is an instance of `C`; when the the method `m()` in invoked on `c1`, it passes its own reference to the method `m2` in `c2`.

do we perform this comparison? Suppose `temp` is a variable that refers to a `StudentNode` object within `studentList`. The call `temp.getData()` retrieves the `Student` object, and `temp.getData().getName()` gets the name of the student. To check if this name is equal to the given name, we can use the `equals()` method defined in `String`. The code first checks if the list is empty; if so, there is nothing to be done. With a non-empty list, it checks if the name of the student at the front of the list is the same as the name supplied in the parameter. If they match, the `Student` object at the front of the list is deleted from the list by moving the head to the next object (which may not exist, if we have a `null`). If the element at the front of the list is not what we want, execution proceeds to a loop that examines all the elements starting at the second position until the end of the list is reached or the student with the given name is located. The variable `previous` always refers to the object preceding the object referred to by `temp`. Once it is located, the object can be deleted using `previous`.

The code for the `delete()` method is given below.

```
public void delete(String studentName) {
  if (head == null) {
     return;
  }
  if (head.getData().getName().equals(studentName)) {
     head = head.getNext();
  } else {
     for (StudentNode temp = head.getNext(), previous = head;
          temp != null;
          previous = temp, temp = temp.getNext()) {
       if (temp.getData().getName().equals(studentName)) {
          previous.setNext(temp.getNext());
          return;
       }
     }
  }
}
```

## 2.5 Interfaces

Another powerful concept in the object-oriented paradigm is that of interfaces. This section introduces the concept and shows how to program using interfaces.

### 2.5.1 Why Use Interfaces?

In the previous section, we successfully separated the collection class (`StudentLinkedList`) from the client class that used the collection (`Section`). This level of separation still leaves some unwanted coupling between the client class and the collection class. For instance, the method `addStudent` in `Section` invokes the `add` method of `StudentLinkedList`. The code in the client class is, therefore, coupled with specific methods in the collection class. Now consider a situation where we later find that an array implementation of the collection is more desirable. Say, we have a readymade implementation for the class `StudentArrayList`. We can switch to the new collection by replacing

```
studentList = new StudentLinkedList();
```

with

```
studentList = new StudentArrayList();
```

Next, we must make sure that the method names for the new class are being used. For instance, it is possible that the method for adding a student in `StudentAarrayList` is `addStudent`, instead of `add`. This requires us to go through all the code in `Section` and make the necessary changes. This is not an efficient way of reusing code.

### 2.5.2 Improving Reuse with an Interface

Reuse can be improved through the use of an interface, which is one way of partially specifying the requirements for a class. When we create a list of students, we should be able to add a student, remove a student, and print all the students in the list. We can specify the syntax for the methods by creating an interface as given below.

```
public interface StudentList {
  public void add(Student student);
  public void delete(String name);
  public void print();
}
```

Notice that the syntax of the first line resembles the syntax for a class with the keyword `class` replaced by the keyword `interface`. We have specified three methods: `add` with a single parameter of type `Student`; `delete` with the name of the student as a parameter, and `print` with no parameters. Notice that we have not given a body for the methods; there is a semi-colon immediately after the right parenthesis that ends the parameters.

Let us see how to utilize the above entity. We can now create a class that implements the above three operations as below.

```
public class StudentLinkedList implements StudentList {
  // fields for maintaining a linked list
  public void add(Student student) {
    // code for adding a student to the list
  }
  public void delete(String name) {
    // code for deleting a student from the list
  }
  public void print() {
    // code for printing the list
  }
  // other methods
}
```

The first line states that we are creating a new class named `StudentLinkedList`. The words `implements StudentList` mean that this class will have all of the methods of the interface `StudentList`. It is a syntax error if the class did not implement the three methods because it has claimed that it implements them. A `StudentArrayList` would be similarly created:

```
public class StudentArrayList implements StudentList {
  // fields for maintaining an array-based list
  public void add(Student student) {
    // code for adding a student to the list
  }
  public void delete(String name) {
    // code for deleting a student from the list
  }
  public void print() {
    // code for printing the list
  }
}
```

Just as a class introduces a new type, an interface also creates a new type. In the above example, `StudentList`, `StudentLinkedList` are both types. All instances of the `StudentLinkedList` and `StudentArrayList` classes are also of type `StudentList`.

We can thus write

```
StudentList students;
students = new StudentLinkedList();
// example of code that uses StudentList;
Student s1 = new Student(/* parameters */);
students.add(s1);
s1 = new Student(/* parameters */);
students.add(s1);
```

```
students.print();
```

We created an instance of the `StudentLinkedList` class and stored a reference to it in `students`, which is of type `StudentList`. We can invoke the three methods of the interface (and of the class) through this variable.

To a beginner, defining the interface `StudentList` and then defining `StudentLinkedList` may appear to be unnecessary. To understand our motivation for doing this, consider the following facts:

- The class `StudentLinkedList` implements the interface `StudentList`, so variables of type `StudentLinkedList` are also of type `StudentList`.
- We declared `students` to be of type `StudentList` and not `StudentLinkedList`.
- We restricted ourselves to using the methods of the interface `StudentList`.

This means that although the variable `students` holds a reference to an object of `StudentLinkedList`, all our code is written such that `students` is an object of type `StudentList`. When we wish to replace the class `StudentLinkedList` with the class `StudentArrayList`, we can rewrite the code that manipulates `students` as below.

```
StudentList students;
students = new StudentArrayList();
// code that uses StudentList;
```

The only change that we need to make in our code to use the list is the one that creates the `StudentList` object. Since we restricted ourselves to using the methods of `StudentList` in the rest of the code (as opposed to using methods or fields unique to the class `StudentLinkedList`), we do not need to change anything else. This makes maintenance easier.

We saw the implementation of `StudentLinkedList` earlier. It is instructive to complete the code for `StudentArrayList` as well. We proceed to do that now.

### 2.5.3 Array Implementation of Lists

We need to set up an array of `Student` objects. This is done as follows:

1. Declare a field in the class `StudentArrayList`, which is an array of type `Student`.
2. Allocate an array of the required size. We will allocate storage for as many students as the user wishes; if the user does not specify a number, we will allocate space for a small number, say, 10, of objects. In any case, when this array fills up, we will allocate more.

Therefore, we need two constructors: one that accepts the initial capacity and the other that accepts nothing. The code for the array field and the constructors is given below.

```
public class StudentArrayList implements StudentList {
  private Student[] students;
  public StudentArrayList() {
    students = new Student[10];
  }
  public StudentArrayList(int capacity) {
    students = new Student[capacity];
  }
  // other methods
}
```

Note that the code for the first constructor is a special case of the second constructor. Such repetition is undesirable, since the code in the second constructor is general enough to handle both cases. To avoid the repetition, we need to do the following: when the user does not supply an initial capacity, we should somehow invoke the second constructor with a value of 10. This can be achieved by rewriting the first constructor as follows:

```
  public StudentArrayList() {
    this(10);
  }
```

In this case, `this(10)` invokes the other constructor of the class, with the appropriate parameter. The net effect would be the same as that of the user writing `new StudentArrayList(10)`.

The following approach is employed to manage the list. We will have two variables: `first` that gives the index of the first occupied cell and `count` that counts the number of objects in the list. When the list is empty, both are 0. When we add an object to the list, we will insert it at `(first + count)` % `array size` and increment `count`.

```
public class StudentArrayList implements StudentList {
  private Student[] students;
  private int count;
  public StudentArrayList() {
    this(10);
  }
  public StudentArrayList(int capacity) {
    students = new Student[capacity];
  }
  public void add(Student student) {
    if (count == students.length) {
```

```
            reallocate(count * 2);
        }
        students[count++] = student;
    }
    public void delete(String name) {
        for (int index = 0; index < count; index++) {
            if (students[index].getName().equals(name)) {
                students[index] = students[(count - 1)];
                students[(count - 1)] = null;
                count--;
                return;
            }
        }
    }
    public Student get(int index) {
        if (index >= 0 && index < count) {
            return students[index];
        }
        return null;
    }
    public int size() {
        return count;
    }
    public void print() {
        for (int index = 0; index < count; index++) {
            System.out.println(students[index]);
        }
    }
    public void reallocate(int size) {
        Student[] temp = new Student[size];
        System.arraycopy(students, 0, temp, 0, count);
        students = temp;
    }
}
```

**Using `this` in a constructor versus using `this` in an instance method**

The use of `this` in the constructor should not be confused with the use of `this` when an object refers to itself in instance methods. The code we wrote for `createSection()` used `this` in the second context.

```
public Section createSection(String semester, String place,
String time) {
  return new Section(this, semester, place, time);
}
```

Since this code is executed by the `Course` object, `this` refers to the particular instance of `Course`.
On the other hand, when we write:

```
  public StudentArrayList() {
    this(10);
  }
```

we are in a constructor (that is, no instance has been defined), and `this(10)` invokes the other constructor for the class.
Also, note the following aspects:

- There can be no code before the statement `this()`. In other words, this call should be the very first statement in the constructor.
- You can have code in the constructor after the call to another constructor.
- You can call at most one other constructor from a constructor.

## 2.6 Abstract Classes

In a way, classes and interfaces represent the two ends of the spectrum of type definitions. When we write a class, we code every field and method; in other words, a complete implementation of the type. In an interface, we need to specify only the method signatures, that is, a minimal definition of the type.

Sometimes, we might know the specifications for a class, but might not have the information needed to implement the class completely. For example, consider the set of possible shapes that can be drawn on a computer screen. While the set is infinite, let us consider only three possibilities: triangles, rectangles, and circles. We know that the set of fields needed to represent each object is different, but there are some commonalities as well: for example, all shapes have an area.

In such cases, we can implement a class partially using what are called abstract classes. In the case of a shape, we may code

```
public abstract class Shape {
  private double area;
  public abstract void computeArea();
  public double getArea() {
    return area;
  }
  // more fields and methods
}
```

The class is declared as abstract (using the keyword `abstract` prior to the keyword `class`), which means that the class is incomplete. Since we know that every shape has an area, we have defined the `double` field `area` and the method `getArea()` to return the area of the shape. We require that there be a method to compute the area of a shape, so we have written the method `getArea()`. However, since the formula to compute the area is different for the three possible shapes, we have left out the implementation and declared the method itself as abstract.

Any class that contains an abstract method must be declared abstract. The converse, however, is not true: an abstract class need not contain any abstract methods. We cannot create an instance of an abstract class. The utility of an abstract class comes from the fact that it provides a basic implementation that other classes can "extend." This is done using the technique of inheritance, which is explained later in this chapter.

## 2.7 Dealing with Run-time Errors

In most object-oriented languages, run-time errors are manifested as **exceptions**. Consider the following lines of code:

```
public class Except0 {
  public static void main(String[] s) {
    Student s1 = null;
    s1.toString();
  }
}
```

We have declared the reference `s1` to be of type `Student`, but it does not contain a reference to any object. Such a reference is known as a `null` reference. If we place this code in the main method of a Java program, it would compile correctly. When the program containing this piece of code is executed, we get something like the following error message:

```
Exception in thread "main" java.lang.NullPointerException
       at Except0.main(Except0.java:4)
```

We say then that the program has thrown an exception. The programmer did not anticipate the possibility of the exception, and any code after the invocation of toString() will not be executed. In an object-oriented language, there is an object corresponding to each exception. We can access this object through a try-catch block, and handle the exception as shown below:

```
public class Except1 {
  public static void main(String[] s) {
    Student s1 = null;
    try {
      s1.toString();
    } catch (NullPointerException ne) {
      System.out.println(" Null Pointer Exception on s1. \n
      Continue(yes/no)?");
      Scanner myScanner = new Scanner(System.in);
      String answer = myScanner.next();
      if (answer.equals("no")) {
        System.exit(0);
      }
      myScanner.close();
    }
    System.out.println("continuing \n");
  }
}
```

The piece of code where an exception might be thrown is placed in braces after the keyword try (called the try block). Following the try block is the catch block, which names the exception that it is supposed to catch, and contains the code that should be executed before proceeding with the rest of the program. In our program, we handle the error by listing the problem (since we know what is happening) and ask if the user wishes to continue. If the user answers "no," the system exits; otherwise the program continues execution with the statement that follows the catch block.

Exceptions can be more complicated and can propagate back up the calling chain, until they are caught and handled. If they are not caught, the program will terminate. Consider the following example, with the simplified classes Course and Section:

```
class Course {
  private String name;

  public String getName() {
    return name;
  }
}

class Section {
  private Course course;
  private String id;

  public Section(Course course) {
    this.course = course;
  }

  public Section() {
  }

  public String toString() {
    return (course.getName() + id);          // line 21
  }
}

public class Except2 {
  public static void main(String[] args) {
    Section section1 = new Section();
    System.out.println(section1.toString()); // line 28
  }
}
```

Note that `Section` has two constructors: one which assigns a course and one which does not. In the `main()` method of `Except2`, we are creating a `Section` object where the `Course` reference is `null`. When this code is executed, an exception is thrown when `getName()` is invoked. The resulting error message shows all the methods and classes in the calling chain:

```
Exception in thread "main" java.lang.NullPointerException
        at Section.toString(Except2.java:21)
        at Except2.main(Except2.java:28)
```

The code at line 28 made a call, which resulted in a crash in line 28. The exception can be handled at any point along the calling chain; in that case, no error message appears.

```
public class Except3 {
  public static void main(String[] argss) {
    Section section1 = new Section();
    try {
      System.out.println(section1.toString());
    } catch (NullPointerException ne) {
      System.out.println("Continue(yes/no)?");
      Scanner myScanner = new Scanner(System.in);
      String answer = myScanner.next();
      if (answer.equals("no")) {
        System.exit(0);
      }
      myScanner.close();
    }
    System.out.println("continuing \n");
  }
}
```

The Java language defines many exceptions. In addition, a programmer can define custom exceptions for specific errors that are thrown by methods in the user-defined classes.

## 2.8 Inheritance

As we have noted earlier, classes are user-defined types created in the course of constructing an object-oriented program. With larger systems, it is common to encounter situations where there are several variants of a user-defined type. Trying to capture all the variants in a single class can lead to very complex code inside the class. At the same time, creating multiple independent classes will result in complicated code in the client class. In such situations, it is beneficial to create a set of classes that are related by an **inheritance hierarchy**. Any object-oriented programming language, therefore, has to provide a mechanism to construct such a hierarchy.

In any object-oriented programming language, inheritance is a relationship characterized by a **superclass** and a **subclass**, which are also respectively termed **ancestor** or **base** class and **descendant** or **derived** class, represented using UML notation as shown in Figure 2.4. We draw one box per class and an arrow from each derived class to the base class.

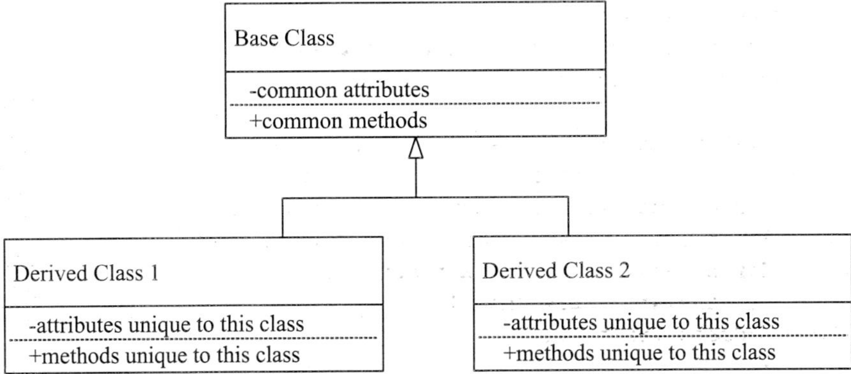


**Fig. 2.4** Basic idea of inheritance. We have a single base class that is common to multiple derived classes. The base class represents the commonality of all classes, and the derived class(es) represent the uniqueness.

### 2.8.1 An Example of a Hierarchy

Consider a company that sells various products such as television sets and books. Obvious differences between the products imply that they have different attributes to be tracked, and thus, we need two classes, `Television` and `Book`. One way to accomplish this task is to create a class for television sets, say, `Television`, and a second class, for books, say, `Book`. However, in many situations, the company would like to think of books and televisions as simply products. For instance, the company needs to keep track of sales, profits (or losses), etc. for all products. Now, add to the above scenario, more products, say, CDs, DVDs, cassette players, pens, etc. Each may warrant a separate class, but, as just discussed, they all have common properties and behaviors; and to the company, they are all products.

What we see is an example of a situation where two classes have a great deal of similarities, but also substantial differences. The need to view different entities such as televisions and books as products suggests that we may benefit by having a new type `Product` introduced into the system. Since there is a fair amount of common functionality between the two products, we would like `Product` to be a class that implements the commonality found in `Television` and `Book`.

In Java, we do this as follows. We start off with a class that captures the essential properties and methods common to all products.

```
public class Product {
  // functionality for a product
}
```

The above class may have attributes such as the number of units sold and unit price. It will also have constructors and methods for recording sales, computing profits, and so on.

We are now ready to create a class that represents a single kind of TV set. For this, we note that a television is a product, and that we would like to utilize the functionality that we just implemented for products. In Java, we do this as below:

```
public class Television extends Product {
  // functionality that is unique for televisions
  // modifications
}
```

Informally speaking, the `Television` class inherits all of the properties and methods from the class `Product`. All we have done is add properties and methods unique to televisions, which will not, for obvious reasons, be implemented in `Product`.

In a similar manner, we implement the class `Book`.

```
public class Book extends Product {
  // functionality that is unique for books
  // modifications
}
```

The relationship between the three classes is depicted in Figure 2.5.

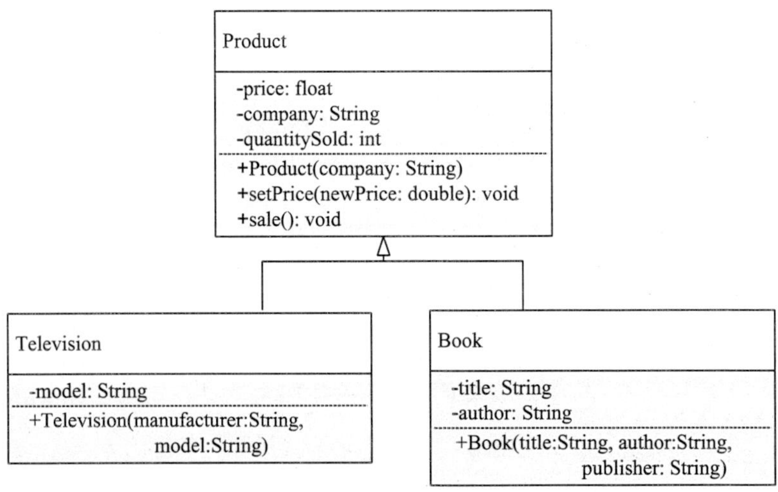


**Fig. 2.5** The derived classes, `Television` and `Book`, inherit from the base class, `Product`. The attributes common to `Book` and `Television` are available in `Product`.

Now, notice the similarities and differences between the two classes: both classes, since they represent products, carry the fields `quantitySold` and `price` with their obvious meanings. The method `sale()` in both classes is invoked whenever one unit (a book or a TV set) is sold. The meaning of the `setPrice()` method should be obvious.

The two classes are somewhat different in other respects: `Book` has attributes `title` and `author` whereas the `Television` class has the attribute `model`.

The `manufacturer` attribute is named differently from, but is not dissimilar to, `publisher`. Both essentially denote the company that produced the product. As we shall see, we will pass this information to the superclass for it to store.

Here is where the power of the object-oriented paradigm comes into play. It allows the development of a base class or superclass that reflects the commonalities of the two classes and then enables us to extend or subclass this base class to arrive at the functionalities we discussed before. The class `Product` keeps track of the common attributes of `Book` and `Television` and implements the methods necessary to act on these attributes. `Television` and `Book` are now constructed as subclasses of `Product`; they will both inherit the functionalities of `Product`, so that they are now capable of keeping track of the sales of these two products.

The code for `Product`, given below, is fairly simple. The variable `company` stores the manufacturer of the product. We will also make it a requirement to specify the price at object construction time. Otherwise, there are no special features to be discussed.

```
public class Product {
  private String company;
  private double price;
  private int quantitySold;

  public Product(String company, double price) {
    this.company = company;
    this.price = price;
  }
  public void sell() {
    quantitySold++;
  }
  public void setPrice(double newPrice) {
    price = newPrice;
  }
  public String toString() {
    return "Company: " + company +  " price: " +
      price + " quantity sold " + quantitySold;
```

```
  }
}
```

Let us now construct `Television`, which extends `Product`. Any object of type `Television`, the subclass, can be thought of as having two parts: one that is formed from `Television` itself and the other from `Product`, the superclass. Thus, this object has four fields in it: `model`, `quantitySold`, `price`, and `company`. Typically, the code within the subclass is responsible for managing the fields within it, and the code in the superclass deals with the fields in the superclass.

Recall that objects are initialized through code in the constructor. When inheritance is involved, the part of the object represented by the superclass must be initialized *before* the fields of the subclass are given values; this is because the subclass is built from the superclass and thus the former may have fields that depend on the fact that the superclass's attributes are initialized. An analogy may help: When a house is built, the roof is put on only after the walls have been erected, which takes place only after the foundation has been laid. Here, the roof depends on the walls, and therefore, the latter must be built first.

To create a `Television` object, we need to invoke a constructor of that class as below, where we pass the brand name, manufacturer name, and price:

```
Television set = new Television("RX3032", "Modern Electronics",
230.0);
```

Thus the constructor of `Television` must be defined as below.

```
public Television(String model, String manufacturer, double
price) {
  // code to initialize the Product part of a television
  // code to initialize the television part of the object
}
```

The constructor of `Product` initializes the fields of a `Product` object. We therefore call that constructor, by the statement

```
super(/* parameters for superclass constructor go here*/)
```

Here, `super` is a Java keyword. The call `super` with proper parameters always invokes the superclass's constructor. The superclass's constructor call can be invoked only as the very first statement from the code within a constructor of a subclass; it cannot be placed later in the code.

In this example, the parameters to be passed would be the manufacturer's name and price. The code for the constructor is then

```
public Television(String model, String manufacturer, double
price) {
```

```
  super(manufacturer, price);
  // store the model name
}
```

The fields of the superclass are initialized before the fields in the subclass. What this means in the context of object creation is that the constructor of `Television` can begin its work only after the constructor of the superclass `Product` has completed execution. Of course, when you wish to create a `Television` object, you need to invoke that class's constructor, but the first thing the constructor `Television` does (and must do) is invoke the constructor of `Product` with the appropriate parameters: the name of the company that manufactured the set and the price.

The result of `super(manufacturer, price)` is, therefore, to invoke `Product`'s constructor, which initializes `company` and `price` and then returns. The `Television` class then gives a value to the `model` field and returns to the invoker.

As is to be expected, the class `Television` needs a field for storing the model name. We thus have a more complete piece of code for this class as given below.

```
public class Television extends Product {
  private String model;
  public Television(String model, String manufacturer, double
price) {
    super(manufacturer, price);
    this.model = model;
  }
  public String toString() {
    return super.toString() + " model: " + model;
  }
}
```

The `toString()` method of `Television` works by first calling the `toString()` method of `Product`, which returns a string representation of `Product` and concatenates to it the model name.

The ideas explained above are formalized as follows:

Suppose $C_1$ and $C_2$ are two independent but related classes that we would like to connect through a hierarchy. We extract the common aspects of $C_1$ and $C_2$ and create a class, say, $B$, to implement that functionality. The classes $C_1$ and $C_2$ could then be smaller, containing only properties and methods that are unique to them. This idea is called inheritance: $C_1$ and $C_2$ are said to *inherit* from $B$. $B$ is said to be the base class or superclass, and $C_1$ and $C_2$ are termed derived classes or subclasses. The superclasses are generalizations or abstractions – we move toward a more general type, an "upward" movement

– and the subclasses denote specializations – toward a more specific class, a "downward" movement. The class structure then provides a hierarchy.

### 2.8.2 Inheriting from an Interface

Sometimes we have a group of classes, say, $C_1$, $C_2$, and $C_3$, all of which implement a set of common methods, say $m_1()$ and $m_2()$. Programmers may instantiate objects of type $C_1$ or $C_2$ or $C_3$ and invoke methods $m_1()$ and $m_2()$ on those instances. In such a situation, it is useful to place the set of common methods (in this case $m_1()$ and $m_2()$) in an interface.

Earlier on, we defined an interface as a collection of methods that can be implemented by a class. Since an interface specifies the methods, and the implementing class implements them, an interface has been likened to a contract signed by the class implementing the interface. Implementing the interface is, therefore, viewed as a form of inheritance; the implementing class inherits an abstract set of properties from the interface. All the classes implementing the interface can be viewed as subclasses of the same superclass.

Java recognizes an interface as a type (as do several other object-oriented languages), which means that objects that belong to classes that implement a given interface also belong to the type represented by the interface. Likewise, we can declare a variable as belonging to the type of the interface, and we can then use it to access the objects of any class that implements the interface.

```
public interface I {
  // details of I
}

public class  A implements I {
  //code for A
}

public class  B implements I {
  //code for B
}

I i1 = new A(); // i1 holds a reference to an object of type A

I i2 =  new B(); // i2 holds a reference to an object of type B
```

In the UML notation, this kind of a relationship between the interface and the implementing class is termed **realization** and is represented by a dotted line with a large open arrowhead that points to the interface, as shown in Figure 2.6.

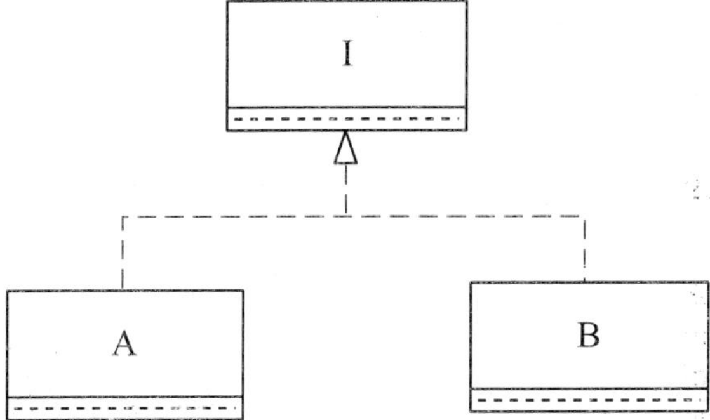


**Fig. 2.6** Interfaces. I is an interface that is implemented by both A and B.

### 2.8.3 Polymorphism and Dynamic Binding

Consider a university application that contains, among others, three classes that form a hierarchy, as shown in Figure 2.7. A student can be either an undergraduate student or a graduate student. Just as in real life, where we would think of an undergraduate or a graduate student as a student, in the object-oriented paradigm as well, we consider an `UndergraduateStudent` object or a `GraduateStudent` object to be of type `Student`. Therefore, we can write

```
Student student1 = new UndergraduateStudent();
Student student2 = new GraduateStudent();
```

The two references `student1` and `student2` are declared to be of type `Student`. We say that the **declared type** of these references is `Student`. A variable has only one declared type and that is determined at compile time. (There could be multiple references with the same name, but they have different scopes.) On the other hand, `student1` happens to be assigned a reference to an instance of `UndergraduateStudent`. After execution of the statement, we say that the actual type of `student1` is `UndergraduateStudent`. Similarly, the actual type of `student2` after execution of the second line is `GraduateStudent`. Unlike declared types, the actual type of a reference is determined only at execution time and can change as the program executes.

This is a powerful idea. We can now write methods that accept a `Student` and pass either an `UndergraduateStudent` or a `GraduateStudent` object to it as below.

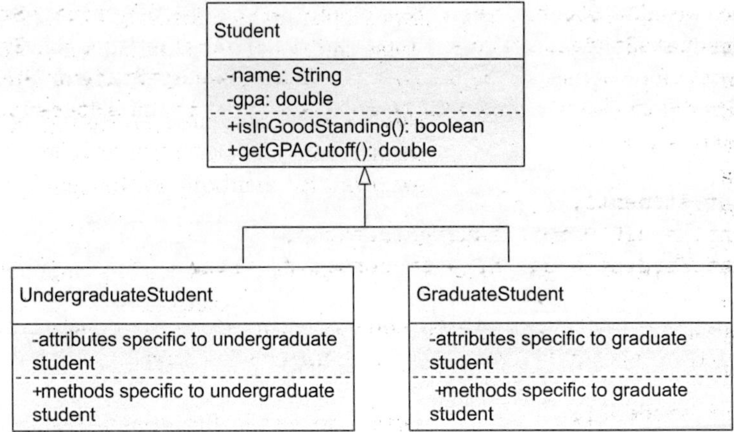


**Fig. 2.7** Student hierarchy. The class `Student` holds the features common to all students, while `GraduateStudent` and `UndergraduateStudent` hold the features unique to each.

```
public void storeStudent(Student student) {
  // code to store the Student object
}
```

We can then create `UndergraduateStudent` and `GraduateStudent` objects and pass them to the above method.

```
storeStudent(new UndergraduateStudent());
storeStudent(new GraduateStudent());
```

The parameter `student` in `storeStudent()` is a **polymorphic** reference. The adjective polymorphic is applied to anything that can take many forms. In this case, we see that the parameter `student` can take the form `UndergraduateStudent` or `GraduateStudent`. We can also write the following code:

```
Student student1 = new GraduateStudent();
Student student2 = new UndergraduateStudent();
```

Here we have two **polymorphic assignments**; objects of type `GraduateStudent` and `UndergraduateStudent` are stored in `student1` and `student2`, respectively.

In real life, we usually do not think of a graduate student as an undergraduate student or vice-versa. In the same way, we cannot write the following code in Java.

```
UndergraduateStudent student1 = new GraduateStudent(); // wrong
GraduateStudent student2 = new UndergraduateStudent(); // wrong
```

Since we allow `Student` references to point to both `UndergraduateStudent` and `GraduateStudent` objects, we can see that some, but not all, `Student` references may point to objects of type `UndergraduateStudent`; similarly, some `Student` references may refer to objects of type `GraduateStudent`. Thus, we cannot write

```
Student student1;
student1 = new UndergraduateStudent();
GraduateStudent student2 = student1; // wrong!
```

The compiler will flag that the code is incorrect. The following code is intuitively correct, but the compiler will flag it as incorrect.

```
Student student1;
student1 = new GraduateStudent();
GraduateStudent student2 = student1; // compiler generates a
syntax error.
```

The reason for this error is that the compiler *does not execute the code* to realize that `student1` is actually referring to an object of type `GraduateStudent`. It is trying to protect the programmer from the absurd situation that could arise if `student1` held a reference to an `UndergraduateStudent` object. It is the responsibility of the programmer to tell the compiler that `student1` actually points to a `GraduateStudent` object. This is done through a cast as shown below.

```
Student student1;
student1 = new GraduateStudent();
GraduateStudent student2 = (GraduateStudent) student1; // O.K.
Code works.
```

To reiterate, while casting a reference to a specialized type, the programmer must ensure that the cast will work correctly; the compiler will happily allow the code to pass syntax check, but carelessly written code will crash when executed. See the following code.

```
Student student1;
student1 = new UndergraduateStudent();
GraduateStudent student2 = (GraduateStudent) student1;
    // crashes
```

`Student1` does not point to a `GraduateStudent` object in the last line, so the system's attempt to cast the instance of `UndergraduateStudent` as an instance of `GraduateStudent` fails and a `ClassCastException` is thrown by the system. (`ClassCastException` is a kind of `RuntimeException` thrown to indicate that the code has attempted to cast an object to a subclass of which it is not an instance.)

**When can we store an object in a reference of another type?**

Consider the simple hierarchy shown in Figure 2.8.

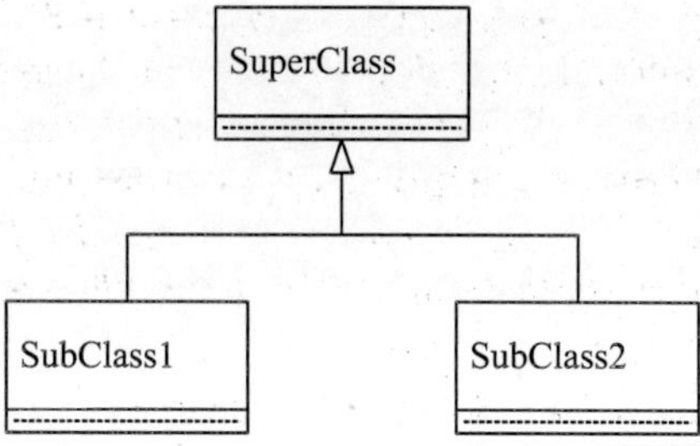


**Fig. 2.8** A simple hierarchy showing a class, `SuperClass`, with two subclasses, `SubClass1` and `SubClass2`

The general rules are as follows.

- Any object of type `SubClass1` or `SubClass2` can be stored in a reference of type `SuperClass`.
- No object of type `SubClass1` (`SubClass2`) can be stored in a reference of type `SubClass2` (`SubClass1`).
- A reference of type `SuperClass` can be cast as a reference of type `SubClass1` or `SubClass2`. If the cast fails, a `ClassCastException` is thrown by the system.

A reference is able to point to objects of different types as long as the actual types of these objects *conform* to the type of the reference. The above rules informally give the notion of **conformance.**

It is instructive to compare the assignments and casts given above with the rules for assignments and casts of variables of primitive types. Some type conversions, for example, from `int` to `float`, do not need any casting: `float` variables have a wider range than `int` variables. This is analogous to the situation we have with polymorphism, where the set of all superclass objects is a superset of the objects in any subclass. Some others, `double` to `int` being an instance, are fine with casting; however, the programmer must be prepared for loss of precision. This is similar to the loss of information that occurs when a subclass object is stored in a superclass reference. The rest – any casts from (to) `boolean` to (from) any other type – are disallowed always.

We have so far seen examples of polymorphic assignments. In one of these, we store a reference to an object of the class `GraduateStudent` in an entity whose declared type is `Student`. This is equivalent to taking a bunch of bananas and storing them in a box labeled "fruit." The declared contents of the box (as given by the label) is fruit, just as the declared type of entity `student1` on the left-hand side of the assignment is `Student`. By doing this, we have lost some information, since we can no longer find out what kind of fruit we have in the box without examining the contents. Likewise, when we operate on the entity `student1`, all we can assume is that it contains a reference to a `Student` object. *Thus, there is loss of information in this kind of assignment in the sense that we cannot access the members of the subclass using just the superclass reference.*

The second kind of polymorphic assignment is the one where we moved a reference from an entity whose declared type is `Student` to an entity whose declared type is `GraduateStudent`. (This would amount to taking the fruit out of the box labeled "fruit" and putting them in the box labeled "bananas"; we do this only if we know that the fruit are bananas.) As we saw with our cast and exception, this can only be done after ensuring that the entity being used is of type `GraduateStudent`. This is therefore an operation that "recovers" information lost in assignments of the previous kind.

What we conclude from this is that using polymorphism does result in loss of information at run time. Why, then, do we use this? The answer lies in **dynamic binding.** This ability allows us to invoke methods on members of a class hierarchy without knowing what kind of specific object we are dealing with. To make a rough analogy with the real world, this would be like a manager in a supermarket asking an assistant to put the fruits on display (this is analogous to applying the "display" method to the "fruit" object). The assistant looks at the fruit and applies the correct display technique. Here, the manager is like a client class invoking the "display" method and the assistant plays the role of the system and applies dynamic binding.

To get a concrete understanding of how dynamic binding works, let us revisit the example of the `Student` hierarchy. The code for `Student` – once again, in a simplistic manner – is written as below.

```
public abstract class Student {
  private String name;
  private double gpa;
  // more fields
  public Student(String name) {
    this.name = name;
  }
  public String getName() {
    return name;
  }
```

```
  public boolean isInGoodStanding() {
    return (gpa >= getGPACutoff());
  }
  public abstract double getGPACutoff();
  // more methods
}
```

We assume that periodically, perhaps at the end of each semester or quarter, the university will check students to see if they are in "good standing." Typically, it would mean ensuring that the student is progressing in a satisfactory manner. We assume that for a student, good standing means that the student's GPA meets a certain minimum requirement. The minimum GPA expected of students may change depending on whether the student is an undergraduate or a graduate student. The method `getGPACutoff()` returns the minimum GPA a student must have to be in good standing. We will assume that this value is 2.0 and 3.0 for undergraduate and graduate students, respectively. Note that the method is declared abstract in the `Student` class. Let us now focus on the code for `UndergraduateStudent`, which is given below.

```
public class UndergraduateStudent extends Student {
  public UndergraduateStudent(String name) {
    super(name);
  }
  public double getGPACutoff() {
    return 2.0;
  }
}
```

The constructor gets the name of the student as its only parameter and calls the superclass's constructor to store it. Since this is a non-abstract class, the `getGPACutoff` method, which returns the minimum GPA is implemented.

All of the public and protected (explained shortly) methods of a superclass are inherited in the two subclasses. So the method `isInGoodStanding()` can be instantiated on an instance of `UndergraduateStudent` as well. Thus the following code is valid:

```
UndergraduateStudent student = new UndergraduateStudent("Tom");
// code to manipulate student
if (student.isInGoodStanding()) {
   // code
} else {
   // code
}
```

When the method is called, the `isInGoodStanding()` method in the superclass `Student` will be invoked.

Finally, we have the code for the class for graduate students. The constructor for the class is quite similar to the one for the `UndergraduateStudent` class. To make the class non-abstract, this class, too, should have an implementation of `getGPACutoff()`. In addition, we assume that to be in good standing, graduate students must meet the requirements imposed on all students and they cannot have more than a certain number of courses in which they get a grade below B.

What we would like is a redefinition or **overriding** of the method `isInGoodStanding()`. Overriding is performed by defining a method in a subclass with the same name, return type, and parameters as a method in the superclass, so the subclass's definition takes precedence over the superclass's method. The modified code for the `isInGoodStanding()` method is shown below.

```
public class GraduateStudent extends Student {
  public GraduateStudent(String name) {
    super(name);
  }
  public double getGPACutoff() {
    return 3.0;
  }
  public boolean isInGoodStanding() {
    return super.isInGoodStanding() && checkOutCourses();
  }
  public boolean checkOutCourses() {
    // implementation not shown
    // checks to ensure that the student has
    // a grade below B in  in at most 3 courses
  }
}
```

Now, suppose we have the following code:

```
GraduateStudent student = new GraduateStudent("Dick");
// code to manipulate student
if (student.isInGoodStanding()) {
   // code
} else {
   // code
}
```

In this case, the call to `isInGoodStanding()` results in a call to the code defined in the `GraduateStudent` class. This in turn invokes the code in the

Student class and makes further checks using the locally declared method checkOutCourses to arrive at a decision.

Recall the StudentArrayList class we defined earlier, which stores Student objects. The method to add a Student in this class was as follows:

```
public void add(Student student) {
  // code
}
```

Since a Student reference may point to an UndergraduateStudent or a GraduateStudent object, we can pass objects of either type to the add() method and have them stored in the list. For example, the code

```
StudentArrayList students = new StudentArrayList();
UndergraduateStudent student1 = new UndergraduateStudent("Tom");
GraduateStudent student2 = new GraduateStudent("Dick");
students.add(student1);
students.add(student2);
```

stores both objects in the list students.

Suppose the class also had a method to store a Student object at a certain index, as below.

```
public Student getStudentAt(int index) {
  // Return the Student object at position index.
  // If index is invalid, return null.
}
```

Let us focus on the following code that traverses the list and checks whether the students are in good standing:

```
for (int index = 0; index < students.size(); index++) {
  if (students.getStudentAt(index).isInGoodStanding()) {
    System.out.println(students.get(index).getName()
                           + " is in good standing");
  } else {
    System.out.println(students.getStudentAt(index).getName()
                           + " is not in good standing");
  }
}
```

We assume that students Tom, an undergraduate student, and Dick, a graduate student, are in the list as per the code given a little earlier. The loop will iterate twice, first accessing the object corresponding to Tom and then getting the object for Dick. In both cases, the isInGoodStanding() method will be called.

What is interesting about the execution is that the system will determine at run time the method to call, and this decision is based on the actual type of the object. In the case of the first object, we have an instance of `UndergraduateStudent`, and since there is no definition of the `isInGoodStanding()` method in that class, the system will search for the method in the superclass, `Student`, and execute that. But when the loop iterates next, the system gets an instance of `GraduateStudent`, and since there is a definition of the `isInGoodStanding()` method in that class, the overriding definition will be called.

This is a general rule: Whenever a method call is encountered, the system will find out the actual type of the object referred to by the reference and check if there is a definition for the method in the corresponding class. If so, it will call that method. Otherwise, the search proceeds to the superclass and the process is repeated. The actual code to be executed is bound dynamically; hence this process is called dynamic binding.

The above code shows the power of dynamic binding. The reader should understand that the code indeed performed correctly. In our calls to `isInGoodStanding()`, we were unaware of the type of the objects. Simply by examining the code that calls the method, we cannot tell which definition of the `isInGoodStanding()` method will be invoked, that is, *dynamic binding gives us the ability to hide this detail in the inheritance hierarchy.*

### 2.8.4 Protected Fields and Methods

Consider the hierarchy shown in Figure 2.9. `ClosedFigure` has an attribute `area`, which stores the area of a `ClosedFigure` object. Since the classes `Polygon` and `ClosedCurve` are of the type `ClosedFigure`, we would like to make this attribute available to them. This implies that the attribute cannot be private; on the other hand, making it public could lead to inappropriate usage by other clients. The solution to this is found in the `protected` access specifier. Loosely speaking, what this means is that this field can be accessed by `ClosedFigure` and its descendants as shown below.

```
public class ClosedFigure extends Figure {
  protected  double area;
  //other fields and methods
}

public class Polygon extends ClosedFigure {
  public void insertVertex(Point point, int index) {
    // code to insert vertex point at position index
    area = computeArea();
```

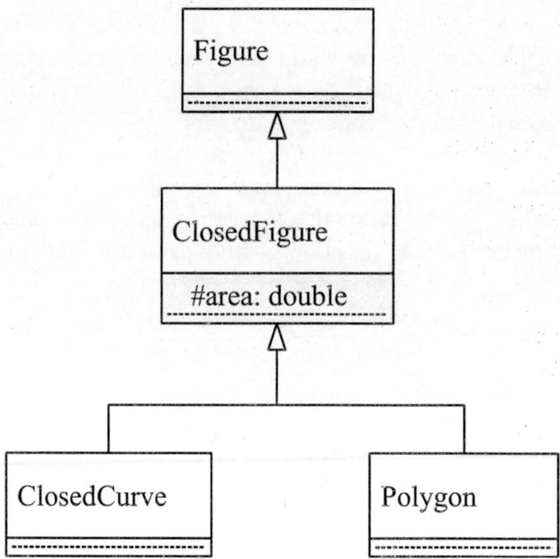


**Fig. 2.9** Figure hierarchy. The class `ClosedFigure` has a protected attribute `area`, which is available to `ClosedCurve` and `Polygon`.

```
    }
    private double computeArea() {
      //code to compute the area
    }
  }
```

Declaring it `protected` ensures that the field is available to the descendants, but cannot be accessed by code that resides outside the hierarchy rooted at `ClosedFigure`.

The above example is a simple one, since the class `Polygon` is modifying the field of a `Polygon` object. Consider the following situation:

```
public class ClosedCurve {
  // other fields and methods
  public void areaManipulator(Polygon polygon) {
    polygon.area = 0.0;
  }
}
```

Here the class `ClosedCurve` is modifying the area of a polygon. Our loose definition says that `area` is visible to `ClosedCurve` which would make this valid. However, `ClosedCurve` is a sibling of `Polygon` and is therefore not party to the design constraints of `Polygon`, and providing such access could compromise the integrity of our code. In fact, an unscrupulous client could easily do the following:

```
public class BackDoor extends ClosedFigure {
  public void setArea(double area,
                              ClosedFigure someClosedFigure) {
    someClosedFigure.area = area;
  }
}
```

We therefore need the following stricter definition of protected access. *The code residing in a class A may access a protected attribute of an object of class B only if B is at least of type A, that is, B belongs to the hierarchy rooted at A.*

With this definition, methods such as `setArea()` in `BackDoor` would violate the protected access (since `ClosedFigure` is not a subclass of `BackDoor`) and the violation can be caught at compile time. The compiler will not raise an objection if `someClosedFigure` is cast as `BackDoor` as shown below:

```
((BackDoor) someClosedFigure).area = area;
```

If `someClosedFigure` contained a reference to a `Polygon` object, the cast would fail at run time, preventing access to the protected field.

## 2.9 Design Patterns

As one may expect, a software engineer who has had experience developing a number of application systems is able to utilize the expertise so gained in future projects. Although two applications may not be alike and exhibit relatively little similarity at the outset, delving deeper into the design may exhibit a number of similar issues. Working on a variety of projects, a software engineer is exposed to problems that are common to multiple scenarios, which hones his/her ability to identify repeated instances of problems and spell out solutions for them fairly quickly. From an object-oriented perspective, what it means is that two different applications may provide design issues that are alike; the solutions may involve the development of a set of classes with similar functionalities and relationships. Thus, the class structures for the two sub-problems may end up being the same although there may be differences in the details.

An example from the imperative paradigm may help the reader better understand the above discussion. Consider two applications, one a university course registration system and the other a Human Resource (HR) system for some organization. In the first example, we may wish to provide screens that allow students to register for classes that can be selected from a list. Let us say that we will list courses sorted according to the departments in the university and that within the department, the courses will be listed in ascending order of course identifiers; the information is to be retrieved from disk before it can be displayed. In the second application, let us assume that we want to retrieve employee-related information from disk and print the information in the sorted order of departments, and within each department, in the ascending order of employee names. Although the applications are quite different, the scenarios have similarity: both involve reading information, which is data related to some application, from disk and then sorting the data based on some fields in it. An efficient sorting mechanism should be used in both cases. We could envisage similar processing in many other applications as well. A professional who has some experience in application design and is conversant with such scenarios should be able to identify the proper approach to be taken for solving the problem and employ it effectively.

In object-oriented systems, we break up the system into objects and develop classes that serve as blueprints for creating objects. Therefore, unlike the imperative world where we need to recognize the appropriate algorithms for solving a problem, the task in object-oriented systems is to recognize the necessary classes, interfaces, and relationships between them for solving a specific design problem. Such an approach, which can then be tailored to solve similar design problems that recur in a multitude of applications, is called a **design pattern**.

Here are some quotes from the literature:

> "Design patterns are partial solutions to common problems, such as separating an interface from a number of alternate implementations, wrapping around a set of legacy classes, protecting a caller from changes associated with specific problems. A design pattern is composed of a small number of classes that, through delegation and inheritance, provide a robust and modifiable solution. These classes can be adapted and refined for the specific system under construction." [1]
>
> "A pattern is a way of doing something, or a way of pursuing an intent." [7]
>
> "... a software design pattern is a general reusable solution to a commonly occurring problem within a given context in software design. It is not a finished design that can be transformed directly into source or machine code. It is a description or template for how to solve a problem that can be used in many different situations. Design patterns are formalized best practices that the programmer can use to solve common problems when designing an application or system." (Wikipedia)

A number of design patterns are known, and as one may expect, they vary in difficulty to comprehend and use. We will introduce several design patterns throughout this book, and most of them are presented in a context that explains their significance. Next, we present a commonly used design pattern.

### 2.9.1 Iterating over the Items in a List

In many applications, we need to maintain collections, which are objects that store other objects. For example, a telephone company system could have a collection object that stores an object for each of its customers; an airline system will likely maintain information about each of its flights and references to them may be stored in a collection object. In all such situations, there is often a need to go through each item in the collection and perform a common task. For instance, a telephone company may want to generate a monthly billing statement for all its customers; this would require the billing method to iterate over the collection of customers.

Depending on the type of application, the actual data structure employed may differ. Popular data structures that implement collections include linked lists, queues, stacks, double-ended queues, binary search trees, B-trees, and hash tables. One way to iterate over the collection is to access the underlying data structure and work through it. This requires the client class (the class holding a reference to a collection class and wanting to perform the iteration) to have knowledge of the details of the specific collection data structure. Such an approach makes the client too coupled to the internals of the collection class. It is therefore considered good practice for all collection classes to support a common mechanism for iterating over all the items.

### 2.9.2 Need for a Common Mechanism

Consider the class `StudentList` that stores a list of `Student` objects. Say that some university process requires going through all the objects in the list to perform some action on each. This process would use an algorithm that carries out the following:

```
while (the list has at least one unprocessed student)
     student = get an unprocessed student object from the list
     process student
```

If the `studentList` object was of type `StudentArrayList`, this code would look something like this:

```
StudentArrayList studentList;
Student student;
// other code deleted

for (int index = 0; index < studentList.size(); index++) {
    student = studentList.getStudent(index); //get next student
    student.process();
```

```
}
```

If the studentList object was of type StudentLinkedList, the code would look quite different and would be along the following lines:

```
StudentLinkedList studentList;
Student student;
for (StudentNode studentNode = studentList.getHead();
    studentNode != null;
    studentNode = studentNode.getNext()) {
    student = studentNode.getData(); //get next student
    student.process();
}
```

Such an approach suffers from two problems:

- The code for processing must be aware of how studentList is implemented. We can see that the methods being invoked in the code are different for StudentArrayList and StudentLinkedList.
- The code for traversing the list must be modified if we change the implementation for studentList. If a new data structure is available, it is likely to have different methods.

One possible solution is for the studentList interface to specifiy methods for going through the list. These methods could be as follows:

1. A method void startIteration() that performs the necessary housekeeping to permit the iteration. For StudentArrayList, this would set the index to zero; for StudentLinkedList, it would set a pointer to the head of the list.
2. A method Student getNext() that returns the next student from the list. For StudentArrayList, this would return the Student object from the array location specified by the index; for StudentLinkedList, it would return the Student object in the StudentNode that the pointer is pointing to.
3. A method boolean hasMore() that returns false if there are no more elements, true otherwise. For StudentArrayList, this would return true only when the index is less than the size; for StudentLinkedList, it would return true only when the pointer is not null.

With these methods, our code for processing a list of students would look the same for both StudentArrayList and StudentLinkedList. However, this is not a satisfactory solution for the following reasons:

- The traversal process is continuously modifying the collection object. Although the request for traversing the list originates outside the collection object, there are variables stored inside the collection that are actually controlling the process. Thus the collection object is being modified by this process. The collection class is less cohesive.

- We may have multiple traversals at the same time. There is only one variable that keeps track of where the traversal has reached. If two or more simultaneous traversals are needed, things will get complicated.
- There are several kinds of iterators. Some collections may provide both forward and backward iterators (see Exercises). If a collection has a binary tree-like structure, we can have three kinds of iterators for each of the three traversals. This interface cannot accommodate that.

### 2.9.3 The Iterator Pattern

Going back to our problem, what common mechanism should each collection provide to facilitate traversal? The traversal is a process, and we would like to keep this process separate from the data on which it is acting, that is, the collection. We therefore *encapsulate the traversal process as an object*, and store the necessary data within that object. This object has a standard interface that the client can access. At the same time, it has knowledge of and access to the implementation details of the collection over which the iteration is taking place. Changes are inevitable in almost all applications, so we must ensure that these changes do not have widespread ramifications.

In the Iterator design pattern, we have every collection class support a method, sometimes called `iterator()`, that returns an object (`Iterator` object), using which elements of the collection can be accessed. If every collection class supports this pattern, clients can use the `Iterator` object to traverse the collection, making the process independent of the collection implementation. This insulates the client code from changes in the collection class.

For example, if `myCollection` refers to an object of type `Collection`, the expression

```
myCollection.iterator()
```

returns an `Iterator` object.

The iterator supports a method called `next()`, which returns an element from the collection each time it is called. No element is returned more than once and if enough calls are made, all elements will be returned. The caller may check whether all elements have been returned by using the method `hasNext()`, which returns `true` if not all the elements have been returned.

Thus, in our scheme, we have the following classes and interfaces:

**The Iterator pattern**

An iterator allows an external object to traverse the items in a collection object without any knowledge of the data structures used by the collection. It is a behavioral pattern, that is, it identifies a common communication pattern between objects and realizes this communication pattern. This communication is realized by having the collection provide the client with an `Iterator` object with a standard interface. The iterator can traverse the collection and access the items; through the standard interface, the iterator provides the same functionality to the client. The consequence of this pattern is that it decouples a client class from a collection class.

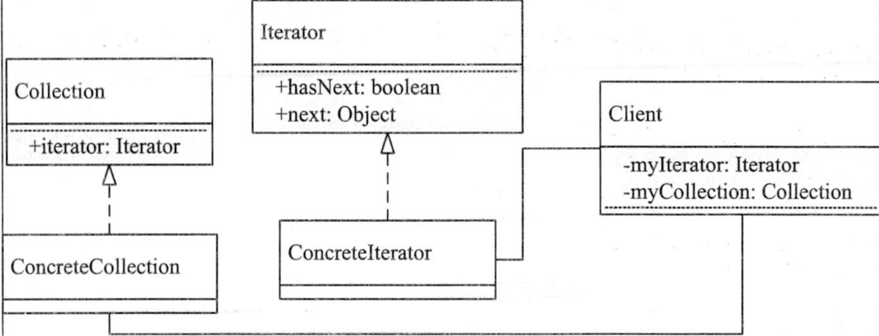


**Fig. 2.10** Class diagram for the Iterator pattern

Figure 2.10 shows the relationship between the participants. The interface `Collection` includes the method `iterator` that provides an `Iterator` object with the standard `Iterator` interface. The class `ConcreteCollection` implements this interface, and has the ability to generate a `ConcreteIterator` object that implements the `Iterator` interface. The client can then traverse the collection and access its items through the following code:

```
Collection myCollection = new ConcreteCollection();
// code to perform various functions
...
Iterator myIterator = myCollection.iterator(); // start an
iteration
Object object;
while (myIterator.hasNext()) { //traverse the collection
  object = myIterator.next();
  // other code to work with object
}
```

1. `Collection`, an interface that allows the usual operations to add and delete objects, plus the method `iterator()` that returns an `Iterator` object.
2. `Iterator`, an interface that supports the operations `hasNext()` and `next()` described earlier.
3. Implementation of the `Collection` interface. Obviously, every implementation must implement the `iterator()` method by creating an `Iterator` object and returning it.
4. Implementation of the `Iterator` interface. This class must cooperate with the code in (3) above to properly access and return the elements of the collection.
5. Client code that uses the collection.

Let us look at the class `LinkedList` in Java, which implements `Collection` and supports the `iterator()` method.

```
Collection collection = new LinkedList();
collection.add("Element 1");
collection.add(new Integer(2));
for (Iterator iterator = collection.iterator(); iterator.
hasNext(); ) {
  System.out.println(iterator.next());
}
```

The first line creates a `LinkedList` object, whose reference is stored in the variable `collection`. We add two elements to the collection, a `String` object and an `Integer` object. Every object of type `Collection` supports the `iterator()` method, and this method is invoked in the initialization of the `for` loop. The returned object `iterator` is of type `Iterator`. Before entering the loop the first time or in any succeeding iteration, we make sure that we have not processed all the elements. The method call `iterator.hasNext()` returns `true` if there is at least one element in the collection not yet retrieved since `iterator` was created. Such a collection element is retrieved in the body of the loop by the call `iterator.next()`. In this code, we simply print the elements. Thus we will end up printing `Element 1` and 2 in successive lines.

### Iterator Implementation

In this section, we describe how to implement an iterator in Java. Suppose we have an interface `Queue`, which enables us to add and remove objects using queue discipline (FIFO).

```
public interface Queue {
  public boolean add(Object value);
  public Object remove();
```

```
}
```

We implement the above interface in LinkedQueue. The inner class Node stores an object and the reference to the next element in the linked list. The head and tail of the queue are stored in the variables head and tail, respectively.

```
import java.util.*;
public class LinkedQueue implements Queue {
  private Node head;
  private Node tail;
  private int numberOfElements;
  private class Node {
    private Object data;
    private Node next;
    private Node(Object object, Node next) {
      this.data = object;
      this.next = next;
    }
    public Object getData() {
      return data;
    }
    public void setNext(Node next) {
      this.next = next;
    }
    public Node getNext() {
      return next;
    }
  }
  // Queue methods
}
```

The add method creates an instance of Node and inserts it at the tail of the list. The code is straightforward.

```
  public boolean add(Object value) {
    Node node = new Node(value, null);
    if (tail == null) {
      tail = head = node;
    } else {
      tail.setNext(node);
      tail = node;
    }
    numberOfElements++;
    return true;
  }
```

The `remove` method also employs the standard approach to deleting from a queue. Before changing the value of `head`, we retrieve the contents of the first node in the queue, so we can return the deleted element.

```
public Object remove() {
  if (head == null) {
    return null;
  }
  Object value = head.getData();
  head = head.getNext();
  if (head == null) {
    tail = null;
  }
  numberOfElements--;
  return value;
}
// The iterator method returns a new Iterator.
public Iterator iterator() {
  return new QueueIterator();
}
```

The iterator is implemented as an inner class. In the interface `java.util.Iterator`, there are three methods: `hasNext()`, `next()`, and `remove()`, the last operation being optional.

The `Iterator` object must have access to the list of elements in the queue that are not yet returned to the client. For this we take advantage of the fact that the `LinkedQueue` class itself has a linked list and that list is accessible from code within `QueueIterator`. However, the `Iterator` class must not modify the field `head` in `LinkedQueue`; for this, we maintain a field called `cursor` within `QueueIterator`. This field is initialized to `head` when the `Iterator` object is created.

```
private class QueueIterator implements Iterator {
  private Node cursor;
  public QueueIterator() {
    cursor = head;
  }
  // hasNext, next, and remove
}
```

Our plan is to return the elements as they appear in the queue. Therefore, the code for `hasNext` is quite simple: we just need to make sure that `cursor` is not `null`. Hence we have

```
  public boolean hasNext() {
```

```
    return cursor != null;
  }
```

To retrieve the next element, we must first make sure that there is at least one element not supplied to the client. That is, `hasNext()` does not return a `null` value. Then, we just move one element forward by setting `cursor` to `cursor.getNext()`.

```
public Object next() {
  if (!hasNext()) {
    return null;
  }
  Object object = cursor.getData();
  cursor = cursor.getNext();
  return object;
}
```

We will not support the `remove()` method, so it is coded as below.

```
public void remove() {
}
```

The above implementation shows the clean separation between the collection and the iterator. Another advantage of this approach is that we incur no additional complexity if multiple iterators are employed simultaneously. The following code illustrates this:

```
LinkedQueue collection = new LinkedQueue();
collection.add(new Integer(1));
collection.add(new Integer(2));
for (Iterator iterator1 = collection.iterator();
iterator1.hasNext(); ) {
  Integer int1 = (Integer) iterator1.next();
  int count = 0;
  for (Iterator iterator2 = collection.iterator();
  iterator2.hasNext(); ) {
    Integer int2 = (Integer) iterator2.next();
    if (int1.equals(int2)) {
      count++;
    }
  }
  System.out.println(int1 + count);
}
```

## 2.10 Run-Time Type Identification

An inheritance hierarchy can involve a large number of classes. In addition, more classes can be added to the hierarchy over a period of time to allow for new functionality. Although dynamic binding is a powerful tool, there are situations when it is not sufficient. Such situations typically occur when the original designer did not anticipate all possible changes. As a simple example, consider a `Shape` class with several subclasses like `Square` and `Circle`, and a `ShapeList` class, which holds a collection of `Shape` objects. If we access an item from this collection, we know that it will be of type `Shape`, but we do not know whether it will be a `Square` or a `Circle`. In a typical application, one would expect that new kinds of shapes would be added over time.

Say we have a new client application that needs to know the number of `Circle` objects in a `ShapeList` collection. We cannot modify `ShapeList`, since other applications are using it. The problem can be solved if the client iterates over all the `Shape` objects and checks which ones are circles. In such a situation, one approach would be to perform dynamic type checking, or **run-time type identification (RTTI)**. Java provides the `instanceof` operator, which could be used as follows:

```
public class ShapeClient {
  private ShapeList shapeList = new ShapeList();
  public void countCircles() {
    int count = 0;
    Iterator shapeIterator = shapeList.iterator();
    while (shapeIterator.hasNext()) {
      if (shapeIterator.next() instanceof Circle) {
         count++;
      }
    }
    System.out.println("count " + count);
  }
}
```

The `instanceof` operator returns `true` if the object returned by `shapeIterator.next()` is an instance of the class `Circle`. An alternative approach would be to downcast the object as a `Circle` and increment the counter in a `try` block and then catch the `ClassCastException`, as shown below.

```
public void countCircles() {
  int count = 0;
  Circle circle;
  Iterator shapeIterator = shapeList.iterator();
  while (shapeIterator.hasNext()) {
```

```
    try {
      circle = (Circle) (shapeIterator.next());
      count++;
    } catch(ClassCastException cce){
    }
  }
  System.out.println("count " + count);
}
```

As is obvious, the first approach is more elegant. A third approach is possible in Java through the reflection mechanism which we shall see in the next section. Use of RTTI can be minimized by employing good design principles. (In the above example, if the designer had anticipated the need for adding new functionality, the `Shape` class could have been designed to *accept visitors*, which would have avoided the need for RTTI; we shall learn about visitors in a later chapter.) However, it is not possible to anticipate all situations, and when the need arises, RTTI provides a quick way of dealing with them.

## 2.11 The `Object` Class

Java has a special class called `Object` from which every class inherits. In other words, `Object` is superclass of every class in Java, and it is at the root of the class hierarchy. Thus we can declare a reference to be of type `Object`, and store a reference to any object, without regard to the class to which the object belongs. The `Object` class serves two important functions: providing utility methods and system support. Utility methods are for general purpose operations that have been found to be useful for all classes. By defining these in `Object`, Java provides a shared understanding of their syntax and semantics. Java runs on a virtual machine (JVM), which is connected to the operating system. The `Object` class provides some methods that the JVM can invoke, without any knowledge of the class to which the object belongs.

### 2.11.1 Using `Object` as a General Reference

When we declare a class in Java that does not extend any other class, it automatically becomes a direct descendant of the `Object` class. Therefore every class in Java is either a direct or indirect descendant of `Object`. From our knowledge of polymorphic assignments, we can see that a variable of type

Object can store the reference to an object of any other type. The following code is thus legal:

```
Object anyObject;
anyObject = new Student();
anyObject = new Integer(4);
anyObject = "Some string";
```

In the above code, the variable anyObject first stores a Student object, then an Integer object, and finally a String object.

We can use an Object reference when we need to refer to objects that belong to any one of several unrelated classes. An example of where this ability is required is the equals() method (discussed in the next subsection) which checks if two object references are referring to the same object. Since this can be applied to any two objects, the parameter to the method is of type Object.

Having an identifier that can reference any object is very unusual in well-designed applications; in fact, such a situation can often indicate that some principle of good design is being violated. In earlier versions of Java (up to Java SE 1.4), there were no generics. In those versions, the Object class was used to create library classes that could be used for a variety of applications. For instance, in the LinkedList class in JDK 1.4, we see the method

```
void add(int index, Object element)
```

This method inserts the specified element at the specified position in this list. The parameter element is declared as belonging to the class Object. A programmer could employ an instance of this class, and add items belonging to any class. Such an approach was replaced by generics in Java SE 1.5, but may still be encountered in legacy code.

## 2.11.2 Utility Methods Provided by Object

Java designers have decided that some methods are useful for all classes and should be invoked in a uniform way. This is accomplished by defining these methods as a part of the Object class.

### 2.11.2.1 The equals() and hashCode() Methods

The equals() method provides a mechanism for checking if two objects are equal in value. Given any two variables of the same *primitive type*, it is easy for Java to decide whether they are equal: the variables are equal if they have the same value, which can be checked using the == operator. However, consider a class such as `Student`, which is a user-defined class. How should we decide that two `Student` objects are equal? Here are some interpretations of equality:

- *The two objects are equal if they occupy the same physical storage.* In this case, the language would have to provide some mechanism to determine if this is the case.
- *The two objects are equal if all the corresponding fields of the objects are equal.* This is a recursive definition. For example, in the `Student` class, the fields are `name`, `address`, and `gpa`. To decide if the `name` fields of two objects are equal, we need to know when two `String` objects are equal. Since `gpa` is a `double`, that field presents no problems.
- *The two objects are equal if some subset of the corresponding fields of the objects are equal.* This would only check some key field, say, the `id` of a person.

The Java language supports the first interpretation through the `==` operator. To use one of the other interpretations, Java provides an `equals()` method which can be defined by the author of the class; if this is not defined, the `equals()` method defaults to the `==` operator. The `equals()` method has the following template:

```
public boolean equals(Object anObject) {
  // implement the policy for comparison in this method.
  // return true if and only if this object is equal to anObject
}
```

We are given two objects: `this`, the one on which we invoke `equals()`, and `anObject`, which is an arbitrary object and can be of any type. The author of the class is free to choose a mechanism that decides whether `anObject` is equal to `this`.

For example, let us say that a `Student` object is equal to another object only if that object is a `Student` object, and the names are equal, and they have the same address.

```
public boolean equals(Object anObject) {
  Student student = (Student) anObject;
  return student.name.equals(name) &&
  student.address.equals(address);
}
```

The first thing that the `equals()` method does is to cast the incoming object as a `Student` object; the resulting reference is used to access all of the members of the corresponding `Student` object, and, in particular, the `name` and `address` fields.

After the cast, we check if the `name` field of the cast object is equal to the `name` field of `this`; note that we perform this by invoking the `equals()` method on the object `student.name`, which is a `String`; thus, we are invoking the `equals()` method of the `String` class. It turns out that the `equals` method of the `String` class is defined to return `true` if and only if every character in one string is equal to the corresponding character of the other string.

The `address` fields are compared in a similar way. The method returns `true` if and only if the two fields match. The method is placed inside the `Student` class and is invoked as below.

```
Student student1 = new Student("Tom");
student1.setAddress("1 Main Street");
// some other code
Student student2 = new Student("Tom");
student2.setAddress("1 Main Street");
// more code
if (student1.equals(student2)) {
  System.out.println("student1 is the same as student2");
} else {
  System.out.println("student1 is not the same as student2");
}
```

After creating the two `Student` objects with the same name and address, we invoked the `equals` method on `student1` with `student2` as the actual parameter.

There is more to the issue of making comparisons reliable. When a class redefines the `equals()` method, it is expected that the redefinition satisfies the following conditions:

- *Implements an equivalence relation*: For any two objects belonging to `C`, the boolean relation defined by `equals()` should be *symmetric, reflexive*, and *transitive*.
- *Is consistent*: If two objects belonging to `C` are compared, we will get the same result as long as the objects have not been modified.
- *Distinguishes the* `null` *reference*: For any reference `c` of type `C`, `c.equals(null)` should return `false` as long as `c` is not `null`.

These requirements mean that the `equals()` method should return `true` only if the objects being compared belong to the exact same class. Consider a different implementation of `Student`, in which we use the ID as a unique key. We may then use the ID to search a `StudentList` for a particular student. It is tempting to use `equals()` to compare a given ID with the ID of each `Student` in the list. The following code in the class `Student` would compile correctly:

```
public class Student {
  private String name;
  private double gpa;
  private String id;

  // other code deleted

  public boolean equals(Object anObject) {
    return ((String) obj).equals(id);
  }

}
```

The `equals()` method returns `true` if the current object's `id` field matches the given `String`. The method can be invoked as:

```
Student student = new Student("John", "X1");
String ids = new String("X1");
if (student.equals(ids)) {
// some code
}
```

The problem in the above code is that `equals()` compares `student`, a `Student`, with `ids` which is a `String`, and finds them to be equal. Such a relationship between objects is *not symmetric*. Symmetry implies that if we swap the two entities being compared for equality, the result should be the same. In the above code, we invoked `equals()` on `student` and passed `ids` as a parameter. If we invoke `equals()` on `ids` and pass `student` as a parameter, we get the following expression:

```
ids.equals(student)
```

This expression will use the `equals()` method of `String` with a `Student` as parameter and therefore find them to be unequal. The `equals()` method in `Student` therefore violates the condition that `equals()` should implement an equivalence relation. Clearly a pair of objects cannot be included in an equivalence relation if they belong to different classes. Our first order of business in the `equals()` method should therefore be to verify that `anObject` is of type `Student`, which can be done using the `instanceof` operator. This guard should be placed at the beginning of the template for `equals()`; our earlier code for checking the equality of `Student` objects by comparing `name` and `address` should therefore be rewritten as:

```
public boolean equals(Object anObject) {
  if (!(anObject instanceof Student)) {
       return false;
  }
```

```
    Student student = (Student) anObject;
    return student.name.equals(name) &&
    student.address.equals(address);
  }
```

The definition of equals() should also be in agreement with the way in which objects of the class are placed in hash-based data structures. If two objects considered equal can hash to different locations, our search operations will not be correct. To address this, the Object class includes a hashCode() method which must be defined to comply with the definition of equals(). Every object in Java has a **hashcode**, which is a 32-bit signed integer, which is used when the object has to be managed by a hash-based data structure. When we invoke the hashCode() method on an object, it returns an int, which is the hashcode for the object. The requirements of this method are:

- The hashcode of an object should not change during the execution of a program as long as no information used in the computation of the equals() method has been modified.
- If we have objects, o1 and o2, such that o1.equals(o2) returns true, then they must have the same hashcode. However, if o1.equals(o2) returns false, o1 and o2 are not required to have different hashcodes.

Enforcing this relationship between equals() and hashcode() is not trivial. Consider again our class Student, in which two Student objects are considered equal if their IDs are equal. To comply with the above requirements, we need to ensure that having equal ID values would ensure equal hashcodes. One way to do that would be to use the hashcode() method for String.

```
public class Student {

  // other code deleted

  public int hashCode()  {
    return  id.hashcode();
  }

}
```

#### 2.11.2.2 The toString() Method

The toString() method, as we have seen earlier, gives us a textual representation of the object. By including this in the Object class, operations like System.out.println() can be completed without worrying about the specific object that is being printed to the output stream.

#### 2.11.2.3 The getClass() and clone() Methods

In the field of computing, **reflection** is defined as the ability of a process to obtain knowledge of, and examine, its own structure and behavior. Reflection should be used only by developers who have a strong grasp of the language and of the software development process. It is a very powerful technique that allows us to to perform operations which would otherwise be impossible.

Central to Java's support for reflection is the `Class` object. For each class, Java defines a `Class` object that represents the run-time class, and contains all the information specific to the class. Say we have a class `C` and an object `c1` belonging to `C`. Any application program can access the `Class` object for `C` through the `getClass()` method.

```
C c1 = new C();
Class classObject = c1.getClass();
```

The object `classObject` is declared to be a reference to a `Class` object; after the second statement, it holds a reference to an object that contains all the information about the class `C`. The `Class` object provides us with several methods through which can get information about the class.

A simple application of reflection is in run-time type identification using the `getName()` method in `Class`. This method returns a `String` which represents the name of the class. In the context of the above code, `classObject.getName()` returns the `String` "`C`", which is the name of `C`. We can use this method as an alternative to the `instanceof` operator. As an example, we had a piece of code in the previous section with the conditional expression

```
(allShapes.next() instanceof Circle)
```

This expression can be replaced by

```
if (allShapes.next().getClass().getName().equals("Circle"))
```

Here, we are explicitly getting the name of the class to which the `Shape` object belongs, and checking it against the string "Circle". One drawback of using reflection for RTTI is that code with typographical errors can compile and return an incorrect result. For instance, the conditional

```
(allShapes.next().getClass().getName().equals ("Circule"))
```

will compile, but will fail to identify any object as belonging to `Circle`. Such an error will be detected by the compiler when we employ the `instanceof` operator, unless we have also defined a class named `Circule`.

**Cloning** in the context of object-oriented programming refers to the making of an exact copy of an object. By providing the `clone()` method as part of `Object`, Java provides a standard way of invoking this feature. It is not required that all classes provide a `clone()` method. Hence the method is declared to be `protected`, allowing all user-defined classes to deal with clonability as they see fit. However, it is expected by convention that any subclass of `Object` that makes itself clonable will invoke `super.clone()`. If this convention is followed, we can ensure that the `getClass()` method will work correctly for the cloned copy of the object. Since an object can contain references to objects of other classes, making a clone is complicated. We shall look at this in greater detail in a later chapter.

### 2.11.3 Methods for System Support

Since the JVM is like a virtual computer, it performs operating system operations and also communicates with the underlying physical computer system. As a result, there are several operations that the JVM needs to perform on individual objects. These operations must necessarily be invoked without knowledge of the class to which the object belongs, and are therefore placed in the `Object` class. By overriding these methods, a user-defined class can send specific instructions to the JVM and the operation system.

#### 2.11.3.1 Memory Management

Computer systems have two kinds of memory: statically allocated memory on the *stack* and dynamically allocated memory on the *heap*. Static allocation is carried out when the program starts execution, and the amount of memory allocated does not change during execution. Dynamic allocation occurs as the program executes, and the amount of memory allocated varies depending on the specific execution path. Memory management in Java involves dynamically allocating space on the heap for new objects and removing unused objects to make space for new object allocations.

**Garbage collection** is the process of freeing unused space for new objects. An object is considered to be **garbage** if it cannot be reached, directly or indirectly, through any reference. Consider the following code that creates a `Student` object with name "John" and ID "X1" and adds the object to a list:

```
Student s1 = new Student("John", "X1");
StudentList slist = new StudentList();
slist.add(s1);
```

At this point, the `Student` object (with name "John" and ID "X1") exists on the heap, and the reference to this object is stored in two places: in the variable `s1` and inside the `StudentList` object referenced by `slist`. This means that both `s1` and `slist` store the address of the memory word(s) in which this `Student` object is stored. Later in the execution, we may no longer need to track this student and may execute the code

```
slist.remove("X1")
```

which removes the reference to the `Student` object with ID "X1" from `slist`. This object is no longer needed, but `s1` still holds a reference to the object. If we free the memory word(s) in which the `Student` object was stored, those words may be allocated to some other object. However, `s1` stores the address of those words, and the statement `System.out.println(s1.getName());` will access those word(s) and print out whatever data is stored there. In such a situation, `s1` is termed a **dangling reference.**

To avoid creating dangling references, JVM employs a sophisticated garbage collection process to detect the garbage objects. It may, however, be possible that a useful object is identified as garbage, or that an object requires some specific clean-up operations to be performed before it is discarded. To take care of these possibilities, the JVM invokes the `finalize()` method on the object, when it is identified as garbage for the first time. If the object is identified as garbage a second time, it is discarded. The `finalize` method is never invoked more than once by a Java virtual machine for any given object.

#### 2.11.3.2 Thread Support

Modern operating systems use the concept of **threads**, which serve as a mechanism for dividing a program into two or more simultaneously (or pseudo-simultaneously) running tasks. The JVM allows an application to have multiple threads of execution running concurrently. Threads in Java are associated with objects, and it follows that the `Object` class should provide methods for supporting thread-based execution.

The `notify()` method is used when we have situations where multiple threads want to access an object, but only one thread can access the object at a given time. The threads that do not have access to the object are said to be **waiting**. The `notify()` method is used to wake up (reactivate) one of the waiting threads. The `notifyAll()` method is used to wake up all the waiting threads. While these two methods are used to reactivate waiting threads, the `wait()` method is invoked when a thread that is currently accessing the object has to be asked to wait. Threads are discussed in greater detail in Chapter 8.

## 2.12 An Introduction to Generics in Java

Genericity is a mechanism for creating entities that vary only in the types of their parameters, and this notion can be associated with any entity (class or method) that requires parameters of some specific types. As we have seen before, in the definition of any entity, the types of the parameters involved are specified. In the case of a method, we specify the types of the arguments and the return type. In the case of a class, the types of the arguments to the constructor(s), the return types and argument types of the methods are all specified. In any instance of the entity, the actual types of all these parameters must conform to the corresponding types specified in the definition. When we specify a generic entity, the types of the parameters are replaced by placeholders, which are called *generic parameters.* The entity is therefore *not fully specified* and cannot be used as such to instantiate any concrete objects. At the time of creating artifacts (objects, if our generic entity was a class), these placeholders must be replaced by actual types.

To understand the usefulness of genericity, consider the following implementation of a stack:

```
public class Stack {
  private class StackNode {
    Object data;
    StackNode next;
    // rest of the class not shown
  }
  public void push(Object data) {
    // implementation not shown
  }
  public Object pop() {
    // implementation not shown
  }
  // rest of the class not shown
}
```

Elements of the stack are stored in the `data` field of `StackNode`. Notice that `data` is of type `Object`, which means that any type of data can be stored in it.

We create a stack and store an `Integer` object in it.

```
Stack myIntStack = new Stack(); // line 1
myIntStack.push(new Integer(5)); // line 2
Integer x = (Integer) myIntStack.pop(); //line 3
```

This implementation has some drawbacks. In line 2, there is nothing that prevents us from pushing arbitrary objects into the stack. The following code, for instance, is perfectly valid:

```
Stack myIntStack = new Stack();
myIntStack.push("A string");
```

The reason for this is that the `Stack` class creates a stack of `Object` and will, therefore, accept any object as an argument for `push`. The second drawback follows from the same cause; the following code will generate an error:

```
Stack myIntStack = new Stack();
myIntStack.push("A string");
Integer x = (Integer) myIntStack.pop(); // erroneous cast
```

We could write extra code that handles the errors caused by the erroneous cast, but it does not make for readable code. On the other hand, we could write a separate `Stack` class for every kind of stack that we need, but then we would be unable to reuse our code.

Generics provides us with a way out of this dilemma. A generic `Stack` class would be defined as something like this:

```
public class Stack<E> {
  //code for fields and constructors
   public void push(E item) {
     // code to push item into stack
   }
   public E pop() {
     // code to push item into stack
   }
}
```

A `Stack` that stores only `Integer` objects can now be defined as

```
Stack<Integer> myIntStack = new Stack<Integer>();
```

The statement

```
  myIntStack.push("A string");
```

will trigger an error message from the compiler, which expects that the parameter to the `push` method of `myIntStack` will be a subtype of `Integer`.

## 2.13 Discussion and Further Reading

The concept of a class is fundamental to the object-oriented paradigm. As we have discussed, it is based on the notion of an abstract data type and one can trace its origins to the Simula programming language. This chapter also discussed some of the UML notation used for describing classes. In the next chapter, we look at how classes interconnect to form a system, and the use of UML to denote these relationships.

The Java syntax and concepts that we have described in this chapter are quite similar to the ones in C++, so the reader should have little difficulty in learning that language. A fundamental difference between Java and C++ is in the availability of pointers in C++, which can be manipulated using pointer arithmetic in ways that add considerable flexibility and power to the language. However, pointer arithmetic and other features in the language also make C++ more challenging to someone new to this paradigm.

Since our intention is to cover just enough language features to complete the implementations, some readers may wish to explore other features of the language. For those who want an exposure to the numerous features of the language, we suggest Core Java by Cornell and Horstmann [5]. A more gentle and slow exposure to programming in Java can be found in Liang [6]. If the syntax and semantics of Java come fairly easy to you, but you wish to get more insights into Java usage, you may wish to take a look at Eckel [4].

It is important to realize that the concepts of object-oriented programming we have discussed are based on the Java language. The ideas are somewhat different in languages such as Ruby, which abandons static type checking and allows much more dynamic changes to class structure during execution time. For an introduction to Ruby, see Cooper [2].

A thorough knowledge of inheritance is vital to anyone engaging in OOAD. While the notion of a class helps us implement abstract data types, it is inheritance that makes the object-oriented paradigm so powerful. Inheriting from a superclass makes it possible not only to reuse existing code in the superclass, but also to view instances of all subclasses as members of the superclass type. Polymorphic assignments combined with dynamic binding of methods makes it possible to allow uniform processing of objects without having to worry about their exact types.

Dynamic binding is implemented using a table of method pointers that give the address of the methods in the class. When a method is overridden, the table in the extending class points to the new definition of the method. For an easily understandable treatment of this approach, the reader may consult Eckel[3].

There is some overhead associated with dynamic binding. In C++, the programmer can specify that a method is *virtual*, which means that dynamic binding will be used during method invocation. Methods not defined as virtual will be called using the declared type of the the reference used in the call. This helps the programmer avoid the overhead associated with dynamic binding in method calls that do not really need the power of dynamic binding. In C++ parlance, all Java methods are virtual.

## Projects

1. A consumer group tests products. Create a class named Product with the following fields:

   a. Model name
   b. Manufacturer's name
   c. Retail price
   d. A reliability rating (based on consumer survey) that is a double number between 0 and 5
   e. The number of customers who contributed to the survey on the reliability rating

   Remember that names must hold a sequence of characters and the retail price may have a fractional part.

   The class must have two constructors:

   a. The first constructor accepts the model name, the manufacturer's name, and the retail price in that order.
   b. The second constructor accepts the model name and the manufacturer's name in that order, and this constructor must effectively use the first constructor.

   Write methods to obtain every field. Write a method to set the retail price.

   Reliability rating is the average of the reliability ratings by all customers who rated this product. A method called `rateReliability` should be written to input the reliability rating of a customer. This method has a single parameter that takes in the reliability of the product as viewed by a customer. The method must then increment the number of customers who rated the product and update the reliability rating using the following formula:

   New value of Reliability rating = (Old value of reliability rating * Old value of number of customers + Reliability rating by this customer) / New value of number of customers.

   For example, suppose that the old value of reliability was 4.5 based on the input from 100 customers. If a new customer gives a reliability rating of 1.0, then the new value of reliability would be

   ```
   (4.5 * 100 + 1.0) / 101
   ```

   which is 4.465347

   Override the `toString()` method appropriately, so we can see the value stored clearly when the string is printed.

2. Write a Java class called `LongInteger` according to the following specifications. Objects of this type are immutable.

   Objects of this class store integers that can be as long as 50 digits. The class must have the following constructors and methods:

   a. `public LongInteger()`: Sets the integer to 0.
   b. `public LongInteger(short[] otherDigits)`: Sets the integer to the given integer represented by the parameter. A copy of `otherDigits` must be made to prevent accidental changes. Assume that the length of `otherDigits` is no more than 50.
   c. `public LongInteger(int number)`: Sets the integer to the value given in the parameter.
   d. `public LongInteger add(int number)`: Adds `number` to the integer represented by this object and returns the result. (Remember that `LongInteger` is immutable.) Assume the result can be represented in 50 digits.
   e. `public LongInteger add(LongInteger number)`: Adds `number` to the integer represented by this object and returns the result. (Remember that `LongInteger` is immutable.) Assume the result can be represented in 50 digits.
   f. `public String toString()`: Returns a `String` representation of the integer.

   Use an array of 50 `shorts` to store the digits of the number.

3. Study the interface `Extendable` given below.

```
public interface Extendable {
  public boolean append(char c);
  public boolean append(char[] sequence);
}
```

   A class `C` that implements this interface maintains a sequence of characters. The method `append(char c)` appends a character to the character sequence. The second version of the method appends all characters in the array to this sequence. If for some reason the character(s) cannot be appended, the methods return `false`; otherwise they return `true`.

4. Consider the interface `Shape` given below:

```
public interface Shape {
  public double getArea();
  public double getPerimeter();
  public void draw();
}
```

Design and code two classes `Rectangle` and `Circle` that implement `Shape`. Put as many common attributes and methods as possible in an abstract class from which `Rectangle` and `Circle` inherit. Ensure that your code is modular. For drawing a shape, simply print the shape type and other information associated with the object.

Next, implement the following interface using any strategy you like. The interface maintains a collection of shapes. The `draw` method draws every shape in the collection.

```
public interface Shapes {
  public void add(Shape shape);
  public void draw();
}
```

Then, test your implementation by writing a driver that creates some `Shape` objects, puts them in the collection, and draws them.

5. The following interface specifies a data source, which consists of a number of x-values and a corresponding set of y-values. The method `getNumberOfPoints` returns the number of x-values for which there is a corresponding y-value. `getX` (`getY`) returns the x-value (y-value) for a specific index (0 ≤ `index` < `getNumberOfPoints`).

```
public interface DataSource {
  public int getNumberOfPoints();
  public int getX(int index);
  public int getY(int index);
}
```

The next interface is for a chart that can be used to display a specific data source.

```
public interface Chart {
  public void setDataSource(DataSource source);
  public void display();
}
```

A user will create a `DataSource` object, put some values in it, create a `Chart` object, use the former as the data source for the latter, and then call `display()` to display the data.

Here is a possible use. Note that `MyDataSource` and `LineChart` are implementations of `DataSource` and `Chart`, respectively.

```
DataSource source = new MyDataSource();
Char chart = new LineChart();
chart.setDataSource(source);
chart.display();
```

Implement the interface DataSource in a class MyDataSource. Create methods in it to store x and y values.

Provide two implementations of Chart: LineChart and BarChart. For displaying the chart, simply print out the x and y values and the type of chart being printed. If needed, put the common functionality in an abstract superclass.

6. Implement three classes: BinaryTreeNode, BinaryTree, and BinarySearchTree. The first class implements the functionality of a node in a binary tree, the second is an abstract class that has methods for visiting the tree, computing its height, etc., and the third class extends the second to implement the functionality of a binary search tree to add data.
7. Create a Java program with the following classes and meet the given specifications:

   - An abstract class named Position, which stores the degree and minute of either a longitude or a latitude.
   - A subclass of Position named Latitude, which represents the latitude of a position. It should have an extra attribute (of type char) to store either 'N' or 'S.'
   - A subclass of Position named Longitude, which represents the longitude of a position. It should have an extra attribute (of type char) to store either 'E' or 'W.'
   - A class named WeatherInformation to store the maximum and minimum temperature of a point on the earth. It should have attributes to store the latitude, longitude, minimum temperature ever recorded, and maximum temperature ever recorded at that position.
   - The class WeatherInformation must implement the following interface:

```
public interface WeatherRecord {
  /**
    * Sets the maximum temperature
 * @param maxTemperature the new maximum temperature
  */
  public void setMaxTemperature(double maxTemperature);
  /**
    * Sets the minimum temperature
    * @param minTemperature the new minimum temperature
    */
    public void setMinTemperature(double minTemperature);
}
```

   - A driver to test the above implementation.

## Exercises

1. Given the following class, write a constructor that has no parameters, but uses the given constructor so that x and y are initialized at construction time to 1 and 2, respectively.

```
public class SomeClass {
  private int x;
  private int y;
  public SomeClass(int a, int b) {
    x = a;
    y = b;
  }
  // write a no-argument (no parameters)
  // constructor here, so that x and y are
  // initialized to 1 and 2 respectively.
  // You MUST Utilize the given constructor.
}
```

2. In Section 2.3, we had a class called `Course`, which had a method that creates `Section` objects. Modify the two classes so that:

   a. `Course` class maintains the list of all sections.

   b. `Section` stores the capacity and the number of students enrolled in the section.

   c. `Course` has a search facility that returns a list of sections that are not full.

3. Trace the following code and write what the program prints.

```
public class A {
  protected int i;
  public void modify(int x) {
    i = x + 8;
    System.out.println("A: i is " + i);
  }
  public int getI() {
    System.out.println("A: i is " + i);
    return i;
  }
}
public class B extends A {
  protected int j;
  public void modify(int x) {
    System.out.println("B: x is " + x);
```

```
      super.modify(x);
      j = x + 2;
      System.out.println("B: j is " + j);
    }
    public int getI() {
      System.out.println("B: j is " + j);
      return super.getI() + j;
    }
  }
  public class UseB {
    public static void main(String[] s) {
      A a1 = new A();
      a1.modify(4);
      System.out.println(a1.getI());
      B b1 = new B();
      b1.modify(5);
      System.out.println(b1.getI());
      a1 = b1;
      a1.modify(6);
      System.out.println(a1.getI());
    }
  }
```

4. Consider the class `Rectangle` in Project 4. Extend it to implement a square.
5. A manager at a small zoo instructs the zoo-keeper to "feed the animals." Explain how a proper completion of this task by the zoo-keeper implies that the zoo operations are implicitly employing the concepts of inheritance, polymorphism, and dynamic binding. (Hint: Defining a class `Animal` with method `feed` could prove helpful.)
6. Write the `equals()` method in a situation where two `Student` objects are considered equal if their IDs are equal. There should be no exceptions thrown by the code.
7. Suggest an implementation for `hashcode()` when two `Student` objects are considered equal if their names and addresses are identical.

## References

1. Bruegge, B and Dutoit, AH. 2000. *Object-Oriented Software Engineering.* Prentice Hall International: Englewood Cliffs, NJ, USA.
2. Cooper, P. 2007. *Beginning Ruby: From Novice to Professional.* Apress: New York, NY, USA.

3. Eckel, B. 2000. *Thinking in C++, Volume 1 (2nd Edition).* Prentice Hall: Upper Saddle River, NJ, USA.
4. Eckel, B. 2006. *Thinking in Java (4th Edition).* Prentice Hall: USA.
5. Horstmann, CS and Cornell, G. 2007. *Core Java, Volume I–Fundamentals (8th Edition).* Sun Microsystems.
6. Liang, YD. 2007. *Introduction to Java Programming, Comprehensive Version.* Pearson Prentice Hall: USA.
7. Metsker, SJ. 2002. *Design Patterns Java Workbook.* Addison-Wesley: USA.

# Chapter 3
# Modeling Object-Oriented Systems

Before creating software, it is very helpful to have a representation of what the program is supposed to do. Consider a simple program that checks if a given number is a prime number. The requirement for this program is simply stated: given a positive integer, decide if it is a prime number. However, to create a program, some questions need to be answered: how will the number be given to us (through a keyboard, verbally, or in a file)? How does the program tell the user it has "decided" if the number is a prime? Is there any other information that the program should give us? These ambiguities can be avoided if we can agree on a standard template as follows:
Input: A number typed in using the keyboard.
Output: Print "Yes" on the screen if the number is prime; print "No" otherwise.
This restatement in a simple standard format (sometimes referred to as the *Input-Output model*) gives us a clearer picture of what the program is required to do. We say that we have modeled the program requirements.

If the requirements for a simple program can be ambiguous, it is easy to imagine that more complex requirements will be harder to capture accurately. It is therefore important that we have a good process for modeling the requirements. Models are useful for other purposes too. A simple program can be modeled as a *flowchart*, which gives us a visual representation of how control will flow when the program is executed. Another kind of representation is *pseudocode* which looks like a program, but gives a compact representation of the essence of the program. Both these representations are useful for different reasons. For instance, flowcharts are helpful for beginners in visualizing the process, while pseudocode can be helpful for analyzing the algorithm.

We can recognize the importance of modeling from two perspectives. Object-oriented software construction is a result of the need to create large programs. For large programs, having a high-level understanding of the entire system becomes critical to the construction process. To enable this understanding, we need a language for representing various aspects of the system. **Modeling** is the process by which we construct representations for these various aspects. From another perspective, even a moderate-sized object-oriented program consists of numerous classes. If we tried to identify these classes and design each of them without a systematic process, the result can be quite haphazard. By placing information in standard templates all through the construction process, we can follow a systematic process and avoid costly errors.

A few different models are created in the process of building a moderately large program, and to describe these models we need a suitable **modeling language.** In this chapter, we introduce one such language called the **Unified Modeling Language** or **UML**. UML was first developed in 1994–95 by Grady Booch, Ivar Jacobson, and James Rumbaugh at Rational Software, and has been managed by the Object Management Group (OMG) since 1997. The OMG specification states:

"The Unified Modeling Language (UML) is a graphical language for visualizing, specifying, constructing, and documenting the artifacts of a software-intensive system. The UML offers a standard way to write a system's blueprints, including conceptual things such as business processes and system functions as well as concrete things such as programming language statements, database schemas, and reusable software components."

UML 2.5 specifies 19 possible diagrams (this number includes some variants) that can be used to represent various aspects of a system, and also the elements that are used to construct these diagrams.

## 3.1 A First Example

In the previous chapter, we presented several examples of classes, and the relationships between classes. We also discussed the use of class diagrams in UML. Class diagrams model the class by presenting the data fields and methods. Thus the class diagram defines a model for the data element that it represents. Class diagrams can also represent the relationships between classes, that is, the relationship between the data elements.

Consider a simple example where we have data elements to represent a course, a section of a course, and a student. The Java code for these classes is summarized below:

```
public class Student {
  private String name;
  private String address;
  private double gpa;
  public Student(String studentName) {
    name = studentName;
```

```
  }
  // methods to access and modify data for a student
}

public class Course {
  private String id;
  private String name;
  private int numberofCredits;
  private String description;
  public Course(String courseId, courseName) {
    id = courseId;
    name = courseName;
  }
  // methods to access and modify data for a course
}

public class Section {
  private StudentLinkedList studentList;
  private String semester;
  private String place;
  private String daysAndTimes;
  private Course course;
  public Section(Course theCourse, String theSemester,
                 String thePlace, String theDaysAndTimes) {
    course = theCourse;
    place = thePlace;
    daysAndTimes = theDaysAndTimes;
    semester = theSemester;
    studentList = new StudentLinkedList();
  }
  // methods to access and modify data for a course
}
```

Each of these data entities can be represented by a class diagram. In addition, we can capture the nature of the relationships between them. A section has a collection of zero or more students, and a reference to the course associated with that section. The section depends on the course, since it is a particular offering of the course. All of this can be presented in a single class diagram (Figure 3.1), which would also constitute a data model for these three entities.

While this gives us a simple example of what we mean by a model, it should be kept in mind that this model is far from adequate. It does not tell us anything about the purpose of the data or why we have chosen to represent it this way. It does not tell us who will be using the data and how they will be accessing it. From this model, we cannot determine how the data will be used

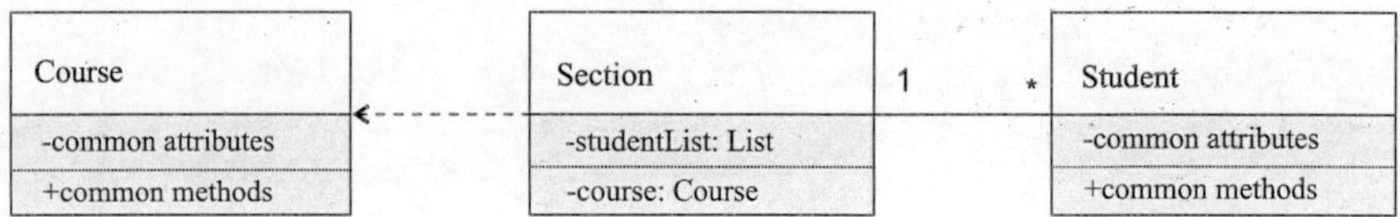


**Fig. 3.1** A data model showing the relationship between Student, Section and Course. A section is dependent on a course (dashed arrow) and has any number of students enrolled (one-many relationship) in it.

or modified in conjunction with other activities. To answer such questions, we need to take a broader look at system modeling. In the rest of the chapter, we cover the tools employed for this purpose.

## 3.2 Choosing the Diagrams to Describe an Object-Oriented System

Having decided to create a model for the software we are going to construct, we need to decide what diagrams should be created to represent the system. To make this decision, we need to develop an understanding of two things:

- *What aspects of the system we want to represent.* The aspects to be represented depend on the kind of system we are building and what stage of the construction process we are at. These aspects will inform us about the kinds of models that we need to build.
- *The suite of possible diagrams to choose from.* UML provides several diagrams, but there is considerable overlap between them, in terms of the information they provide. It is important to choose a good subset of these so that we have a complete but non-redundant characterization of the system.

### 3.2.1 Building Models to Represent the System

There are many kinds of models and it is important to pick the appropriate set of models for a given system. Constructing all possible models can be confusing and could lead to inconsistencies.

Before constructing any system, we need to define what the system should be capable of. This collection of capabilities is called a **requirements model.** Building a good requirements model is vitally important in the software engineering process. In the context of this text, we start the object-oriented construction process with a set of functional requirements, that is, what the system will do. In addition, the requirements model would typically contain non-functional requirements, which describe the performance constraints.

Business rules and a glossary of terms are also commonly included in the model.

When we look at the system as a whole, it is important to recognize the *boundaries of the system.* For instance, a search engine returns a set of links to various websites. Interaction with a search engine begins when we type in keywords and hit Enter; this point is therefore a boundary of the search engine system. Interaction ends when we see the page displaying the websites, which defines another boundary of the system. If we click on a link and visit a site, we are outside the system. Closely tied to the boundaries is the manner in which an external actor interacts with the system. In a search engine system, this could include the manner in which search terms can be qualified or the format in which results should be presented. To represent such information, we construct a **user interface model** that describes the boundary and interaction between the system and users. In an object-oriented construction process, the user interface model is one of earliest models we build; therefore, the requirements must specify how the system should interact with the external world.

In an object-oriented construction process, the system we build will have objects and classes. As we progress through the various stages, we develop a clearer understanding of what these objects and classes will contain, how they will be connected to each other, and how they will interact with each other. In the process of analysis, we make our first attempt to identify the classes and their interconnections. This yields the **class model** or the **logical model** of the system. During the object-oriented analysis process, we create a more abstract version of the classes, which are called **conceptual classes**, but as we progress, we define the **software classes** which are more concrete, and the **implementation classes** which specify the precise way in which each class is implemented.

The models we described above were **static models**, which represent aspects of the system that do not change with time. **Dynamic models** represent aspects that change with time. A **communication model** describes how the objects will communicate with each other to accomplish a task. As the system operates, the properties of objects change, and along with that, there is a change in the way objects respond to input. A **state model** is constructed to describe states that objects assume over time. These models also capture what causes an object to change state, and how the object's behavior changes from one state to another.

Other models are used to describe the system as a whole. An **architectural model** could describe how the system is decomposed into subsystems. A **physical component model** describes the software (and sometimes hardware components) that make up the system. A **physical deployment model** describes the physical architecture and the deployment of components on that hardware architecture.

Models can vary widely with regard to the level of precision. At one end of the spectrum, models can be defined very loosely, just to give an idea about the system. At the other end, we have models defined using very formal syntax and semantics that precisely capture the requirements. Such precise models, called **formal models**, are used in critical systems where it is essential to capture the exact behavior, since the cost of failure is very high. These models use **formal specifications** which have precise syntax and semantics, are mathematically based, and allow for automated detection of inconsistencies. Specialized languages like Object-Z, CASL and VDM are employed for this.

Modeling is a complex activity and, as described above, there is a wide variety of models. The best way to understand the use of models and the associated notation is look at several examples of systems and how they are modeled. To illustrate all these concepts, we will construct appropriate models as we go through various stages of the construction process.

### 3.2.2 Diagrams Supported by UML

Once we have decided on the models, we can choose the appropriate UML diagrams. The important point to note here is that UML is a "language" for specifying, and not a method or procedure. The UML is used to define a software system, to detail the artifacts in the system, to document and construct – it is the language that the blueprint is written in. The UML may be used in a variety of ways to support a software development methodology (such as the Rational Unified Process), but in itself, it does not specify that methodology or process. UML can be seen as a mechanism for defining the notation and semantics for several kinds of models.

UML diagrams can be broadly divided into **structure** diagrams, which show the static structure of the system, and **behavior** diagrams, which describe the dynamic behavior. **Interaction** diagrams, which capture dynamic behavior by describing an interaction, are sometimes categorized separately. The structure diagrams are **class diagram, object diagram, package diagram, composite structure diagram, component diagram, deployment diagram**, and **profile diagram. Use case diagram, activity diagram** and **state machine diagram** are types of behavior diagrams. While **sequence diagram, communication diagram, timing diagram** and **interaction overview diagram** are types of interaction diagrams.

Describing the various aspects of all the diagrams can be confusing, and often not very useful. We shall therefore focus on the modeling used during the object-oriented construction process and learn about the applicable UML notation for each stage.

## 3.3 Building a User Interface Model

Let us start with an example. Consider a small bank with a collection of ATMs. The bank has several customers, and each customer has an account and a debit card. The customers can access their accounts through the ATMs, and can deposit money, withdraw money, or check the balance. We will build a user interface model for this system. As we discussed earlier, we start with the set of requirements.

### 3.3.1 Requirements for an ATM System

We can describe the associated processes that the system is required to support, as follows:

- *Withdraw cash:* The user enters an ATM to withdraw cash. The user provides a debit card, a valid pin, and the amount of cash needed. The system validates the pin and the debit card, verifies that the requested amount can be withdrawn (according to the bank's rules of operation), debits the account, dispenses the cash and prints a statement showing the balance in the account.
- *Make a deposit:* The user enters an ATM to make a deposit. The user provides a debit card, a valid pin, and the deposit instrument (cash or check to be deposited). The system validates the pin and the debit card, accepts the deposit instrument and prints a receipt.
- *Check the balance:* The user enters an ATM to check their balance. The user provides a debit card and a valid pin. The system validates the pin and the debit card and prints a statement showing the balance in the account.

In each of the above processes, we have described the nature of the activity, the roles of the players, and any related information that may be useful for a more detailed specification. Each of these corresponds to a particular way in which the system will be used by the customer, and can therefore be mapped to use cases. A **use case** describes a certain way in which a user can interact with the system, and usually captures a desired functionality of the system. A use case is thus a single unit of some useful work.

The **UML use case diagram** captures the set of actions (use cases) that the system should perform. Each action involves collaboration(or interaction) with one or more external users of the system, and provides some observable and useful results. Each kind of external user (or actor) is represented by a humanoid figure, and each use case is represented by an oval with the name of the use case written inside. To represent the collaboration with a user, a line is drawn connecting the oval with the corresponding humanoid figure. The use case diagram for the ATM system is shown in Figure 3.2, following the UML syntax. The diagram symbolically represents the interaction between an

**actor**, which could be a human or a piece of software or hardware, and the **system**. It does *not* specify *how* the system carries out the task.

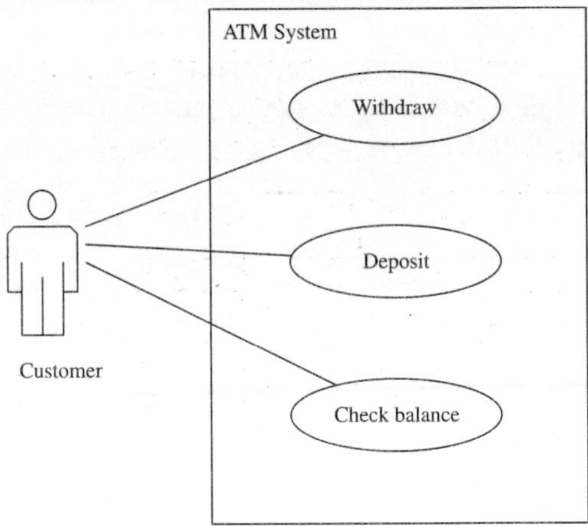


**Fig. 3.2** Customer use cases for the ATM subsystem. A use case diagram captures the set of actions (use cases) that the system should perform.

### 3.3.2 Detailed Use Cases for the ATM

The use case diagram gives the list of interactions; the detailed exchange for each of these interactions can be captured using a two-column format. When we do that, we need to make some choices about the kind of user interface that is being provided. Based on our everyday experience with ATMs, we can see two options here:

- **Option 1.** *The customer's first action is to validate their identity by inserting a debit card.* The ATM then allows the customer to perform multiple operations of any kind.
- **Option 2.** *The customer's first action is to choose the kind of operation that they wish to perform.* Only one operation can be performed; for each operation, the customer must start over again.

Option 1 has the advantage of convenience for the customer, and may be preferable in some situations. Option 2 is simpler since it keeps the use cases completely separate, which is what we prefer (pedagogically) for our initial examples.

With this interface, we can write the detailed interaction for each use case. Table 3.1 describes the use case interaction for withdrawing cash. Note that the exact rule for deciding whether the amount can be withdrawn has not

| Customer action | Response from the system |
|---|---|
| 1) Goes to the ATM, and requests to withdraw cash. | |
| | 2) Asks the customer to insert the Debit Card. |
| 3) Inserts the Debit Card in the "Insert Card" slot. | |
| | 4) If the card is unreadable or the system is unavailable, displays an error and goes to Step 11. Otherwise, asks for the PIN. |
| 5) Enters the PIN. | |
| | 6) Verifies the PIN. If the PIN is invalid, displays an error and goes to Step 11. |
| | 7) Asks for the amount. |
| 8) Enters the amount. | |
| | 9) If the amount is not valid as per bank rules, displays the necessary message and goes back to Step 7. Otherwise, dispenses the amount, updates the balance, and prints a balance statement. |
| 10) Takes the cash and the statement. | |
| | 11) Ejects the card. |
| 12) Takes the card. | |
| | 13) Closes the transaction. |

**Table 3.1** Use case: Withdraw Cash

| Customer action | Response from the system |
|---|---|
| 1) Goes to the ATM, and requests to make a deposit. | |
| | 2) Asks the customer to insert the Debit Card. |
| 3) Inserts the Debit Card in the "Insert Card" slot. | |
| | 4) If the card is unreadable or the system is unavailable, displays an error and goes to Step 10. Otherwise, asks for the PIN. |
| 5) Enters the PIN. | |
| | 6) Verifies the PIN. If the PIN is invalid, displays an error and goes to Step 10. Otherwise, opens a receptacle for placing the deposit instrument. |
| 7) Places the deposit instrument in the receptacle and closes the receptacle. | |
| | 8) Records the transaction and prints a receipt. |
| 9) Takes the receipt. | |
| | 10) Ejects the card. |
| 11) Takes the card. | |
| | 12) Closes the transaction. |

**Table 3.2** Use case: Make a Deposit

| Customer action | Response from the system |
|---|---|
| 1) Goes to the ATM, and requests to make a deposit. | |
| | 2) Asks the customer to insert the Debit Card. |
| 3) Inserts the Debit Card in the "Insert Card" slot. | |
| | 4) If the card is unreadable or the system is unavailable, displays an error and goes to Step 8.<br>Otherwise, asks for the PIN. |
| 5) Enters the PIN. | |
| | 6) Verifies the PIN. If the PIN is invalid, displays an error and goes to Step 8.<br>Otherwise, determines the available balance, and prints the amount. |
| 7) Takes the printout. | |
| | 8) Ejects the card. |
| 9) Takes the card. | |

**Table 3.3** Use case: Check the Balance

been specified. These are typically documented separately and provided to the person designing the system. The use case in Table 3.2 describes the deposit process. Note that the system is not required to immediately validate the deposit; this is because the validation is expected to take a longer period of time. The last use case, in Table 3.3, involves a customer checking the available balance in their account.

### 3.3.3 A Simple Interface for Course Registration

Consider a small college that has a set of course offerings (also referred to as offerings). Students can enroll in (or drop out of) these offerings, and instructors can assign grades. Let us say our business model lists the following processes:

1. *Add/Remove a course offering.*
2. *Add/Remove students in the registration system.*
3. *Enroll a student in an offering.*
4. *Drop a student from an offering.*
5. *Assign a grade to a student for an offering.*

We can look at these processes as the set of use cases for the user interface model. However, there is the question of who performs each of these operations. The college must have an administrator to add or remove offerings and to add students. Students should be able to enroll in or drop out from an offering, and instructors should assign the grades. We can use this definition of roles to construct a use case diagram with three actors, as shown in Figure 3.3. To complete the requirements, we need to specify what is expected for each of these processes. Adding students would require the following:

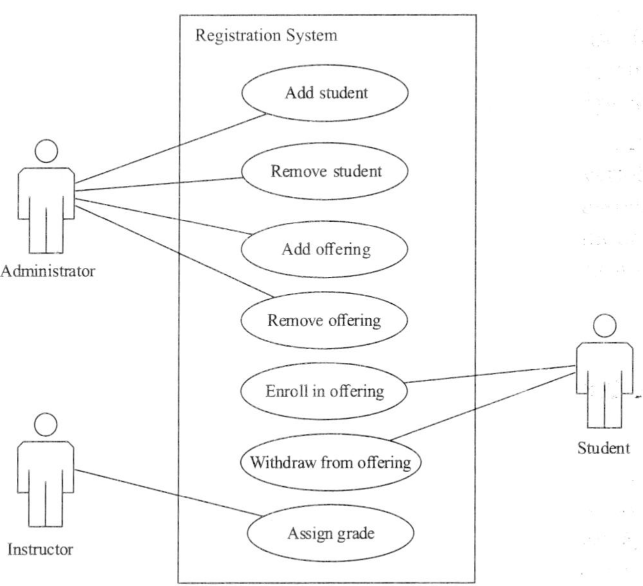


**Fig. 3.3** Use case diagram for the registration system showing multiple actors

*Add students.* The administrator establishes his/her identity and provides the information for individuals seeking to enroll as students. For each student, the administrator enters the name, address and contact information. The system registers the student as enrolled in the college, and generates an ID; if the student cannot be added, an error message is displayed.

The requirements for assigning a grade could be as follows:

*Assign a grade to a student for an offering.* The instructor establishes his/her identity and provides the student's ID, the ID of the offering, and the new grade. The system records this information and confirms the grade. If the operation cannot be accomplished, an error message is displayed.

Systems are rarely built as one unit, since that can make the complexity unmanageable. Even for a simple system like the one above, we will probably have two subsystems: a back-end that stores the data and a front-end with which the actors interact. As represented in Figure 3.4, the users communicate with the front-end to request operations and provide input; the front-end communicates with the back-end to complete the tasks.

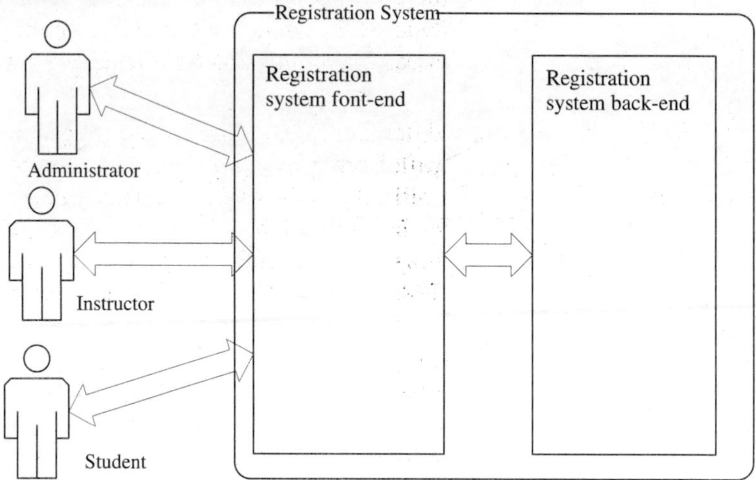


**Fig. 3.4** Block diagram showing the subsystems within the registration system

When constructing the back-end, we can view it as a separate system that interacts only with the front-end, but should be capable of supporting all the operations that users request from the front-end. To construct the back-end, we would model the user interface with a single user; the use case diagram would be as shown in Figure 3.5.

The functionality is essentially the same, but we are assuming the front-end can be trusted; the back-end is dealing with a *trusted actor, that is, the front-end does not have to establish its identity when performing operations.* Accordingly, the specification for adding students is modified as follows:

> *Add students.* The actor provides the information for individuals seeking to enroll as students. For each student, the actor provides the name, address, and contact information. The system registers the student as enrolled in the college and generates an ID; if the student cannot be added, an error message is displayed.

The specification for assigning a grade is rewritten as:

> *Assign a grade to a student for an offering.* The actor provides the student's ID, the ID of the offering, and the new grade. The system records this information and confirms the grade. If the operation cannot be accomplished, an error message is displayed.

The detailed use cases would be written to reflect these requirements.

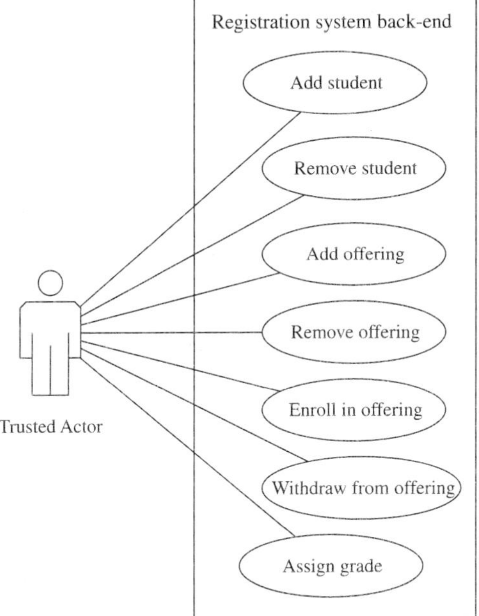


**Fig. 3.5** Use case diagram for the registration system back-end with a single trusted actor

## 3.4 Building a Logical Model

Constructing the logical model (or class model) is usually the next step for an object-oriented system. The logical model represents the classes and their interconnections. This involves the following:

- Determining what concepts should be modeled as classes
- Defining the relationships between these classes

The logical model is the most important model for an object-oriented system, since it leads us to the set of classes that need to be defined. In selecting the classes, it is important to distinguish between concepts that are independent classes, concepts that are part of another concept, and concepts connected with relationships. The logical model is complex and is refined frequently in the software construction process. Broadly, we can identify three stages: in the first stage we define the *conceptual model*, which recognizes concepts and relationships that need to be modeled; in the second stage we define the *software model*, which defines how these concepts and their relationships will appear in the software; and in the third stage we define the *implementation model*, which works with the accommodations needed for a specific language.

### 3.4.1 A Logical Model for the ATM System

The conceptual model shows all the conceptual entities and their relationships. The ATMs, accounts, and customers are clearly the three prominent entities involved. Customers, however, are independent entities and will not be tracked by the system. From the details of the interactions, we can see that there are other concepts involved, such as PIN and Debit Card. The PIN is an attribute associated with the account, and Debit Card is an independent physical object. Thus our ATM management system has only two conceptual entities: ATM and account. Our system has several customers, some ATM machines, and several accounts. We can represent this as shown in Figures 3.6 and 3.7. Figure 3.6, shows a snapshot in time, where customer C1 accesses account A3 through machine M1, and customer C4 accesses account A7 through machine M4.

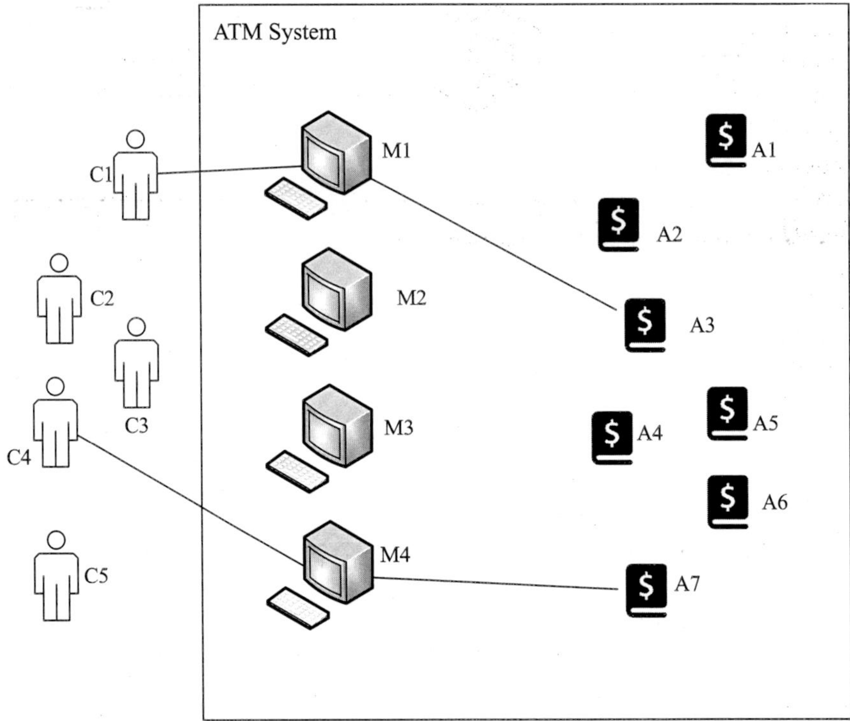


**Fig. 3.6** Customers using the ATM subsystem

In Figure 3.7, we have customer C3 accessing account A2 through machine M2 and customer C5 accessing account A4 through machine M4. Thus, at any time, any machine can access at most one account. If such a system were

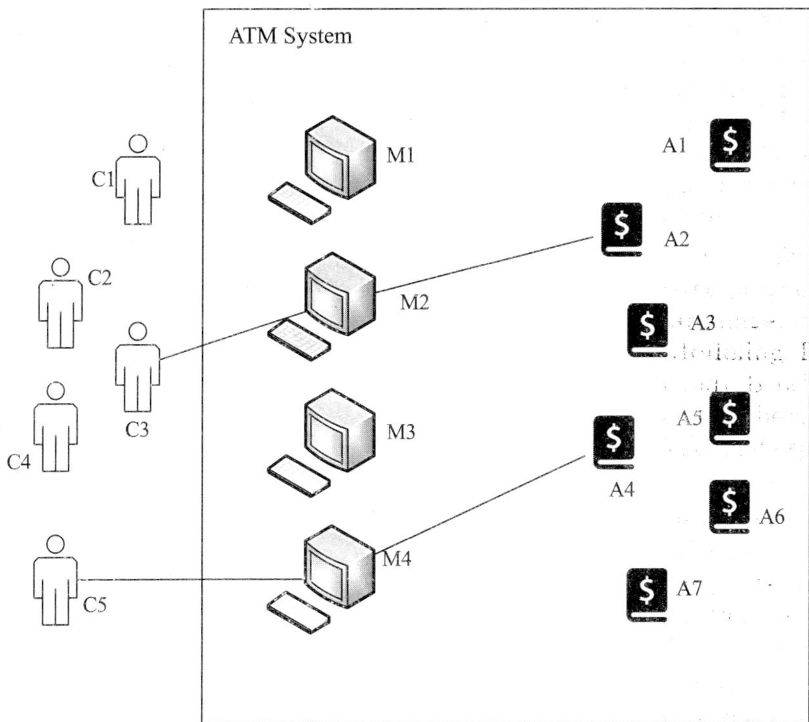


**Fig. 3.7** Customers using the ATM subsystem

to be built, it must keep track of which account is being accessed by each ATM and the relationship between them, which is such that at any given time an ATM can be connected with either one account or no account. The ATM system itself is the concept that holds the entire system. These entities and their relationships can therefore be expressed as shown in Figure 3.8.

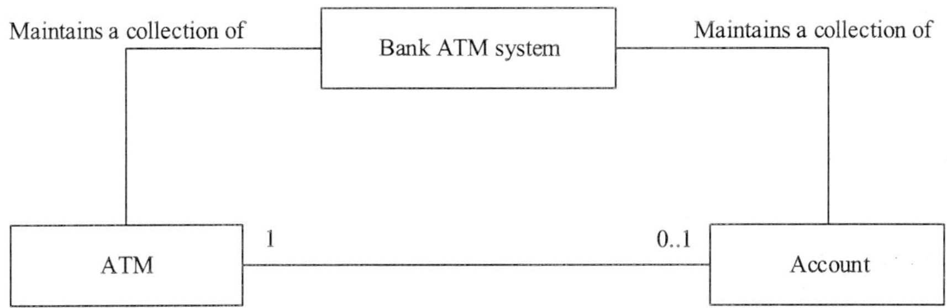


**Fig. 3.8** Conceptual entities and their relationships for the ATM system

### 3.4.2 A Logical Model for a College Registration System

Looking at the requirements for the system, we can identify the following concepts: registration system, administrator, instructor, student, course offering, and grade. We need to decide which of these concepts will be represented by classes. Student details like name and address will not be independent concepts, so we can include them in student. The system is populated with students and course offerings, hence both these concepts should be represented by classes. Administrator and instructor are external entities that make changes to the system; based on the given details they need not be represented inside the system, and hence will not become classes.

The concepts registration system, student, and course offerings are related to each other as follows:

- The registration system maintains records about several students.
- The registration system maintains records about several course offerings.
- A student can be enrolled in or may have completed several course offerings.
- A course offering enrolls several students.

Since there is only one registration system, the relationship between registration system and student is a one-to-many relationship; likewise there is a one-to-many relationship between registration system and course offering. Since a student can be associated with many course offerings and vice-versa, the relationship between student and course offering is many-to-many. A placeholder for a grade results when a student registers in a course offering; initially it may be shown as incomplete, and the final grade is assigned when the student completes the course. Say we have students `s1, s2`, and `s3`, and offerings `o1, o2`, and `o3`. Depending on which students are enrolled in each offering, we can create a picture like the one shown in Figure 3.9.

Figure 3.9 shows that `s1` is enrolled in `o1` and `o3`; this means that we should have a grade (or placeholder) for the pair `(s1, o1)` and one for the pair `(s1, o3)`. Thus each `(student offering)` pair that represents an enrollment should have an associated grade; to enable this, UML provides the concept of an **association class**. An association class is used when an association has its own set of features, that is, *features that do not belong to either of the classes being connected.* In this case, in addition to the grade, we could also have information like the date on which the student enrolled in the offering. All this information is placed in the `registration record`, which is attached to the link connecting `student` and `course offering` by a line, as shown in Figure 3.10. (A dashed line is sometimes used to connect the association class with the link.)

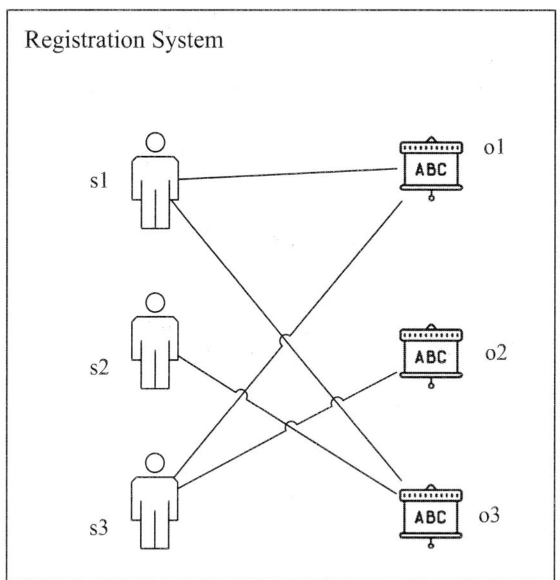


**Fig. 3.9** Registration system showing enrollments: student s1 in o1, o3; s2 in o3; s3 in o1, o2.

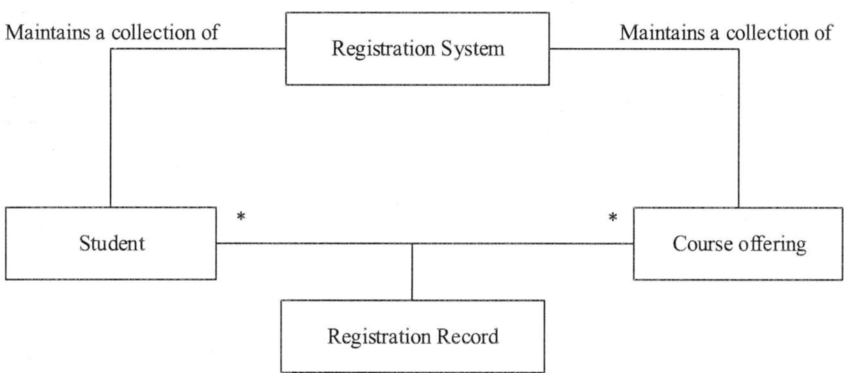


**Fig. 3.10** Conceptual entities in the registration system: registration record is an association class.

### 3.4.3 Logical Models in Various Stages of Development

Logical models form the basis of object-oriented development. This model evolves as we work through the process of construction. In the analysis phase, we identify some concepts that are good candidates to be represented as classes, and also identify some concepts that are not appropriate for being turned into classes. The good candidate concepts are important in the system, whether or not we create software to deploy the system. This picture changes as we move into the design phase; here, we are looking at the concepts that will become *software classes.* In identifying these, we rely on our knowledge of how object-oriented programs are structured and also on our experience with software construction. We recognize new concepts that are required for implementing the system as a piece of software, and drop some concepts that are not independently represented in the software. As we do this, the logical model evolves and depicts the relationship between the software classes.

In object-oriented design, software classes may be conceived assuming the general capabilities of an object-oriented language. It is also impractical and possibly not advisable to specify every potential class that would be in the implemented system. Once we begin implementation, we may have to adjust the design classes to suit the intricacies of the chosen language. The resulting classes are sometimes referred to as the *implementation classes.*

## 3.5 Modeling the Interaction Between Entities

The use cases describe the dynamic interaction between the system and the external world, and the logical model describes the internal static structure. The use cases lay out what the system is expected to do, and this task is accomplished by the classes. Describing how the task is to be completed is a part of the software construction process. This description lays out how responsibilities will be distributed among the classes (and objects) and how the objects interact and communicate with one another.

### 3.5.1 Sequence Diagrams

A sequence diagram gives us one way of modeling an interaction between various participating entities in the system. Each participant in the interaction is represented by a **lifeline,** which consists of a rectangular box (sometime accompanied by a special symbol) labeled with the name of the entity, and a dashed vertical line representing the passage of time as it extends downwards. Each sequence diagram usually describes a single complex task, which is broken up into several simpler sub-tasks performed by participating entities. At some periods of time a participant may be active, that is, executing some task. These periods are denoted by replacing the dashed line with a solid rectangle. Horizontal arrows are drawn to represent communication between the entities, and dotted arrows are used to indicate a response.

Figure 3.11 gives an example of a sequence diagram. This diagram describes how the system will handle the task of cash withdrawal. The use case Withdraw Cash lays down the details of how the system is expected to behave. In the use case, all the system actions were described in a single column. When we built the logical model for the ATM system, we identified the conceptual entities: the ATM machines, the bank's ATM system and the accounts. All three entities are represented by timelines in the sequence diagram, and we see how the system responsibilities from the use case are divided among these entities.

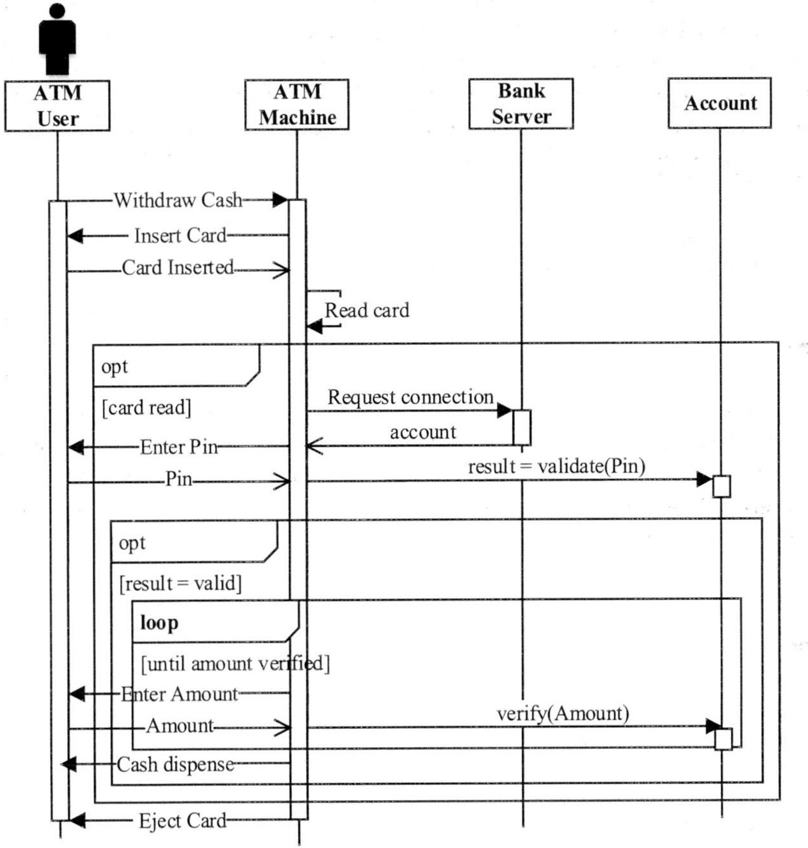


**Fig. 3.11** Sequence diagram showing cash withdrawal in the ATM system

The diagram itself proceeds along the lines specified in the detailed use case for withdrawing cash. The user communicates only with the ATM machine; the machine communicates with either the server or the account, depending on what action needs to be performed. The first arrow represents the user's request to withdraw cash. The machine requests that the user insert a card, in response to which a card is expected to be inserted. The arrow labeled "read card" denotes that the action of reading is performed within the machine.

The box labeled "opt" indicates that the actions inside it are performed only if certain conditions are met. In this case, the condition is that the card is read and determined to be a valid card. The machine then requests the bank's ATM system (presumably hosted on a remote server) to make the connection. In response the system returns a reference to the particular account associated with the card. The machine then requests a PIN, and validates the entered PIN by communicating with the account. Note that if the card were to be invalid, none of the actions inside the opt box are carried out and the card is ejected.

If the PIN is valid, the machine initiates a loop and requests the user to enter an amount. The loop executes until the account entity verifies that the requested amount can be withdrawn. Following this, the machine dispenses the cash and then ejects the card.

### 3.5.2 Communication Diagrams

A **communication diagram** also captures an interaction between participant objects. The lifelines do not have anything to represent the passage of time; instead, the messages are sequenced by numbering them in the order in which they are dispatched.

## 3.6 Modeling the Behavior of a System

We have seen that the use cases help us model the behavior of a system by describing the user interactions. State transition diagrams and activity diagrams are two other models which capture system behavior.

### 3.6.1 State Transition Diagrams

State transition diagrams are used to capture the various states that the system (or the object) could be in and also capture the transitions between those states. They are also called state machine diagrams.

State transition diagrams are used to model the behavior of a system in two kinds of situations. A **behavioral state machine** captures the behavior of an object or a system by defining a set of states, each of which models a situation is which some condition(s) hold. For each state, the diagram specifies how the system responds to input, and when and how the system transitions to another state.

Consider the ATM machine we discussed earlier. The user interface of a single machine can be described as follows:

1. In the *idle state*, it displays the three user options for withdrawal, deposit, or balance enquiry.
2. Based on the user's choice, the ATM transitions to a *cash withdrawal state, deposit state,* or a *balance enquiry state.* Each state is responsible for performing the actions required for that menu operation.
3. When the balance inquiry operation terminates, the ATM returns to the idle state.
4. When the cash withdrawal operation succeeds, the ATM transitions to an *cash dispense* state; when this state completes its actions, the ATM returns to the idle state. If the cash withdrawal fails, the ATM returns to the idle state.
5. When the deposit operation succeeds, the ATM transitions to an *accept deposit* state; when this state completes its actions, the ATM returns to the idle state. On the other hand, if the deposit operation fails, the ATM goes directly from the deposit state to the idle state.

Figure 3.12 shows how this behavior can be described using a finite state machine. Each state is responsible for performing the necessary ATM actions for that operation.

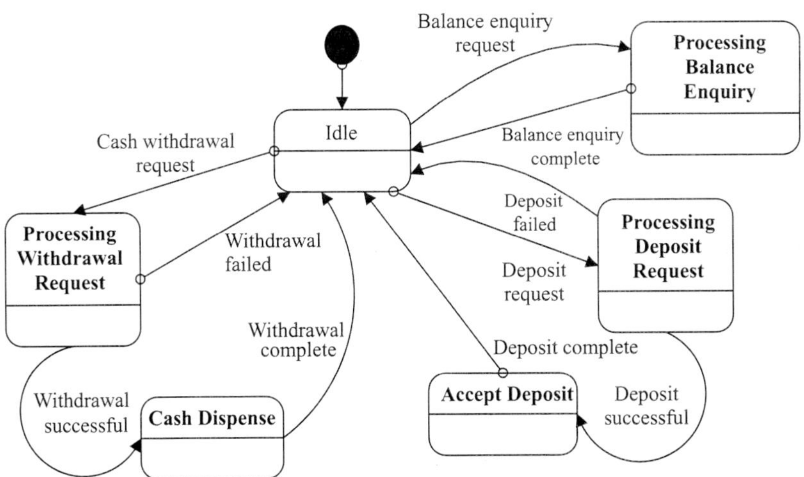


**Fig. 3.12** State machine for modeling the ATM interface

A **protocolar state machine** captures the behavior of a system as it moves through the steps of a protocol employed for a transaction. Consider, for instance, an ATM machine having to ensure that the customer goes through the proper process to withdraw cash. The bank then defines the sequence of steps for this process, which we refer to as the *protocol.* At each step, this ATM is looking for a different kind of input, and this continual change in the expected input can be captured through a state transition diagram. We therefore have the following states, as shown in Figure 3.13:

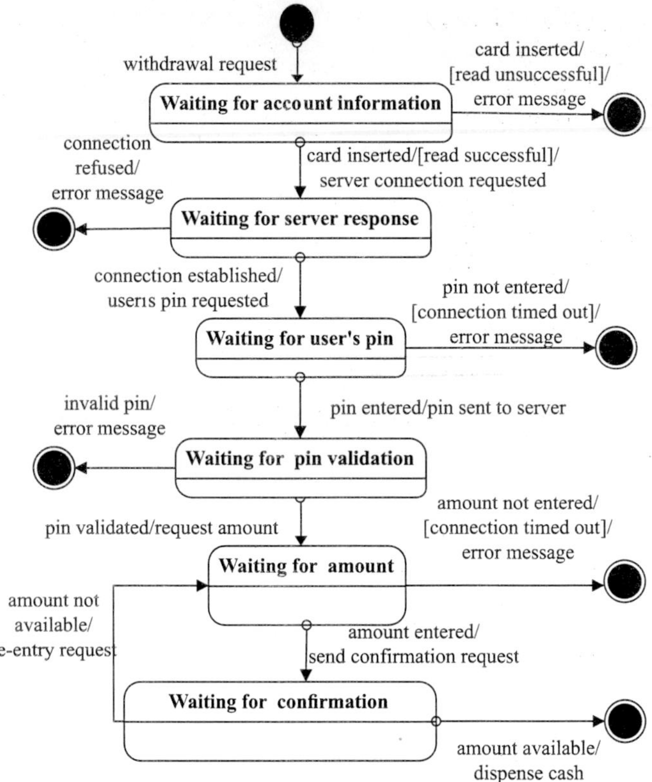


**Fig. 3.13** State machine for the Cash Withdrawal Protocol

- *Waiting for account information.* This state is entered when the user makes a request to withdraw cash and is the point where the protocol begins. It represents the fact that a cash withdrawal has been requested and the ATM is waiting for the user to swipe the card.
- *Waiting for connection state.* If the ATM can successfully read the swiped card, it enters the next state where it attempts to connect with the bank's server.

- *Waiting for pin.* Once the connection is made, the ATM waits for the user to enter the pin.
- *Validating account number and pin.* After the pin input is available, the ATM sends this information to the server and waits for validation.
- *Waiting for cash amount.* This state is entered after the server has validated the pin. The ATM waits for the user to enter the amount of cash needed.
- *Verifying availability of cash.* When the amount of cash is entered, the ATM sends the amount to the server and waits for verification of availability of funds.
- *Dispensing cash.* If availability of funds is verified, the ATM dispenses the cash; otherwise, it requests the user to enter a different amount.

Once the cash is dispensed, the protocol is complete; note that we add two pseudo states: the black circle representing an *initial* state from which we start the protocol, and the black circle within an outer circle that represents a *final* state indicating termination (successful or unsuccessful) of the withdrawal process.

### 3.6.2 Activity Diagrams

An activity diagram presents a view of system behavior by describing the sequence of actions in a process or activity. They are similar to flowcharts because they show the flow between the actions in an activity; however, they go beyond flowcharts since they show different actors performing actions and also show parallel or concurrent flows and alternate flows.

The actions are triggered when some conditions are satisfied; these conditions include the availability of objects and data, completion of other actions, or events external to the flow. The activity diagram in Figure 3.14 shows the actions that are performed when a customer withdraws cash from an ATM.

Through this example, we can identify the following aspects of activity diagrams:

1. *Recognize the roles played by various actors.* In our example, there are three actors: the *customer*, the *ATM machine* and the *Bank Server*, each of which has clearly separated roles. The server holds the account information, the customer seeks banking services, and the ATM machine connects the customer with the server, collects the deposit items, and dispenses cash. Each of these is represented by a separate column, called a **swimlane.** Swimlanes can be drawn either horizontally or vertically as shown; these lanes partition all the actions in the diagram, based on the responsibilities

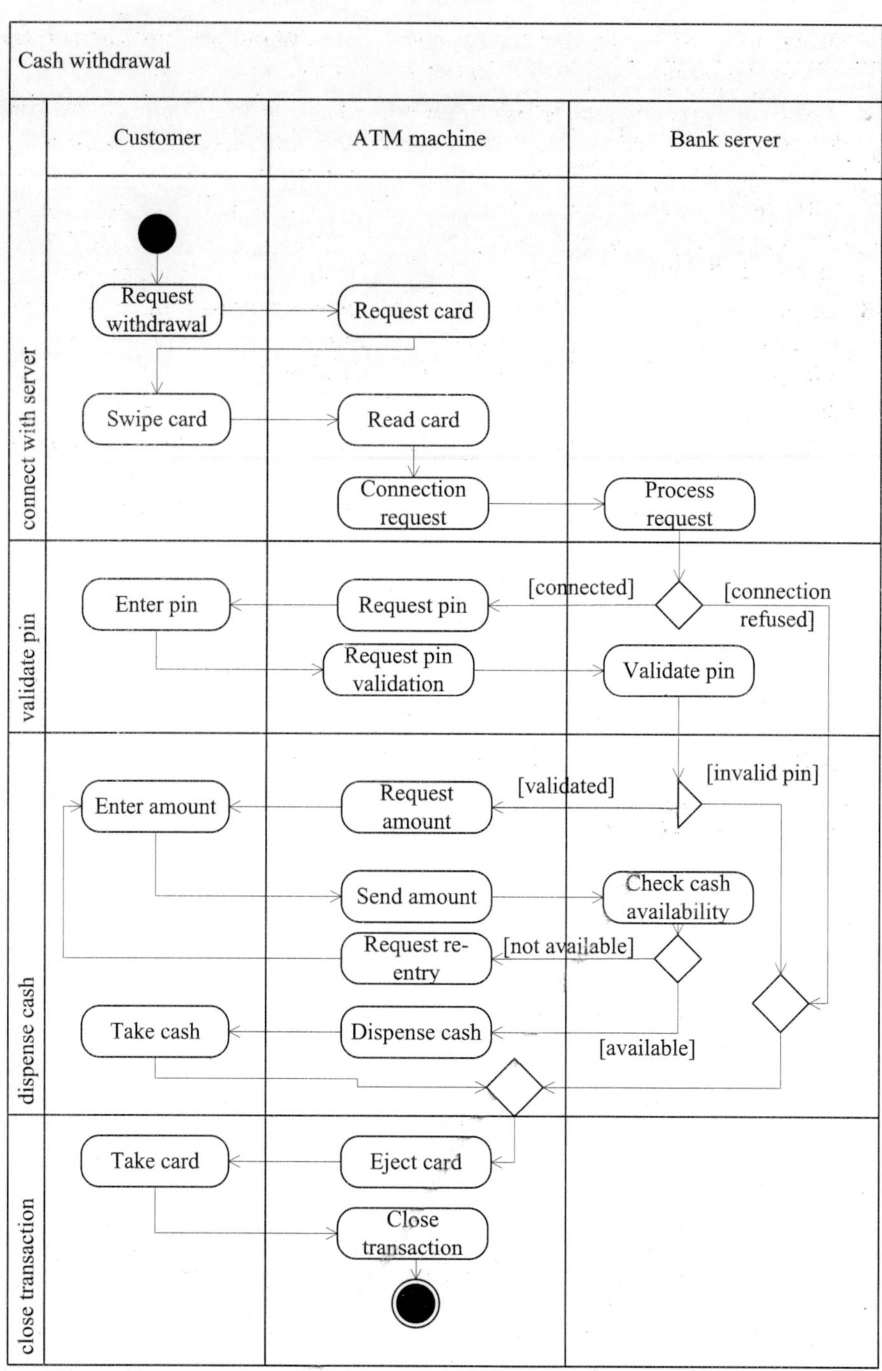


**Fig. 3.14** Activity diagram for Cash Withdrawal

of the actors. The diagram can also be drawn without separating the roles of the actors, in which case all actions are in the same "swimarea."

2. *List the actions.* The actions are represented by the rectangular shape with rounded corners. Each action is placed in the swimlane of the performing actor. In our example, we see the customer perform actions like "request withdrawal", "swipe card", etc. The ATM machine performs actions like "read card" and "request connection (to server)". The activity diagram is drawn on the understanding that each actor performs actions as stated.
3. *Divide the entire activity into phases.* The phases represent different stages of the completion of the activity. In the figure, we see four phases: *connect with server, validate pin, dispense cash*, and *close transaction*.
4. *Represent alternate flows.* Alternate flows occur when a decision has to be made. They cause the activity to branch into different paths depending on the result. **Decision nodes** represented by diamonds are used to represent decisions being made and the outgoing arcs are labeled with **guards** that describe the associated result. Alternate flows must merge together at some point in the activity; this is accomplished by using **merge** nodes, which are also represented by diamonds. In our figure, we see decision nodes associated with making the server connection and validating the pin. The successful connection path goes on to get the pin, and if the pin is validated, the cash is dispensed. The paths representing unsuccessful connection and invalid pin merge together; the unsuccessful paths then merge with the path representing a successful withdrawal.
5. *Initiate and terminate activity.* Initiation of the activity is shown by the black circle, and termination is shown by the black circle with a border around it. These are usually placed in the swimlanes of the actors responsible for the initiation and termination, respectively. In our example, the customer initiates the operation by requesting a transaction, and the ATM terminates it when the customer removes the card.

Activity diagrams can also represent *concurrent flows*, which appear when two or more actions can be performed simultaneously by different actors. Concurrent flows originate at a **fork** node, and combine together at a **join** node. Unlike alternate flows where only one of the alternate flows can be executed, concurrent flows require that all concurrent flows be executed. Figure 3.15 shows an activity diagram for processing an order. Once the order is complete, we have the twin tasks of generating invoice and packaging products, which can occur concurrently. When these two tasks are completed, the two flows join together. In this figure, we also see objects that are being created during the activity. These are called **action objects** and are placed on the arcs leading out of the action nodes; these objects can be physical objects or software objects depending on the context. When the order is complete, we see that a *completed order object* is generated; objects are also created when the invoice is prepared and the package is assembled for shipping.

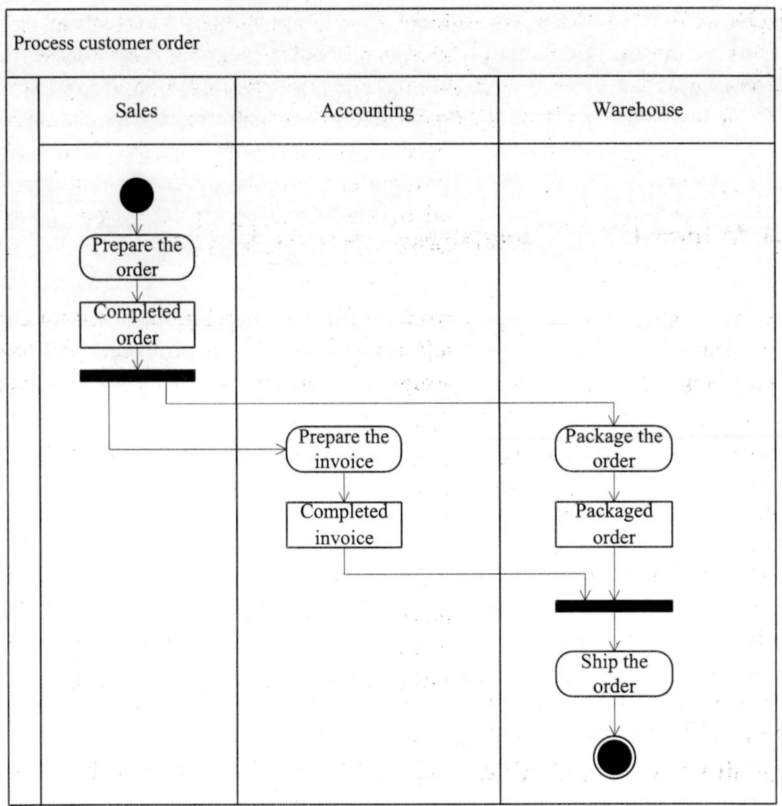


**Fig. 3.15** Activity diagram for processing a customer order

## 3.7 Discussion

The objective of this chapter was to introduce the concept of modeling. In the process of creating the models, the stakeholders in the software creation process refine their understanding of various aspects of the software that is being constructed. This understanding also makes it easier to effectively and efficiently test the system.

There are several reasons for defining and using standardized modeling languages. Due to widespread use, they become a common language that all stakeholders understand. It is more graphical than text-based, which is helpful in a global environment. The standardized notation contributes to clarity in the communication between the stakeholders, and can also be useful when specifying the terms of a contract.

The downside of using them is the sheer size and complexity. The entire UML manual runs into hundreds of pages, and specifies a lot of detail. It is a vast body of knowledge and a chapter like this barely scratches the surface in terms of detail. This complexity deters software creators from using it; however, the models it specifies through the various diagrams are the tools of choice for developers in the software construction process.

### 3.7.1 Which UML Diagrams should we Choose?

One of the things that beginners find confusing is the amount of information that overlaps between various UML diagrams that can be used to model a system. This confusion dissipates with experience, as the designer learns to pick an appropriate selection of diagrams.

Consider the ATM system that we have presented in this chapter. We have seen four different ways of describing how the ATM system interacts with the user:

- The **use case model** and the detailed use cases capture the expectations of the system as a whole. With each operation, we describe what is expected of the user and what are the responsibilities of the system. The detailed use cases describe each operation in a two-column format, specifying what is expected of the system at each step. This captures not only the behavior of an ATM machine, but that of the entire system.
- The **finite state machine** for the ATM interface describes how a single ATM machine changes its interface as it performs various requests. This does not provide us with any deeper understanding of system behavior.
- The **protocolar state machine** describes the detailed protocol that an ATM machine follows when it is performing a specific operation. This is important for someone who is implementing the code for this operation.
- The **activity diagram** describes the interactive sequence of actions that need to be performed by the customer, ATM machine, and the bank server to complete a specific operation.

There is clearly at lot of overlap in the information that these diagrams convey. The activity diagram is very much like a detailed use case, but has three swimlanes, which distinguish the ATM system (the back-end) from the machine (the front-end). In a situation where we have constructed such an activity diagram, the detailed use case may be unnecessary. Likewise, the activity diagram also captures the protocol that is followed by the machine. The finite state machine for the ATM interface tells us that the machine may be performing one of three tasks at any given time. Given the way the state changes occur, all the necessary information is conveyed through a use case diagram and the detailed use cases for each operation.

## Projects

1. Implement the class given in the figure below. Pay attention to the access specifiers, names of all fields and methods. For the `play()` method, simply print a message saying the DVD is playing.

| **Dvd** |
|---|
| -title: String<br>-playingTime: int |
| +Dvd(title:String,playingTime:int)<br>+getTitle(): String<br>+getPlayingTime(): int<br>+play() |

## Exercises

1. A person can be employed by a company both in full-time and part-time capacity. How would you depict these associations?
2. Consider a simple alarm clock. The behavior of the alarm clock can be described as follows:

    a. In the normal operating state, it displays the current time.

    b. When the "set alarm" button is held down, the alarm time is displayed; if the "hour" button is pressed simultaneously, the hour for the alarm time increases and cycles through the 24-hour cycle; if the "minute" button is pressed simultaneously, the minute for the alarm time increases and cycles through the 60-minute cycle.

    c. The "alarm on/off" switch can be used to turn the alarm on or off.

    d. If the clock is in the "alarm on" state, and the current time changes to match the alarm time, the alarm rings until the "alarm on/off" switch is used.

    Model this behavior using a finite state machine.
3. Construct a protocol state machine for making a deposit.
4. Construct a protocol state machine for balance inquiry.

# Chapter 4
# Analyzing a System

Analysis is a fundamental part of any problem solving process. In our case, the solution we seek is a piece of software developed using the object-oriented methodology. This solution consists of many classes and their instances interacting with each other to achieve the desired result. Before any programming effort, it is therefore essential to identify the classes and the manner in which these classes and their instances interact. The process of analysis helps us extract this information from the problem requirements.

At the enterprise level, when new software is to be developed, considerable effort has to be expended to gather all the requirements. These are spelled out in a document known variously as "The Requirements Specification," "System Requirements," etc. Using these, the system analyst creates a model of the system, enabling the identification of some of the components of the system and the relationships among them. The end product of this phase is a *user interaction model*, which describes the functionality of the system and the manner in which it interacts with the user, and a *conceptual model* for the system, which identifies the conceptual entities and describes the nature of the associations between these entities.

We can view the analysis process as a combination of the following three activities:

1. Gathering the requirements. This involves interviews of the user community, reading of any available documentation, etc.
2. Precisely specifying the functionality required of the system and the manner in which it interacts with the user.
3. Developing a conceptual model of the system, listing the conceptual classes and their relationships.

It is not always the case that these activities occur in the order listed. In fact, as the analysts gather the requirements, they will analyze and document what they have collected. This may point to holes in the information, which may necessitate further requirements collection.

This chapter uses the case study of a library system to explain the process of analysis. We go through the processes of requirements specification, precise documentation of functionality, and development of the conceptual model.

## 4.1 Gathering the Requirements

The purpose of *requirements analysis* is to define what the new system should do. The importance of performing this correctly cannot be overemphasized. Since the system will be built based on the information garnered in this step, any errors made in this stage will result in the implementation of an inadequate system. Once the system is implemented, it is expensive to modify it to overcome the mistakes introduced in the analysis stage.

Imagine a scenario where you are asked to construct software for an application. The client may not always be clear in his/her mind as to what should be constructed. One reason for this is that it is difficult to imagine the workings of a system that is not yet built. Only when we actually use a specific application, such as a word processor, do we start realizing the power and limitations of that system. Before actually dealing with it, one may have some general notions of what one would like to see, but may find it difficult to provide many details.

Incompleteness and errors in specifications can also occur because the client does not have the technical skills to fully realize what technology can and cannot deliver. Once again, the general concepts can be stated, but specifics are harder. A third reason for omissions is that it is all too common to have a client who knows the system very well and consequently either assumes a lot of knowledge on the part of the analyst or simply skips over "obvious details."

Requirements for a new system are determined by a team of analysts by interacting with teams from the company paying for the development (clients) and the user community, which ultimately uses the system on a day-to-day basis. This interaction can be in the form of interviews, surveys, observations, studies of existing manuals, etc.

Broadly speaking, the requirements can be classified into two categories:

- *Functional Requirements:* These describe the interaction between the system and its users, and between the system and any other systems, which may interact with the system by supplying or receiving data.
- *Non-Functional Requirements:* Any requirement that does not fall in the above category is a non-functional requirement. Such requirements include response time, usability, and accuracy. Sometimes, there may be

considerations that place restrictions on system development; these may include the use of specific hardware and software and budget and time constraints.

It should be mentioned that initiating the development cycle for a software system is usually preceded by a phase that includes the initial conception and planning. A developer would be approached by a client who wishes to have a certain product developed for his/her business. There would be a *domain* associated with the business, which would have its own jargon. Before approaching the developer, one would assume that the client has determined that a need for the product exists. Once all these issues are sorted out, the developer(s) would meet with the client and, perhaps, several would-be end-users, to determine what is expected of the system. Such a process would result in a list of requirements for the system.

### 4.1.1 The Library Case Study

Let us proceed under the assumption that the requirements have been gathered and the developers of our library system have available to them a document that describes how the business is conducted. To keep things simple, we have only one type of user, the library clerks, who perform all the actions requested by the members and also the tasks required to manage the library. These operations are commonly called *business processes*. It is also assumed that human actors will follow up on the interactions and perform the necessary actions. For instance, when the system says that a book is now available for a member who had placed a hold, a clerk will take the actions necessary to inform the member. The system also does not have the ability to perform specialized tasks like generating call numbers for the Dewey Decimal System. The business processes of the library system are listed below:

- **Register new members:** The library receives applications from people who want to become library members, whom we alternatively refer to as **users**. While applying for membership, a person supplies his/her name, phone number, and address to the library. The system records this information and assigns each member a unique identifier (ID), which is required for transactions such as issuing books.
- **Add books to the collection:** We will make the assumption that the collection includes only books. For each book, the system stores the title, the author's name, and a unique ID. The ID is generated externally; that is, it is provided as input to the system. (For simplicity, let us assume that there is only one author per book. If there are multiple authors, let us say that the names will have to be concatenated to get a pretty huge name such as "Brahma Dathan and Sarnath Ramnath." As a result, to the

system, it appears that there is still just one author.) When it is added to the collection, a book is given a unique identifier by the clerk. This ID is based on some standard system of classification.

- **Issue a book to a member (or user):** To check out books, a user (or member) must identify himself to a clerk and hand over the books. The clerk inputs the IDs, and the system records that the books have been checked out to the member. Any number of books may be checked out in a single transaction.
- **Record the return of a book:** To return a book, the member gives the book to a clerk, who submits the information to the system, which marks the book as "not checked out." If there is a hold on the book, the system should remind the clerk to set the book aside so that the hold can be processed.
- **Remove books from the collection:** From time to time, the library may remove books from its collection. This could be because the books are worn out, are no longer of interest to the users, or other sundry reasons. The clerk inputs the ID and the system verifies that it is safe to remove the book.
- **Print out a user's transactions:** There may be a need to check the interactions (book check-outs, returns, etc.) between a specific user and the library on a certain date. The clerk provides the user's ID and a date; the system displays the relevant information.
- **Place/Remove a hold on a book:** When a user wants to put a hold, he/she supplies the clerk with the book's ID, the user's ID, and the number of days after which the book is not needed. The clerk inputs this information and the system adds the user to a list of users who wish to borrow the book. If the book is not checked out, a hold cannot be placed. To remove a hold, the system should be provided with the book's ID and the user's ID.
- **Renew books issued to a member:** Customers may walk in and request that several of the books they have checked out be renewed (re-issued). The clerk inputs the user's ID; the system displays the relevant books, allows the clerk to make a selection, and displays the result.
- **Notify a member of a book's availability:** Customers who had placed a hold on a book are notified when the book is returned. This process is performed once at the end of each day. The clerk enters the ID of each book that was set aside, and the system returns the name and phone number of the user who is next in line to get the book.

In addition, the system must support three other requirements that are not directly related to the workings of a library, but which, nonetheless, are essential:

- A command to save the data on a long-term basis.
- A command to load data from a long-term storage device.

- A command to quit the application. At this time, the system must ask the user if data is to be saved before termination.

To keep the process simple, we restrict our attention for the time being to the above operations. A real library would have to perform additional operations like generating reports of various kinds, imposing fines for late returns, etc. Many libraries also allow users to check out books themselves without approaching a clerk. Whatever the case may be, the analysts need to learn the existing system and the requirements. As mentioned earlier, they achieve this through interviews, surveys, and study.

Our goal here is to present the reader with the big picture of the entire process so that the beginner is not overwhelmed by the complexity or bogged down in minutiae. Keeping this in mind, we will be designing a system that the reader may find somewhat simplistic, particularly if one compares this with the kinds of features that a "real" system in today's market can provide. While there is some truth to this observation, it should be noted that the simplification of the system has been done with a view to reducing unnecessary detail so that we can focus instead on the development process, elaborate on the use of tools described previously, and explain through an example how good design principles are applied. In the course of applying the above, we have come up with a somewhat simplified *sample development process* that may be used as a template by someone who is getting started on this subject.

Assuming that we have a good grasp of the requirements, we need to document the functional requirements of the application and determine the system's main entities and their relationships.

## 4.2 Building the User Interaction Model

It is important that the requirements be precisely documented. The requirements specification document serves as a contract between the users and the developers. When it is time to deliver the system, there should be no confusion as to what the expectations are. Equally or perhaps even more importantly, it also tells the designers the expected functionality of the system. Moreover, as we attempt to create a precise documentation of the requirements, we will discover errors and omissions.

An accepted way of accomplishing this task is by *use case analysis*, which we study now.

### 4.2.1 Use Case Analysis

Use case analysis is a case-based way of describing the uses of a system with the goal of defining and documenting the system requirements. It is essentially a narrative describing the sequence of events (actions) of an external agent (actor) using the system to complete a process. It is a powerful technique that describes the kind of functionality that a user expects from the system. Use cases have two or more parties: *agents* who interact with the system and the *system* itself. In our simple library system, the members do not use the system directly. Instead, they obtain services through the library staff.

To initiate this process, we need to get a feel for how the system will interact with the end-user. We assume that some kind of a user interface is required, so that when the system is started, it provides a menu with the following choices:

1. Add a member.
2. Add books.
3. Issue books.
4. Return books.
5. Remove books.
6. Place a hold on a book.
7. Remove a hold on a book.
8. Process holds: Find the first member who has a hold on a book.
9. Renew books.
10. Print out a member's transactions.
11. Store data on disk.
12. Retrieve data from disk.
13. Exit.

The above menu gives us the list of ways in which the system is going to be used. There are some implicit requirements associated with these operations. For instance, when a book is checked out, the system must output a due date so that the clerk can stamp the book. This and other such details will be spelled out when we elaborate on the use cases.

The actors in our system are members of the library staff who manage the daily operations. This idea is depicted in the use case diagram in Figure 4.1, which gives an overview of the system's usage requirements. Notice that even in the case of issuing books, the functionality is invoked by a library staff member, who performs the actions on behalf of a member.

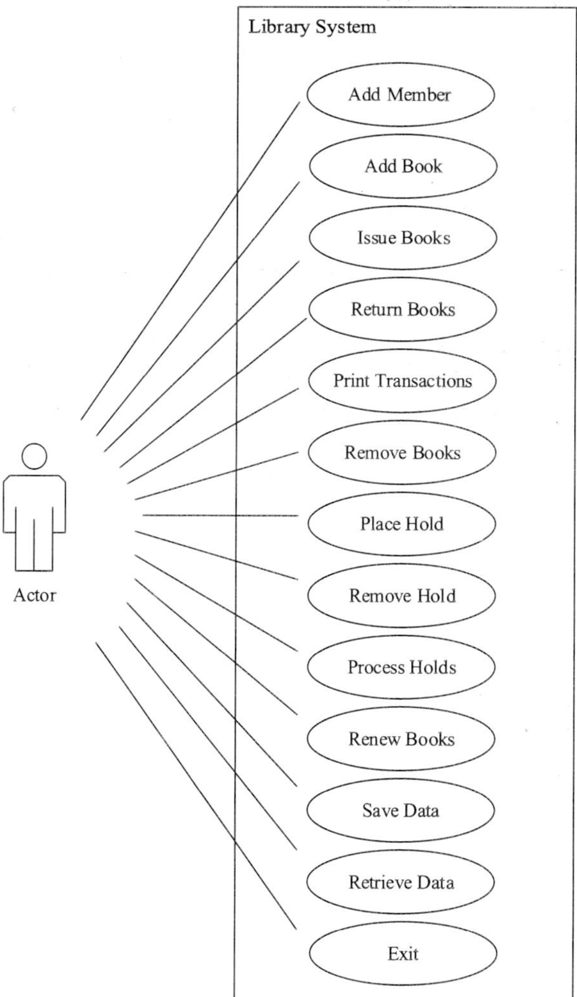


**Fig. 4.1** Use case diagram for the library system

### 4.2.2 Detailed Use Cases for the Library System

We now take up the task of specifying the individual use cases. In order to keep the discussion within manageable size and not lose focus, we make the following assumption: while the use cases will state the need for the system to display different messages prompting the user for data and informing the results of operations, the user community is not fussy about the minute details of what the messages should be; any meaningful message is acceptable. For example, we may specify in a use case that the system "informs the clerk if the member was added." The actual message could be any one of a number of possibilities such as "Member added," "Member registered," etc.

**Use Case for Registering a User:** Our first use case is for registering a new user and it is given in Table 4.1.

| Action performed by the actor | Response from the system |
|---|---|
| 1. The customer fills out an application form containing the customer's name, address, and phone number and gives this to the clerk. | |
| 2. The clerk issues a request to add a new member. | |
| | 3. The system asks for data about the new member. |
| 4. The clerk enters the data into the system. | |
| | 5. The system reads in data, and if the member can be added, generates an identification number (which is not necessarily a number in the literal sense, just as social security numbers and phone numbers are not actually numbers) for the member and remembers information about the member. The system then informs the clerk if the member was added and outputs the member's name, address, phone, and ID. |
| 6. The clerk gives the user his identification number. | |

**Table 4.1** Use case: Register New Member

This example illustrates several aspects that all use cases must exhibit:

- Every use case must be identified by a name. We have given the name Register New Member to this use case.
- It should represent a reasonable-sized activity in the organization. It is important to note that not all actions and operations should be identified as use cases. As an extreme example, stamping a due date on the book should not be a use case. A use case is a relatively large end-to-end process description that captures some business process that a client purchasing the software needs to perform. In some instances, a business process may be decomposed into more than one use case, particularly when there is some intervening real-world event(s) for which the agent has to wait for an unspecified length of time. An example of such a situation is presented later in this chapter.

- The first step of the use case specifies a "real-world" action that triggers the exchange described in the use case. This is provided mainly for the sake of completeness and does not have much bearing on the actual design of the system. It does, however, serve a useful purpose: by looking at the first steps of all the use cases, we can verify that all external events that the system needs to respond to have been taken care of.
- The use case does not specify how the functionality is to be implemented. For example, the details of how the clerk enters the required information into the system are left unspecified. Although we assume that the user interacts with the system through the menu, which was briefly described earlier, we do not specify the details of this mechanism. The use case also does not state how the system accomplishes the task of registering a user: what software components form the system, how they may interact, etc.
- The use case is not expected to cover all possible situations. While we would expect that the sequence of events that are specified in the above use case is what would actually happen in a library when a person wants to be registered, the use case does not specify what the system should do if there are errors. In other words, the use case explains only the most commonly occurring scenario, which is referred to as the *main flow*. Deviations from the main flow due to occurrences of errors and exceptions are not detailed in the above use case.

**Use Case for Adding Books:** Next, we look at the use case for adding new books as shown in Table 4.2. Notice that we add more than one book in this use case, which involves a repetitive process captured by a *go-to* statement in the last step. Notice that details of how the identifier is generated are not specified. From the point of view of the system analyst, this is something that the actor is expected to take care of independently.

**Use Case for Issuing Books:** Consider the use case where a member comes to the check-out counter to issue a book. The user identifies himself/herself to a clerk, who checks out the books for the user. It proceeds as in Table 4.3.

There are some drawbacks to the way this use case is written. One drawback is that it does not specify how due dates are computed. We may have a simple rule (example: due dates are one month from the date of issue) or something quite complicated (example: due dates are dependent on the member's history, how many books have been checked out, etc.). Including these details in the use case may make it messy and harder to understand; they are therefore documented separately as **business rules.** Keeping them separate also has the advantage that they can be updated independently. Our rules here are quite simple, but in general, business rules can deal with several kinds of situations. The box on the next page describes various situations where business rules are employed.

| Action performed by the actor | Response from a system |
|---|---|
| 1. The library receives a shipment of books from a publisher. | |
| 2. The clerk issues a request to add a new book. | |
| | 3. The system asks for the identifier, title, and author name of the book. |
| 4. The clerk generates the unique identifier, and enters the identifier, title, and author name of the book. | |
| | 5. The system attempts to enter the information in the catalog and echoes to the clerk the title, author name, and ID of the book. It then asks if the clerk wants to enter information about another book. |
| 6. The clerk answers in the affirmative or in the negative. | |
| | 7. If the answer is in the affirmative, the system goes to Step 3. Otherwise, it exits. |

**Table 4.2** Use case: Adding New Books

We will refer to the rule for due-date generation as *Rule 1.* Let us document all the business rules for our system before we proceed. These are shown in Table 4.4.

A second drawback with the use case is that as written above, it does not state what to do in case things go wrong. For instance,

- The person may not be a member at all. How should the use case handle this situation? We could abandon the whole show or ask the person to register.
- The clerk may have entered an invalid book ID.

To take care of these additional situations, we modify the use case as given in Table 4.5. We have resolved these issues in Step 7 by having the system check whether the book is issuable, which can be expressed as a business rule. This could check one (or more) of several conditions: *Is the member in good standing with the library? Is there some reason the book should not be checked out? Has the member checked out more books than permitted (if such limits were to be imposed)?* The message displayed by the system in Step 7 informs the clerk about the result of the transaction. In a real-life situation, the client will probably want specific details of what went wrong; if they are important

| Action performed by the actor | Response from the system |
|---|---|
| 1. The member arrives at the check-out counter with a set of books and supplies the clerk with his/her identification number. | |
| 2. The clerk issues a request to check out books. | |
| | 3. The system asks for the user ID. |
| 4. The clerk inputs the user ID to the system. | |
| | 5. The system asks for the ID of the book. |
| 6. The clerk inputs the ID of the book that the user wants to check out. | |
| | 7. The system records the book as having been issued to the member. It also records the member as having possession of the book. It generates a due date. The system displays the book title and due date and asks if there are any more books. |
| 8. The clerk stamps the due date on the book and replies in the affirmative or negative. | |
| | 9. If there are more books, the system moves to Step 5; otherwise, it exits. |
| 10. The customer collects the books and leaves the counter. | |

**Table 4.3** Use case: Book Check-out

| Rule number | Rule |
|---|---|
| *Rule 1* | *Due date for a book is one month from the date of issue.* |
| *Rule 2* | *All books that are not already issued are issuable.* |
| *Rule 3* | *A book is removable if it is not checked out and if it has no holds.* |
| *Rule 4* | *A book is renewable if it has no holds on it.* |
| *Rule 5* | *When a book with a hold is returned, the appropriate member will be notified.* |
| *Rule 6* | *Holds can be placed only on books that are currently checked out.* |

**Table 4.4** Business rules for the library system

to the client, these details should be expressed in the use case. Since our goal is to cover the basics of requirements analysis, we sidestep the issue.

Let us proceed to write more use cases. For the most part, these are quite elementary, and we suggest that the reader try them first as an exercise.

### How do business rules relate to use cases?

Business rules can be broadly defined as the details through which a business implements its strategy. Business analysts perform the task of gathering business rules, and these belong to one of four categories:

- **Definitional rules**, which explain what is meant when a certain word is used in the context of the business operations. These may include special technical terms or common words that have a particular significance for the business. For instance, the term *Book* in the context of the library refers to a book owned by the library.
- **Factual rules**, which explain basic things about the business's operations; they explain how the terms connect to each other. A library, for instance, would have rules such as "Books are issued to Members" and "Members can place holds on Books."
- **Constraints**, which are specific conditions that govern the manner in which terms can be connected to each other. For instance, we have a constraint that says "Holds can be placed only on Books that are currently checked out."
- **Derivations**, which denote the knowledge that can be derived from facts and constraints. For instance, a bank may have the constraint, "The balance in an account cannot be less than zero," from which we obtain the derivation that if an amount requested for withdrawal is more than the balance, the operation will not be successful.

When writing use cases, we are mainly concerned with constraints and derivations. Typically, such business rules are in-lined with the logic of the use case. The use case may explicitly state the test that is being performed and cite the appropriate rule or it may simply mention that the system will respond in accordance with a specific rule.

In addition to the kinds of rules we have presented for this case study, there are always implicit rules that permeate the entire system. A common example of this is validation of input data; a zip code, for instance, can be validated against a database of zip codes. Note that this rule does not deal with how entities are connected to one another, but specifies the required properties of a data element. Such constraints do not belong in use cases, but could be placed in classes that store the corresponding data elements.

**Use Case for Returning Books:** Users return books by leaving them on a library clerk's desk; the clerk enters the book IDs one by one to return them. Table 4.6 gives the details of the use case. Here, as in the use case for issuing books, the clerk may enter incorrect information into the system, which the

| Action performed by the actor | Response from the system |
|---|---|
| 1. The member arrives at the check-out counter with a set of books and supplies the clerk with his/her identification number. | |
| 2. The clerk issues a request to check out books. | |
| | 3. The system asks for the user ID. |
| 4. The clerk inputs the user ID to the system. | |
| | 5. If the ID is valid, the system asks for the ID of the book; otherwise, it prints an appropriate message and exits the use case. |
| 6. The clerk inputs the identifier of the book that the user wants to check out. | |
| | 7. If the ID is valid and the book is issuable to the member, the system records the book as having been issued to the member. It records the member as having possession of the book and generates a due date as in *Rule 1*. It then displays the book's title and due date. If the book is not issuable as per *Rule 2*, the system displays a suitable error message. The system asks if there are more books. |
| 8. The clerk stamps the due date, prints out the transaction (if needed) and replies positively or negatively. | |
| | 9. If there are more books for checking out, the system goes back to Step 5; otherwise, it exits. |
| 10. The clerk gives the user the checked-out books. The customer leaves the counter. | |

**Table 4.5** Use case: Book Check-out (Revised)

use case handles. Notice that if there is a hold on the book, that information is printed out for use by the clerk at a later time.

**Use Cases for Removing (Deleting) Books, Printing Member Transactions, Placing a Hold, and Removing a Hold:** The next four use cases deal with the scenarios for removing books (Table 4.7), printing out member transactions (Table 4.8), placing a hold (Table 4.9), and removing a hold (Table 4.10). In the second of these, the system does not actually print out the transactions, but only displays them on the interface. We are assuming that the necessary facilities to print will be a part of the underlying platform.

In Step 5 of Table 4.7, we allow for the possibility that the deletion may fail. In this event, we assume that there will be some meaningful error message so that the clerk can take corrective action. We shall revisit this issue when we discuss the design and implementation in Chapter 5.

| Action performed by the actor | Response from the system |
|---|---|
| 1. The member arrives at the return counter with a set of books and leaves them on the clerk's desk.<br>2. The clerk issues a request to return books. | |
| | 3. The system asks for the identifier of the book. |
| 4. The clerk enters the book identifier. | |
| | 5. If the identifier is valid, the system marks that the book has been returned and informs the clerk if there is a hold placed on the book; otherwise, it notifies the clerk that the identifier is not valid. It then asks if the clerk wants to process the return of another book. |
| 6. The clerk answers in the affirmative or in the negative and sets the book aside in case there is a hold on the book. (See *Rule 5.*) | |
| | 7. If the answer is in the affirmative, the system goes to Step 3. Otherwise, it exits. |

**Table 4.6** Use case: Return Book

| Action performed by the actor | Response from the system |
|---|---|
| 1. The librarian identifies the books to be deleted.<br>2. The clerk issues a request to delete books. | |
| | 3. The system asks for the identifier of the book. |
| 4. The clerk enters the ID for the book. | |
| | 5. The system checks if the book can be removed using *Rule 3*. If the book can be removed, the system marks the book as no longer in the library's catalog. The system informs the clerk about the success of the deletion operation. It then asks if the clerk wants to delete another book. |
| 6. The clerk answers in the affirmative or in the negative. | |
| | 7. If the answer is in the affirmative, the system goes to Step 3. Otherwise, it exits. |

**Table 4.7** Use case: Removing Books

There may be some variations in the way these scenarios play out. When placing or removing a hold, the library staff may actually want to see a message that the operation was successfully completed. These requirements would modify the manner in which the system responds in these use cases. While such information should be gleaned from the client as part of the requirements analysis, it is often necessary to go back to the client after the use cases are

| Action performed by the actor | Response from the system |
|---|---|
| 1. The clerk issues a request to get member transactions. | |
| | 2. The system asks for the user ID of the member and the date for which the transactions are needed. |
| 3. The clerk enters the identity of the user and the date. | |
| | 4. If the ID is valid, the system outputs information about all the transactions completed by the user on the given date. For each transaction, it shows the type of transaction (book borrowed, book returned or hold placed) and the title of the book. |
| 5. The clerk prints out the transactions and hands them to the user. | |

**Table 4.8** Use case: Member Transactions

written to ensure that the system interacts in the desired manner with the operator.

| Action performed by the actor | Response from the system |
|---|---|
| 1. The clerk issues a request to place a hold. | |
| | 2. The system asks for the book's ID, the ID of the member, and the duration of the hold. |
| 3. The clerk enters the identity of the user, the identity of the book, and the duration. | |
| | 4. The system checks that the user and book identifiers are valid and that *Rule 6* is satisfied. If yes, it records that the user has a hold on the book and displays that; otherwise, it outputs an appropriate error message. |

**Table 4.9** Use case: Place a Hold

| Action performed by the actor | Response from the system |
|---|---|
| 1. The clerk issues a request to remove a hold. | |
| | 2. The system asks for the book's ID and the ID of the member. |
| 3. The clerk enters the identity of the user and the identity of the book. | |
| | 4. The system removes the hold that the user has on the book (if any such hold exists), prints a confirmation, and exits. |

**Table 4.10** Use case: Remove a Hold

**Use Case for Processing Holds:** Given in Table 4.11, this use case deals with processing the holds at the end of each day. In this case, once the contact information for the member has been printed out, we assume that the library will contact the member. The member may not come to collect the book within the specified time, at which point the library will try to contact the next member in line. All this cannot be included in the use case. If we were to do so, the system would, in essence, be waiting on the user's response for a long period of time, and the process would not be temporally cohesive. Also, since our proposed system is not expected to have the ability to contact the members, we cannot add this to the system responsibilities. We therefore leave out these steps and when the next user has to be contacted, we simply process holds on the book once again.

| **Action performed by the actor** | **Response from the system** |
|---|---|
| 1. The clerk issues a request to process holds (so that *Rule 5* can be satisfied). | |
| | 2. The system asks for the book's ID. |
| 3. The clerk enters the ID of the book. | |
| | 4. The system returns the name and phone number of the first member with an unexpired hold on the book. If all holds have expired, the system responds that there is no hold. The system then asks if there are any more books to be processed. |
| 5. If there is no hold, the book is then shelved back to its designated location in the library. Otherwise, the clerk prints out the information, places it in the book, and replies in the affirmative or negative. | |
| | 6. If the answer is yes, the system goes to Step 2; otherwise, it exits. |

**Table 4.11** Use case: Process Holds

**Use Case for Renewing Books:** This use case (see Table 4.12) deals with situations where a user has several books checked out and would like to renew some of these. The user may not remember the details of all of them and would perhaps like the system to prompt him/her. We shall assume that users only know the titles of the books to be renewed (they do not bring the books or even the book IDs to the library) and that most users would have borrowed only a small number of books. In this situation, it is entirely appropriate for the system to display the title of each book borrowed by the user and ask if that book should be renewed.

| Action performed by the actor | Response from the system |
|---|---|
| 1. The member makes a request to renew several of the books that he/she has currently checked out. | |
| 2. The clerk issues a request to renew books. | |
| | 3. The system asks for the member's ID. |
| 4. The clerk enters the ID into the system. | |
| | 5. The system checks the member's record to find out which books the member has checked out. If there are none, the system prints an appropriate message and exits; otherwise, it moves to Step 6.<br>6. The system displays the title of the next book checked out to the member and asks whether the book should be renewed. |
| 7. The clerk replies yes or no. | |
| | 8. The system attempts to renew the book using *Rule 4* and reports the result. If the system has displayed all checked-out books, it reports that and exits; otherwise, the system goes to Step 6. |

**Table 4.12** Use case: Renew Books

It may be the case that a library has additional rules for renewability: if a book has a hold or a member has renewed a book twice, it may not be renewable. In the above interaction, the system displays all the books and determines the renewability only if the member wishes to renew the book. A different situation could arise if we require that the system display only the renewable books. (The system would have to have a way for checking renewability without actually renewing the book, which places additional requirements on the system's functionality.) For our simple library, we go with the scenario described in Table 4.12.

## 4.3 Defining Conceptual Classes and Relationships

As discussed earlier, the last major step in the analysis phase involves determination of the conceptual classes and the establishment of their relationships. For example, in the library system, some of the main conceptual classes include members and books. Members borrow books, which establishes a relationship between them.

**Guidelines to remember when writing use cases**

- A use case must provide something of value to an actor or the business; when the scenario described in the use case has played out, the actor must have accomplished some task. The system may have other functions that do not provide value; these will be just steps within a use case. This also implies that each use case has at least one actor.
- Use cases should be *functionally cohesive,* that is, they should encapsulate a single service that the system provides.
- Use cases should be *temporally cohesive.* This notion applies to the time frame over which the use case occurs. For instance, when a book with a hold is returned, the member who has the hold needs to be notified. The notification is done after some delay; due to this delay, we do not combine the two operations into one use case. Another example could be a university registration system. When a student registers for a class, he or she should be billed. Since the billing operation is not temporally cohesive with the registration, the two constitute separate use cases.
- If a system has multiple actors, each actor must be involved in at least one, and typically, several use cases. If our library allowed members to check out books by themselves, "member" is another possible actor.
- The model that we construct is a *set* of use cases, that is, there is no relationship between individual use cases.
- Exceptional exit conditions are not handled in use cases. For instance, if a system should crash in the middle of a use case, we do not describe what the system is supposed to do. It is assumed that some reasonable outcome will occur.
- Use cases are written from the point of view of the actor in the active voice.
- A use case describes a scenario, that is, it tells us what the visible outcome is and does not give details of any other requirements that are being imposed on the system.
- Use cases specify the functionality of the system. Hence we should ensure that we have the technology necessary to handle the stated responsibilities.

We could justify the usefulness of this step in several ways:

- **Design Facilitation.** Through use case analysis, we determined the functionality required of the system. Obviously, the design stage must determine how to implement the functionality. For this, the designers should be in a position to determine the classes that need to be defined, the objects to be created, and how the objects interact. This is better facilitated if the analysis phase classifies the entities in the application and determines their relationships.

- **Added Knowledge.** The use cases do not completely specify the system. Some of these missing details can be filled in by the class diagram.
- **Error Reduction.** In carrying out this step, analysts are forced to look at the system more carefully. The result can be shown to the client who can verify its correctness.
- **Useful Documentation.** Classes and relationships provide a quick introduction to the system for someone who wants to learn it. Such people include personnel who join the project to carry out the design or implementation or subsequent maintenance of the system.

In practice, an analyst will probably use multiple methods to come up with the conceptual classes and their relationships. In this case study, however, we use a simple approach: we examine the use cases and pick out all the nouns in the description of the requirements. We then refine the selection through analysis to obtain concepts that deserve to be classes and look for the relationships between them.

### 4.3.1 Conceptual Classes for the Library System

Let us start with the text of the first use case, registering new users, and pick out the nouns. Here is the text of that use case, once again, with all nouns bold-faced:

> 1) The **customer** fills out an **application form** containing the **customer's name, address,** and **phone number** and gives this to the **clerk.** 2) The **clerk** issues a **request** to add a new **member.** 3) **The system** asks for **data** about the new **member**. 4) The **clerk** enters the **data** into the **system**. 5) **The system** reads in **data**, and if the **member** can be added, generates an **identification number** for the **member** and remembers **information** about the **member.** It informs the **clerk** if the **member** was added and outputs the **member's name**, **address**, **phone**, and **ID**. 6) The **clerk** gives the **user** his **identification number**.

Let us examine the nouns. First, let us eliminate duplicates to get the following list: **customer**, **application form**, **customer's name**, **address, phone number**, **clerk, request**, **system**, **data**, **identification number**, **member**, **user**, **member information,** and **member's name**. Some of the nouns such as **member** are composite entities that qualify to be classes.

While using this approach, we must remember that natural languages are imprecise and that synonyms may be found. We can eliminate the others as follows:

1. **customer**: Becomes a member, so it is effectively a synonym for member.
2. **user**: The library refers to members alternatively as users; so this is also a synonym.
3. **application form** and **request**: Application form is an external construct for gathering information, and request is just a menu item; so neither actually becomes part of the data structures.
4. **customer's name, address,** and **phone number**: They are attributes of a customer, so the `Member` class will have them as fields.
5. **clerk:** This is just an agent for facilitating the functioning of the library; so it has no software representation.
6. **identification number**: This will become part of a member.
7. **data**: Gets stored as a member.
8. **information**: This is the same as the data related to a member.
9. **system**: This is a collective reference to all the entities that help track the necessary information.

The noun **system** implies a conceptual class that represents all of the software; we call this class `Library`. Although we do not, as yet, have any specifics of this class, we note its existence and represent it in UML without any attributes and methods (Figure 4.2). (Recall from Chapter 2 that a class is represented by a rectangle.)

A member is described by the attributes name, address, and phone number. Moreover, the system generates an identifier for each user, so that also serves as an attribute. The UML convention is to write the class name at the top with a line below it and the attributes listed just below that line. The UML diagram is shown in Figure 4.3. Obviously, members and books are the most central entities in our system: the sole reason for the library's existence is to provide service to its members and that is effected by letting them borrow books. Just as we reasoned for the existence of a conceptual class named `Member`, we can argue for the need for a conceptual class called `Book` to represent a book. It has attributes `id`, `title`, and `author`. A UML description of the class is shown in Figure 4.4.

Library

**Fig. 4.2** UML diagram for the class `Library`

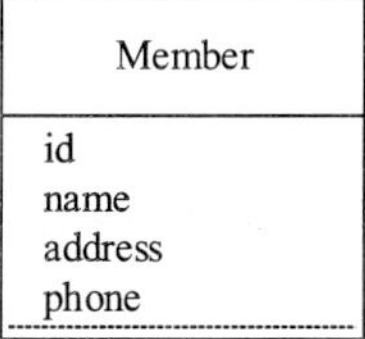


**Fig. 4.3** UML diagram for the class `Member`

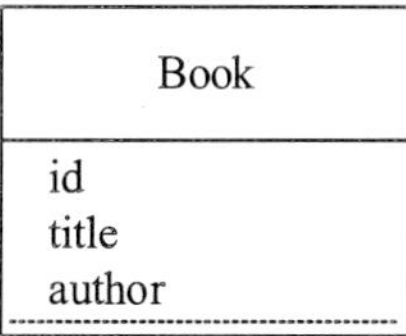


**Fig. 4.4** UML diagram for the class `Book`

### 4.3.2 Identifying the Relationships Between the Classes

Recall the notion of association between classes, which we know from Chapters 2 and 3 as a relationship between two or more classes. We note several examples of association in our case study. The use case Register New Member says that the system "remembers information about the member." This implies an association between the conceptual classes `Library` and `Member`. This idea is shown in Figure 4.5; note the line between the two classes and the labels 1, *, and "maintains a collection of" just above it. They mean that one instance of the `Library` maintains a collection of zero or more members.

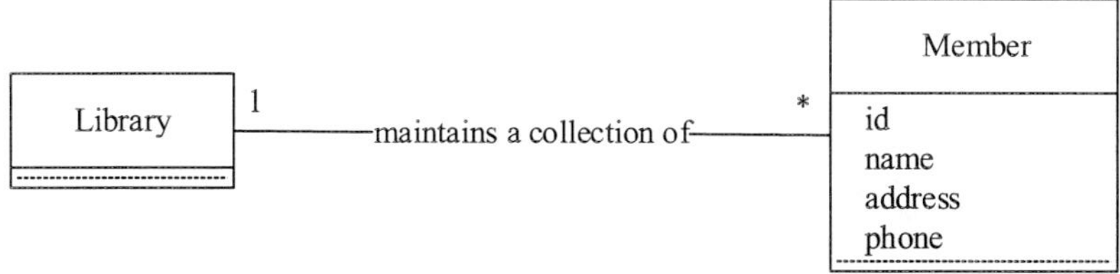


**Fig. 4.5** UML diagram showing the association of `Library` and `Member`

It should come as no surprise that an association between the classes `Library` and `Book`, shown in Figure 4.6, is also required. We show that a library has zero or more books. (Normally, you would expect a library to have at least one book and at least one member; but our design takes no chances!)

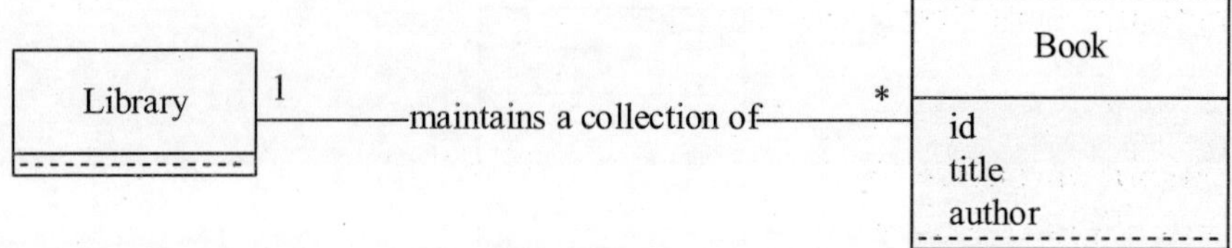


**Fig. 4.6** UML diagram showing the association of `Library` and `Book`

Some associations are *static*, that is, permanent, whereas others are *dynamic*. Dynamic associations are those that change as a result of the transactions being recorded by the system. Such associations are typically associated with verbs.

As an example of a dynamic association, consider members borrowing books. This is an association between `Member` and `Book`, as shown in Figure 4.7. At any instant in time, a book can be borrowed by one member and a member may have borrowed any number of books. We say that the relationship `has borrowed` is a one-to-many relationship between the conceptual classes `Member` and `Book` and indicate it by writing 1 by the side of the box that represents a user and the * near the box that stands for a book.

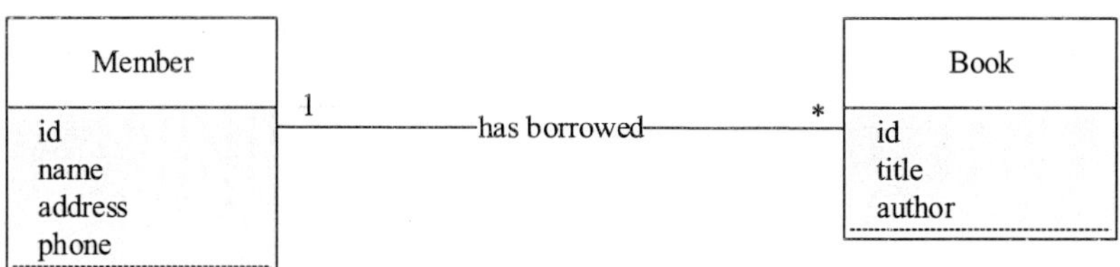


**Fig. 4.7** UML diagram showing the association `Borrows` between `Member` and `Book`

This diagram actually tells us more than what the Issue Book use case does. That use case does not state some of the considerations that come into play when a user borrows a book: for example, how many books a user may borrow. We may have forgotten to ask that question when we learned about the use case. However, now that we are looking at the association and are forced to put labels at the two ends, we may end up capturing missing information. In Figure 4.7, we state that there is no limit. It also states that two users may not borrow the same book at the same time. This is a dynamic relationship. When a member borrows books, the corresponding member object and the corresponding book objects become associated in this way. When a member returns books, the associations are removed.

Another action that a member can undertake is to place a hold on a book. Several users can have holds placed on a book, and a user may place holds on an arbitrary number of books. In other words, this relationship is many-to-many between users and books. We represent this in Figure 4.8 by putting a * at both ends of the line representing the association.

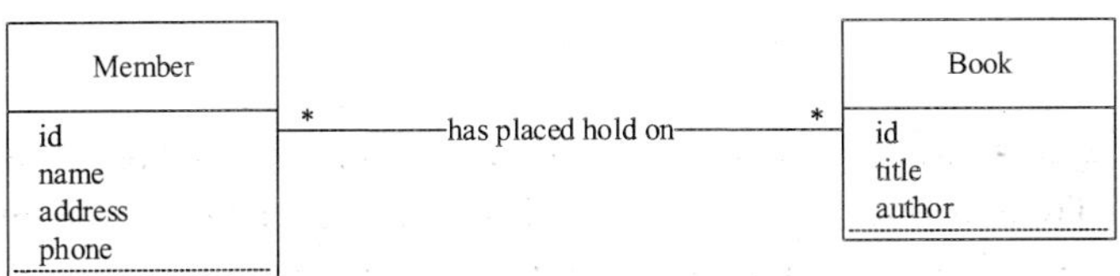


**Fig. 4.8** UML diagram showing the association `Holds` between `Member` and `Book`

We capture all of the conceptual classes and their associations in a single figure, as shown in Figure 4.9. To reduce complexity, we have omitted the attributes of `Library`, `Member`, and `Book`.

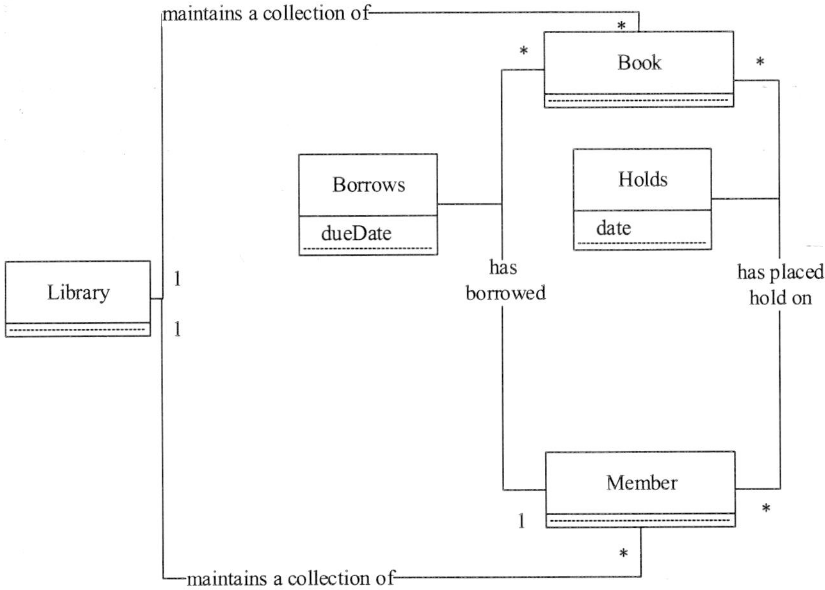


**Fig. 4.9** Conceptual classes and their associations for the library system

As seen before, a relationship formed between two entities is sometimes accompanied by additional information. This additional information is relevant only in the context of the relationship. There are two such examples in the inter-class relationships we have seen so far: when a user borrows a book and when a user places a hold on a book. Borrowing a book introduces new information into the system, namely, the date on which the book is due to be returned. Likewise, placing a hold introduces some information, namely, the date after which the book is not needed. The lines representing the association are augmented to represent the information that must be stored as part of the association. For the association `Borrows` and the line connecting `Member` and `Book`, we come up with a conceptual class named `Borrows` having an attribute named `dueDate`. Similarly, we create a conceptual class named `Holds` with the attribute called `date` to store the information related to the association `Holds`. Both these conceptual classes are attached to the line representing the corresponding associations.

It is important to note that the above conceptual classes or their representations do not, in any way, tell us how the information is going to be stored or accessed. Those decisions will be deferred to the design and implementation phase. For instance, there may be additional classes to support the operations of the `Library` class. We may discover that while some of the conceptual classes have corresponding physical realizations, some may disappear and the necessary information may be stored as fields distributed over multiple classes. We may choose to move fields that belong to an association elsewhere. For instance, the field `dueDate` may be stored as a field of the book or as a separate object, which holds a reference to the book object and the user object involved. Upon making that choice, the designer decides how the conceptual relationship between User and Book is going to be physically realized. The conceptual class diagram is simply that: **conceptual.**

## 4.4 Using the Knowledge of the Domain

Domain analysis is the process of analyzing related application systems in a domain so as to discover what features are common between them and what parts are variable. In other words, we identify and analyze common requirements from a specific application domain. In contrast to looking at a certain problem completely from scratch, we apply the knowledge we already have from our study of similar systems to speed up the creation of specifications, design, and code. Thus one of the goals of this approach is reuse.

Any area in which we develop software systems qualifies to be a **domain**. Examples include library systems, hotel reservation systems, university registration systems, etc. We can sometimes divide a domain into several interrelated domains. For example, we could say that the domain of university applications includes the domain of course management, the domain of student admissions, the domain of payroll applications, and so on. Such a domain can be quite complex because of the interactions of the smaller domains that make up the bigger one.

**Finding the right classes**

In general, finding the right classes is non-trivial. It must be remembered that this process is iterative, that is, we start with a set of classes and complete a conceptual design. In the process of walking through the use case implementations, we may find that some classes need to be dropped while some others need to be added. Familiarity with design patterns also helps in recognizing the classes. The following thumb rules and caveats come in handy:

- In general, do not build classes around functions. Write a class description. If it reads "This class performs...," we most likely have a problem. If the class name is imperative, for example, print, parse, etc. it is likely that either the class is wrong or the name is wrong.
- Remember that a class usually has more than one method; otherwise, it is probably a method that should be attached to some other class.
- Do not form an inheritance hierarchy too soon unless we have a pre-existing taxonomy. (Inheritance is supposed to be a relationship among well-understood abstractions.)
- Be wary of classes that have no methods, (or only query methods) because they are not frequent. Some situations in which they occur are:
  (i) Representing objects from the outside world
  (ii) Encapsulating facilities, constants or shared variables.
  (iii) Applicative classes used to describe non-modifiable objects. For example, the `Integer` class in Java generates new integers, but does not allow modification of integers.
- Check for the following properties of an ideal class:
  (i) A clearly associated abstraction, which should be a data abstraction (as opposed to a process abstraction).
  (ii) A descriptive noun/adjective for the class name.
  (iii) A non-empty set of run-time objects.
  (iv) Queries and commands.
  (v) Abstract properties that can be described as pre/post conditions and invariants.

Before we analyze and construct a specific system, we first need to perform an exhaustive analysis of the class of applications in that domain. In the domain of libraries, for example, there are things we need to know, including the following:

- The environment, including customers and users. Libraries have loanable items such as books, CDs, periodicals, etc. A library's customers are members. Libraries buy books from publishers.
- Terminology that is unique to the domain: for example, the Dewey Decimal Classification (DDC) System for books.
- Tasks and procedures currently performed. In a library system, for example:

  1. Members may check out loanable items.
  2. Some items are available only for reference; they cannot be checked out.
  3. Members may put holds on loanable items.
  4. Members will pay a fine if they return items after the due date.

One of the major activities of this analysis is discovering the business rules, which are the rules that any properly functioning system in that domain must conform to.

Where does the knowledge of a specific domain come from? It could be from sources such as surveys, existing applications, technical reports, user manuals, and so on. As shown in Figure 4.10, domain analysis uses this knowledge to improve the design of the resulting system.

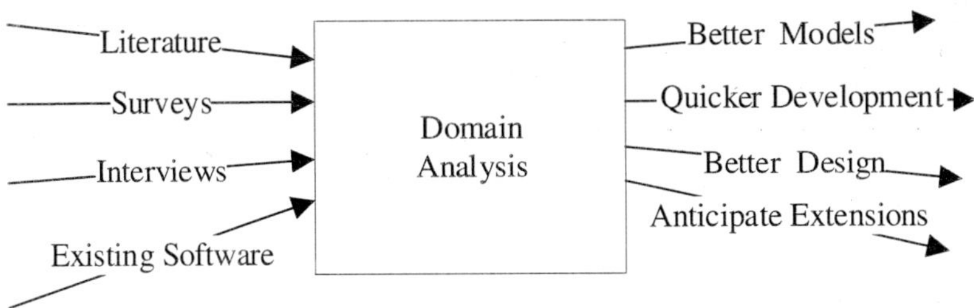


**Fig. 4.10** Domain analysis: inputs and potential benefits

Clearly, a significant amount of effort has to be expended on domain analysis before undertaking the specific problem. The benefit is that after the initial investment of resources, the products (such as specifications, designs, code, test data, etc.) can be reused for the development of any number of applications in that domain. This reduces development time and cost.

## 4.5 Discussion and Further Reading

A detailed treatment of object-oriented analysis methods can be found in [4]. The rules for finding the right classes are condensed from [5].

Obtaining the Requirements Specification is typically part of a larger *"plan and elaborate phase"* that would be an essential component of any large project. In addition to specification of requirements, this phase includes such activities as the *initial conception*, *investigation of alternatives, planning, budgeting,* etc. The end product of this phase will include such documents as the *Plan* showing a schedule, resources, budget etc.; a *Preliminary Investigation Report* that lists the motivation, alternatives, and business needs; *Requirements Specification*, a *Glossary* as an aid to understanding the vocabulary of the domain; and, perhaps, a *rough Conceptual Model.* Larger systems typically require more details before the analysis can proceed.

Use case modeling is one of the main techniques of a more general field of study called *Usage Modeling.* Usage Modeling employs the following techniques: *essential use cases, system use cases*, *UML use case diagrams, user stories* and *features* [1]. What we have discussed here are essential use cases, which deal only with the fundamental business task without bringing technological issues into account. These are used to explore usage-based requirements.

Making sure that our use cases have covered all the business processes is in itself a non-trivial task. This area of study, called *Business Process Modeling*, employs tools such as *data flow diagrams, flowcharts,* and *UML activity diagrams*, [1] and is used to create process models for the business.

There are several UML tools available for analysis, and new variants are being constantly developed. What a practitioner chooses often depends on the development package being employed. A good, compact reference to the entire language can be found in [3]. The use case table and the class diagram with associations exemplify the very basic tools of object-oriented analysis.

There is no prescribed analysis or design technique that a software designer must follow at all costs. There are several methodologies in vogue, and these ideas continue to evolve over time. In [2] it has been pointed out that while some researchers and developers are of the opinion that object-oriented methodologies are a revolutionary change from the conventional techniques, others have argued that object-oriented techniques are nothing but an elaboration of structured design. A comparative study of various object-oriented and conventional methodologies is also presented in that article.

**The object-oriented analysis process**

The object-oriented analysis process explained in this chapter can be captured by the Figure 4.11 below.

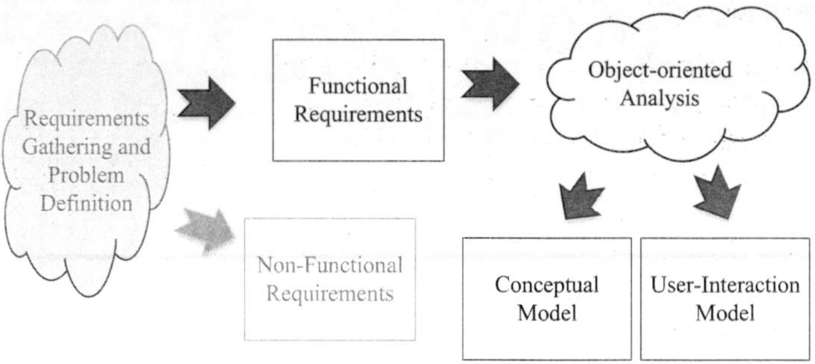


**Fig. 4.11** The object-oriented analysis process

When a piece of software needs to be created, we go through a process of gathering requirements and defining the problem. This task is carried out as part of any good problem solving or software engineering process. This process is not specific to object-oriented analysis, and is not within the scope of this book. This process produces two artifacts: the functional requirements and the non-functional requirements.

Our focus in this book is mainly on the functional requirements, which can be expressed as a set of business processes. The object-oriented analysis process that we describe here starts with this artifact. It is important that these business processes be defined clearly enough for our purpose, which means the person undertaking the object-oriented analysis must recognize when the businesses processes are poorly written.

Our object-oriented process uses the functional requirements to generate the **user interaction** model and the **conceptual** model. The user interaction model defines how the system responds to the various inputs and is captured in the detailed use cases. Such a model of a system is useful for any kind of design process. The conceptual model identifies the particular concepts specific to such a system, and the nature of the relationships between these concepts. These concepts are the conceptual classes that define the types of objects that our system will need and are the building blocks of the object-oriented design process.

## Projects

1. **A database for a warehouse.**

   A large warehousing corporation operates as follows:

   a. The warehouse stocks several products, and there are several manufacturers for each product.
   b. The warehouse has a large number of registered clients. The clients place orders with the warehouse, which then ships the goods to the client. This process is as follows: The warehouse clerk examines the client's order and creates an invoice, depending on the availability of the product. The invoice is then sent to the shop floor where the product is packed and shipped along with the invoice. The unfilled part of the order is placed in a waiting list queue.
   c. When the stock of any product runs low, the warehouse orders that product from one of the manufacturers, based on the price and terms of delivery.
   d. When a product shipment is received from a manufacturer, the orders in the waiting list are filled in first. The remainder is added to the inventory.

   **The business processes:** The warehouse has three main operational business processes:

   a. Receiving and processing an order from a client.
   b. Placing an order with the manufacturer.
   c. Receiving a shipment.
   d. Receiving payment from a client.

   Let us examine the first of these. When an order is received from a client, the following steps are involved:

   1. The clerk receives the order and enters the order into the system.
   2. The system generates an invoice based on the availability of the product(s).
   3. The clerk prints the invoice and sends it over to the storage area.
   4. A worker on the floor picks up the invoice, retrieves the product(s) from the shelves and packs them, and ships the goods and the invoice to the client.
   5. The worker requests the system to mark the order as having been shipped.
   6. The system updates itself by recording the information.

This is an interesting business process because the steps of printing the invoice and retrieving the product from the shelves are performed by different actors. This introduces an indefinite delay into the process. If we were to translate this into a single end-to-end use case, we have a situation where the system will be waiting for a long time to get a response from an actor. It is therefore appropriate to break this up into two use cases as follows:

1. Use case create-invoice.
2. Use case fill-invoice.

In addition to these operational business processes, the warehouse will have several other querying and accounting processes, such as:

a. Registering a new client.
b. Adding a new manufacturer for a certain product.
c. Adding a new product.
d. Printing a list of clients who have defaulted on payments.
e. Printing a list of manufacturers who are owed money by the warehouse.

Write the use cases and determine the conceptual classes and their relationships.

2. **Managing a university registration system.**

A small university would like to create a registration system for its students. The students will use this system to obtain information about courses, when and where the classes meet, register for classes, print transcripts, drop classes, etc. Faculty will be using this system to find out what classes they are assigned to teach, when and where these classes meet, get a list of students registered for each class, and assign grades to students in their classes. The university administrative staff will be using this database to add new faculty and students, remove faculty and students who have left, put in and update information about each course the university offers, enter the schedules for classes that are being offered in each term, and any other housekeeping tasks that need to be performed.

Your task is to analyze this system, extract and list the details of the various business processes, develop the use cases, and find the conceptual classes and their relationships.

In finding the classes for this system, one of the issues that will come up is that of distinguishing a course from an offering of the course. For instance "CS 430: Principles of Object-Oriented Software Construction" is a course listed in the university's course bulletin. The course is offered once during the fall term and once during the spring term. Each offering may be taught at a different time and place and, in all likelihood, will have a different set of students. Therefore all offerings have some information in common and some information that is unique to that offering. How will you choose a set of classes that models all these interactions?

3. **Creating an airline reservation and staff scheduling database.**

   An airline has a weekly flight schedule. Associated with each flight is an aircraft, a list of crew, and a list of passengers. The airline would like to create and maintain a database that can perform the following functions:

   For passengers: Add a passenger to the database, reserve a seat on a flight, print out an itinerary, request seating and meal preferences, and update frequent flier records.

   For crew: Assign crew members to each flight, allow crew members to view their schedule, keep track of what kinds of aircraft the crew member has been trained to operate.

   For flights: Keep track of crew list, passenger list, and aircraft to be used for that flight.

   For aircraft: Maintain all records about the aircraft and a schedule of operation.

   Make an exhaustive list of queries that this system may be required to answer. Carry out a requirements analysis for the system and model it as a collection of use cases. Find the conceptual classes and their relationships.

## Exercises

1. In the use case Issue Book, the system displays the transaction details of each book. Modify this so that there is only one display of transactions at the very end of the process.
2. (Discussion) In a real library, there would be several other kinds of query operations that would be performed. Carry out a brainstorming exercise to come up with a more complete list of use cases for a real library system.
3. A Hotel Reservation System supports the following functionality:

   a. Room reservation
   b. Changing the properties of a room (for example, from non-smoking to smoking)
   c. Customer check-in
   d. Customer check-out

   Come up with system use cases for the above functionality.

4. We are building a system to track personal finances. We plan an initial version with minimal functionality: we track the expenditure items. (Each expenditure has a description, date, and amount.) We show the use case given below for creating a new expenditure item and a new income item.

| Actor | System |
|---|---|
| 1) Inputs a request to create a new expenditure item | |
| | 2) Asks for description, date, and amount |
| 3) Supplies the data | |
| | 4) Creates an expenditure item and notifies the user |

| Actor | System |
|---|---|
| 1) Inputs a request to create a new income item | |
| | 2) Asks for description, date, and amount |
| 3) Supplies the data | |
| | 4) Creates an income item and notifies the user |

a. The use cases are quite weakly specified. In what ways? (Hint: Compare with the addition of a new member or book in the library system.)

b. What are the alternate flows in the use cases? Modify the two use cases to handle the alternate flows.

c. Identify the conceptual classes.

5. Consider the policies maintained by an automobile insurance company. A policy has a primary policy holder, a set of autos insured, and a list of people who are covered by the insurance. From your knowledge of insurance, come up with system use cases for:

a. Creating a new policy

b. Adding a new person to a policy

c. Adding a new automobile to a policy

d. Recording a claim

6. Consider an information system to be created for handling the business of a supermarket. For each of the following, state if it is a possible class. If not, explain why not. Otherwise, why would you consider it to be a class? What is its role in the system?

a. Customer

b. Vegetable

c. Milk
d. Stock
e. Tinman's 8oz baked beans
f. Quantity on hand for a product

7. A company has several projects, and each employee works on a single project. The human resource system evaluates the personnel needs of each project and matches them against the personnel file to find the best possible employees to be assigned to the project. Come up with the conceptual classes by conducting use case analysis.
8. Explain why mistakes made in the requirements analysis stage are the costliest to correct.
9. Among the following requirements, which are functional and which are non-functional?

   a. Paychecks should be printed every two weeks.
   b. Database recovery should not take more than one hour.
   c. The system should be implemented using the C++ language.
   d. It should be possible to selectively print employee checks.
   e. Employee list should be displayed in lists of size 10.

10. In Problem 6, assume that a customer may pay with cash, check, or credit/debit cards. Should this aspect be taken into consideration while developing the use case for purchasing grocery? Justify your answer.
11. Again, in Problem 6, suppose that a user may check out independently in an automated check-out counter. Should there be two versions of the grocery purchase use case? Explain.
12. What are the advantages of ignoring implementation-related aspects while performing analysis?

## References


1. Ambler, S. 2004. *The Object Primer: Agile Model-Driven Development with UML 2.0.* Cambridge University Press: New York, NY, USA.
2. Fichman, R and Kemerer, C. 1995. *Object-Oriented and Conventional Analysis and Design Methodologies.* IEEE Computer Society Press.
3. Fowler, M and Scott, K. 1997. *UML Distilled.* Addison-Wesley Longman Publishing Co: Boston, MA, USA.
4. Larman, C. 1998. *Applying UML and Patterns.* Prentice Hall PTR.
5. Meyer, B. 1997. *Object-Oriented Software Construction.* Prentice Hall: Upper Saddle River, NJ, USA.

# Chapter 5
# Designing a System

During analysis, we constructed a conceptual model and a behavioral model for the proposed system. In the design step, we use the class structure defined in the conceptual model to design a system that behaves in the manner specified by the behavioral model. The main UML tool that we employ here is the sequence diagram. In a sequence diagram, the designer details how the behavior specified in the model will be realized. This process requires the system's actions to be broken down into specific tasks, and the responsibility for these tasks to be assigned to the various players (classes and objects) in the system. In the course of assigning these responsibilities, we determine the public methods of each class and also describe the function performed by each method. Since the stage after design is implementation, which is coding, testing, and debugging, it is imperative that we have a full understanding of how the required functionality will be realized through code. The designer thus breaks down the system into smaller units and provides enough information so that a programmer can code and test each unit.

As we shall see in this chapter, the design process involves making several choices. This is quite typical of any engineering design and should come as no surprise. For instance, when a structure is designed, an engineer may be starting with an architect's plan and making choices about how various aspects of the plan are going to be realized; in doing this, the engineer is typically guided by principles that have been formulated through years of experience. Likewise, we have principles that guide the process of designing object-oriented software. A natural question that arises is: *Can we review the completed design and determine if the principles were applied correctly?* Fortunately, there are some things that can guide us in this. Experienced practitioners have identified *code smells* and *design smells* that help us identify parts of the completed design that do not square with best practice. The principles of *refactoring* may prove to be useful in this context. Refactoring is most commonly used to improve an existing system, and refactoring rules guide us through this process. However, we can also apply these rules as we design the system, thereby avoiding mistakes that can be expensive to correct after deployment. In the later part of this chapter, we examine a situation where reviewing a completed design helps us to refactor and improve it.

## 5.1 Initiating the Design Process

In the broadest sense, the design process requires a number of questions to be answered:

1. On what platform(s) (hardware and software) will the system run? For example, will the system be developed for just one platform, say, Windows running on 386-type processors? Or will we be developing for other platforms such as Unix?
2. What languages and programming paradigms will be used for implementation? Often, the choice of the language will be dictated by the expertise the company has. But sometimes the functionality will also heavily influence the choice of the language. For example, a business application may be developed using an object-oriented language such as Java or C++, but an artificial intelligence application may be programmed in Lisp or Prolog.
3. What will the software architecture be, that is, the major subsystems and their relationships?
4. What user interfaces will the system provide? These include GUI screens, printouts, and other devices (for example, library cards).
5. What classes and interfaces need to be coded? What are their responsibilities?
6. How is data stored on a permanent basis? What medium will be used? What model will be used for data storage?
7. What happens if there is a failure? Ideally, we would like to prevent data loss and corruption. What mechanisms are needed for realizing this?
8. Will the system use multiple computers? If so, what are the issues related to data and code distribution?
9. What kind of protection mechanisms will the system use?

However, our focus in this book is on object-oriented design and development using the the Java programming language. Hence, we will not be distracted by considerations of the exact platform on which the system will run. Our main focus throughout the book is the identification of the software structure: *the major subsystems, and the classes and interfaces that make up the system.* Although we discuss user interface (UI) design and long-term storage issues, we do not address protection and recovery mechanisms since the development of these is largely orthogonal to the issues that we are attempting to address. In general, systems typically employ some combination of application software, firewalls, database management system support, manual procedures, etc. to provide the necessary mechanisms for protection, concurrency control, and recovery. The choices made when designing solutions for these issues should have little or no impact on the design of the application software itself.

### 5.1.1 The Major Subsystems

The first step in our design process is to identify the major subsystems. We can view the library system as composed of two major subsystems:

- **Back-end:** This part deals with input data processing, data creation, queries, and data updates. This module will also be responsible for interacting with external storage, storing and retrieving data.
- **User Interface:** This subsystem interacts with the user, accepting and outputting information.

It is important to design the system in such a way that the above parts are separated from each other, so they can be varied independently. That way, we get good cohesion within each subsystem. Our focus in this chapter is mainly on the design and implementation of the back-end.

We put together a rudimentary, text-based UI that enables to test the system. We also implement a simple mechanism for storing and retrieving data by interacting with external storage devices. While the UI and external storage management modules are adequate to carry out functional testing of our system, a more sophisticated design (and implementation) would be in order for a full-blown system.

### 5.1.2 Identifying the Software Classes

The next step is to identify and create the software classes. During analysis, after defining the use case model, we came up with a set of conceptual classes and a conceptual class diagram for the entire system. As mentioned earlier, these come from a conceptual or essential perspective. The software classes are more "concrete" in that they correspond to the software components that make up the system. Let us examine each of the conceptual classes and decide which conceptual classes have corresponding software classes.

- **Member** and **Book:** These are central concepts. Each `Member` object comprises several attributes such as name and address, stays in the system for a long period of time, and performs a number of useful functions. Books stay part of the library over a long time, and we can perform a number of useful actions on them. We need to instantiate books and members quite often. Clearly, both are classes that require representation in software.

- **Library:** Do we really need to create a class for this? To answer the question, let us ask what the real library – not a possible object – has. It keeps track of books and members. When a member thinks of a library, he/she thinks of borrowing and returning books, placing and removing holds, that is, the *functionality* provided by the library. To model a library with software, we need to mimic this functionality, which we did by creating a use case model. The use case behavior is what is exhibited by the UI, and to meet the required specifications, the UI must perform some other computations that involve the module that implements the business logic. One of the important principles of object-oriented design is that every computation must be represented as an application of a method on a given object, which is then treated as the current object for the computation. All the computation required of the business logic module must be executed on some current object; that object is a `Library`. This requires that `Library` be a class in its own right, and the operations required of the business logic module correspond to the methods of this class.

  We therefore create a `Library` class that provides a set of methods for the interface, and serves as a single point of entry to and exit from the business logic module. In the language of design patterns, what we created is known as a **facade.**
- **Borrows:** This class represents the one-to-many relationship between members and books. *In a typical one-to-many relationship, the association class can be efficiently implemented as a part of the two classes at the two ends.* To verify this for our situation, for every pair of member $m$ and book $b$ such that $m$ has borrowed $b$, the corresponding objects simply need to maintain a reference to each other. Since a member may borrow multiple books, this arrangement entails the maintenance of a list of `Book` objects in `Member`, but since there is only a single borrower for a book, each `Book` object needs to store a reference to only one instance of `Member`. Further examining the role played by the information in `Borrows`, we see that when a book is checked out, the due date can be stored in `Book`. In general, this means that all attributes that are unique to the relationship may be captured by storing information at the "many" end of the relationship. When the book is returned, the references between the corresponding `Member` and `Book` objects as well as the due date stored in `Book` can be "erased." This arrangement efficiently supports queries arising in almost any situation: a user wanting to find out when her books are due, a staff member wanting to know the list of books borrowed by a member, or an anxious user asking the librarian when he can expect the book on which he placed a hold. In all these situations, we have operations related to some `Member` and `Book` objects.
- **Holds:** Unlike `Borrows`, this class denotes a many-to-many relationship between the `Member` and `Book` classes. *In a typical many-to-many relationship, implementation of the association without using an additional class is unlikely to be clean and efficient.* To attempt to do this without an

### The Facade pattern

The Facade pattern provides a unified interface to a subsystem, allowing external objects to use the subsystem without any knowledge of the details. It is a **structural** pattern, since it provides a simple way to realize the relationship between external objects and the subsystem. The relationship here is that the external object is invoking the functionality provided by the subsystem. The subsystem has several individual classes, each with its own set of public methods. Without the facade, the external object would require knowledge of the public methods of each individual class. The facade shields the client from this requirement, thus enabling loose coupling between the subsystem and its clients. Facades are typically designed to prevent the client from accessing the components within the subsystem.

The facade provides a single point of entry through which external objects can interact with a subsystem, enabling abstraction. It also allows the entire system to adapt to changes in individual classes within the subsystem, as long as the functionality of the subsystem remains unchanged. Figure 5.1 shows how the relationship between the external (client) objects and the subsystem changes when we have a facade.

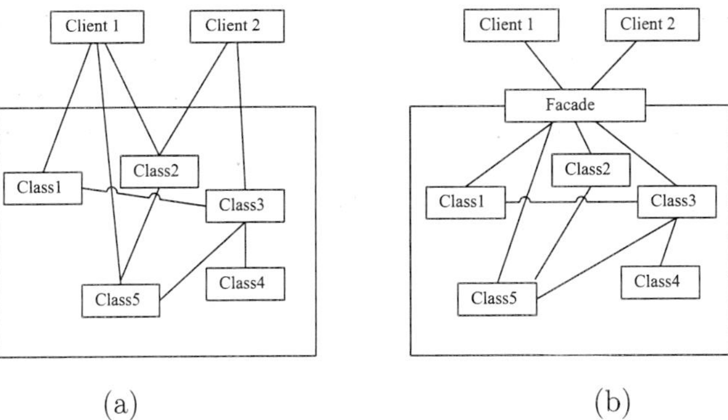


**Fig. 5.1** The facade pattern. Contrast the two ways in which the clients interact with the system. In (b), the two clients access the facade to utilize a subset of the functionality provided by the five classes.

Perhaps the most ubiquitous example of the use of facade is in designing the interface of an operating system. The system provides various menus through which the users may invoke the standard operations of the operating system, thus shielding the user from its complexity. The interface does not prevent users from writing a script to customize operations, which gives them access to the components of the system.

One apparent downside is that a facade is a largely "custom-written" class that cannot be reused. However, the actual coding is quite simple, and the advantage gained by simplifying the interactions between other entities is worth this effort.

additional class in the case of holds, we would need to maintain within each `Member` object references to all `Book` instances for which there is a hold, and keep "reverse" references from the `Book` objects to the `Member` objects. This is, however, incomplete because we also need to maintain for each hold the number of days for which it is valid. But there is no satisfactory way of associating this attribute with the references. We could have queries like a user wanting a list of all of his holds that expire within 30 days. The reader can verify that implementations without involving an additional class will be complicated and inefficient. It is, therefore, appropriate that we have a class for this relationship and make the `Hold` object accessible to the instances of `Member` and `Book`.

Finding Other Classes

The conceptual classes are a rich source of software classes. However, they do not provide a complete set of software classes. We can find other classes using our experience with programming and software creation, and also by thinking about how the system will be implemented.

From analysis, we see two important aspects of the `Library` class: the `Library` instance must keep track of the members of the library as well as the books, which obviously implies maintenance of two collections. The functionality of these two collections is again to be determined, but it is likely that we need two different classes, `MemberList` and `Catalog`, which may be alike in certain respects.[1] These two collections last as long as the library itself, and we make modifications to them very frequently. The actions that we perform are not supported by programming languages although there may be some support in the associated packages such as the list classes in the Java Development Kit. All these would suggest that they be classes.

At this point, we do not see the need for any more classes. As we look at ways to implement the use cases, it often happens that we eliminate some of these classes, discover more, and determine the attributes and methods for all of the concrete classes.

## 5.2 Assigning Responsibilities to the Classes

Having decided on an adequate set of software classes, our next task is to assign responsibilities to them. Since the ultimate purpose of these classes is to enable the system to meet the responsibilities specified in the use cases, we shall work with these system responsibilities to find the class responsibilities.

---

[1] Although we use the name `MemberList`, we do not imply that this class has to be organized as a list.

The next step is, therefore, to spell out the details of how the system meets its responsibilities by devolving these down to the software classes. The UML tool that we employ to describe this devolution is the sequence diagram.

It should be noted that the sequence diagram is only a concise, visual way of *representing* the devolution, and we need to make our design choices *before* we start drawing our arrows. For each system response listed in the right-hand column of the use case tables, we need to specify the following:

- The sequence in which the operations will occur.
- How each operation will be carried out.

For the first item above, we need a complete algorithm; the second item describes which classes will be involved in each step of the algorithm and how the classes will be engaged. In specifying the second item, we spell out detailed definitions of the classes: the methods that need to be invoked and the parameters that should be passed to these methods. The first item specifies what is done in each step; since each step is a method call, we are specifying what each method is supposed to accomplish. In the course of figuring out how the method computes what is needed, we make other design choices. In the end, all of these things come together to give us a complete system.

### Returning the Result

The detailed use cases tell us what result the system returns for each business process. Presenting these results is the responsibility of the UI, but the necessary information has to be returned by the `Library` class. As we get into the design, we need to specify the type of result in each business process. In some cases, all the necessary information is contained in an existing object, which can be returned to the UI. In other cases, we may need to display a message that can be returned as a string, or return a result code (an integer) and allow the UI to decide what kind of message should be displayed. The two principles that guide us in these decisions are:

- Allow the UI the freedom to design the input and output.
- Avoid coupling between the UI and the back-end.

If the result is, say, a string, the UI has little choice but to display it; on the other hand, if the result is a complex object that the UI has to decode, it could cause unwanted coupling. Since we have conflicting constraints, we will try and make the best decision individually for each case.

In all cases, it is necessary to return a result code (we will use an integer) that indicates whether the operation was successful, and if there was a problem, the result code would specify that too. Many operations require supplemental information to be delivered as well, which would be data contained in one or more existing business objects such as the `Member` and `Book` objects. The user interface can use the result code and any other data contained in the message to clearly display the result.

It is important to note here that the sequence diagrams represent the kind of information that the back-end returns to the UI, but to keep the discussion in this chapter focused on the business logic, we will defer discussion of the interface between the UI and the business logic to Chapter 6. This decision depends, among other considerations, upon non-functional requirements like security and performance.

Saving and Retrieving Data

The business processes for *saving the data* and *retrieving the data* are not discussed here, since these operations depend heavily on the choice of programming language for implementation. The design for these is quite simple, and the difficulty lies in the implementation. We therefore defer the discussion of these to the next chapter.

### 5.2.1 Actions that Add New Entities (Populating the System)

The simplest of the operations for setting up a database is that of populating it with all the basic entities. Our system has only two kinds of basic entities: *member* and *book*. We therefore start with designing the operations for adding a member and for adding books.

#### 5.2.1.1 Register a Member

The sequence diagram for the use case for registering a member is shown in Figure 5.2. The clerk issues a request to the system to add a new member. The system responds by asking for data about the new member. This interaction occurs between the library staff member and the `UserInterface` instance. The clerk enters the requested data, which the `UserInterface` accepts.

Obviously, at this stage, the system has all the data it needs to create a new `Member` object. The role of the UI is to interact with the user and not to perform business logic. So if the UI were to assume all responsibility for creating a `Member` object and adding that object to the `Library` instance, the consequence will be unnecessary and unwanted coupling between the business logic module and the UI class. We would like to retain the ability to develop the UI knowing as little as possible about the application classes. For this purpose, it is ideal to have a method, namely, `addMember()`, within `Library` to perform the task of creating a `Member` and storing it in `MemberList`. All

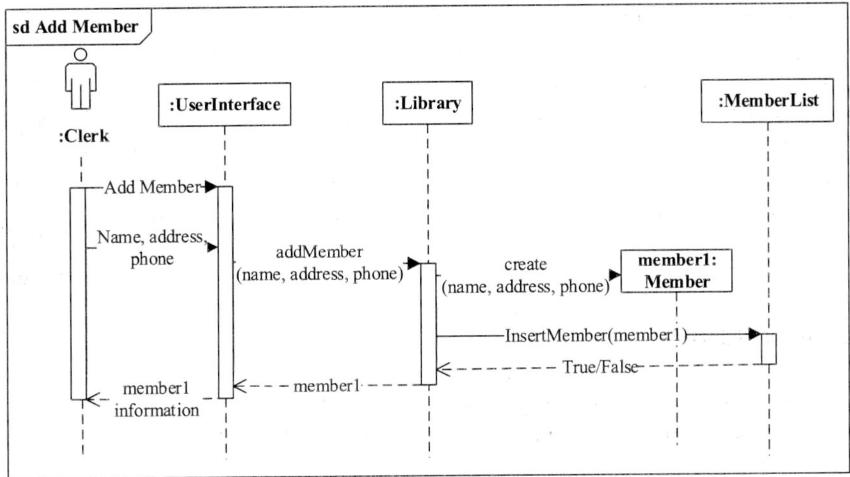


**Fig. 5.2** Sequence diagram for adding a new member. `Library` invokes the constructor to create the object `member1`, and then adds the object to `MemberList`.

that `UserInterface` needs to do is pass the three pieces of information – name, address, and phone number of the applicant – as parameters to the `addMember()` method, which then assumes full responsibility for creating and adding the new member.
Let us see details of the `addMember` method. The algorithm here consists of three steps:

1. Create a `Member` object.
2. Add the object to the list of members.
3. Return the result of the operation.

To carry out the first two steps, we have two options:

- **Option 1:** Invoke the `Member` constructor from within the `addMember()` method of `Library`. The constructor returns a reference to a `Member` object and an operation, `insertMember()`, is invoked on `MemberList` to add the new member.
- **Option 2:** Invoke the `addNewMember()` method on `MemberList` and pass as parameters all the data about the new member. `MemberList` creates a `Member` object and adds it to the collection.

Let us examine what the purpose of the `MemberList` class is: *to serve as a container for storing a large number of members, adding new ones, removing existing ones, and performing search operations.* The container should not, therefore, concern itself with details of a member, especially, its attributes. If we choose this option, `addNewMember()` must take in as parameters, the details of a member (name, address, and phone) so that it can call the constructor of the `Member` class. This introduces unnecessary coupling between `MemberList` and `Member`. As a result, if changes are later made to the `Member` constructor, these will also affect `MemberList`, even though the intended functions of `MemberList` do not warrant these changes.

Therefore, we prefer Option 1 to implement the `addMember()` method. A second issue crops up in the generation of `memberID`. Once again, we have two options:

- **Option 1:** Generate the ID in `Library` and pass it through the constructor.
- **Option 2:** Generate the ID in `Member`, through the constructor.

Here, it is important to note that we need a mechanism to ensure that no two members get the same ID, that is, there has to be some central place where we keep track of how IDs are generated. It is tempting to perform this in the `Library` class, but it is a poor design choice since this reduces the cohesiveness of the design by adding irrelevant responsibilities to the facade. The difficulty with performing this in `Member` is that we need to remember the history of previous IDs to avoid duplication. This difficulty can be overcome by using static fields and static methods. These details depend on the language, and are laid out when we implement the design.

The last step is to return the result, so that `UserInterface` can adequately inform the actor about the success of the operation. The requirements for this are spelled out in Step 5 in Table 4.1 (see Chapter 4), which reads: "(The system) informs the clerk if the member was added and outputs the member's name, address, phone, and ID." This can be achieved if `Library` returns information about the `Member` object that was created. The result code would indicate to the UI whether the operation was successful; otherwise, the necessary information is accessed from the result object and reported.

#### 5.2.1.2 Add Books

The next sequence diagram (Figure 5.3) is for the Add Books use case. This use case allows the insertion of an arbitrary number of books into the system. In this case, when the request is made by the actor, the system enters a loop. Since the loop involves interacting repeatedly with the actor, the loop control mechanism is in the UI itself. The first operation is to get data about the book to be added. The algorithm here consists of the following steps: (i) create a `Book` object, (ii) add the `Book` object to the catalog and (iii) return the result of the operation. This is handled in a manner similar to the previous use case.

The UI displays the result and continues until the actor indicates an exit. This repetition is shown diagrammatically by a special rectangle that is marked `loop`. All activities within the rectangle are repeated until the clerk indicates that there are no more books to be entered.

In Figures 5.2 and 5.3, note that `Library`, `MemberList`, and `Catalog` are in the top row. Placing the entity in the top row indicates that it is in existence at the beginning of the process. This contrasts with the entities `member1`

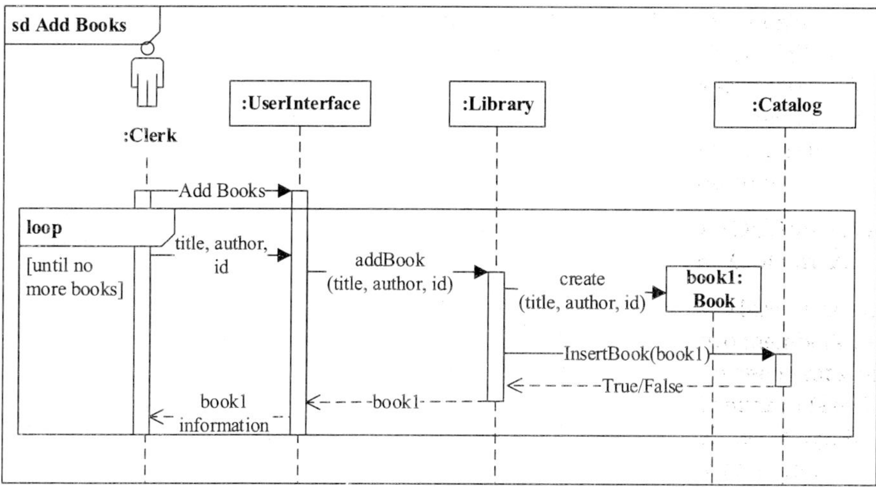


**Fig. 5.3** Sequence diagram for adding books. For each book, `Library` invokes the constructor, and adds the `Book` object to `Catalog`.

and `book1`, which do not exist at the beginning, but are created by invoking constructors. This is indicated by placing these boxes at the end of the arrow representing the call to the constructor. This box is at a lower level, to signify the later point in time when the entity comes into existence.

### 5.2.2 Adding/Removing the Relationship Between Existing Entities

The operation for checking out a book requires that the system record the book as being issued to the member and the member as having possession of the book. This is accomplished by modifying both the `Book` object and the `Member` object to reflect this relationship. Consequently, the operation for returning a book must modify the `Book` object and the `Member` object to indicate that the relationship no longer exists. Likewise, when a hold is placed, the system must record that the member has placed a hold on the book, and that the book is being held by the member. In all these situations, different parts of the operation are performed on different objects. `Library` provides the glue code that ties all these operations together.

#### 5.2.2.1 Issue Books

The sequence diagram for the Issue Books use case is given in Figure 5.4. From the detailed use case, we see two steps:

1. Get the user's ID and verify that it is valid.
2. Issue the books, one at a time, to the user.

To enable these steps, `Library` provides two methods: `searchMember()` and `issueBook()`. Since there are several books, the `issueBook()` method will be invoked several times, from within a loop.

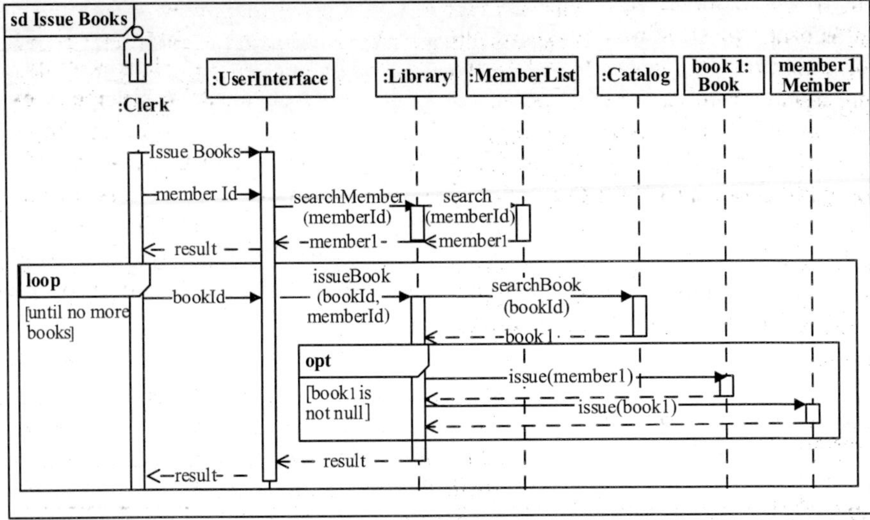


**Fig. 5.4** Sequence diagram for issuing books. The UI first verifies the member, then invokes the `issue()` method for each book.

Two options suggest themselves for implementing the `searchMember()` method in `Library`:

- **Option 1:** Get an enumeration of all `Member` objects from `MemberList`, get the ID from each and compare with the target ID.
- **Option 2:** Delegate the entire responsibility to `MemberList`.

Option 1 places too much detail of the implementation in `Library`, which is undesirable. Option 2 is more attractive because search is a natural operation that is performed on a container. The flip side with the second option is that in a naive implementation, `MemberList` will now become aware of the implementation details of `Member` (that `memberID` is a unique identifier, etc.), causing some unwanted coupling between `Member` and the container class `MemberList`. This coupling is not a concern because it can be removed using generic parameters, as we shall see later in the text.
The `issueBook()` method involves the following steps:

1. Verify that the book ID is valid.
2. If the book is issuable:

- Record that the book is being issued to the member
- Record that the member has possession of the book
- Renerate and record a due date for returning the book

3. Return the result.

Once again, searching for the `Book` object is delegated to `Catalog`. Next, the `Book` and `Member` objects are updated to indicate that the book is checked out to the member, and that the member is in possession of the book.

Another question we need to address is this: *Where should the responsibility for generating the due date lie?* In our simple system, the due date is simply one month from the date of issue, and it is not determined by other factors such as member privileges. Consequently, computing the due date is a simple operation, and since we are storing the due date as a field in `Book`, we can fold this detail into the `issue()` method of `Book`. As before, we must decide the return type of the method `issueBook()`. The use case requires that the system generate a due date and display the book title and due date and ask if there are any more books. This can be easily done by returning an appropriate result code and associated information such as the due date.

#### 5.2.2.2 Return Books

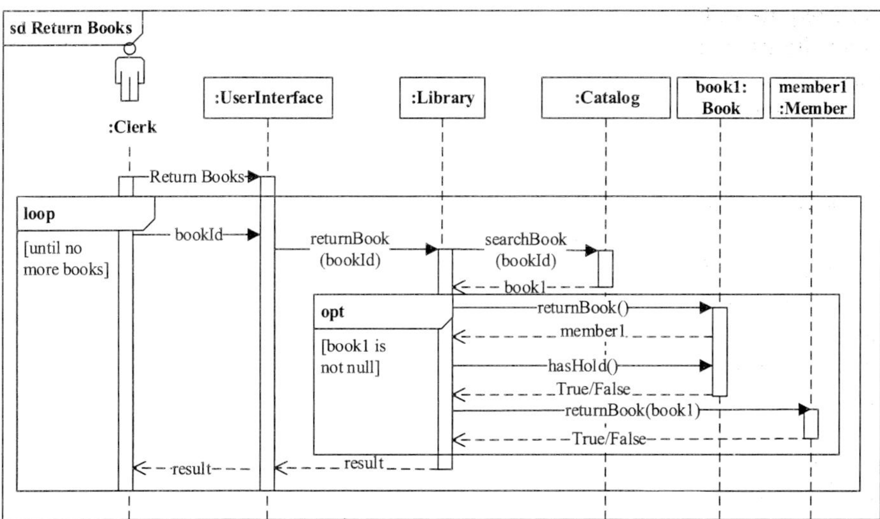


**Fig. 5.5** Sequence diagram for returning books. The clerk can return several books issued to various members; both `Book` and `Member` are updated to reflect the return.

The sequence diagram for the Return Books use case is given in Figure 5.5. From the detailed use case, we see that for each book, a return operation is performed. To enable this, `Library` provides the method `returnBook()`, which performs the following steps:

1. Verify that the book ID is valid.
2. If the book ID is valid:
   - Record that the book has no borrower
   - Record that the member has returned the book
   - Check if the book has any holds
3. Return the result.

**Cohesion and coupling**

In deciding how specific details of the implementation are carried out, we have to keep in mind the twin issues of cohesion and coupling. We must have *good cohesion* among all the entities that are grouped together or placed within a subsystem. Simultaneously, entities within the group must be *loosely coupled.* In our example, when issuing a book, we have chosen to implement the system so that `Library` calls the `issue()` methods of `Book` and `Member`. Contrast this with a situation where `Book` calls the `issue()` method of `Member`; in such a situation, the code in `Book` depends on the method names of `Member`, which causes tight coupling between these two classes. Instead, we have chosen a solution where each of these classes is tightly coupled with `Library`, but there is very loose coupling between any other pair of classes. This means that when the system has to adapt to changes in any class, this can be done by modifying `Library` only. `Library`, therefore, serves as "glue" that holds the system together and simultaneously acts an interlocutor between the entities in the library system.

We have also consciously chosen to separate the design of the business module from the UI through which the actors will interact with the system. This is to ensure good cohesion within the system's "back-end."

A related question that we face at a lower level is that of how responsibilities are assigned. We ask this question when a class is being designed. Responsibilities are assigned to classes based on the fields that the class has. These responsibilities turn into the methods of the class. The principle that we are following here can be tersely summarized in an Italian saying (attributed to Bertrand Meyer), *"The shoemaker must not look past the sandal."* In other words, the only responsibilities assigned to an object/class should be the ones that are relevant to the data abstraction that the class represents. This, in turn, ensures that we avoid unnecessary coupling between classes.

For each book returned, we obtain the corresponding `Book` object from `Catalog`. The `returnBook()` method is invoked on this object, and it returns the `Member` object corresponding to the member who had borrowed the book. The `returnBook()` method is then invoked on the `Member` object to record that the book has been returned. This business process has three possible outcomes that the use case requires the system to distinguish (Step 5 in the use case Return Book):

1. The book's ID was invalid, which would result in the operation being unsuccessful.
2. The operation was successful.
3. The operation was successful and there is a hold on the book.

The result returned by `returnBook()` must enable `UserInterface` to make the distinction between these. This can be done by having `Library` return an integer result code.

### 5.2.2.3 Place a Hold

As discussed earlier, we create a separate `Hold` class for representing the holds placed by members. Each `Hold` object stores references to a `Member` object and a `Book` object, and the date when the hold expires. The use case shows that the system accepts the book ID and the member ID and places the hold.

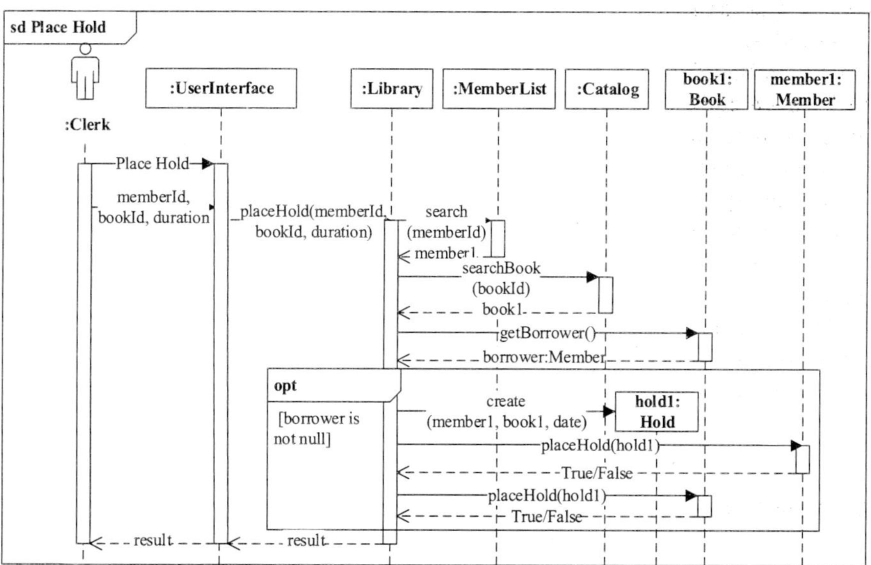


**Fig. 5.6** Sequence diagram for placing a hold. We create the object `hold1`, that connects `book1` and `member1`.

To enable this, as can seen in the sequence diagram (Figure 5.6), `Library` provides the method `placeHold()`, which performs the following steps:

1. Verify that the book ID is valid.
2. Verify that the member ID is valid.
3. If both IDs are valid:
   - Create the `Hold` object
   - Store a reference to the `Hold` object in the `member` object
   - Store a reference to the `Hold` object in the `book` object
4. Return the result.

To store the reference to the `Hold` object, the `placeHold()` method is provided in both the `Book` class and the `Member` class. It is instructive to consider what alternative structures may be used for tracking the holds. One possibility is that both `Book` and `Member` create their own individualized `Hold` objects (`BookHold` and `MemberHold`), with the `BookHold` class storing the date and a reference to `Member` and `MemberHold` storing the date and a reference to `Book`. Such a solution is less preferable because it creates additional classes, and if not carefully implemented, could also lead to inconsistency due to multiple copies of the date.

### 5.2.3 Actions that Remove Objects

Actions that remove objects can be tricky due to the fact that multiple objects may be holding references to the object removed. Verifying that these references are removed is critical, and this verification requires knowledge of all the associations between the classes.

#### 5.2.3.1 Remove a Hold

Removing a hold removes a relationship between a book and a user. However, since we have created a separate `Hold` object, we need to observe the precautions associated with removing objects. A request is issued to `Library` through the method `removeHold()`. As presented in the detailed use case, the user specifies the book ID and the member ID. We need to ensure that all references to the `Hold` object are removed before the object is removed. We know from our design that the only objects that ever store references to a `Hold` object are the corresponding `Book` and `Member` objects; furthermore, these are stored at the time the `Hold` object is constructed, and no additional references to the `Hold` object are created during its lifetime.
The `removeHold()` method in `Library` therefore performs the following steps:

1. Retrieve the `Book` object using the book ID.
2. Retrieve the `Member` object using the member ID.
3. If both objects are successfully retrieved:

- Inform the `Member` object to remove the hold on the specified book
- Inform the `Book` object to remove the hold by the specified member
- Delete the `Hold` object

4. Return the result.

To enable this, a `removeHold()` method is provided in both the `Book` class and the `Member` class. The sequence diagram is given in Figure 5.7.

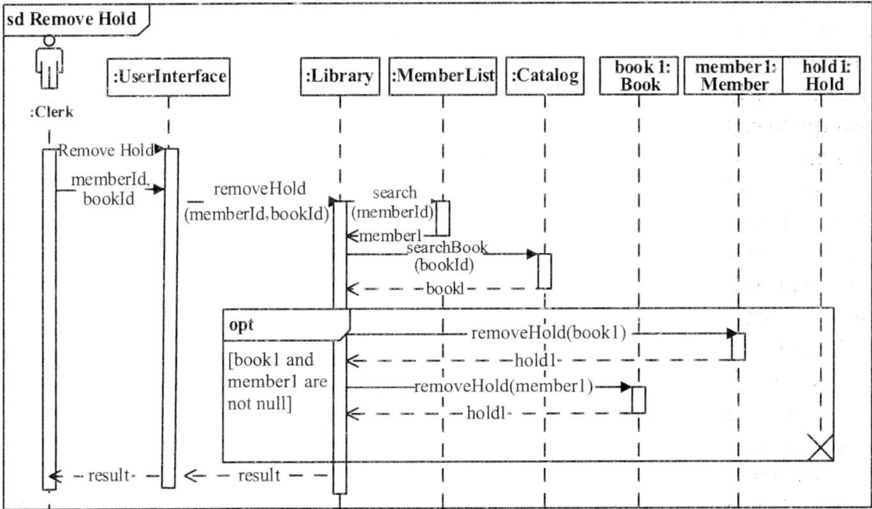


**Fig. 5.7** Sequence diagram for removing a hold. References to `hold1` must be removed from `book1` and `member1`.

### 5.2.3.2 Remove Books

Removing a `Book` object is complicated by the fact that during a book's lifetime, several objects store and delete references to it. However, from our structure we know that the only objects that can store references to a `Book` object are `Catalog`, any one `Member` object, and multiple `Hold` objects. Accordingly, as discussed in the use case, we remove only those books that are not checked out and do not have a hold.
The `removeBook()` method in `Library` therefore performs the following steps:

1. Retrieve the `Book` object using the book ID.
2. If the object is successfully retrieved:
   - Check if anyone has borrowed the book
   - Check if there are any holds on the book
3. If there are no holds and no borrower, remove the book.
4. Return the result.

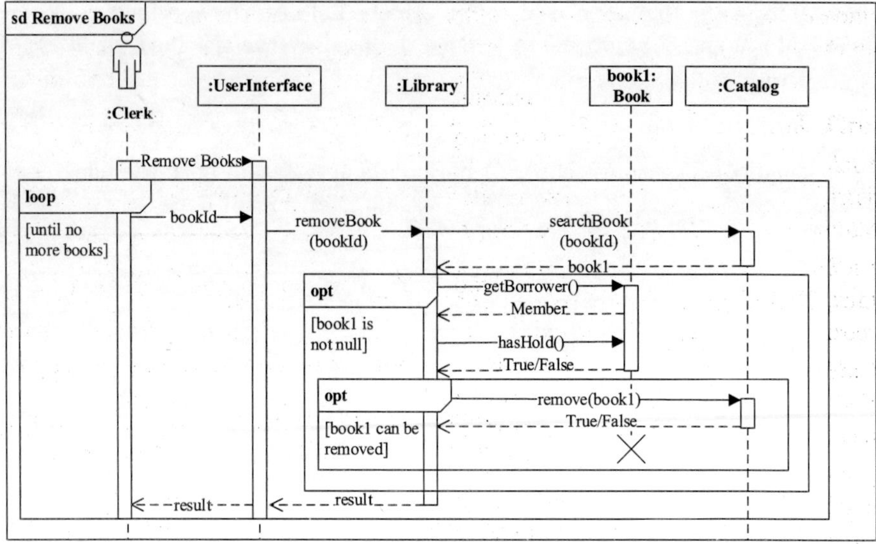


**Fig. 5.8** Sequence diagram for removing books. We ensure that no references to `book1` exist in any other object.

To enable this, the `getBorrower()` and `hasHold()` methods are provided in the `Book` class, and a `remove()` method is provided in `Catalog`. Figure 5.8 shows the sequence diagram for removing books from the collection. The square brackets before the invocation of `remove()` contain the condition "book1 can be removed," indicating that the `Book` object is deleted only if this condition is met. `Library` returns a specific code for each possible outcome, which `UserInterface` translates into an appropriate message.

### 5.2.4 Actions that Involve Queries

Some actions require some data to be retrieved and displayed to the user. The simplest situation is that where the retrieved data is simply displayed. In more complex situations, additional actions may be needed depending on the results of the query.

#### 5.2.4.1 Member Transactions

As described in the use case, the user specifies the member ID and a date, and prints the information about all the transactions by the corresponding member on the specified date. To access information about all transactions would be difficult if there was no record of the operations performed by a member. Accordingly, we create a `Transaction` class and maintain a list of `Transaction` objects for each member, and for all the relevant business processes, we generate the appropriate `Transaction` object and store it in the list for the member. This query can be easily answered by accessing this list. There are two steps that `UserInterface` performs:

1. Query the system to get the transactions.
2. Display the transactions.

We have two options for structuring this process:

- **Option 1:** Provide a method `getTransactions()` in `Library` that returns a list of transactions for the given member, on the given date only. The UI simply displays all the items in the list in the required format.
- **Option 2:** Provide a method `getTransactions()` in `Library` that returns the entire list of transactions for the given member. The UI filters the list, and displays only transactions on the specified date in the required format.

Option 1 is attractive because it reduces the coupling between the UI and the back-end. The UI does not have to be involved in any details of how the answer to the query is generated, and deals only with displaying the result. Option 2 is attractive because we can easily accommodate variations in the query. Say, we want all the transactions since the specified date. This change can be easily made in the code in the UI, and other classes are not affected. The question then arises: *Under what circumstances is it acceptable to allow this coupling between the UI and the back-end?*

To answer this, we need to look at the specifics of the situation. We are maintaining a record of each transaction. Note that the use case is limited to displaying transactions for a specific member on a given date. A simple way to record transactions would be a descriptive string and a date, and to keep the UI from performing business logic, the filtering process (member and date) should be built into the result supplied to it. The limited scope of the query does not warrant too much machinery to be built into the system and complicate the design. We will keep matters simple, so the UI does not have to know any details of what is happening in the back-end, and the process would still not increase coupling between the UI and the back-end. We can therefore go with Option 1.

The above choice may have to be reconsidered if the scope of the system is more extensive. In a full-blown system, we are likely to have many more queries on different types of entities such as members, books, holds, etc., with each query based on multiple selection criteria. See the exercises at the end of the chapter for a reconsideration of the choice in a more demanding set of use cases.

`UserInterface` therefore does the following:

1. Query the system to get all the transactions for the specified member for the specific date.

2. Display the result, which are transactions for the specified member and date.

The method `getTransactions()` in `Library` does the following:

1. Verify that the member ID is valid.
2. If valid, retrieve the list of transactions for the member for the specific date.
3. Return the result.

The sequence diagram in Figure 5.9 describes the details. The `Member` class stores the necessary information about the transactions, but the UI would make the decision about the format. It would, therefore, be desirable to provide the information to the UI as a collection of objects, each object containing information about a particular transaction. This can be done by defining a class `Transaction` that stores the type of transaction (issue, return, place, or remove hold), the date, and the title of the book involved. `Member` stores a list of transactions, and the method `getTransactions()` returns an enumeration (`Iterator`) of the `Transaction` objects. `Library` returns this to the UI, which extracts and displays the required information.

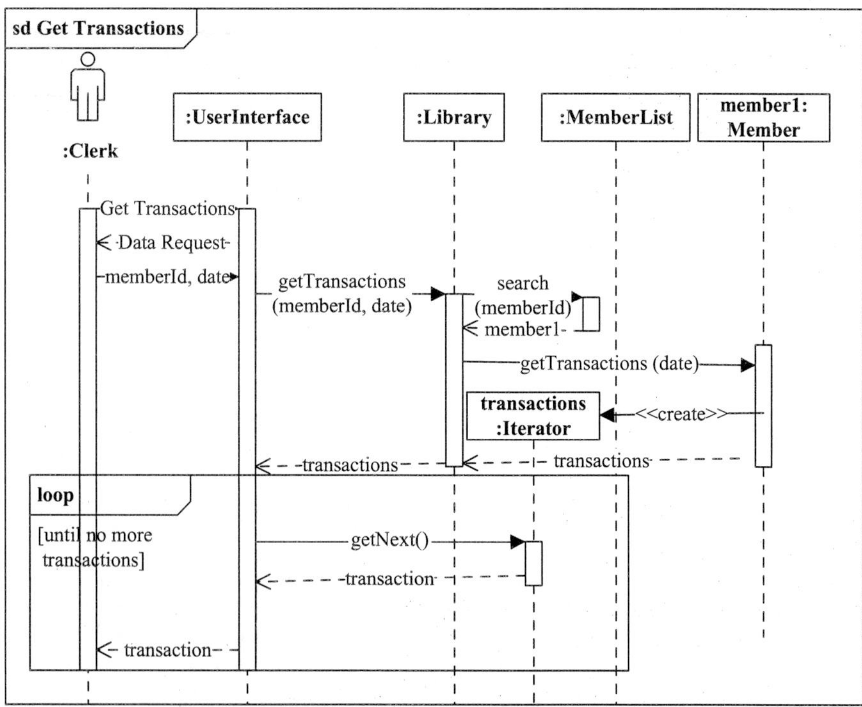


**Fig. 5.9** Sequence diagram for printing a member's transactions on a given date. The relevant transactions are extracted from `Iterator` in `UserInterface`.

### 5.2.4.2 Process Holds

The operation here is to retrieve the next valid hold, delete the `Hold` object, and display the relevant information. This operation is not strictly a query, but performs one when the next hold is retrieved. The input here is only the ID for the book.
The `processHold()` method in `Library` therefore performs the following steps:

1. Retrieve the `Book` object using the book ID.
2. If `Book` exists, get the next valid hold.
3. If there is a hold:
   - Get the associated `Member` object
   - Remove the hold from the book
   - Remove the hold from the member
4. Return the result.

To enable this, we add the method `getNextHold()` to the `Book` class, and the method `getMember()` to the `Hold` class. Figure 5.10 shows the sequence diagram for processing holds. Since we process several books in this use case, a loop is placed around the steps described above.

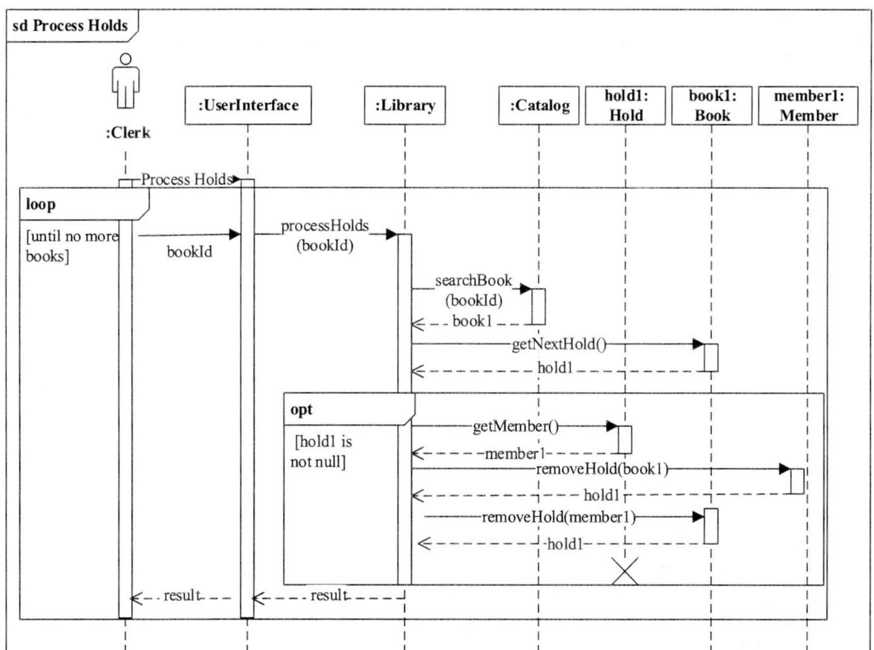


**Fig. 5.10** Sequence diagram for processing holds. The next valid hold is identified and processed.

### 5.2.4.3 Renew Books

As described in the use case, the system displays the books checked out to the member and allows the actor to specify the ones that need to be renewed. There are two steps in this process:

1. Query the system to get the books.
2. Display the books and perform the requested operation on each book.

This operation is not strictly a query, but performs a query to get a list of all the books issued to a user.

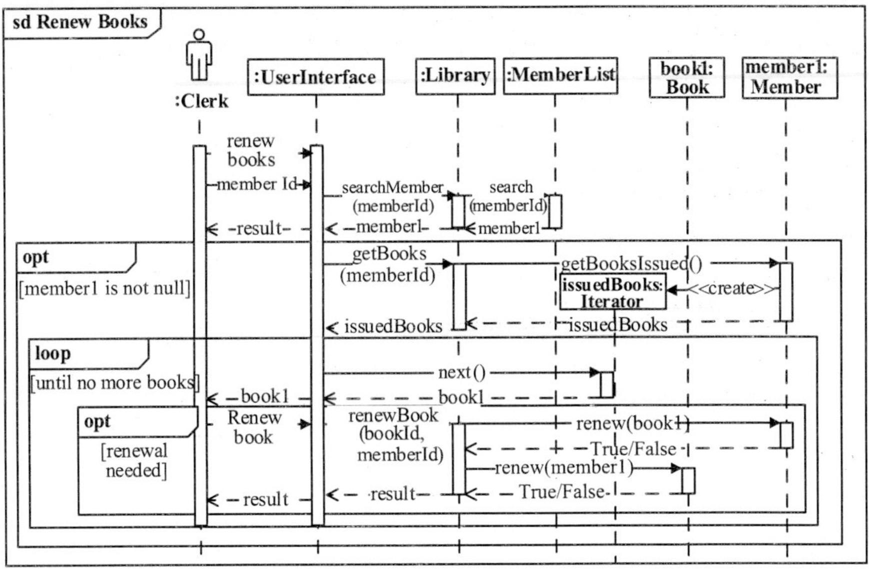


**Fig. 5.11** Sequence diagram for renewing books. `UserInterface` queries the actor about each book.

We provide a query operation, `getBooks()` in `Library`, to get the list of books issued to a member, and a `renewbook()` method in `Library` to renew a single book. The UI uses these methods to carry out both the steps described above. A beginner may wonder why we do not provide a method `renewBooks()` in `Library`, that is invoked by the UI, and which renews all the books. This approach may seem more compact, since it can handle both the steps described above. This is not an option because after getting the list of books, the `renewBooks()` method in `Library` has to seek user input for each book. This makes a method in `Library` responsible for user interaction, which is unacceptable. The `renewBooks()` method in `UserInterface` therefore gets the member ID and performs the following steps:

1. Query `Library` to get the list of books issued to the member.

2. For each `Book` object, perform the following:

   - Display details of the `Book` object and ask if the user wants to renew
   - If yes, call the `renewBook()` method in `Library`
   - Display the result

The `renewBook()` method in `Library` does the following:

1. Retrieve the `Book` and `Member` objects using the book ID and member ID.
2. If the objects are successfully retrieved:

   - Call the `renew()` method on the `Book` object
   - If renewed, call the `renew()` method on the `Member` object

3. Return the result.

Figure 5.11 shows the sequence diagram for renewing books.

## 5.3 Designing the Classes

From the previous section, we can see that we have the following software classes:

- `Library`
- `MemberList`
- `Catalog`
- `Member`
- `Book`
- `Hold`
- `Transaction`

The relationships between these classes are shown in Figure 5.12. Note that `Hold` is not shown as an association class, but as an independent class that connects `Member` and `Book`. The new class `Transaction` is added to record transactions; this has a dependency on `Book` since it stores the title of the book.

### 5.3.1 Designing the `Member` and `Book` Classes

In the course of the design, we have seen that the details of the operations are performed on the `Member` and `Book` objects. Specifying these classes correctly is therefore critical. The relationships between these classes are shown in Figure 5.12. Note that `Hold` is not shown as an association class, but as an independent class that connects `Member` and `Book`. The new class `Transaction` is added to record transactions; this has a dependency on `Book` since it stores

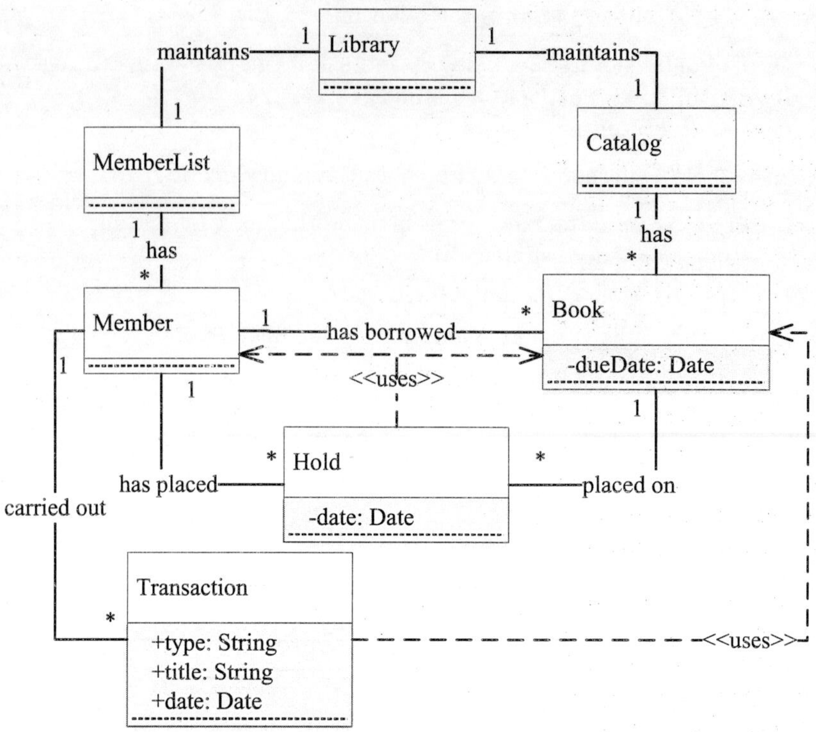


**Fig. 5.12** Software classes for the library system. The figure represents all the entities identified as software classes. Some fields (such as `dueDate` for `Book`) represent design decisions and are included. Other details are deferred to the diagrams for individual classes.

the title of the book. It is important to note that the collection classes `Catalog` and `MemberList` are introduced for `Book` and `Member`, respectively, but we choose not to have a collection class for `Hold`. Table 5.1 explains why this is the correct choice.

#### 5.3.1.1 The `Member` Class

Let us examine the `Member` class. From Figure 5.12, we can see that a `Member` object may store several references to `Book` objects, zero or more references to `Hold` objects, and multiple references to `Transaction` objects. Accordingly, the `Member` class has a list of books, a list of holds, and a list of transactions. In addition, we store the personal data for the member. To decide the list of methods for the `Member` class, we perform the following:

- Provide accessors and modifiers for all the appropriate data fields.

**When should we define a new class for a collection?**

Let us take a closer look at the software class diagram in Figure 5.12. We see a few one-many relationships. When we look back at the conceptual class diagram from the previous chapter, we see a one-many relationship (maintains a collection of) between `Library` and `Book`, and also a one-many relationship (borrows) between `Member` and `Book`. In the case of `Library` we argued in favor of creating an additional software class (`Catalog`); for the borrows relationship no such class is created.

The `Member` class clearly maintains a list of all the books issued to the member, and one could argue that this list provides a functionality similar to a catalog. In the case of `Catalog`, we made a case for defining a separate class. Part of our reasoning here is that this is a distinguished feature of the library, and the functions performed by a catalog should be captured in this class.

It is also useful to examine what the solution would look like if we did not define a new class. In that case, `Library` would hold a reference to a list of books, and all catalog operations would be done through `Library`. This would make the `Library` class bigger and violate the interface segregation principle, discussed later in this chapter. Another issue is that of collections that have a distinguished role in the system. These may be accessed from various places in the system. As we shall see in the next chapter, this access is facilitated by defining a new class and making it a singleton.

- Provide the methods needed to implement the designs described in our sequence diagrams.

Accessors are provided for all the data fields. The methods should have the appropriate return type. For instance, `name`, `address`, `id`, etc., are strings. Hence the return type for `getName()`, `getAddress()`, `getId()`, etc., is `String`. We provide modifiers for `name` (`setName()`) and `address` (`setAddress()`), but not for `id`, since the member ID is generated by the system. Note that in specifying the types of attributes, we may have to make language-specific choices; some of these decisions may therefore be deferred to the implementation stage.

Let us now examine all the sequence diagrams and check what methods are needed. This can be succinctly done, as shown in Table 5.1. Using information about the `Member` attributes and information from this table, we can generate a class diagram for `Member`.

| Sequence diagram | Method(s) to add | Description |
|---|---|---|
| Add Member | constructor | Parameters are name, address, phone number; generates the ID |
| Issue Books | `issue()` | Stores a reference to the given `Book` object in the `Member` object; records the transaction |
| Place Hold | `placeHold()` | Stores a reference to the given `Hold` object in the `Member` object; records the transaction |
| Return Books | `returnBook()` | Removes the reference to the given book from the `Member` object; records the transaction |
| Process Holds | `removeHold()` | Removes the reference to the given hold from the `Member` object; records the transaction |
| Remove Hold | `removeHold()` | Removes the reference to the given hold from the `Member` object; records the transaction |
| Renew Books | `getBooksIssued()` | Returns a list of all the books currently issued to the member |
| | `renew()` | Verifies that a reference to the given book is in the `member` object; records the transaction |
| Get Transactions | `getTransactions()` | Returns a list of all the transactions of the member |

**Table 5.1** Collecting the methods of the `Member` class. Each sequence diagram tells us what methods need to be invoked on the objects of the `Member` class, and what task the method should perform.

#### 5.3.1.2 The `Book` Class

The approach to developing the class diagram for `Book` parallels that for the `Member` class. A table similar to 5.1 is created from the sequence diagrams (see Exercises). Fields are identified from the requirements and the appropriate accessor methods are added. However, there are no setters for the `Book` class because we do not expect to change anything in a `Book` object. The class diagrams for `Book` and `Member` given in Figure 5.13.

### 5.3.2 Building the Collection Classes

All the collection classes would be built around an existing `List` class. Typical operations on a list would be add, remove, and search for objects. Our collection classes are `Catalog` and `MemberList`, each of which stores a reference to an object of type `List`. These `List` objects store references to `Book` objects and `Member` objects, respectively. In `Catalog`, we have the method `getBooks`, whose return type is `Iterator`. This enables `Library` to get an enumeration of all the books so that any specialized operations that have to be applied to the collection are facilitated. Since the requirements did not ask for the functionality of removing a member, there is no `remove()` method in the `MemberList` class. The resulting class diagrams are shown in Figure 5.14

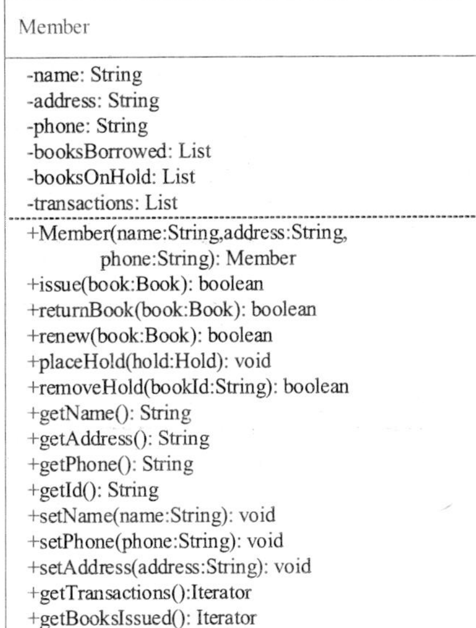


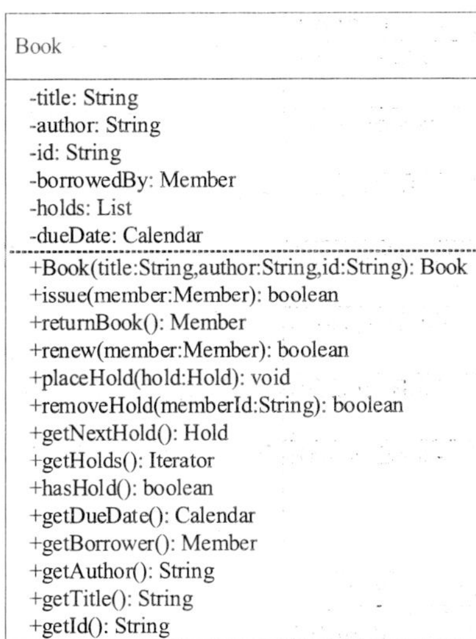


**Fig. 5.13** Class diagram for the `Member` and `Book` classes. The fields are derived from the requirements and from the design process. In addition to the necessary accessor and modifier methods for the fields, we include the methods required by the sequence diagrams.

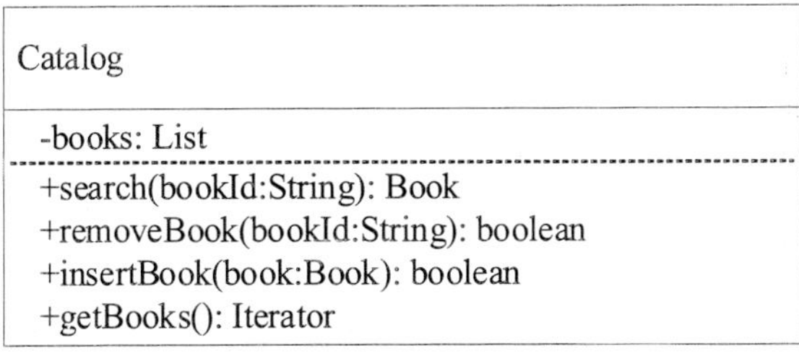


MemberList
-members: List
+search(memberId:String): Member
+insertMember(member:Member): boolean
+getMembers(): Iterator

**Fig. 5.14** Class diagram for `Catalog` and `MemberList`. The collection classes comprise a `List` and methods for list operations.

### Exporting and importing objects

The classes that we have implemented for the business logic form an object-oriented system, which can be accessed and modified through the methods of `Library`. When dealing with object-oriented systems, one must keep in mind that there are often several references to one object, stored in multiple locations. For instance, a reference to every `Member` object is stored in `MemberList`, but when the member checks out a book, the `Book` object also holds a reference. In a lot of situations it is convenient to have a query return a reference to an object. This multiplicity of references means that we need to observe some caveats to ensure that data integrity is not compromised. In the context of importing and exporting references through the facade, the following deserve mention:

- *Do not export references to mutable objects.* All the objects that we are creating in the library system are **mutable**, that is, the values stored in their fields can be changed. Within the system, objects store references to each other (`Book` and `Member` in our case study) and this is unavoidable. Our worries start with situations like the implementation we have for Issue Books, in which a reference to a `Member` object is being returned to `UserInterface`. Here a reference to a mutable object is being exported from the library subsystem, and in general we do not have any control over how this reference could be (mis)used. In a system that has to be deployed for widespread use, this is a serious matter, and some mechanism must be employed to make sure that the security and integrity of the system are not compromised. Several mechanisms have been proposed and we can create simple ones by defining additional classes (see Exercises).
- *The system must not import a reference to an internal object.* Objects of type `Book` and `Member` belong to the system and their methods are invoked to perform various operations. To ensure integrity, it is essential that these methods behave exactly in the expected manner, that is, *the objects involved belong to the classes we have defined and not to any malicious descendants.* This means that our library system cannot accept as a parameter a reference to a `Book` object. This can be seen in the sequence diagram for Renew Books. The UI has the references to the `Book` and `Member` objects, but the `Library` does not accept these as parameters for `renewBook()`. Working with the ID may mean an additional overhead to search for the object reference using the ID, but it certifies that when the `renew()` methods are invoked, these are on objects that belong to the system.

### 5.3.3 Designing the `Hold` and `Transaction` Classes

These classes are created for a single purpose and are quite simple. The `Hold` class is defined for the purpose of capturing a relationship between `Book` and `Member`. Besides the accessors, `getMember()`, `getBook()`, and `getDate()`, the `Hold` class needs the `isValid()` method, which checks whether a certain hold is still valid.

The `Transaction` class needs a date, which could itself be a class. Since languages may provide this (Java's `util` package has a class `Calendar`), for the time being we will designate the class as `Date`. We also need the title of the associated book and a descriptive string. Accessors are provided for each field. Since this object is used only to record the details of a transaction, no mutators are provided. The class diagrams are shown in Figure 5.15.

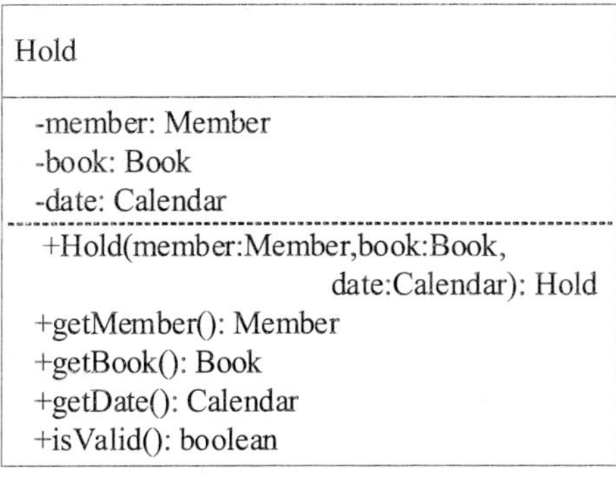


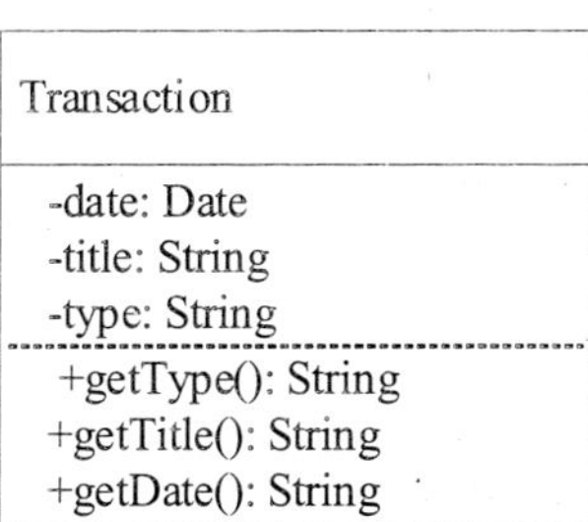


**Fig. 5.15** Class diagrams for `Hold` and `Transaction`. These classes are created for specific purposes and need to store only the relevant data and methods.

### 5.3.4 Designing the `Library` Class

This class contains methods with their parameters as given in the sequence diagrams. However, we have specified their return types, which were not clearly specified in the sequence diagrams. Whenever something is added to the system such as a member or a book or a hold, some information about the added object is returned, so that the clerk can verify that the data was correctly recorded.

We have already seen that the class must maintain references to `Catalog` and `MemberList`. Figure 5.16 shows the class diagram for `Library`.

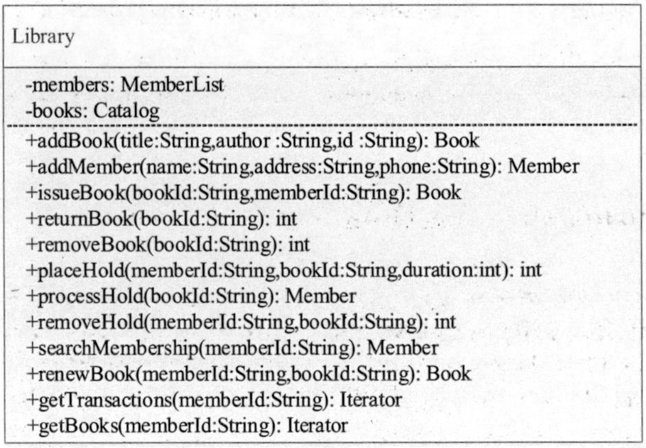

| Library |
| --- |
| -members: MemberList<br>-books: Catalog |
| +addBook(title:String,author :String,id :String): Book<br>+addMember(name:String,address:String,phone:String): Member<br>+issueBook(bookId:String,memberId:String): Book<br>+returnBook(bookId:String): int<br>+removeBook(bookId:String): int<br>+placeHold(memberId:String,bookId:String,duration:int): int<br>+processHold(bookId:String): Member<br>+removeHold(memberId:String,bookId:String): int<br>+searchMembership(memberId:String): Member<br>+renewBook(memberId:String,bookId:String): Book<br>+getTransactions(memberId:String): Iterator<br>+getBooks(memberId:String): Iterator |

**Fig. 5.16** Class diagram for `Library`. Methods are provided to ensure that all the business processes can be carried out. Fields are provided for the collections.

### 5.3.5 Constructing the User Interface

As discussed earlier, all input/output will be through a simple text interface. The system will present a menu with user choices, and will accept input from and display output to the user. All of this will be accomplished through an imperative program, and is, therefore, not of interest for an object-oriented design. The details are deferred to the implementation phase.

## 5.4 Designing for Safety and Security

Building adequate safety and security into a system is a complex task, and it is usually handled at several levels. At the level of our design, it is important to know what kind of vulnerabilities can exist, and what design choices must be made to secure the system. Distinguishing between safety and security is tricky: safety generally refers to accidental threats, while security refers to intentional threats. However, if a system is unsafe due to poor construction, this could lead to the presence of vulnerabilities that can be exploited by malicious actors. Being aware of these vulnerabilities enables us to build some protections into the software during the design. For a system like the library, let us examine three situations that can compromise the safety and security of our system:

- An error during the data update causes the data to become inconsistent.
- Data updates are performed through imported objects not created within the system.

- The data being exported is accessed by unauthorized objects.

Each of these illustrates a different example of how the system ends up in an undesirable state. We shall examine each of these in detail below.

### 5.4.1 Ensuring that the Data is not Inconsistent

In any object-oriented system, all the data items (objects and classes) must satisfy certain **integrity constraints**. For example, in the library system, if a `Member` object `m1` is shown as having checked out `b1`, then `b1` must indicate `m1` as its borrower. It is in general difficult, if not impossible, to list all integrity constraints in a collection of data items; but bug-free application programs preserve them. That is, every application program that reads a consistent set of data items leaves the data items in a consistent state, when it completes. In the context of this textbook, we consider three ways in which data integrity constraints could be violated:

1. The data could end up in an inconsistent state due to system errors. Suppose in the course of issuing a book, the system manages to mark a book as borrowed by a member, but as it attempts to mark the member as having borrowed the book, it encounters an error. The system would be in an inconsistent state.
2. Untrusted, malicious code could get unauthorized access to insufficiently-protected data. For example, classes in the user interface side could obtain a reference to the `Catalog` object. Or they could find a way to access the database stored on external storage. After gaining access to the catalog, the user interface program could wreak havoc, deleting books as it pleases, making incorrect updates, and so on.
3. The design calls for the business logic to provide references of business objects to untrusted code, which could result in a security leak. In our design, for example, suppose `Library` returns a `Member` reference in the course of issuing a book. This reference could then be used to make updates to that object (mark the member as having not checked out a book, for instance) or any objects accessible through that object (for example, access and make changes to `Hold` objects accessible through the `Member` reference).

Cases 2 and 3 are discussed in the next two subsections. In case 1, we can apply various practices like formal verification and validation, testing and debugging to arrive at reasonably correct code. Commercial database management systems could then be employed to store and maintain application data. They have mechanisms to handle failures of the kind outlined in this category. All these techniques are important, but they are orthogonal to the design of object-oriented systems, so we will not discuss this further.

### 5.4.2 Preventing Unauthorized Objects from Making Data Updates

In our design, all the operations are carried out through actions taken by the objects we have created within the library system. In such a situation, the methods discussed in the previous section can be employed to ensure consistency, but for this to be effective, we also need to ensure that no action can be taken by any object not created within our system. For example, how do we ensure that `UserInterface` is unable to get hold of the `Catalog` object?

Providing a degree of safety to the objects would require actions at different levels: proper design, employment of relevant language features, following proper manual and automated procedures, and so on. Since our scope is limited to design and implementation, our focus will be on these. The reader is cautioned that our approaches are presented as examples of what can be done, and do not cover all possible safety issues.

#### 5.4.2.1 Actions Taken During Implementation

Secure coding practices play a big role in ensuring safety. These practices range from very basic things like using good variable names, comments, and structured programming. They are often dependent on the programmer's familiarity with the idioms of the language being used. Knowledge of the language libraries and the manner in which design patterns are implemented also play a big role.

We have decided to use Java for implementation, so we will need to see some of the Java features to use in this connection. This will be dealt with in a following chapter. The reader may wish to explore facilities supported in other languages, should they choose to use a different language.

#### 5.4.2.2 Good Safety Practices During Design

Applying good class design principles and design patterns plays a big role in ensuring safety. Software vulnerabilities caused by violating these cannot be easily corrected at later stages of development. For our specific situation, we look at two concepts that have been applied

- *Using the design patterns to restrict access.* Restricting unnecessary access is often done implicitly through design patterns. The facade hides details of a subsystem, but also enables us to prevent external client classes from accessing objects directly. The iterator provides a way of returning the data in a collection with an external client without allowing any access to the collection itself.

The design is flexible enough to support multiple "views" of `Book`, if the situation warrants it. For instance, we could have a version of `Book` that supports renewal but not removal or one that supports removal but not renewal. For every combination of requirements, we simply create a new class, all of them object adapters of `FullBook`, with the `FullBook` object maintaining a reference to each type of object. All these objects can be instantiated in the constructor of `FullBook`. The design is depicted in Figure 5.17.

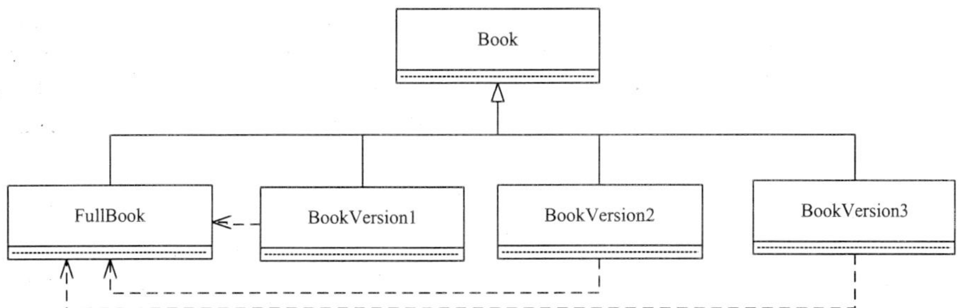


**Fig. 5.17** A single "entity" can be implemented with multiple rights. Here, `FullBook`, `BookVersion1`, `BookVersion2`, and `BookVersion3` all afford different access privileges. It is assumed that `FullBook` allows "full" rights, whereas the other three have limited access to some of the functionalities of a book. All of them inherit from `Book`, an abstract class. `BookVersion1`, `BookVersion2`, and `BookVersion3` depend on `FullBook` to complete their work, but `FullBook` maintains references to each of these. Note that `FullBook`'s relationship with each of the other sibling classes is shown as composition; so deletion of `FullBook` also implies deletion of the other three.

## 5.5 Evaluating the Quality of the Software Design

In the process of assigning responsibilities, we have explored all the choices we could think of, applied the rules of good design, and picked the best. Using this process exclusively may not be wise, since we may fail to see the impact of these design choices on the system as a whole. In this context, it is useful to examine the resulting structure and look for anomalies. Two questions that naturally arise are:

- How can we recognize poor design choices in a system?
- Is there a systematic process for fixing the bad choices?

**Code smells** and **design smells** are terms that are used to refer to structures that appear in a system when design principles are violated. Familiarity with these helps us recognize when a poor design choice has been made. If we look for these smells as we are making the design decisions, correcting them is easier.

### The Proxy pattern

Consider a client accessing some object (an image on the internet or a remote service, for example) to get some service, perform some data manipulation, or any set of methods supported by that object. Let us use the term target to refer to the object the client is trying to access. In these situations, it is sometimes desirable to introduce a surrogate or stand-in between the client and the target. This object is termed a proxy, and the the intent of the Proxy pattern is to provide an object that manages all requests to the original object. This management can take various forms depending on what the application requires:

- *Serve as remote proxy.* This is seen when we have a distributed system and we have a local object that represents a remote object.
- *Serve as a virtual proxy.* This happens when we have an original object that is "heavy" and expensive to load. A proxy serves as a front which manages a partial or complete loading of the original in response to queries from a client.
- *Serve as a protection proxy.* This aspect is invoked when we do not wish to make a reference to the original object available to a client, and would like to place restrictions on the amount of access to the original object.

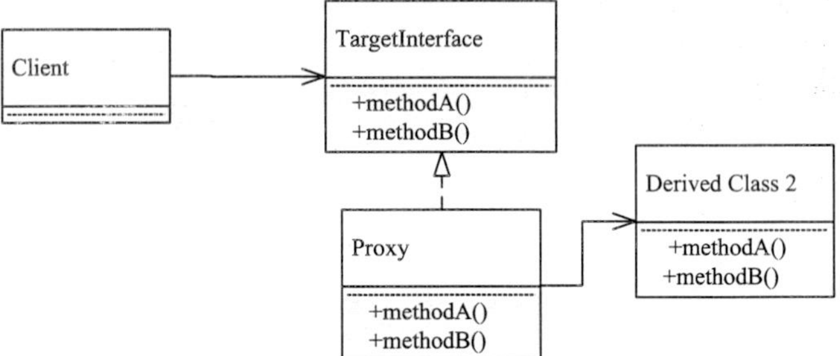


**Fig. 5.18** Structure of the Proxy pattern

The class diagram (Figure 5.18) shows the connection between the client object, the proxy object and the real (target) object. The client has a reference to the proxy, which implements the same interface that the original target implements. The client is not necessarily aware that it is dealing with a proxy and not the actual object.

With the introduction of a proxy, we can solve some problems related to the interactions between the client and the target. For example, a protection proxy could filter the requests and provide only a subset of the services provided by the target. Or an image proxy could allow for lazy loading of images over a potentially slow network.

Proxy is a structural design pattern since it deals with the static structure of the modules involved.

Code smells can be classified based on the level at which they are recognized and eliminated. At the highest level are the smells that are recognized by looking at the entire system. An example of this is the smell *Duplicated Code* which refers to a situation where identical or very similar code is present in multiple locations. At the next level are the smells identified by looking at an entire class and its relationship with other classes. The smell *Inappropriate Intimacy* refers to a situation where a class depends on the implementation details of another. When a class uses the features of another class excessively, the resulting smell is called *Feature Envy*. Some smells are recognized at the method level, which is the lowest level at which we recognize smells. An example of this is *Long Method*, which is characterized by a method, function, or procedure that has become too long.

**The object-oriented design process**

The object-oriented design process we have followed in this chapter can be summarized in the figure below:

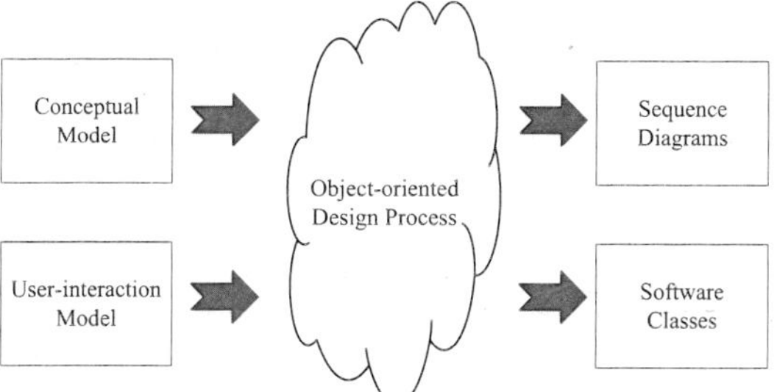


The inputs to this process are the conceptual model, defined by the conceptual classes and their relationships, and the behavioral model, detailed in the use cases. These artifacts are the result of the object-oriented analysis that we have described earlier in the text.

We start the object-oriented design process by examining the conceptual classes and making decisions on what software classes will be needed. Next, we look at each use case and decide how the system functionality specified in the use case is to be realized through the software classes. This realization is described through sequence diagrams. It should be noted that this is not a linear process. For instance, as we construct the sequence diagrams, we may discover the need for additional software classes.

Once we have the sequence diagrams, we know all the software classes and the methods required in each. This completes the design process.

**Refactoring** is defined as the process of improving the internal structure (design and code) of a piece of software without altering the module's external behavior. The process is often applied to a system in production, but we can use this process just as effectively during design and development. Practitioners have developed a set of rules that can be used systematically to refactor code. Once we have identified a bad smell in the code, we apply the appropriate refactoring rules to remove the smell. It is easier to understand these concepts and processes through an example, and to that end, we add a new requirement to one of the business processes in our library system.

### 5.5.1 A New Requirement: Charging Fines for Overdue Books

Consider the situation where the library decides to cut down on truancy by imposing fines. When an overdue book is returned, the librarian would like to know the amount of the fine and send out a notice to the user regarding the fine payable. The system should therefore compute the fines and display the relevant information. The resulting changes in the business process are captured in the use case in Table 5.2.

| Action performed by the actor | Response from the system |
|---|---|
| 1. The member arrives at the return counter with a set of books and gives the clerk the books. | |
| 2. The clerk issues a request to return books. | |
| | 3. The system asks for the identifier of the book. |
| 4. The clerk enters the book identifier. | |
| | 5. If the identifier is valid, the system marks that the book has been returned and informs the clerk if there is a hold placed on the book; otherwise (that is, in case of an invalid ID), it notifies the clerk that the identifier is not valid. If there is a fine involved, the system computes the amount of the fine using *Rule 7* and adds it to the user's account; information about the member is displayed. It then asks if the clerk wants to process the return of another book. |
| 6. If there is a hold on the book, the clerk sets it aside. He/She then informs the system if there are more books to be returned. | |
| | 7. If the answer is in the affirmative, the system goes to Step 3. Otherwise, it exits. |

**Table 5.2** Use case Book Return with Fines. If a book is overdue, a fine is calculated and charged to the user.

This use case for Book Return with Fines is similar to what we had earlier, with one addition – the amount of fine owed is computed whenever a book is returned. Also, notice that the use case does not say anything about actually collecting fines from a member and updating the corresponding `Member` object after the fine is paid. These are left as exercises.

We have the following business rule for computing the fine:

*Rule 7: New books (less than a year old) are charged \$0.25 for the first day and \$0.10 for every subsequent day. Older books are charged \$0.15 for the first day and \$0.05 for every subsequent day. If a book has a hold on it, the amount of fine is doubled.*

### 5.5.2 The Initial Design

Before we construct the modified sequence diagram, we need to decide where the amount of fine owed will be computed. There are three possible options: `Library`, `Book`, and `Member`. We can make a case for each option: `Book` would be appropriate since it is the return of the book that incurs a fine; `Member` is where the fine is stored and is therefore the place it could be computed; since both `Book` and `Member` are involved in this, `Library` is perhaps the best place to do the computation. Lets say we decide (somewhat arbitrarily) that `Library` is the place where the fine is computed.

Having made this decision, let us take a look at the pseudocode for the new `returnBook()` method in `Library`. As a result of these decisions, `Book` now has an `acquisitionDate` field and an associated accessor. The `returnBook()` method in `Library` involves the following steps:

1. Search the catalog for the book; if not found, exit.
2. From the book, get the member who issued the book; if none, exit.
3. From the book, get the date of acquisition and the due date, and check if the book has any holds.
4. Compute the fine (if any) as follows:
   - if (current date is past the book's due date), compute fine as follows:
     - if (365 days have elapsed since the book's acquistion date) fine $= 0.15 + 0.05 \times$ (days elapsed since due date);
     - otherwise, fine $= 0.25 + 0.1 \times$ (days elapsed since due date);
   - if (book has any holds), double the amount of the fine.
5. Record that the member has returned the book.
6. If there was a fine, record the information in the member.
7. If the book has any holds, add that to the results.
8. Return the results.

The resulting sequence diagram for returning books is shown in Figure 5.19. The `returnBook()` method in `Library` must now check if a fine is involved: if so, it computes the fine and updates the corresponding `member` object by invoking the `addFine()` method. The book's title is also passed, so a transaction can be created to keep a record of the fine.

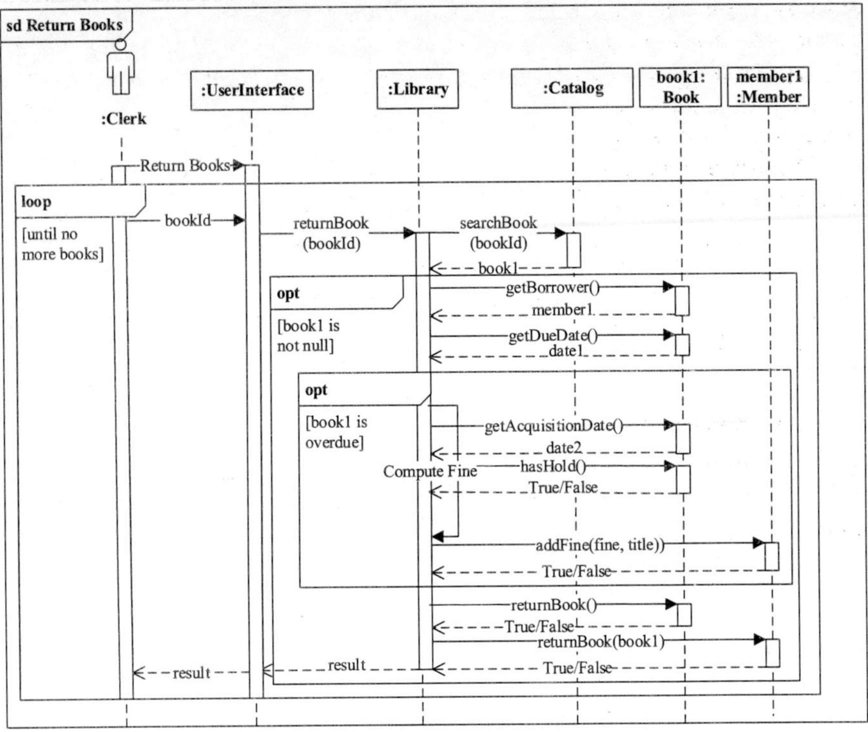


**Fig. 5.19** Returning a book and checking for fines. If `Book` is overdue, `Library` gets the relevant data, computes the fine, and adds the fine to `Member`.

The `returnBook()` method returns a code that indicates if a fine was involved, so the interface can alert the library clerk. The assumption is that the code in the user interface will take appropriate action to notify the clerk in the above circumstances.

### 5.5.3 Evaluating and Improving the Solution

In the process of evaluation, we perform two tasks: *recognize poor design* and *identify a process for fixing it.* We begin by noting that our process takes eight steps, which is large in comparison to the designs we had for the other processes. In the jargon of code smells, this is called a Long Method, and we look for the possibility of refactoring it.

When methods or classes become too large, we try to remove parts that do not fit very well with the rest of the method or class. The simplest kind of removal is one where we identify a part of a method that can be pulled out as a subprogram. This leads us to our first refactoring rule: Extract Method. Considerations involved in applying this rule and the steps for carrying it out are detailed in the box below.

**Extract method rule**

*If you have a code fragment that can be grouped together, turn the fragment into a method, and assign it a name that explains the purpose of the method.* It is easy to recognize these fragments from the comments added by the programmer. These comments, which typically take the form of a verb phrase, also suggest how the extracted method should be named. If a code fragment does not appear to have a simple name, it is often unlikely to be a good candidate for extraction into a method. Another indicator is the number of local variables that are modified; if the code fragment modifies only one variable, this strengthens the case for extraction. If a large number of variables are modified, the code fragment should probably be left in place.
The steps involved in applying this rule are as follows:

1. Identify the code fragment and copy it into a method named for the intention of that code fragment.
2. In the extracted code, locate the references to variables local to the original method and pass these as parameters to the new method.
3. For all temporary variables that are used in the fragment, declare corresponding variables in the new method.
4. Determine the local variable that is modified by the extracted code and set its type as the return type of the new method.
5. Replace the code fragment in the original code with a call to the new method and store the value returned in the local variable identified in the previous step.

The first step of the process is key: identifying what can be extracted. In our design for the business process, notice that each of these steps, *except Step 4*, is an application of a single method, which is computed on some object (`Catalog`, `Book`, or `Member`). Step 4, by contrast, deals with a lot of detail about how the fine is to be computed. This kind of detail is unusual for a method in a facade, and causes a significant increase in the size and complexity of the method for returning a book. Hence this step is a good candidate for extraction.

The next part of the process is to figure out how Step 4 will be extracted. The data used in Step 4 is accessed from `Book` in Step 3; this data will have to be passed as parameters to the new method. However, we can also see that the data accessed in Step 3 is used only in Step 4; it therefore makes sense to move both these steps and make the `Book` object a parameter.

The two steps together perform the task of computing the amount of time. We therefore extract this code and create the method `computeFine()` with `Book` as a parameter. This method will return the amount of the fine. The new `returnBook()` method is as follows:

1. Search the catalog for the book; if not found, exit.
2. From the book, get the member who issued the book; if none, exit.
3. Call the `computeFine()` method to compute the fine.
4. Record that the member has returned the book.
5. If there was a fine, record the information in the member.
6. Check if the book has any holds.
7. Return the results.

The method `returnBook()` looks much cleaner now. All it is doing is getting the relevant information by invoking appropriate methods and then compiling all the results. The `computeFine()` method does the following:

1. Get the due date of the book.
2. Get the date of acquisition of the book.
3. Check if the book has any holds.
4. Compute the fine(if any) as follows:
   - If the current date is past the book's due date, compute fine as follows:
     - if 365 days have elapsed since the book's acquistion date fine $= 0.15 + 0.05 \times$ (days elapsed since due date);
     - otherwise, fine $= 0.25 + 0.1 \times$ (days elapsed since due date);
   - If the book has any holds, double the amount of fine.
5. Return the amount of fine.

Let us take a closer look at the method that we have extracted. The logic employed by `computeFine()` involves examining the fields of `Book` and making decisions based on the values stored in these fields. To get these values, the method repeatedly invokes the accessor methods of book. In the jargon of code smells, this is referred to as Inappropriate Intimacy between the `Library` class and the `Book` class. This leads to tighter coupling between the classes.

One of the rules of good object-oriented design is called the Law of Inversion, which states that

*"If your routines exchange too many data, put your routines in your data."*

What this means is that our focus should be more on the data and less on the process. In a process-oriented design, we do not think adversely about importing all the data elements into the function that implements the process. In a data-centered approach, the parts of the process that are close to one data element are encapsulated as methods and placed into the class corresponding to that data element. The computation for the encapsulated part of the process is then carried out by calling the method on the data element.

The above design principle leads us to the next refactoring rule, Move Method. The `computeFine()` method is moved from `Library` to `Book` using the principles set forth in the box on the next page. This process has helped resolve our dilemma about where the fine should be computed. The resulting sequence diagram is shown in Figure 5.20.

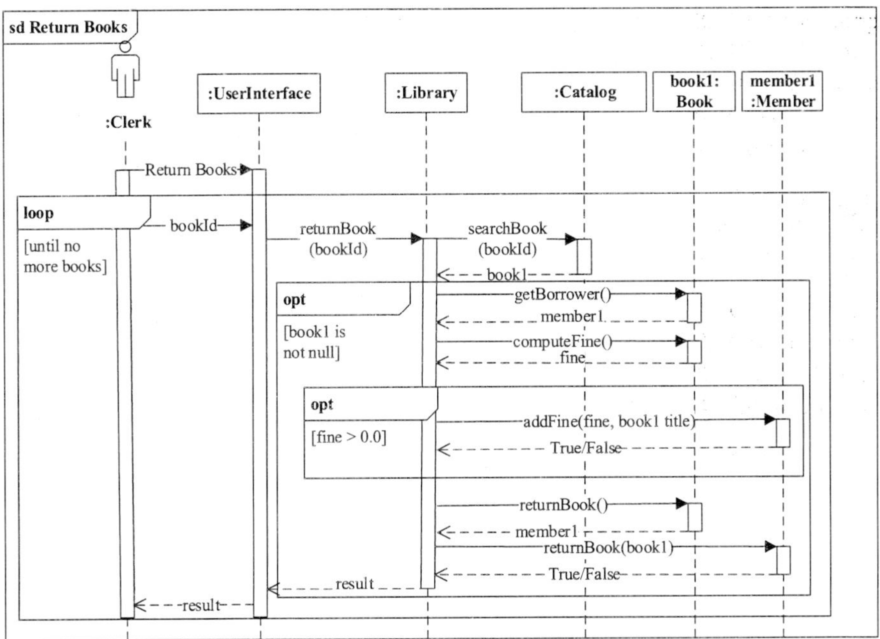


**Fig. 5.20** Refactored process for returning a book and checking for fines. `Library` invokes a method provided by `Book` for computing the fine and then invokes a method in `Member` to add the fine.

In the initial stages of design, we need not go through the entire process of refactoring to correct our errors. Nonetheless, beginners may often find themselves in a quandary as to where the responsibilities for a certain task should be placed. The exercise of refactoring helps to formalize some of the basic principles of object-oriented design so that such errors can be caught early in the design process and suitably corrected.

**Move method rule**

If we have a method that is using more features of another class than the class on which it is defined, then the method needs to be moved to the class whose features it is using the most.

This rule is a manifestation of the process of assigning responsibilities to the appropriate class and is perhaps the most frequently applied rule in refactoring. When a method uses too many features of another class, we have a situation where the classes are either collaborating too much or are too tightly coupled. It is not always the case that such a problem will be resolved by moving a method. Sometimes, other patterns may have to be applied that allows objects to communicate without getting too entangled in each other's methods. The simplest and most obvious situation is when a method accesses several fields of another class and almost all its computation is done on these fields.
The steps involved in applying this rule are as follows:

1. Make a list of all features used by the method in question.
2. Identify the target class for the move, that is, the class whose features are most frequently employed in the computation.
3. Examine other features that are not in the most frequently used class and decide if those features need to be moved to the target class as well.
4. It could be that the features from the source that are being moved to the target are being used by other methods in the source. The possibility that these methods also need to be moved should be taken into consideration. It is sometimes easier to move a set of methods and fields instead of a single method.
5. Declare the method(s) and field(s) in the target class, and move the code to the new method. Make the necessary adjustments so that the code works in the target class. This would involve changing the names of the features being used.
6. Change the code in the source class to reflect the movement of the fields and methods.

As is evident from this description, moving a collection of methods and fields can affect several methods of the source class. Care must be taken to ensure that the new code reflects the changes. When this rule is applied in the presence of inheritance, we have to exercise an additional caveat: *If super-classes and sub-classes of the source class have also declared the method, then the method cannot be moved unless the polymorphism can also be expressed in the target class.*

## 5.6 Discussion and Further Reading

Converting the model into a working design is by far the most complex part of the software design process. In this chapter, we have attempted to capture some of this complexity through an example, and also tried to raise and deal with the questions that may appear troublesome. Although there are only a few principles of good object-oriented design that the designer should be aware of, the manner in which these should be applied in a given situation can be quite challenging at first. Indeed, the only way these can be mastered is through repeated application and critical examination of the designs produced. Perhaps needless to say, it is also extremely useful to discuss design issues with more experienced colleagues.

The sequence of topics so far suggests that the design would progress linearly from analysis to design to implementation. In reality, what usually happens is more like an iterative process. In the analysis phase, some classes and methods may get left out; worse yet, we may not even have spelled out all the functional requirements. These shortcomings could show up at various points along the way, and we may have to loop through this process (or a part of this process) more than once, until we have an acceptable design. It is also instructive to remember that we are not by any means prescribing a definitive method that is to be used at all times, or even coming up with the perfect design for our simple library system. As stated before, our goal is to provide a condensed, but complete, overview of the object-oriented design process through an example. At the end of the previous chapter, several student projects were presented. To maximize benefit, the reader is encouraged to apply the concepts to one or more of these projects as he/she reads through the material. From our experience, we have seen that students find this practice very beneficial.

### 5.6.1 Conceptual Classes and Software Classes

Finding the classes is a critical step in the object-oriented methodology. In the analysis phase, we found the *conceptual* classes. These correspond to real-world concepts or things and present us with a conceptual or essential perspective. These are derived from and used to satisfy the system requirements at a conceptual level. At this level, for instance, we can identify a piece of information that needs to be recognized as an entity and make it a class; we can talk of an association between classes without any thought to how this will be realized.

In the design phase, we deal with *software* classes, that is, classes which can be built using typical programming languages. We need to deal with the following issues:

- How conceptual classes will be manifested in the software
- What additional classes will be needed to build such a system in a typical programming language

We identify the conceptual classes that will become software classes, the conceptual classes that are dropped, and the additional classes to be added. For the software classes we identify all the fields and the methods and their parameters. In the library case study, we added the collection classes `Catalog` and `MemberList`, and a `Transaction` class as new software classes. The conceptual class `Borrows` was not included in the set of software classes. Methods were identified when we created the sequence diagrams.

### 5.6.2 The Single Responsibility Principle

The single responsibility principle captures a lot of the the essence of the ideas of cohesion and coupling. It was coined by Robert C. Martin in 2005, and is stated as follows:

*Each software module should have one and only one reason to change.*

He revisited it in a 2014 blog post, attributing its inception to a 1972 article by David L. Parnas, wherein the author compared two different strategies for decomposing and separating the logic in a simple algorithm. One of the conclusions of Parnas' article is as follows:

> We have tried to demonstrate by these examples that it is almost always incorrect to begin the decomposition of a system into modules on the basis of a flowchart. We propose instead that one begins with a list of difficult design decisions or design decisions which are likely to change. Each module is then designed to hide such a decision from the others.

Starting with this, Martin leads up to the single responsibility principle, restating it as:

*Gather together the things that change for the same reasons. Separate those things that change for different reasons.*

The above approach looks at the construction of a module as a process of grouping together the related responsibilities. In the software development process used in this text, the software modules are identified based on the conceptual model that came from our analysis. We are therefore looking at responsibilities from the other end: *given a responsibility, identify the best module.*

Some of the design decisions made in this chapter can be justified from this point of view. The chosen option in each case is the one that does not violate the single responsibility principle; in case there is a responsibility that does not fit well into any module, we either add another module(class) or revisit our conceptual model. Consider, for instance, our decision to invoke the `Member` constructor from `Library`. If we had chosen the other option, all the parameters would be passed to `MemberList`; we can identify two reasons for changing `MemberList`:

- The parameters needed for constructing `Member` objects are changed
- The mechanism used for managing the `MemberList` collection is changed

These two reasons stem from two different responsibilities. From this point of view, we can see the violation of the single responsibility principle, justifying our choice. In a later chapter, we shall examine other mechanisms that are employed to accommodate possible changes in object construction.

### 5.6.3 The Interface Segregation Principle

The interface segregation principle (ISP) states that no client should be forced to depend on methods it does not use. Consider for instance, our initial choice of software classes, where we decided to add modules named `Catalog` and `MemberList` for managing the collections. Let us consider the other option where we would not have had seperate modules for collections. Instead, we would store references to, say, a `LinkedList` within `Library`, and invoke the list management methods on these.

A collection like `Catalog` plays a significant role in the system. Services that invoke the methods of such a collection may be needed by several other modules within the system. Say for instance that another internal class is looking up a reference to a `Book` object. If we did not have a class `Catalog`, the relevant `search()` method would have to be invoked on `Library`. Being a facade, `Library` contains a lot of other methods. These other methods would be largely for external clients and therefore irrelevant to classes within the system. However, the internal class that is searching for a book will invoke a method on `Library`, making the internal class dependent on the large interface of the facade. Since the methods in the facade are irrelevant to the internal class, this would be a violation of ISP.

### 5.6.4 Recognizing Bad Smells and Design Flaws in Object-oriented Programs

Software design problems have been studied under different terms, such as code smells, flaws, non-compliance to design principles, violation of heuristics, excessive metric values, and anti-patterns. They can be identified in many different stages of the software lifecycle and can usually be removed by applying an appropriate refactoring. Several aspects of quality, such as maintainability, comprehensibility, and reusability, are often improved as a consequence of correcting the flaws.

Attempts have been made to classify the code smells based on the nature of their appearance. Since there are a large number of smells, such a classification can help identify them in different settings. The Long Method smell has been grouped along with some others as a "bloater," that is, something that causes a method or class to become unnecessarily large. Smells like Inappropriate Intimacy and Feature Envy are classified as "couplers," due to their tendency to increase coupling. The classification can also help identify the kind of refactoring: bloaters require part of the method or class to be extracted, and couplers require part(s) of the class to be moved elsewhere.

Some attempts have been made to automate the process of finding and correcting design flaws. JDeodorant is an Eclipse plug-in that identifies design problems in software, known as bad smells, and resolves them by applying appropriate refactorings. JDeodorant employs a variety of novel methods and techniques in order to identify code smells and suggest the appropriate refactorings that resolve them. For the moment, the tool identifies five kinds of bad smells, namely, Feature Envy, Type Checking, Long Method, God Class, and Duplicated Code.

### 5.6.5 Building a Commercially Acceptable System

The reader with familiarity with software systems may be left with the feeling that our example is too much of a "toy" system, and our assumptions are too simplistic. This criticism is not unjustified, but should be tempered by the fact that our objective has been to present an example that can give the learner a "big picture" of the entire design process, without letting the complexity overwhelm the beginner.

#### 5.6.5.1 Non-Functional Requirements

A realistic system would have several non-functional requirements. Giving a fair treatment to these is beyond the scope of the book. Some issues like portability are automatically resolved since Java is interpreted and is thus platform independent. Response time (run-time performance) is a sticking point for object-oriented applications. We can examine this in a context where design choice affects performance, and this is addressed briefly in a later case study.

#### 5.6.5.2 Functional Requirements

It can be argued that for a system to be accepted commercially, it must provide a sufficiently large set of services, and if our design methodologies are not adequate to handle that complexity, then they are of questionable value. We would like to point out the following:

- *Additional features can be easily added.* Our decision to exclude several such features has been made based on pedagogical considerations.
- *Allowing for variability among kinds of books/members.* This variability is typically incorporated by using inheritance. To explain the basic design process, inheritance is not essential. However, using inheritance in design requires an understanding of several related issues, and we shall in fact present these issues and extend our library system in a later chapter.
- *Having a more sophisticated interface.* Once again, we may want a system that allows members to log in and perform operations through a GUI. This would only involve the interface and not the business logic. We shall see how a GUI can be modeled as a multi-panel interactive system and how such features can be incorporated later on.
- *Allowing remote access.* Now-a-days most systems of this kind allow remote access to the server. Technologies can be incorporated into the UI to accomplish this, but are beyond the scope of this book.

It should be noted that in practice, several of the non-functional requirements would actually be provided by a database management system. What we have created with the use case model, the sequence diagrams, and the class diagrams is in fact an object-oriented schema, which can be used to create an application that runs on an object-oriented database system. Such a system would not only address issues of performance and portability but also take care of issues like persistence, which can be done more efficiently using relations rather than reading and writing the objects. Details of this are beyond the scope of this text.

### 5.6.6 Further Reading

The book by Meyer [6] devotes an entire chapter to the problem of class design and makes valuable reading. As we discussed earlier in the book, the notion of design patterns captures the idea that many design situations are similar in nature and a knowledge of the solution to these problems can make a designer more productive. The reader is encouraged to read the book by Gamma et al. [3] to get exposure to the common design patterns. There are hundreds of other lesser patterns and a catalog of these can be found in [7, 8].

The book by Fowler [2] is the main reference for refactoring. Among other things, the book emphasizes the importance of the role that refactoring can play in keeping a system from falling into decay. While the benefits of refactoring are many, there are also a few caveats one should follow to avoid going overboard, and there are also situations and systems whose characteristics make refactoring difficult. The reader would be well advised to engage in a deeper study of this process before attempting a wider application.

Fowler points out that refactoring, when added to the design process, has the capacity to present us with an alternative to the conventional "up-front" design, which views the development of the design as a blueprint and considers coding to be just a process of going through the mechanics of implementation. While this up-front approach is certainly the one recommended by most textbooks, the process can be tempered by refactoring. Instead of getting the design down to the last detail and then coding it, we work with a loosely defined design, start the coding and "firm-up" (and correct) the design with some refactoring as we go through the implementation process. This process may be a better description of what happens in practice and has the added advantage of giving the designers some flexibility in the choices that they make.

The notions of code smells and design smells were first introduced by Kent Beck in the 1990s. The book by Martin [5] lists several bad smells and case studies, explaining how these can be detected and removed. The research in [4] attempts a classification of code smells, and [1] discusses how bad smells evolve throughout the software lifecycle.

## Projects

1. Complete the designs for the case study exercises from the previous chapter.

## Exercises

1. Consider a situation where a library wants to add a feature that enables the librarian to print out a list of all the books that have been checked out at a given point in time. Construct a sequence diagram for this use case.
2. Explain the rationale for separating the user interface from the business logic.
3. Suppose the due date for a book depends not only on the date the book is issued, but also on factors such as member type (assume that there are multiple types of membership), number of books already issued to the member, and any fines owed by the member. Which class should then be assigned the responsibility to compute the due date and why?
4. (Discussion) There is fairly tight coupling in our system between the `Book`, `Member` and `Hold` classes. Code in `Book` could inadvertently modify the fields of a `Member` object. One way to handle this is to replace the `Member`

reference with just the member's ID. What changes would we have to make in the rest of the classes to accommodate this? What are the pros and cons of such an approach?

5. Continuing with the previous question, the `Hold` object stores references to the `Book` and `Member` objects. This may not be necessary. What specific information does `Book` (`Member`) require from `Hold`? Define an interface that contains the relevant methods to retrieve this information. What are the pros and cons of an implementation where `Hold` implements these interfaces, over the design presented in this chapter?
6. (Keeping mutables safe.) Suggest a simple scheme for creating a new class `SafeMember` that would allow us to export a reference to a `Member`. The classes outside the system should be unaware of this additional class and access the reference like a reference to a `Member` object. However, the reference should not allow the integrity of the data to be compromised.
7. Create a table similar to Table 5.1 showing all the methods for the `Book` class.
8. Without modifying any of the classes other than `Library`, write a method in `Library` that deletes all invalid holds for all members.
9. (Discussion) Instead of having `renew()` methods, would it be simpler to return the book and issue it again? What problems might this cause?
10. Consider the use case in a university registration system where a student drops a course. The amount of refund to be credited to the student can depend on several factors:

    - A student can always drop a course for a full refund within 24 hours of registration
    - The amount of refund depends on the current date and the starting date of the course

    In which class should the responsibility for computing the amount of refund be placed, given that both the student and section are involved in this process? Write the detailed steps in the process assuming that the `RegistrationSystem` (the facade) is responsible. Look for bad smells and any possible refactoring(s) to remove them.
11. Consider a use case in a warehouse system where a customer is returning an item to the warehouse. The amount of refund could depend on the following:

    - Warehouse return policy and stocking fee for the item
    - The number of days since the purchase

    In which class should the responsibility for computing the amount of refund be placed, given that both the product and the transaction may be involved in this process? Write the detailed steps in the process assuming that the `WarehouseSystem` (the facade) is responsible. Look for bad smells and any possible refactoring(s) to remove them.

12. Consider a use case in an airline reservation system where a customer is cancelling a reservation. The amount of refund could depend on the following:

    - Full refund for any cancellation within 24 hours
    - The amount of refund depends on the kind of reservation
    - The nature of refund (credit towards next reservation vs. cash) depends on the kind of reservation

    In which class should the responsibility for computing the amount of refund be placed, given that the result depends on the kind of reservation but may also affect the passenger? Write the detailed steps in the process assuming that the `ReservationSystem` (the facade) is responsible. Look for bad smells and any possible refactoring(s) to remove them.
13. When we added the a book or a member to the library system, the responsibility for invoking the constructor was assigned to `Library` and not to the respective collection classes. Explain why this is consistent with the single responsibility principle.
14. When we implemented the `searchMember()` method in `Library`, we rejected the idea of getting an enumeration of the members for the collection and performing the search operation in `Library`. Explain how this approach would be a violation of the single responsibility principle.
15. Re-examine the Member Transactions query in the light of the single responsibility principle. We used the fact that query variations could be easily accommodated, to support using Option 2. The query variation can be viewed as a reason for change. Which classes are affected by the change in the query, under each of the two options? Is this consistent with the requirement that "each software module should have one and only one reason to change?"
16. Assume that we have several new use cases in the form of queries. Each query involves a certain type of entity (for example, members). The query should filter entities of a certain type based on one or more criteria. For example, we could say that we want to display members who have not checked out any books but have placed at least one hold. Or we could ask to list books that have more than three holds and are not yet returned even though the due date has come and gone.
    Answer the following questions.

    a. Suppose we proceed as we did for displaying member transactions. What would be the drawback(s) of such an approach?
    b. Come up with a scheme that would help the end user specify the selection criteria and issue a command to display all objects of a certain entity that meet these criteria. The approach should not allow the user interface to perform business logic and leave all classes cohesive and keep the system loosely coupled.

## References

1. Chatzigeorgiou, A and Manakos, A. 2014. Investigating the evolution of code smells in object-oriented systems. *Innov. Syst. Softw. Eng.*, 10(1):3–18.
2. Fowler, M. 1999. *Refactoring: Improving the Design of Existing Code.* Addison-Wesley Longman Publishing Co.: Boston, MA, USA.
3. Gamma, E, Helm, R, Johnson, R and Vlissides, J. 1994. *Design Patterns: Elements of Reusable Object-oriented Software.* Addison-Wesley Professional.
4. Mantyla, M, Vanhanen, J and Lassenius, C. 2003. A taxonomy and an initial empirical study of bad smells in code. In: *International Conference on Software Maintenance (ICSM)*, 2003, Proceedings, pp. 381–384.
5. Martin, RC. 2008. *Clean Code: A Handbook of Agile Software Craftsmanship.* Prentice Hall: NJ, USA.
6. Meyer, B. 1997. *Object-Oriented Software Construction.* Prentice Hall: NJ, USA.
7. Rising, L. 2000. *The Pattern Almanac.* Addison-Wesley Professional.
8. Vlissides, JM, Coplien, JO and Kerth, NL. 1999. *Pattern Languages of Program Design, Volume 2* (Software Patterns Series). Addison-Wesley.

# Chapter 6
# Implementing a System

Having designed the system, we proceed to the implementation stage. In this step, we use the class structures produced by the design to implement a system that behaves in the manner specified by the model. During this process, the programmer should follow good coding and testing practices. Although we mention some of these principles here, we do not spend a significant amount of time on them, since these are concepts common to all software implementations. Our implementation will be carried out in Java. Any new language concepts that need elaboration are dealt with in the context where we employ them.

To a good extent, we follow the blueprints arrived at in the design stage. (Otherwise, there would be little point having a design stage.) However, we will employ support mechanisms provided by the implementation language (Java) to enhance the software structure. There are also situations where programming language restrictions may force us to tweak the design. We wish to emphasize that there will be no deviations that make the implementation too divergent from the design and that all such tweaks will be well justified.

The implementation is about 1500 lines of Java code, without counting documentation. Obviously, we cannot explain every line of code, nor is it necessary. What we will do in this chapter is explain code that cannot be easily inferred from the design itself. As a result, while we may make passing remarks on the following topics that are indicated in the design, we will not spend any significant real estate explaining them:

- Constructors that simply copy the parameter values to fields and/or initialize some fields. An example would be the constructor of `Book`.
- Constants (Java `final` variables) whose identifiers are self-documenting.
- Getter and setter methods.
- Overrides of `Object` methods: `toString()`, `hashCode()`, and `equals()`.

The first section of this chapter describes how the `UserInterface` class is set up, how this class communicates with the `Library` facade, and how the `Library` and the collection classes are structured. Next, we implement the methods for populating the database with books and members. Then we implement the operations that add, remove, and update relationships between books and members, and display transactions. Finally we look at the principles involved in implementing saving, retrieving, and securing the data.

## 6.1 Organization of `UserInterface` and `Library`

As the reader can verify from Chapter 5, the `UserInterface` class interacts with the actor (the library staff), reading commands and processing them. We can execute the library system by using this class.

In its `main()` method, `UserInterface` calls a method named `process()`, which is in a loop: in each iteration of the loop, the code reads a user command and calls the appropriate method in `Library` to process the request. Although we have seen the flow of control between `UserInterface` and `Library`, let us review it here.

1. The `UserInterface` class's `process()` method reads a command. If it is a data processing command (not exit or help), the method invokes an appropriate method in the same class. To add a member, the actor enters the command 1 (`ADD_MEMBER`), which causes a method named `addMember()` to be called. This method reads the member name, address, and phone number of the member to be added.
2. The `addMember()` method submits these values to `Library` using a similarly-named method in that class.
3. The `Library` class's `addMember()` method processes the request and returns a result.
4. The `addMember()` of `UserInterface` examines the result and displays an appropriate message.
5. The control returns to the `process()` method.

The structure of the `process()` method is given below.

```
public void process() {
  int command;
  help();
  while ((command = getCommand()) != EXIT) {
    switch (command) {
      case ADD_MEMBER:      addMember();
                            break;
      case ADD_BOOKS:       addBooks();
                            break;
      case ISSUE_BOOKS:     issueBooks();
                            break;
      // several lines of code not shown
      case HELP:            help();
```

```
                    break;
        }
    }
}
```

The reader will note the semantically-meaningful method names for adding books and issuing books. The `help()` method displays all the options with the corresponding numeric choices. In addition to the methods for each of the menu items, `UserInterface` also has methods `getToken()`, `getName()`, `getNumber()`, `getDate()`, and `getCommand()` for reading different types of data.

To keep things simple, we assume that `UserInterface` can only deal with one user at a time. Similarly, the `Library` class deals with only one request at any instance in time: only after processing a request will `Library` entertain another request. Such a strategy simplifies design and implementation considerably. Moreover, we reduce complexity even further by allowing only one instance of `UserInterface` or `Library`. This helps ensure that only one request ever comes to `Library` and business data is not simultaneously updated by multiple processes.

### 6.1.1 Avoiding the Creation of Multiple Libraries

Consider classes like `Library`, `Catalog`, and `MemberList`. We need only one instance of each of these classes, and if by any oversight, a second instance of any of these classes is created, we may end up with unwanted consequences. We can say that the integrity of software is dependent on ensuring that the modules `Library`, `Catalog`, and `MemberList` are never duplicated. It is therefore imperative that our software not allow a second instance of any of these to be created. A class that should not be instantiated more than once is called a **singleton** class. Many practical systems enforce such restrictions. Both `UserInterface` and `Library` are implemented as singleton classes. Therefore, `Library` has the following code. Note that the code closely follows the pattern given for class `B` in the box.

```
public class Library {
    private static Library library;
    private Library() {
    }
    public static Library instance() {
        if (library == null) {
            return library = new Library();
        } else {
            return library;
        }
    }
```

### The Singleton pattern

The intent of the Singleton pattern is to ensure that there is only one instance of a class, and that there is a global access point to that object. The mechanism chosen to implement this pattern must ensure that the class can never have more than one instance, instantiation of the class is fully controlled, instantiation does not occur until needed by the application, and the only instance is easily globally accessible. To create a class that can only be instantiated once, we note that the constructor cannot have the `public` access specifier. Instead, we provide a method called `instance()` that returns the only instance of the class.

```
public class B {
  private static B singleton;
  private B() {
  }
  public static B instance() {
    if (singleton == null) {
      singleton = new B();
    }
    return singleton;
  }
  // application code
}
```

The main observation to be made here is that to get the only instance of class `B`, a client invokes the static method `instance`. This is because the constructor is private, so code from outside the class cannot instantiate `B`. When the class is loaded, the field `singleton` will be set to `null`. In the very first call to `instance`, an instance of `B` is created and the reference stored in `singleton`. Further calls to `instance` result in no new allocations; the value in `singleton` is returned.

Notice some of the other important features of the implementation:

- Clients need not maintain a variable to keep track of the instance. Simply by invoking the static method `instance`, the instance can be retrieved.
- The class can be subclassed. The subclasses themselves may be singletons.
- Instead of using a singleton, one may have a class with static methods. But since static methods are not virtual, subclassing will not be able to override these methods.

The need for creating a singleton arises quite often. Some software systems require that only a single instance of a certain kind of application (sometimes, a database manager) be in existence; another example would be a global collection.

Singleton is an important design pattern that finds application in many contexts.

#### 6.1.1.1 Passing Data to and Returning Results from Library Methods

As we have seen, UserInterface calls addMember() of Library to create a Member object. The method has three parameters: name, address, and phone, all of type String. This can be problematic from the viewpoint of coding UserInterface. If the parameters are passed out of order, the mistake will not be caught by the compiler and this will be a bug. Likewise consider a situation where a Member object is added to Library. UserInterface would like to get all the information about the Member added, or any resulting error message and display the information in the desired format. Clearly, there are different kinds of data to be sent back, and as we discussed in Chapter 5, there is a security risk involved in returning a reference to the object that was created.

Both the situations above are a result of the lack of a good data transfer arrangement between UserInterface and Library. To facilitate data transfer among different objects, we introduce the concept of a **data transfer object (DTO)** (see Figure 6.1). The DataTransfer class has fields to store most of the Book and Member fields, among other things. Some fields like the due date are never part of the request, so such fields are not in DataTransfer, but will need to be in the information returned to UserInterface. Also, some fields like duration for a hold are part of a request, but do not find a place in the result.

Although the entire library system, as implemented here, resides in a single Java Virtual Machine, using a DataTransfer object makes it easier to have the user interface and business logic located in separate virtual machines. This approach also helps reduce bugs.

The information transferred between UserInterface and Library can be viewed as either request data coming from UserInterface to Library or results of these requests traveling from Library to UserInterface. Thus, we can organize the data shipped between the two classes into a simple hierarchy, as shown in Figure 6.1.

The instance fields of the DataTransfer class are given below. The meaning of each field should be obvious.

```
private String bookId;
private String bookTitle;
private String bookAuthor;
private String bookBorrower;
private String bookDueDate;
private String memberId;
```

```
private String memberName;
private String memberAddress;
private String memberPhone;
```

The class has getters and setters for the fields. The user interface classes use a `Request` object to ship parameters for a specific operation to the facade. A `Result` object is used to return the result of a facade operation. `Request` is a singleton class.

### 6.1.2 Structure of `Library`

As we mentioned before, this is a singleton class. It has methods named as in its class diagram shown in Figure 5.16. Although the relevant parameters are as specified in the class diagram, they are always passed in a `Request` object as described earlier. Each facade method packs the result into a `Result` object and returns it to `UserInterface`. The flow of every method follows the corresponding sequence diagram closely.

## 6.2 Populating the Database

A good way to begin understanding the code is to see how `Member` and `Book` objects are instantiated. The Adapter pattern is applied in creating the collection classes. Then we discuss implementing the data transfer from the user interface, invoking the contructors, and adding items to the collections.

### 6.2.1 Adding a Member

Let us focus on the business process for adding a member. The sequence diagram in Figure 5.2 would be a good reference in this context, because the code closely follows the flow of control in that diagram.
To add a member, `UserInterface` assembles the relevant parameters as given below. The `getName()` method returns a sequence of characters (with possible spaces in it), after prompting the user with the `String` parameter.

```
Request.instance().setMemberName(getName("Enter member name"));
Request.instance().setMemberAddress(getName("Enter address"));
Request.instance().setMemberPhone(getName("Enter phone"));
```

The `Request` object is used to send the parameters to `Library`'s `addMember()` method, which returns a `Result` object.

### The DTO pattern

The data transfer object is an example of an Enterprise pattern. An enterprise application is a large software system usually designed to operate in a business or government environment. There is often a need to integrate applications that were developed independently. Enterprise (Integration) patterns have been identified for developing systems to integrate new and existing software in a business environment. Most other patterns in this book are applied at a lower level.

This original intent of the Data Transfer Object (DTO) pattern was to facilitate data transfer between remotely located processes. A large number of calls between processes hurts performance, and this can be alleviated by transferring more data in each call. A DTO simply carries data that needs to be transferred between processes and does not contain any business logic. Performance is the principal benefit from this pattern when we are integrating independently developed systems, but this concept finds application within a system also. A DTO can be used to pass parameters across two subsystems. The two subsystems can then be developed without a complete knowledge of each other's interfaces, allowing for for more parallelism and independence in the development process. The two subsystems can hide their abstractions from each other, which loosens the coupling between them. The DTO also enables reuse, by allowing a method call to accommodate variations in the parameters and in the return types.

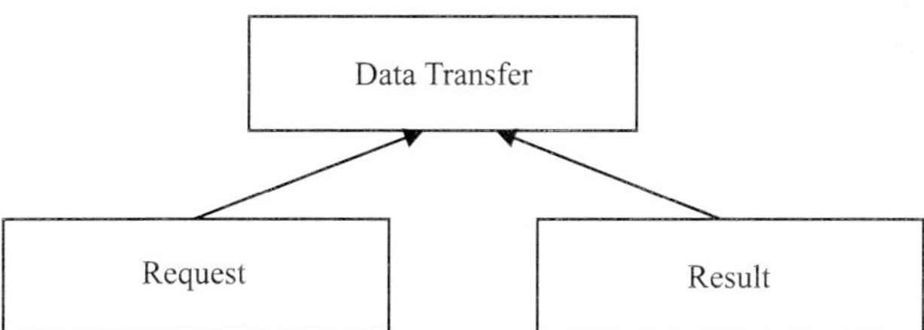


**Fig. 6.1** The Data Transfer Object pattern

The DTO provides fields for all the potential data entities that may need to be transferred, methods to store them, and methods to access them. The DTO is employed to send data, both as a parameter and as a `return` object. Typically there are differences between them, and so we define two classes of DTO; a `Request` type for sending parameters and a `Result` type for return values. Depending on the application, it is likely that there is significant commonality between these signatures. In such situations, it is useful to define the `Request` type and the `Result` type as subclasses of an abstract `DataTransfer` class as shown in Figure 6.1.

```
Result result = library.addMember(Request.instance());
```

The `Result` class has the `int` field `resultCode`, which stores a value specifying the end-result of an operation carried out by `Library`. Constants (`final` variables) declared in the class are used instead of hard-coded numbers to specify the results. Thus, after obtaining the result of requesting member addition, `UserInterface` proceeds to interpret the result of the operation and display an appropriate result. If an operation is successful, `resultCode` is always `Result.OPERATION_COMPLETED`.

```
Result result = library.addMember(Request.instance());
if (result.getResultCode() != Result.OPERATION_COMPLETED) {
    System.out.println("Could not add member");
} else {
    System.out.println(result.getMemberName()
         + "'s id is " + result.getMemberId());
}
```

`Library`'s `addMember()` extracts each of the three values supplied, before following the sequence of steps specified in the sequence diagram. It then assembles the result and returns it to `UserInterface`. For all methods that return a `Result` object, the code for the relevant `Library` method follows the structure given below.

```
create a Result object
follow the steps in the corresponding sequence diagram
     modifying the Result object as and when needed
return the Result object
```

Here is the code for `addMember()` in `Library`.

```
public Result addMember(Request request) {
    Result result = new Result();
    Member member = new Member(request.getMemberName(),
         request.getMemberAddress(), request.getMemberPhone());
    if (members.insertMember(member)) {
        result.setResultCode(Result.OPERATION_COMPLETED);
        result.setMemberFields(member);
        return result;
    }
    result.setResultCode(Result.OPERATION_FAILED);
    return result;
}
```

### 6.2.2 Creation of a `Member` Object

The `Member` object is always instantiated from the facade class, `Library`, in the `addMember()` method. The `Member` class's constructor has a slight complexity. Recall that the system needs to generate a unique ID for every member. The generated ID is a `String` and is stored in the field `id`.
To generate a unique ID, the `Member` class maintains a static field declared as below.

```
private static int idCounter;
```

In its constructor, `Member` assigns to the field `id`, a `String` value concatenated with the value in `idCounter`. `MEMBER_STRING` is currently "M" to denote that the ID is a member ID. The static field `idCounter` is incremented every time a new `Member` object is created.

```
id = MEMBER_STRING + ++idCounter;
```

### 6.2.3 Maintaining the Collection of `Member` Objects

After a `Member` object is created, it should be remembered in the `MemberList` collection. Let us examine the considerations involved in implementing this collection.

- *Difficulty of implementing from scratch*: Implementing from scratch would require knowledge of details of data structures, resulting in an expensive and error-prone exercise. Rather than implementing the collections from the "first principles" (such as arrays or dynamic memory), we should utilize the language facilities to the extent possible. Let us look at the `Collection` interface in the package `java.util`. It provides basic functionality with methods such as `add()`, `remove()`, `iterator()`, and `size()`.
- *Need for a customized collection*: Many of the sub-interfaces of `Collection` and their implementing classes such as `LinkedList` provide rich sets of methods. However, these interfaces do not support functionality of the nature shown in Figure 5.15. For example, there is no way to search for a member with a call such as `search(memberId)`. The supported functionality would have us issue calls such as `memberCollection.get(member)` and that does not meet our requirements. This warrants the creation of a custom collection.
- *Security of the collection object*: The collection should not be accessible from classes outside the business logic. Having them as separate classes and not "exporting" them to the user interface would greatly enhance the security of the business objects.

### 6.2.4 Using Pre-existing Collection Classes

The MemberList class needs to provide the functionality to add a member, search for a member given the member ID, and iterate over the collection. To capture these requirements, MemberList should make the following methods available:

```
public Member search(String memberId);
public boolean insertMember(Member member) ;
public Iterator<Member> iterator();
```

We can view these methods as the desired interface of MemberList. What is the best way to implement the above functionality? As we have been discussing, we do have Java classes with similar, but not precisely the same, set of methods. The interface java.util.List has a number of methods, some of which are quite close in functionality to that of MemberList. A simplified version of this interface is given below with comments borrowed from the official Java documentation.

```
public interface List<E> extends Iterable<E> {
    /**
     * Inserts the specified element at the specified position
     in this list.
     */
    public boolean add(E e);

    /**
     * Returns a list-iterator of the elements in this list
     (in proper sequence),
     * starting at the specified position in the list.
     *
     */
    public E get(int index);

    /**
     * Returns a list-iterator of the elements in this list
     (in proper sequence),
     * starting at the specified position in the list.
     */
    public Iterator<E> iterator() ;

}
```

List is a generic interface. We can see that if we substitute E with Member, the add() and iterator() methods perform the same function as insertMember() and iterator() in the desired interface of MemberList.

One could utilize the `get()` method or the `iterator()` method to implement `search()` in `MemberCollection`. The generic class `LinkedList<E>` implements this interface. If we can use the implementation provided by `LinkedList` to implement the desired interface of `MemberList`, we can avoid the difficulty of implementing those methods from scratch.

The Adapter pattern (see Figure 6.2) comes in handy for the purpose. In this example, we use an Object Adapter. An Object Adapter creates an adapter class that matches the desired interface, using an instance of an existing class, which is the **adaptee**. In the scenario we just described above, the desired interface is the set of methods in `MemberList`, and the adaptee is an instance of `LinkedList`. `MemberList` is built as an adapter that implements the desired methods by invoking the methods of `LinkedList`.
Thus, the class `MemberList` would be structured as below.

```
import java.util.*;
public class MemberList {
  private List<Member> members =  new LinkedList<Member>();
  // methods as dictated by MemberCollection
}
```

The object `members` stores the list of members. When a request to add comes in, we simply invoke the `add()` method of the `members` object. This is done by invoking the `add` method in `List`.

```
  public boolean insertMember(Member member) {
    return members.add(member);
  }
```

We are accessing the methods of `LinkedList` through `members`, and using that implementation to implement the desired functionality for `MemberList`. We are thus adapting the `LinkedList` object, hence the pattern is called an **object adapter.**

Alternatively, we could have accessed the methods of `LinkedList` by defining `MemberList` as a subclass of `LinkedList` and called the methods of the superclass. Such an adapter is called a **class adapter.**

## The Adapter pattern

The intent of the Adapter pattern is to modify the interface of a class to one that the client class expects. As an example, most languages today provide libraries with classes that implement various data structures for maintaining collections, and have a common interface. The common interface typically contains methods like `add()` and `delete()`, whereas the interface of the collection class may contain methods like `addStudent()` and `deleteStudent()`. So we have available to us classes whose application programming interface (API) – the set of methods available to clients – is similar to what the application needs, but the classes cannot be used directly by the application.

Implementing the interface completely from scratch in the application is expensive, so we are better off by tweaking the existing class. We have two options for tweaking: modify the available class directly by changing the source code to arrive at the new functionality, or make the interfaces compatible. Modifying the available class requires the application developer to understand the details of the implementation of the given class; also, later modifications to the original class may necessitate modifications to the application. We therefore try to make the interfaces compatible.

Formally, we have a class $C$ that supports a set, say, $M_C$, of methods. We need to implement interface $I$ that contains a set, $M_I$, of methods. $M_I$ provides all the functionality of $M_C$, but the manner of accessing the functionality is different. The solution is to develop a class $A$ (the adapter) that implements $I$, whereby each method in $M_I$ is realized by a combination of calls to a subset of the methods in $M_C$.

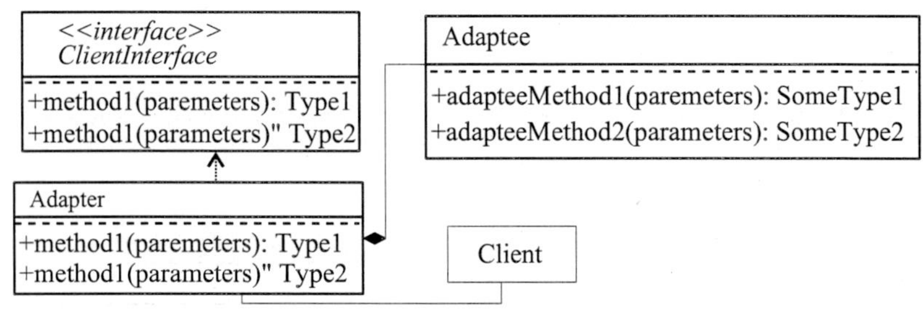


**Fig. 6.2** The Adapter pattern

The structure of the pattern is shown in Figure 6.2. `ClientInterface` corresponds to the interface $I$ that the client (that is, the application) desires. The client maintains a reference to an `Adapter` instance, which implements the methods in `ClientInterface`; in other words, `method1()` and `method2()` form the set $M_I$. The class `Adaptee` is the class $C$, and the methods `adapteeMethod1()` and `adapteeMethod2()` form the set $M_C$. `Adapter` implements `method1()` and `method2()` by invoking `adapteeMethod1()` and `adapteeMethod2()`. This approach is called an **object adapter**; if `Adapter` extends `Adaptee` it is called a **class adapter.**

```
import java.util.*;
public class MemberList extends LinkedList<Member> {
  public boolean insertMember(Member member) {
    return super.add(member);
  }
  // other methods in the desired interface
}
```

In general, this is not as flexible as the object-based approach because we are extending a specific class and that decision is made at compile time. The object adapter has the advantage that the choice of the adaptee class can be postponed until execution time. Moreover, in the case of the class adapter, all of the public methods of the extended class are exposed to the client. For instance, the clients of `MemberList` can invoke both `insertMember()` and the `add()` method; such usage can reduce the readability of the code. The downside to an object adapter is that it introduces one more object, that is, one more method invocation, into the sequence of operations.

### 6.2.5 Implementing `Catalog` and `MemberList`

The implementation of `Catalog` and `MemberList` follows the design shown in Figure 5.15 and they are both object adapters that use `java.util.LinkedList` as an adaptee. We now show the implementation of `Catalog`. The code for `MemberList` is quite similar.

```
public class Catalog implements Iterable<Book>, Serializable {
  private List<Book> books = new LinkedList<Book>();
```

By making the class implement the `Iterable` interface, we are supporting an Iterator for the collection. We will cover the `Serializable` interface later, but for the moment, the reader should just be aware that it is a Java interface that participates in the process of storing the `Catalog` object as a disk file. The following code makes the class a singleton:

```
private static Catalog catalog;
private Catalog() {
}
public static Catalog instance() {
    if (catalog == null) {
        catalog = new Catalog();
    }
    return catalog;
}
```

The process of instantiating a Book object follows a similar flow of control and data. Unlike the constructor of Member, the constructor of Book is a simple assignment of the parameters to the fields.
Adding a book is accomplished by adding it to the books object.

```
public boolean insertBook(Book book) {
    books.add(book);
    return true;
}
```

Given a book ID, the corresponding book is searched for in books as shown below.

```
public Book search(String bookId) {
    for (Iterator<Book> iterator = books.iterator();
    iterator.hasNext();) {
        Book book = (Book) iterator.next();
        if (book.getId().equals(bookId)) {
            return book;
        }
    }
    return null;
}
```

Removal of a book first involves a search to retrieve the object and subsequent removal from books. Note that a Book object is passed to the remove() method of List. That method removes the Book object based on the equals() method implemented in Book. It considers two Book objects to be equal if they have the same book ID.

```
public boolean removeBook(String bookId) {
    Book book = search(bookId);
    if (book == null) {
        return false;
    } else {
        return books.remove(book);
    }
}
```

Implementing the iterator() method is simple.

```
public Iterator<Book> iterator() {
    return books.iterator();
}
```

## 6.3 Modifying Relationships Between Objects

Once the database is populated, we need to perform the bulk of the operations which involves creation and removal of connections between objects.

### 6.3.1 Issuing Books

`UserInterface` begins the process by getting the member's ID and verifying that it is correct.

```
public void issueBooks() {
  Request.instance().setMemberId(getToken("Enter member id"));
  Result result = library.searchMembership(Request.instance());
  if (result.getResultCode() !=
      Result.OPERATION_COMPLETED) {
      System.out.println("No member with id " +
          Request.instance().getMemberId());
      return;
  }
```

If the member ID is valid, `UserInterface` invokes the `issueBook()` method of `Library` repeatedly for each book to be issued. It remembers the member's ID throughout the process.

```
do {
    Request.instance().setBookId(getToken("Enter book id"));
    result = library.issueBook(Request.instance());
    if (result.getResultCode() == Result.OPERATION_COMPLETED) {
        System.out.println("Book " +
          result.getBookTitle() + " issued to " +
          result.getMemberName() + " is due on "
          + result.getBookDueDate());
    } else {
        System.out.println("Book could not be issued");
    }
} while (yesOrNo("Issue more books?"));
```

Some of the representative and interesting lines of `issueBook()` in `Library` are given below. The code verifies that the member ID is valid for each invocation. The `Result` object has been initialized with appropriate default values, such as `"No such book"`, in every field. As a consequence, if the book could not be located because of a bad book ID, the method simply sets `resultCode` to `BOOK_NOT_FOUND` and returns the `Result` object. `UserInterface` could choose to use the book-related fields of `Result` in its messages to the actor. Otherwise, the member-related fields are set to the appropriate values.

```
Member member = members.search(request.getMemberId());
if (member == null) {
    result.setResultCode(Result.NO_SUCH_MEMBER);
    return result;
}
result.setMemberFields(member);
if (!(book.issue(member) && member.issue(book))) {
    result.setResultCode(Result.OPERATION_FAILED);
} else {
    result.setResultCode(Result.OPERATION_COMPLETED);
    result.setBookFields(book);
}
```

The code for setting the fields of the `Result` object is quite simple. Here is the code for setting the fields that correspond to `Book`. Note that if the book is not issued, `book.getBorrower()` is `null` and both `bookBorrower` and `bookDueDate` are set to values that reflect a book that is not checked out. As a result, classes in the user interface will not see a `null` value for any field.

```
public void setBookFields(Book book) {
   if (book.getBorrower() != null) {
      bookBorrower = book.getBorrower().getId();
      bookDueDate = book.getDueDate();
   } else {
      bookBorrower = "Not checked out";
      bookDueDate = "Not applicable (not borrowed)";
   }
   bookId = book.getId();
   bookTitle = book.getTitle();
   bookAuthor = book.getAuthor();
}
```

The `issue()` method in `Book` simply records the fact that the book is issued to the correct member. It generates a due date by adding one month to the date of issue. Note the extra code needed to ensure that the book is due by 11:59:59 on the due date. So no matter what the closing time of the library, the book will not be marked late (if the library had a related policy) if it was returned on the due date. We needed to cater to the quirks of the `GregorianCalendar` class to get this properly set.

```
public boolean issue(Member member) {
    borrowedBy = member;
    dueDate = new GregorianCalendar();
    dueDate.set(Calendar.HOUR, 0);
```

```
        dueDate.set(Calendar.MINUTE, 0);
        dueDate.set(Calendar.SECOND, 0);
        dueDate.add(Calendar.HOUR, 11);
        dueDate.add(Calendar.MINUTE, 59);
        dueDate.add(Calendar.SECOND, 59);
        dueDate.add(Calendar.MONTH, 1);
        return true;
    }
```

We list below the implementation of `issue()` in `Member`. The two collections `booksBorrowed` and `transactions` are implemented using the JDK class `LinkedList`.

```
    private List<Book> booksBorrowed = new LinkedList<Book>();
    private List<Transaction> transactions =
    new LinkedList<Transaction>();
    public boolean issue(Book book) {
        if (booksBorrowed.add(book)) {
            transactions.add(new Transaction("Issued",
            book.getTitle()));
            return true;
        }
        return false;
    }
```

The reader may wonder why we chose to have custom collection classes for the `catalog` and `member` list, but we do not have such classes for `transactions` and `borrowed books`. In general, to choose an appropriate data structure for a data type, we should consider all of the operations acting upon the ADT. It turns out that the operations performed on the `transaction` and `borrowed book` collections are adequately met by the standard. The operations on the `transaction` collection are:

1. Add a `Transaction` object to the collection.
2. Get an iterator to the collection.

It is easy to verify that these are well supported by the JDK collection classes. Regarding books issued, the operations are:

1. Add a `Book` object to the collection.
2. Remove a `Book` object from the collection.
3. Get an iterator to the collection.

Obviously, there is no need to create a custom collection for this as well.

### 6.3.2 Placing a Hold

When a member wants to place a hold on a book, the `placeHold()` method in `UserInterface` is called. This method reads in the book ID, member ID, and duration, and calls `placeHold()` in `Library` with a `Request` object as parameter. After verifying the existence of the member and book, `Library` executes the following code, which essentially follows the sequence diagram in Figure 5.6.

```
Calendar date = new GregorianCalendar();
date.add(Calendar.DATE, request.getHoldDuration());
Hold hold = new Hold(member, book, date);
book.placeHold(hold);
member.placeHold(hold);
result.setResultCode(Result.OPERATION_COMPLETED);
result.setBookFields(book);
return result;
```

The implementation of the `Hold` class is quite simple, with the code being a direct Java translation of the class diagram in Figure 5.15. The constructor, getters and setters need no explanation. The only method with a modicum of complexity is `isValid()`, which checks if a hold is still valid. Validity check is done by comparing the date and time stored in the `Hold` object against the current date and time. `System.currentTimeMillis()` returns the number of milliseconds between the current instant in time and some reference time, say, $T$. Similarly, `date.getTimeInMillis()` is the number of milliseconds between the time stored in `date` (the last valid date of the hold) and the same reference time $T$. If the former is smaller than the latter, clearly the hold is valid.

```
public boolean isValid() {
   return (System.currentTimeMillis() < date.getTimeInMillis());
}
```

Here is how the `placeHold()` method in `Member` is implemented. The method creates a `Transaction` object and adds it to the collection in `Member` and then stores the `Hold` object in a collection named `booksOnHold`, which stores the list of holds placed by this member.

```
public void placeHold(Hold hold) {
   transactions.add(new Transaction("Hold placed",
   hold.getBook().getTitle()));
   booksOnHold.addHold(hold);
}
```

### 6.3.3 Maintaining the Collection of Holds

The question we should address here is how the collection of holds for a member should be implemented. An important method to operate on the collection is removal of a hold. Suppose in the future, the library system would like to delete one or more holds placed by a member. Unless we keep track of the holds placed individually for each member, this operation can be quite time-consuming.

In anticipation of such needs, for efficiency, we store a collection of `Hold` objects in both `Book` and `Member`. With this arrangement, consider the problem of deleting a hold placed by `Member` referred to by `member` for a `Book`, say, `book`. Clearly, there is a `Hold` object, say, `hold`, corresponding to this hold. We need to delete `hold` from both collections. We could arbitrarily select one of the two collections, so let us begin searching the holds collection associated with `member`. We need to look in this collection for a `Hold` object corresponding to `book`. This means testing for each `Hold` object, whether the book ID is equal to the ID of `book`. This type of search involves a loop. Putting such code in `Member` makes that class non-cohesive.

This issue is best handled by the creation of a collection class, which we name `HoldList`. Obviously, this class was not identified during design, and what happened now is a fairly interesting case of refactoring that is not atypical in the implementation phase. To keep matters manageable, we might not always spend a great deal of time identifying every potential class during design, but see the need for one during implementation.
`HoldList` for a book should organize the `Hold` objects in the chronological order of their insertion times. It is implemented as an object adapter, using `LinkedList` as an adaptee.

```
    private List<Hold> holds = new LinkedList<Hold>();
```

The collection is a queue. So a new `Hold` object is added at the end of the list.

```
public boolean addHold(Hold hold) {
   holds.add(hold);
   return true;
}
```

A `Hold` object related to a given book is removed as below. Note the use of `ListIterator`, which allows removal during iteration.

```
public Hold removeHoldOnBook(String bookId) {
   for (ListIterator<Hold> iterator = holds.listIterator();
   iterator.hasNext();) {
      Hold hold = iterator.next();
      String id = hold.getBook().getId();
      if (id.equals(bookId)) {
```

```
            iterator.remove();
            return hold;
        }
    }
    return null;
}
```

Another method removeHoldOnMember() removes holds on a specific member. The code is almost identical, except for the obvious changes needed for matching based on member ID.

When a book is returned, the library must check if there is a valid hold on the book. This is carried out by searching the holds collection related to the book. All invalid holds are removed and the first valid hold is located. The code uses ListIterator to facilitate removal during iteration.

```
public Hold getNextValidHold() {
   for (ListIterator<Hold> iterator = holds.listIterator();
                                        iterator.hasNext();) {
      Hold hold = iterator.next();
      if (hold.isValid()) {
         return hold;
      } else {
        iterator.remove();
      }
   }
   return null;
}
```

The following method checks if there is a valid hold on the book.

```
public boolean hasHold() {
   return holds.getNextValidHold() != null;
}
```

### 6.3.4 Returning Books

To return books, UserInterface has a loop to read and send a book ID to the returnBook() method of Library and display one of different types of messages, depending on the result. The switch statement has a number of cases, most of which are not shown. The missing ones include cases such as book not found, book not checked out, etc.

```
public void returnBooks() {
    do {
        Request.instance().setBookId(getToken("Enter book id"));
```

```
        Result result = library.returnBook(Request.instance());
        switch (result.getResultCode()) {
        // several cases not shown
        case Result.BOOK_HAS_HOLD:
            System.out.println("Book " + result.getBookTitle()
            + "has a hold");
             break;
        }
        if (!yesOrNo("Return more books?")) {
            break;
        }
    } while (true);
}
```

Note that if there is a hold on the book, `returnBook()` of `Library` returns the result code `BOOK_HAS_HOLD`, and `UserInterface` displays an appropriate message on the console. This action requires a follow up, which is discussed in the next section.

After ensuring that the book ID valid and that it was actually issued, `Library` executes the following code.

```
if (!(member.returnBook(book))) {
    result.setResultCode(Result.OPERATION_FAILED);
    return result;
}
if (book.hasHold()) {
    result.setResultCode(Result.BOOK_HAS_HOLD);
    return result;
}
result.setResultCode(Result.OPERATION_COMPLETED);
result.setBookFields(book);
result.setMemberFields(member);
return result;
```

The `hasHold()` method of `Book` returns `true` if and only if there is a valid hold on the book.

The `returnBook()` of `Member` removes the book from its list of borrowed books and generates a `Transaction` object.

```
if (booksBorrowed.remove(book)) {
    transactions.add(new Transaction("Returned",
    book.getTitle()));
    return true;
}
```

### 6.3.5 Process Holds

Recall that the purpose of this use case is to determine the next member who has a valid hold on a certain book. UserInterface's processHolds() method is a do loop, reading in book IDs one by one and calling the processHold() method of Library for each ID, to determine the member who should be issued the book. Part of the code in UserInterface is given below. (We do not show the error cases and the loop isetlf.

```
Request.instance().setBookId(getToken("Enter book id"));
Result result = library.processHold(Request.instance());
if (result.getResultCode() == Result.OPERATION_COMPLETED) {
    System.out.println("Book " + result.getBookTitle() + "
    should be issued to " + result.getMemberName() + "
    phone " + result.getMemberPhone());
}
```

The processHold() method of Library first checks that the book ID is valid and then proceeds as given below.

```
if (book.getBorrower() != null) {
   result.setResultCode(result.BOOK_ISSUED);
   return result;
}
Hold hold = book.getNextHold();
if (hold == null) {
   result.setResultCode(Result.NO_HOLD_FOUND);
   return result;
}
hold.getMember().removeHold(request.getBookId());
hold.getBook().removeHold(hold.getMember().getId());
result.setResultCode(Result.OPERATION_COMPLETED);
result.setMemberFields(hold.getMember());
```

The above code checks that the book is not currently issued and then gets the next valid Hold object on the book. It is possible that all holds have expired. If there is a valid hold, the corresponding Hold object is removed from both Member and Book.

### 6.3.6 Renewing Books

The logic for renewing a book, shown in Figure 5.11, is quite complicated. It requires UserInterface to get information about every book issued to the member and then prompt the user to see if it should be renewed.

A crucial question here concerns the mechanism for getting the information about all checked-out books to `UserInterface`. One option is to return a list of `Book` objects or an `Iterator<Book>`. This approach is risky, because `UserInterface` could misuse the `Book` reference to fulfil any nefarious intentions. To overcome this, we could create a `ReadOnlyBook` object as discussed in Chapter 5. This will work, but the construction is rather elaborate, and, in general, this will mean multiple classes for every type of class we wish to expose.

A slightly easier approach is to supply an `Iterator<Result>` object to `UserInterface`. We arrange matters so that each `Result` object so returned will contain a copy of the fields of the `Book` object. The following is what `Library` does, so `UserInterface` gets an iterator to `Result` objects that contain copies of the fields of the books issued to this member.

```
public Iterator<Result> getBooks(Request request) {
   Member member = members.search(request.getMemberId());
   if (member == null) {
      return new LinkedList<Result>().iterator();
   } else {
      return new SafeBookIterator(member.getBooksIssued());
   }
}
```

`Library` calls the `getBooksIssued()` method in `Member` to get an iterator to all the books issued. Using this object, `Library` creates a `SafeBookIterator` object. As is evident, the constructor of `SafeBookIterator` has as a parameter, an iterator of `Book` objects. Suppose the original `Iterator<Book>` reference is `iterator`. Then `iterator.next()` obviously returns a `Book` object. We create a `Result` object and copy the fields of `Book` using the `setBookFields()` of `Result`. The Java code is given below.

```
    Result result = new Result();
    public Result next() {
        if (iterator.hasNext()) {
            Book book = iterator.next();
            result.setBookFields(book);
        } else {
            throw new NoSuchElementException("No such element");
        }
        return result;
    }
```

The `hasNext()` method simply returns whatever `iterator.hasNext()` returns.

The complete code for `SafeBookIterator` is given below.

```
public class SafeBookIterator implements Iterator<Result> {
    private Iterator<Book> iterator;
```

```
    private Result result = new Result();
    public SafeBookIterator(Iterator<Book> iterator) {
        this.iterator = iterator;
    }
    @Override
    public boolean hasNext() {
        return iterator.hasNext();
    }
    @Override
    public Result next() {
        if (iterator.hasNext()) {
            result.setBookFields(iterator.next());
        } else {
            throw new NoSuchElementException("No such element");
        }
        return result;
    }
}
```

We could employ the same idea to create a safe iterator for `Member` or for any other class.
To complete the business side of things, here is the code for `getBooksIssued()` in `Member`.

```
public Iterator<Book> getBooksIssued() {
    return booksBorrowed.iterator();
}
```

## 6.4 Removing Objects

There are three use cases that require removal of objects: removing books, removing holds, and removing holds that occur while holds are processed. Once all application references to an object are removed, the Java memory management mechanism kicks in and removes the deleted objects from memory. Between these two points in time – removal of all references and the ultimate removal of objects by Java – the object continues to exist but remains unavailable to application code.

### 6.4.1 Removing a Hold

Given a book ID and a member ID for a hold, `Library`'s `removeHold()` method validates the IDs and removes the `Hold` object from both `Member` and

### Memory management in object-oriented systems

Proliferation of objects contributes in large part to the degradation of performance in object-oriented systems, which means that objects must be removed from the system in an expedient manner as soon as they have served their purpose. Objects are typically allocated in the process memory space known as the *heap*. In Java, memory allocated to an object in the heap is not reclaimed until all references to the object are set to `null`. Some languages such as C++ allow and require the user to employ a specific operator in order to free up the space allocated to an object.

The availability of automatic reclamation of storage in Java is often touted as a boon, and it indeed is: it ensures that there are no *dangling references* or *memory leaks* in the traditional sense of these two terms. But it does not absolve the programmer from his/her responsibilities to ensure proper memory management. The reader must be aware that memory shortage and data integrity issues, which are, respectively, the consequences of memory leaks and dangling pointers, may manifest themselves because of design and coding errors.

The problem of memory shortage may still arise in a Java program because we may forget to set to `null` every reference to an object that should be deleted: the language's garbage collection mechanism must be given a chance to kick in, and that will not happen without some cooperation from the application code. Removing objects can be a tricky exercise and to ensure reliable performance, a systematic process is needed for removing the unwanted ones. As systems become more complex, we have more intricate relationships between the objects, which, in turn, make the unwanted objects harder to detect. In our example, `Book` and `Member` objects are relatively stable and introduced into the system in a fairly controlled manner. `Hold` objects, on the other hand, are more ephemeral and can be easily added and removed,which means that there is a potential for their numbers to explode. In the library system, we suggest that this be fixed by removing invalid holds periodically.

Dangling pointers, which imply invalid object references, could ultimately lead to illegal data access and failure. Careless design and development may result in the very same fate in a Java program. While deleting the reference to an object from one part of the system, we must be careful to ensure that any remaining references to the object from other parts of the system will not lead to inconsistencies. When deleting an object from a collection, we typically obtain a reference to the object by searching the container. If there are references to a deleted object stored in other active objects, we may up with *mutual inconsistency*. For instance, assume that we remove a book $b$ from the catalog by deleting the reference to the appropriate `Book` object from `Catalog`. Furthermore, suppose that $b$ has a hold $h$ on it. This could lead to the situation where we obtain the reference to the Book object (corresponding to $b$) from the Hold object (corresponding to $h$) and use $b$'s ID at a later point to search the catalog; obviously, this search will lead to an unexpected failure. There are two possible solutions to overcome this problem: (i) delete the corresponding Hold object while removing the book from the catalog or *(ii) remove the reference from* Catalog *only if there are no holds and the book is not currently checked out.* In our implementation, we have chosen the second solution.

Hold. Note the calls to removeHold() of Member and Book in the same if statement.

```
if (member.removeHold(request.getBookId()) &&
    book.removeHold(request.getMemberId())) {
    result.setResultCode(Result.OPERATION_COMPLETED);
} else {
    result.setResultCode(Result.NO_HOLD_FOUND);
}
```

### 6.4.2 Removing Books

To remove a book with a given book ID, UserInterface gets the book ID from the actor. The code for this is identical to the ones we have seen for some of the other use cases, so we do not repeat it here.

Ultimately, Library gets the book ID through the Request object. It checks for the existence of the book and whether it is borrowed or has a hold. The book is removed if it has no holds and is not borrowed. The outline of the code is given below.

```
Book book = catalog.search(request.getBookId());
if (book == null)
   // return error
if (book.hasHold())
   // return error
if (book.getBorrower() != null)
    // return error
if (catalog.removeBook(request.getBookId())) {
    result.setResultCode(Result.OPERATION_COMPLETED);
    return result;
}
// return error
```

## 6.5 Displaying Transactions

As shown in Figure 5.16, the `Transaction` class has three fields: the type of the transaction, the book title, and the date of the transaction. We keep the collection of all transactions associated with a member in the `Member` class itself. The only query we have regarding transactions is to display them for a specific member on a given date. As a result, the only operations we need to perform on the collection is add new transactions and iterate over existing transactions, which means that a standard Java collection class will suffice.

Let us give some thought to how we might actually display transactions that fall on a given date, or for that matter, satisfy any other criteria. What is the most obvious route? This would be for some class on the business side to iterate over the collection of transactions, select all qualifying transactions, put them in a temporary collection, and supply an iterator to that collection to `UserInterface`. `UserInterface` then iterates over the list of selected transactions.

Is it likely that the transaction list could be small for any specific member? It is conceivable that similar queries could arise in contexts that involve massive collections. In such cases, iterating once over the list and then performing a second iteration on a smaller, but still potentially large, list may be an unattractive prospect.

The above problem can be handled by giving `UserInterface` the collection of all transactions for the member and have the former iterate over this collection and pick and display what it wants. The drawback of such an approach is that `UserInterface` is then performing business logic.

We have come up with an approach that overcomes these problems. Before explaining the underlying technique, let us see the interaction between `UserInterface` and `Library`. Here is the code in `UserInterface`. As the reader can verify from the code, `UserInterface` assembles the member ID and date in the `Request` object and calls `getTransactions()` in `Library`, which returns a reference to an iterator to `Transaction` objects. What is interesting is that `getTransactions()` in `UserInterface` iterates over all elements and displays all of them. (Also observe that even if the member ID is invalid, `UserInterface` gets an iterator, but there will not be any objects to iterate on.)

```
public void getTransactions() {
   Request.instance().setMemberId(getToken("Enter member id"));
   Request.instance().setDate(getDate("Please enter the date "
      + "for which you want records as mm/dd/yy"));
   Iterator<Transaction> result =
        library.getTransactions(Request.instance());
   while (result.hasNext()) {
       Transaction transaction = (Transaction) result.next();
       System.out.println(transaction.getType() + "    " +
```

```
                transaction.getTitle() + "\n");
        }
        System.out.println("\n  End of transactions \n");
}
```

The above code could not work if all transactions associated with the member were "in the" iterator. And as we discussed earlier, there is no selection performed at the outset on the business side. What is happening is that `Library` returns an iterator that supplies only the desired `Transaction` objects when `next()` is called.

Let us examine the code in `Library`. It verifies that the member ID is valid. If it is not, it returns a dummy iterator. We will explain the last executable statement shortly.

```
public Iterator<Transaction> getTransactions(Request request) {
    Member member = members.search(request.getMemberId());
    if (member == null) {
        return new LinkedList<Transaction>().iterator();
    }
    return member.getTransactionsOnDate(request.getDate());
}
```

The `getTransactionsOnDate()` method in `Member` has a declared return type of `Iterator<Transaction>`. But its actual type is `FilteredIterator`, which we now discuss.

### 6.5.1 The Filtered Iterator

A filtered iterator behaves like an iterator, but ignores all objects that do not satisfy a certain property. The class header and fields are given below.

```
public class FilteredIterator implements Iterator<Transaction> {
    private Transaction item;
    private Predicate<Transaction> predicate;
    private Iterator<Transaction> iterator;
```

`Predicate` is a generic Java interface with a single method named `test()`. For a `Transaction`, the signature of this method can be thought of as

```
boolean test(Transaction t)
```

That is, given a `Transaction` reference `t`, `test()` must determine whether the transaction meets a certain condition. When the `FilteredIterator` object is created, it must be supplied two things:

- An iterator to `Transaction` objects. The idea is that `FilteredIterator` will filter and supply only selected objects when `next()` is

### Building a filtered iterator

A filtered iterator is an enhanced iterator that selectively shows a subset of the items in the collection to the client class. Say that a standard iterator is set up to present the items of a collection in the following order:
`A1, B2, C2, D1, E3, F2, G1, H2, I1, J3, K3 L1`
Note that the items in the list above are a symbolic representation of the items in the collection. Let us assume that a client class is interested in seeing only those items that have the numeric value 2, that is, the client class wants to see:
`B2, C2, F2, H2`
The filtered iterator is a wrapper that goes around the filtering predicate and the standard iterator. It has to ensure that the `next()` and `hasNext()` operations always work correctly. In order to make the filtering iterator deliver this result, we perform the following:

1. *Define a Filtering Predicate*: The filtering predicate is essentially a boolean function that looks at the item and returns true only when we have an item that the client wants to see. In our case, the filter checks if the numeral has the value 2.
2. *Set Up the Filtered Iteration Process*: The filtered iterator uses `next()` on the standard iterator to check if there is any item that is accepted by the predicate. If there are none, this is remembered in a boolean flag and `hasNext()` will always return false; if there is an item that is accepted by the predicate then the boolean flag is set to true, and that item is stored in the filtered iterator. In our example, the flag is set to true, and the item `B2` is remembered. Note that the standard iterator would have already processed `B2` and will be on `C2`.
3. *Update the Filtered Iterator*. When the client class calls `hasNext()`, the flag value is returned; this operation does not need any other action. When the client calls `next()`, the filtered iterator returns the stored item, and has to set up the filtered iteration process again, by looking at the rest of the standard iteration sequence. In our example, the standard iterator returns `C2` which is accepted by the predicate, and the boolean flag remains true.

Note that when the underlying standard iterator has reached the end of the sequence, the filtered iterator will always return false on `hasNext()`. In our example, after the filtered iterator has returned `H2` on `next()`, the standard iterator's sequence will be scanned all the way to the end, and the flag will be set to false.

called. Essentially, `FilteredIterator` is an object adapter of `Iterator<Transaction>`.

- The condition for selecting a transaction. This will be a `Predicate<Transaction>` reference.

The constructor header is

```
public FilteredIterator(Iterator<Transaction> iterator,
    Predicate<Transaction> predicate) {
```

Conceptually, what the filtered iterator does is not very difficult. It uses the `next()` method of the adaptee to retrieve each `Transaction` object. It supplies each `Transaction` object as an argument to the `Predicate` object's `test()` method. If the method returns `true`, that is the next `Transaction` object to be returned from `next()`, so it is stored in the field `item`. All of this is accomplished in the method `getNextItem()`. Note that when there are no more items, `item` is set to `null`.

```
private void getNextItem() {
    while (iterator.hasNext()) {
        item = iterator.next();
        if (predicate.test(item)) {
            return;
        }
    }
    item = null;
}
```

The constructor calls `getNextItem()` to initialize `item`.

```
this.predicate = predicate;
this.iterator = iterator;
getNextItem();
```

If `item` is not `null`, it is an indication that there is at least one more transaction. So here is the `hasNext()` method.

```
public boolean hasNext() {
    return item != null;
}
```

The next item to be returned is in `item`. But before returning it, the `next()` method must find the next qualifying transaction and store it in `item`.

```
public Transaction next() {
    if (!hasNext()) {
        throw new NoSuchElementException("No such element");
    }
    Transaction returnValue = item;
    getNextItem();
```

```
        return returnValue;
    }
```

To instantiate a `FilteredIterator` object, `Member` supplies an iterator to the `Transaction` objects and a `Predicate` object. The first one is simply `transactions.iterator()`. To create the `Predicate` object, the following code would work:

```
private class DatePredicate implements Predicate<Transaction> {
    private Calendar date;
    public DatePredicate(Calendar date) {
        this.date = date;
    }
    public boolean test(Transaction transaction) {
        return transaction.onDate(date);
    }
}
```

The method `getTransactionsOnDate()` in `Member` would be

```
public Iterator<Transaction>
getTransactionsOnDate(Calendar date) {
   return new FilteredIterator(transactions.iterator(),
   new DatePredicate(date));
}
```

However, instead of creating a separate class to implement `Predicate` and instantiating it, we can simply supply the essential code in the implementation of the `test()` method. Given the parameter `transaction`, what the method does is evaluate `transaction.onDate(date)` and return the result. This is expressed in a more compact form called a **lambda function**.

```
transaction -> transaction.onDate(date)
```

We can simply pass the above as the second argument. Java will interpret it to mean an instantiation of an anonymous object that implements the `Predicate` interface.
The final code for the method is thus

```
public Iterator<Transaction> getTransactionsOnDate(Calendar
date) {
    return new FilteredIterator(transactions.iterator(),
         transaction -> transaction.onDate(date));
}
```

Since `Transaction` could perhaps some day contain references to other objects on the business side, we would like to protect business data; we apply the principles of safe iterators to `FilteredIterator` and construct a new class as below. The reader can verify that it is a `SafeIterator` that uses a `FilteredIterator` for locating the relevant transactions.

```
public class SafeTransactionIterator implements
                                     Iterator<Result> {
   private FilteredIterator iterator;
   private Result result = new Result();
   public SafeTransactionIterator(FilteredIterator iterator) {
      this.iterator = iterator;
   }
   @Override
   public boolean hasNext() {
      return iterator.hasNext();
   }
   @Override
   public Result next() {
      if (iterator.hasNext()) {
         result.setTransacionFields(iterator.next());
      } else {
         throw new NoSuchElementException("No such element");
      }
      return result;
   }
}
```

The Member class's getTransactions() method has the following form:

```
public Iterator<Result> getTransactionsOnDate(Calendar date) {
   return new SafeTransactionIterator(
      new FilteredIterator(transactions.iterator(),
      transaction -> transaction.onDate(date)));
}
```

We add the following fields and their getters and setters to DataTransfer.

```
private String transactionType;
private String transactionDate;
```

UserInterface now iterates on Result objects, and not on Transaction objects, to display transactions.

## 6.6 Other Requirements

We have now covered the implementation of the business logic of the library system. To make the system usable on a long-term basis, however, we need to store (retrieve) the business data on (from) non-volatile storage. This topic is covered in this section. We also discuss how we protect the data. Both implementations are highly language (Java) specific.

### 6.6.1 Saving and Retrieving Data

Although a full-fledged application would possibly employ a database management system to manage data on a long-term basis, that topic is beyond the scope of this book. Instead, to help us use the system at least on a small scale, we use Java serialization and file management support to store and retrieve data to/from disk.

The Java serialization mechanism takes objects, which have a non-linear structure, and converts them into a linear or serial form. The serialized form can then be shipped across a network, stored in a disk file, etc. Java can reconstruct the objects from the serialized form using a process called deserialization.

From an application perspective, serialization is quite easy to achieve. Any class that needs to be serialized should implement an interface called `Serializable`, which contains no methods. `Serializable` is simply a marker to identify classes that have to be serialized when needed. Thus every class that contains data, that is, all classes except the `UserInterface` and `Iterator` classes, implement this interface. For example, we have declarations such as

```
public class Member implements Serializable {
...
public class Book implements Serializable
...
public class Hold implements Serializable {
...
```

When the command to save data is invoked, `UserInterface` calls the method `save()` in `Library`.

```
 private void save() {
  if (library.save()) {
      System.out.println(" The library has been successfully
      saved"
             + " in the file LibraryData \n");
  } else {
    System.out.println(" There has been an error in saving \n");
  }
}
```

`Library` contains references to the two main collections: the catalog and the list of members.

```
private Catalog catalog = Catalog.getInstance();
private MemberList members = MemberList.getInstance();
```

Both `Catalog` and `MemberList` contain just one field each, for storing the data. For example, in `Catalog`, we have the following reference to all `Book` objects.

```
private List<Book> books = new LinkedList<Book>();
```

`Library`, `Catalog`, and `MemberList` all implement `Serializable`.
Let us follow the steps to store the entire library data onto disk. The code in `Library` to serialize the data and store it in a disk file is given below.

```
public static boolean save() {
    try {
        FileOutputStream file =
        new FileOutputStream("LibraryData");
        ObjectOutputStream output = new ObjectOutputStream(file);
        output.writeObject(library);
        Member.save(output);
        file.close();
        return true;
    } catch (IOException ioe) {
        ioe.printStackTrace();
        return false;
    }
}
```

`Library` creates a disk file named `LibraryData` on disk. It then wraps it in a class called `ObjectOutputStream` and invokes the method `writeObject()` on it. The Java serialization mechanism notes that `Library` has implemented the `Serializable` interface, so it starts to serialize the `Library` object. In the course of serializing `Library`, Java notes the two references `catalog` and `members` and since their respective classes have also implemented `Serializable`, it serializes them as well. To serialize `Catalog`, it serializes the `books` object stored in it, which is actually of type `LinkedList`. It so happens that `LinkedList` implements `Serializable`; so in the course of serializing `Catalog`, Java will serialize `books` and thus succeed in serializing `Catalog`. This takes care of serializing all `Book` objects and all objects referred to by these `Book` objects, which include all `Member` and `Hold` objects stored in them. Serializing the `Hold` objects will also serialize all `Member` objects who have placed a hold. Serialization of `MemberList` will serialize all members not already serialized: that is, the ones who have not borrowed or are holding books. As `Member` objects are serialized, the corresponding `Transaction` objects also get serialized.

Thus serializing `Catalog` and `MemberList` will serialize almost all data in the library system. What will not get serialized is the static field `idCounter` in `Member`, because Java does not serialize any static fields as part of its "automated" serialization process. To store this, we need to explicitly serialize the value in that field.
The following code (which is a repetition from the above method) takes care of that.

```
Member.save(output);
```

The `save()` method in `Member` is

```
public static void save(ObjectOutputStream output) throws
IOException {
   output.writeObject(idCounter);
}
```

The file `LibraryData` can be retrieved and deserialized using the method `retrieve()` in `Library`. The method calls `Member`'s `retrieve()` method to restore the static field `idCounter`.

```
public static Library retrieve() {
   try {
      FileInputStream file = new FileInputStream("LibraryData");
      ObjectInputStream input = new ObjectInputStream(file);
      library = (Library) input.readObject();
      Member.retrieve(input);
      return library;
   } catch (IOException ioe) {
      ioe.printStackTrace();
      return null;
   } catch (ClassNotFoundException cnfe) {
      cnfe.printStackTrace();
      return null;
   }
}
```

The method `retrieve()` in `Member` is

```
public static void retrieve(ObjectInputStream input) throws
          IOException, ClassNotFoundException {
   idCounter = (int) input.readObject();
}
```

### 6.6.2 Protecting the Data Even Further

The implementation as given above allows `UserInterface` free access to all packages and all public members of these packages. This can compromise the safety of the data as a malicious user may use the collection classes and wreak havoc.

The question arises as to how we can protect the data. For this, consider Table 6.1 where we list the packages on the business side and the classes that belong to these packages. (Each package name is prefixed with `org.oobook.libraryv1.business`.)

| Package | Class |
|---|---|
| collections | `MemberList, Catalog, HoldList` |
| entities | `Member, Book, Hold, Transaction` |
| facade | `Library, DataTransfer, Result, Request` |
| iterators | `SafeMemberIterator, SafeBookIterator, SafeTransactionIterator, FilteredIterator` |

**Table 6.1** Organization of the business logic classes into packages

Obviously, the only classes we would like to expose to the outside world are the ones in the `facade` package. To accomplish this, we use the Java **modules** mechanism.

A Java module is a collection of related packages. All of the packages listed above are related and we put them into a single module. Every module is named and specified by a module info file. This module can then specify which packages can be accessed by code in other modules.
The odule file for the business packages is given below.

```
module org.oobook.libraryv1.business {
  exports org.oobook.libraryv1.business.facade;
}
```

What this means is that the business logic is encapsulated into a module named `org.oobook.libraryv1`. The only package the outside world has access to is `org.oobook.libraryv1.business.facade`. The `exports` construct makes that specification. None of the classes in the other packages can be accessed from code outside, even by using Java reflection.

By convention, the package prefix `org.oobook.libraryv1.business` and the module name are the same. We also usually put the source files in a directory that is named the same as the module name.

## 6.7 Discussion and Further Reading

Converting the model into a working design is by far the most complex part of the software design process. Although there are only a few principles of good object-oriented design that the designer should be aware of, the manner in which these should be applied in a given situation can be quite challenging to a beginner. Indeed, the only way these can be mastered is through repeated application and critical examination of the designs produced. It is also extremely useful to study any available design/implementation of software systems and to discuss design issues with more experienced colleagues. In this chapter, we have attempted to capture some of this complexity through an example, and also tried to raise and deal with the questions that trouble the typical beginner.

The sequence of topics so far suggests that a software project would progress linearly from analysis to design to implementation. In reality, what usually takes place is more like an iterative process. In the design phase, some classes and methods may get left out; worse yet, we may not even have spelled out all the functional requirements. These shortcomings could show up at various points along the way, and we may have to loop through this process (or a part of this process) more than once, until we have an acceptable design. It is also instructive to remember that we are not by any means prescribing a definitive method that is to be used at all times, or even coming up with the perfect design for our simple library system. As stated before, our goal is to provide a condensed, but complete, overview of the object-oriented design process through an example.

At the end of the previous chapter, three student projects were presented. To maximize benefit, the reader is encouraged to apply the concepts to one or more of these projects as he/she reads through the material. From our experience, we have seen that students find this practice very beneficial.

### 6.7.1 Summary of the Implementation

As is evident from the pieces of code shown in this chapter, the implementation follows the blueprint established by the design. Of course, we made some tweaks such as introducing the `HoldList` class and the filtered and safe iterators, which were not explicitly specified during design. We made use of language features (like `LinkedList`, lambda functions, Java modules), design patterns (adapter, singleton), and imparted a certain degree of code safety by using the concepts of data transfer objects and safe iterators. We have presented the implementation in sections; when implementing projects of this scale, a beginner would be well-advised to develop incrementally to avoid getting overwhelmed.

### 6.7.2 Conceptual, Software, and Implementation Classes

Finding the classes is a critical step in the object-oriented methodology. In the course of the analysis-design-implementation process, the idea of what constitutes a class goes through some subtle shifts.

In the analysis phase, we found the **conceptual** classes. These correspond to real-world concepts or things, and present us with a conceptual or essential perspective. These are derived from and used to satisfy the system requirements at a conceptual level. At this level, for instance, we can identify a piece of information that needs to be recognized as an entity and make it a class; we can talk of an association between classes without any thought as to how this will be realized.

As we go further into the design process and construct the sequence diagrams, we need to deal with the issue of how these conceptual classes will be manifested in the software, that is, we are now dealing with **software** classes. These can be implemented with typical programming languages, and we need to identify the methods and parameters that will be involved. We have to finalize which entities will be individual classes, which ones will be merged, and how associations will be captured.

The last step is the **implementation** class, which is a class created using a specific programming language such as Java or C++. This step nails down all the remaining details: identification and implementation of helper classes and methods, nitty-gritty details of using software libraries, names of fields and variables, etc.

The process of going from conceptual to implementation classes is a progression from an abstract system to a concrete one and, as we have seen, classes may be added or removed at each step. For instance, `FilteredIterator` was added as an implementation class, whereas the conceptual class `Borrows` was dropped at the design stage.

### 6.7.3 Building a Commercially Acceptable System

A reader having familiarity with software systems may be left with the feeling that our example is too much of a "toy" system, and our assumptions are rather simplistic. This criticism is not unjustified, but should be tempered by the fact that our objective has been to present an example that can give the learner a "big picture" of the entire design process, without letting the complexity overwhelm the beginner.

#### 6.7.3.1 Non-Functional Requirements

A realistic system would have several non-functional requirements. We discussed the issue of code safety to some extent. Giving a complete treatment to this and other non-functional requirements is beyond the scope of the book. Some issues like portability are automatically resolved since Java is interpreted and is thus platform independent. Response time (run-time performance) is a sticking point for object-oriented applications. We can examine this in a context where design choice affects performance, and this is addressed briefly in a later case study.

#### 6.7.3.2 Functional Requirements

It can be argued that for a system to be accepted commercially, it must provide a sufficiently large set of services, and if our design methodologies are not adequate to handle that complexity, then they are of questionable value. We would like to point out the following:

- *Additional features can be easily added*: Some of these will be added in the next chapter. Our decision to exclude several such features has been made based on pedagogical considerations.
- *Allowing for variability among kinds of books/members*: This variability is typically incorporated by using inheritance. To explain the basic design process, inheritance is not essential. However, using inheritance in design requires an understanding of several related issues, and we shall, in fact, present these issues and extend our library system in Chapter 7.
- *Having a more sophisticated interface*: Once again, we might want a system that allows members to log in and perform operations through a GUI. This would only involve the interface and not the business logic. In Chapter 8, we shall see how a GUI can be modeled as a multi-panel interactive system, and how such features can be incorporated.
- *Allowing remote access*: Now-a-days most systems of this kind allow remote access to the server. The reader should consult books on client-server architecture and implementation to learn how such features can be introduced through the use of distributed objects.

It should be noted that in practice several of the non-functional requirements would actually be provided by a database. What we have done with the use case model, the sequence diagrams and the class diagrams is, in fact, an object-oriented schema, which can be used to create an application that runs on an object-oriented database system. A database management system would not only address issues of performance and portability but also take care of issues like persistence and transaction processing. Details of this are beyond the scope of this text.

## Projects

1. Complete the designs for the case study exercises from the previous chapter.

## Exercises

1. Consider a situation where a library wants to add a feature that enables the librarian to print out a list of all the books that have been checked out at a given point in time. Construct a sequence diagram for this use case.

2. Explain the rationale for separating the user interface from the business logic.
3. Suppose the due date for a book depends not only on the date the book is issued, but also on factors such as member type (assume that there are multiple types of membership), number of books already issued to the member, and any fines owed by the member. Which class should then be assigned the responsibility to compute the due date and why?
4. (Discussion) There is fairly tight coupling in our system between the `Book`, `Member`, and `Hold` classes. Code in `Book` could inadvertently modify the fields of a `Member` object. One way to handle this is to replace the `Member` reference with just the member's ID. What changes would we have to make in the rest of the classes to accommodate this? What are the pros and cons of such an approach?
5. Continuing with the previous question, the `Hold` object stores references to the `Book` and `Member` objects. This may not be necessary. What specific information does `Book` (`Member`) require from `Hold`? Define an interface that contains the relevant methods to retrieve this information. What are the pros and cons of an implementation where `Hold` implements these interfaces, over the design presented in this chapter?
6. (Keeping mutables safe.) Suggest a simple scheme for creating a new class `SafeMember` that would allow us to export a reference to a `Member`. The classes outside the system should be unaware of this additional class, and access the reference like a reference to a `Member` object. However, the reference would not allow the integrity of the data to be compromised.
7. Modify the library system to

   a. List the names of all titles put on hold by a specific member. The actor inputs the member ID.
   b. Print the number of books checked out by a specific member. The actor inputs the member ID.
   c. Print the names of all members who have placed a hold on a specific book. The actor inputs the book ID.
   d. Display the names and phone numbers of all members who are late in returning books by a certain number of days. The actor inputs the value.

8. Suppose a book $b_1$ is held by multiple members and member $m_1$ has the earliest hold on $b_1$. Note that the software does not ensure that when $b_1$ is issued, it is to $m_1$ that it is issuing the book. How would you guarantee this? Implement the following approach: When $b_1$ is returned, we do not remove any valid holds. Instead, we notify the member with the first valid hold and adjust his/her hold to be valid for up to a certain number of days. If $m_1$ claims the book in this period, issue the book and delete the hold.
9. Without modifying any of the classes other than `Library`, write a method in `Library` that deletes all invalid holds for all members.

# Chapter 7
# Designing for Reuse

One of the strongest motivations for adopting an object-oriented approach is the facility for reuse. All object-oriented languages provide two mechanisms for reuse: composition and inheritance. The principle of object composition is integral to object-oriented design, and through object composition, objects of any existing class can be used to define new classes. Extending an existing class through inheritance also allows us to use an existing class, but comes with a lot of caveats. Using these mechanisms, we introduce a few basic strategies for enhancing reusability of code.

Construction of reusable code can be viewed as conjoining two pieces: the part of the implementation that exists and the new application or new feature to be introduced. The existing implementation should be implemented to facilitate reuse. How this facilitation is achieved varies across situations and dictates how new features should be implemented. The new application should be implemented in such a way that it fits with the implementation of the existing code.

We look at reuse in two contexts. The first one is when we build a collection of classes, sometimes called a library, that can be used by a variety of applications. We look at examples of three situations where this is done. The first situation is in the implementation of an algorithm. An algorithm that acts on a data set may have broad applicability. In such a situation, reusability is enhanced if the algorithm is implemented in such a manner so that it can be used on a variety of data types. Next, we look at a situation where generic parameters are used to implement a fully reusable class. We introduced generics in Chapter 2. Here, we see a more complex example with two co-dependent parameters. The third situation, presented towards the end of the chapter, is one where we want to use the functionality provided by a pre-defined (or library) class and also inherit its type. In such cases, we can sidestep the pitfalls of substitutability by using a combination of inheritance and composition.

The second context where reusability is critical is when we are creating an application that can adapt to changing requirements. Ensuring such adaptability, in a general setting, can be quite complex, involving more than one design pattern. We introduce this through a simple example where an inheritance hierarchy is sufficient to enable reuse. Along with this, we look at several issues and design principles related to the creation of an inheritance hierarchy.

## 7.1 Reusing through Generic Implementations

Genericity is a mechanism for creating entities that vary only in the types of their parameters, and this notion can be associated with any entity (class or method) that requires parameters of some specific types. This concept was presented in Chapter 2. Here we explain how generics can be employed to develop a searchable collection class.

### 7.1.1 Designing a Generic Collection Class

As a means to reduce system complexity and development and maintenance effort, it is important to look for opportunities where the number of classes in a system can be kept as small as possible, subject, of course, to good object-oriented design principles. Prospects for merging two or more classes arise if they have similar functionality, although they may differ in relatively minor aspects. In the library system, for instance, `MemberList` and `Catalog` are strikingly similar in what they do. Of course, there are some differences: one stores books and the other is a collection of members; `Catalog` has a method to remove books, but no such functionality exists in `MemberList`. Using generics we can develop a class `ItemList`, which can be used to store books or members.

Recall that we separately implemented a `MemberList` class and a `Catalog` class. We now have to tell the system that `ItemList` should be capable of storing either books or members. For this, the type of element to be stored in the `ItemList` object is passed as a parameter to the class name itself as given in the following class declaration:

```
public class ItemList<T> implements Serializable {
// generic code
}
```

To implement the methods of this generic collection class, we utilize the logic used in the corresponding methods of `Catalog`. (As noted before, `Catalog` is slightly more general than `MemberList` because the former contains a method to remove items from the collection.)
We need to modify the places where references to specific types occur with generic type names. Specifically, we need to replace data definitions such as

```
private List books = new LinkedList();
```

with

```
private List<T> elements = new LinkedList<T>();
```

Next, we focus on `search()`. Here is the code from `Catalog`:

```
public Book search(String bookId) {
  for (Iterator iterator =
                        books.iterator();iterator.hasNext();) {
    Book book = (Book) iterator.next();
    if (book.getId().equals(bookId)) {
      return book;
    }
  }
  return null;
}
```

There are two problems with the code:

- In each iteration, the ID value of an object in the catalog is checked against the given book ID. This constitutes fairly tight coupling between `Book` and `Catalog`; the parameter to `search()` is of type `String`, so we build into `Catalog` the information that ID is of type `String`. The iterator's return type is cast as a `Book`. It also assumes the existence of a method called `getId()`. If we want to use generics and factor out the common code, this coupling must be eliminated.
- In the code, note that two books are considered equal (that is, identical) if their `id` fields are equal. If the coupling between `Catalog` and `Book` is to be removed, the decision as to which field(s) should be used in the comparison should be made by `Book`, and not left for the collection class. This suggests that the code for deciding how to match the incoming object against the `Book` object must be extracted and moved to `Book`.

### 7.1.2 A Caveat on Using the `equals()` Method

We have seen that the responsibility for checking whether a specific book's ID is equal to that of some given ID should be delegated to the `Book` class itself. In Chapter 2, we discussed a situation where using `equals()` led to inconsistencies. A similar argument can be applied here. Carefully read the following, which is taken from the Java online documentation.

```
The equals method implements an equivalence relation on non-null object
references:

• It is reflexive: for any non-null reference value x, x.equals(x)
  should return true.

• It is symmetric: for any non-null reference values x and y,
  x.equals(y) should return true if and only if y.equals(x) returns
  true.
```

Suppose that we write the `equals()` method in `Book` as follows:

```
public boolean equals(Object object) {
  String id = (String) object;
  return (this.id.equals(id));
}
```

As we demonstrate below, the relation implemented by the method is asymmetric. Clearly, there is an implication that the `equals()` method expects a `String` object. The `equals()` method of the `String` class, however, will not produce the same result when a `Book` object is passed as its parameter. Trace the following piece of code:

```
String id = "id1";
Book book1 = new Book("title1", "author1", id);
System.out.println(book1.equals(id)); // call 1
System.out.println(id.equals(book1)); // call 2
```

Although invocation of the `equals()` method on `book1` (commented `call 1`) results in a `true` output, calling the method on the corresponding `String` object (commented `call 2`) returns the `false` value.

In other words, the `equals()` method as implemented above will not result in an equivalence relation. We should, therefore, refrain from using that method as the vehicle for comparison. Failure to do so could ultimately result in subtle bugs that are likely to be quite difficult to catch: imagine the plight of a programmer who trusts that the above implementation of `equals()` follows the requirements set forth in the Java documentation and codes as in `call 2` above.

### 7.1.3 A Different Approach

To rectify the situation, we implement a method called `matches()` in `Book`, which does not impose the equivalence relation requirement. To start with, we implement the code as shown below:

```
public boolean matches(String bookId) {
  return this.id.equals(bookId);
}
```

The search method in Catalog is modified as follows:

```
public Book search(String value) {
  for (Book element: elements) {
    if (element.matches(value)) {
      return element;
    }
  }
  return null;
}
```

Next, we eliminate type dependence. For this, we replace the type name Book with the generic type T. (Recall that T is the parameter to the class.)

```
public T search(String value) {
  for (T element: elements) {
    if (element.matches(value)) {
      return element;
    }
  }
  return null;
}
```

This change begs the question: What if id were to be of a type other than String? This additional type dependence is eliminated by introducing a second generic parameter. The class ItemList is now defined as:

```
public class ItemList<T, K> implements Serializable {
  // generic code
}
```

K represents the type of the key on which the container matches items. The search() method is now written as:

```
public T search(K value) {
  for (T element: elements) {
    if (element.matches(value)) {
      return element;
    }
  }
  return null;
}
```

Similar modifications can be made to the other methods. The changes are fairly straightforward.

```
public boolean removeItem(K value) {
  T element = search(value);
```

```
  if (element == null) {
    return false;
  } else {
    return elements.remove(element);
  }
}
public boolean insertItem(T item) {
  elements.add(item);
  return true;
}
public Iterator<T> getItems() {
  return elements.iterator();
}
```

While this solution is satisfactory for our limited case, in a more general situation, one may wish to use `ItemList` to create other collection classes. If we were to replace `T` with some user-defined class `C`, the code would fail to compile if the method `matches()` was not defined for class `C`. In other words, to create instantiations of `ItemList`, we require that `T` satisfy a specific property, that is, have a method named `matches`. This property is named `Matchable` and is extracted as an interface that `T` must implement.

```
public interface Matchable<K> {
  public boolean matches(K other);
}
```

The `Book` and `Member` classes are modified as below.

```
public class Member implements Serializable, Matchable<String> {
  // fields and other methods
  public boolean matches(String id) {
    return this.id.equals(id);
  }
}


public class Book implements Serializable, Matchable<String> {
  // fields and other methods
  public boolean matches(String id) {
    return this.id.equals(id);
  }
}
```

Finally, `ItemList` is defined as:

```
public class ItemList<T extends Matchable<K>, K> implements
Serializable {
  // generic code
}
```

### 7.1.4 Instantiating Catalog and MemberList

With the code developed so far, we can create a new catalog as below.

```
ItemList<Book, String> catalog = new ItemList<Book, String>();
```

Similar code can be used to create a collection for members. However, from the viewpoint of robustness, this approach is unsatisfactory. There can be multiple catalogs and member lists because the constructor can be invoked from the outside. In other words, the class is not a singleton.

Ideally, we would like to put within `ItemList<T, K>` a static method that returns an `ItemList<T, K>` object with the correct parameter. The code should look like the following:

```
private static ItemList<T, K> itemList;
private ItemList() {
}
public static ItemList<T,K> instance() {
  if (itemList == null) {
    itemList = new ItemList<T,K>();
  }
  return itemList;;
}
```

Unfortunately, the above code is not legal. Because of the way Java implements generics, the type name `T` is *erased* from the class definition at compilation time and is not available during execution. Therefore, there can be no useful checks against the type name `T`.
`Catalog` is now declared as an extension of `ItemList<Book, String>`.

```
public class Catalog extends ItemList<Book, String> {
}
```

Now, every `public` and `protected` method of `ItemList<T extends Matchable<K>, K>` is inherited by `Catalog`. `MemberList` is coded in a similar fashion. We make `ItemList` abstract, so no collection objects can be created directly using it.

```
public abstract class ItemList<T extends Matchable<K>, K>
                                implements Serializable {
  // generic code
}
```

We now have two choices for naming the methods of `Catalog` and `MemberList`:

- We could create methods such as `removeBook()` and `insertBook()` inside `Catalog` and similarly named methods in `MemberList`. Thus, instead of having methods with names such as `removeItem()` and `insertItem()`, we end up with the old method names: `removeBook()`, `insertBook()`, etc.

```
public boolean removeBook(String value) {
  return super.removeItem(value);
}
public boolean insertBook(Book item) {
  return super.insertItem(item);
}
public Iterator<Book> getItems() {
  return super.getItems();
}
```

This means that `Catalog` is a *class adapter,* that is, it is a subclass of `ItemList<T extends Matchable<K>, K>` and it implements a different interface by suitably calling the methods of the superclass.

- We simply live with the new names `insertItem()` and `removeItem()`, and then modify the `Library` class to adjust to these changes.

While refactoring a module or a set of modules within a system, it is clearly preferable to ensure that the changes do not require modifications in the rest of the system. In our case, if we choose the second option, `Library` needs to be updated, which would mean that we should go for the first option. The number of places in `Library` that refer to these methods is small, so a case could be made for the second option. In general, that is not advisable, however, because there could be many modules with numerous locations that could be affected.
Making `Catalog` a singleton is not difficult. See the following code:

```
private static Catalog catalog;
private Catalog() throws Exception {
}
public static Catalog instance() {
  try {
    if (catalog == null) {
      return catalog = new Catalog();
    }
  } catch(Exception e) {
    return null;
  }
  return catalog;
}
```

## 7.2 Using Reusable Types to Obtain Reusable Implementations

Consider a class Queue and a method insert() that inserts a given object at the tail of the queue. An insert operation is performed by storing the reference to the given object in the appropriate location. Reusing this method is simple, if we implement a Queue with elements of type Object; since all types conform to Object, no adaptation is needed to reuse the code. On the other hand, consider an algorithm for finding the largest-valued item (the maximum) of a collection. The pseudocode for such an algorithm would look something like this:

```
Algorithm findMax (collection of items L)
    max = first item in the collection
    while L has more items {
        x = next item on L
        if (x is bigger than max) max = x
    }
    return max
```

A reusable implementation of this algorithm should work on all types of collections and all types of objects. From our knowledge of the Iterator pattern, we know that accessing the objects in the collection could be performed as below.

```
Iterator iterator = collection.iterator(); // get an Iterator
if (iterator.hasNext()) // check if there is a next item
Object max = iterator.next(); // get the first object
```

Using the Iterator pattern, we can access the objects in the collection in a uniform way. To make the implementation reusable for all types of objects, we need to find a way to compare two objects and determine which is the smaller (or, equivalently, the larger) of the two. The type Comparable, an important interface in Java, makes it possible to compare two objects in a uniform manner.

The responsibility for checking whether a given object object is smaller than, equal to, or larger than another object other is most appropriately assigned to object itself. (Recall that the task of checking for equality (using the equals() method) is also assigned to the object.) In Java, this is done by using the Comparable interface. Comparable is an interface with just one method, compareTo(), which has the following signature:

```
int compareTo(T other)
```

The method compareTo() is defined with one parameter, the object to be compared. It returns a negative integer, zero, or a positive integer when the this object is less than, equal to, or greater than the specified object. To check if `object1` is smaller than `object2` and perform some actions based on the result, we write:

```
if (object1.compareTo(object2) < 0)
   perform action1
else
   perform action2
```

Consider a class named `ComparableObject`. Suppose we wish to make two objects of type `ComparableObject` comparable to each other, as in the code above. The class `ComaprableObject` is then made to implement the `Comparable` interface. The class header would then be:

```
public class ComparableObject implements
Comparable<ComparableObject> {
```

The `Comparable` interface has exactly one method named `compareTo()`. The pseudocode for the method in `ComparableObject` would be along the following lines:

```
   public int compareTo(ComparableObject other) {
       if this object is smaller than other
          return -1;
       if this object is larger than other
          return 1;
       return 0;
     }
   }
```

The task of determining whether this object compares itself with another object is left entirely to the class itself.

Suppose we wish to employ the `findMax` algorithm for determining the largest of a set of objects of type `City`, which, as the name implies, represents a city. Suppose `City` stores the name, state, and population. Let us say that one `City` object `city1` is larger than another `City` object `city2`, if the name of `city1` is lexicographically larger than the name of `city2`. If the two names are equal, we could resolve the situation by determining which of the two states involved in the two `City` objects is larger.

To make objects of type `City` comparable, we have it implement the `Comparable` interface. Each `City` object maintains a reference to the corresponding `State`, so the `compareTo()` method of the former employs the `compareTo()` method of the latter to complete its work. Here is the code:

```
public class City implements Comparable<City> {
  private String name;
  private State state;
  private int population;
```

```
  public City(String name, State state, int population) {
    this.name = name;
    this.state = state;
    this.population = population;
  }

  public int compareTo(City city) {
    int result = 0;
    if ((result = name.compareTo(city.name)) == 0) {
      return state.compareTo(city.state);
    }
    return result;
  }

  public boolean equals(Object city) {
    // rest of the method not shown
    return compareTo(city) == 0;
  }
}
```

The class State must also be Comparable as shown below.

```
public class State implements Comparable<State> {
  private String name;
  public int compareTo(State state) {
    return name.compareTo(state.name);
  }
  // other fields and methods
}
```

We could then implement the findMax algorithm as below.

```
public static Object findMax
                          (Collection<Comparable> collection) {
  Iterator<Comparable> iterator = collection.iterator();
  Comparable max = null;
  if (iterator.hasNext()) {
    max = iterator.next();
    while (iterator.hasNext()) {
      Comparable item = iterator.next();
      if (item.compareTo(max) > 1) {
        max = item;
      }
    }
  }
  return max;
}
```

Next, we look at how these concepts are applied to reuse Java's sorting algorithms.

### 7.2.1 A Reusable Sorting Algorithm

The vast majority of general purpose sorting algorithms are based on comparing pairs of items in an indexed list, and depending on the result of the comparison, moving the item(s) to different locations. Such an algorithm would contain statements like the following:

```
if (item1 precedes item2)
    perform action1
else
    perform action2
```

There are several algorithms for this, and the performance of these algorithms often depends on the kind of data that is being sorted. These algorithms can also be quite complex, and it is therefore valuable to have a library implementation. Thus we would desire reusability from two points of view:

- Once the algorithm is implemented, it should be available for sorting any indexed collection of objects.
- An application should be able to change the sorting algorithm being used without any undesirable consequences.

Consider the following problems:

- Suppose we have an array of `Student` objects that needs to be arranged in decreasing order by GPA, that is, the student with a higher GPA is placed in the array location with a smaller index. In this case, the comparison of students is done by comparing the GPAs. When we sort an array of `Student`, the references `object1` and `object2` would hold references to `student1` and `student2`. The class `Student` would define `compareTo()` to return $-1$ if `student1` had a higher GPA, return 0 if `student1` and `student2` had the same GPA, and return 1 if `student2` had a higher GPA.
- When we sort an array of `Appliance`, the references `object1` and `object2` would hold references to `appliance1` and `appliance2`. To sort appliances in the increasing order of price, the class `Appliance` would define `compareTo()` to return $-1$ if `appliance1` had a lower price, return 0 if `appliance1` and `appliance2` had the same price, and return 1 if `appliance2` had a lower price.

Thus the conditional statement

```
if (item1 precedes item2) {...}
```

is replaced by

```
if (student1.getGpa() > student2.getGpa()) {...}
```

If, on the other hand, we have a sequence of appliances ordered by increasing price, the replacing statement would be

```
if (appliance1.getPrice() < appliance2.getPrice()) {...}
```

Here we see that the code being reused (the sorting program) uses a single method (`compareTo()`) to make comparisons between items. The application reuses this code by defining the `compareTo()` method for the class of item that needs to be sorted. As we shall see in the following example, the definitions are verified at compile time through the `Comparable` interface.

## 7.3 Building an Inheritance Hierarchy

Inheritance hierarchies allow an application to accommodate new requirements. They are useful when the changes in the requirements can be expressed as a variant of an existing class. This kind of change is difficult to accommodate when the existing class is a concrete class; the new variant may have requirements that contradict the requirements of the existing class. Inheritance can help if the existing class is abstract, with minimal requirements; all the concrete classes can then be defined as extensions of the abstract class. By designing the other classes in the system to work with the abstract superclass, the concrete subclasses with different implementations can coexist.

### 7.3.1 The Situation Without Inheritance

Consider a more sophisticated version of the `Library` system that we created in the last chapter. With the advent of technology, our clients now wish to expand their collection to include non-print media. Thus we now have books in electronic format, CDs, and DVDs, in addition to printed books. Also, the library wants to include some periodicals, which are to be handled differently from the other books. For instance, recent periodicals cannot be checked out. For CDs and DVDs, we wish to keep track of the duration.

If we do not add any other classes, all these variations have to be accommodated within the `Book` class. Consider the use case for issuing a book. The operations needed are the same: check issuability, compute a due date, and record the transaction. We could handle these simply by making changes in the methods of the existing `Book` class.

To simplify the discussion, we restrict ourselves to two types of items that the library lends: books and periodicals. Even with this simplification, we need a mechanism to find out what item (that is, a book or a periodical) we are dealing with when we process these transactions. One approach could be to add a field `bookType` to the class `Book`, which would tell us what kind of a `book` it is. We would make changes in the method that computes the due date by switching on the field `bookType`. Periodicals that are less than three months old are not issuable; otherwise, they can be borrowed for a week. Another difference is that periodicals have no authors.
Let us re-write `Book` with these enhancements. New fields are added to hold the `bookType` and `dateAcquired` and we also declare constants to designate the type of the book

```
private String title;
private String author;
private String id;
private Member borrowedBy;
private List holds = new LinkedList();
private Calendar dueDate;
private int bookType;
private Calendar dateAcquired;
public static final int BOOK = 1;
public static final int PERIODICAL = 2;
```

Since periodicals and books store different values, we need two constructors: to create a periodical, we use the constructor with two parameters because periodicals have no `author` parameter.

```
public Book(String title, String author, String id) {
  this.title = title;
  this.author = author;
  this.id = id;
  this.type = BOOK;
}
public Book(String title, String id) {
  this.title = title;
  this.id = id;
  this.type = PERIODICAL;
  this.dateAcquired = new GregorianCalendar();
  this.dateAcquired.setTimeInMillis(System.currentTimeMillis());
}
```

The user interface should allow the user to specify what kind of item is being added to the library. This will require a conditional that will not ask for an author if the item being added is a periodical.

```
public void addBooks() {
```

```
  Book result;
  do {
    String title = getToken("Enter  title");
    String bookID = getToken("Enter id");
    if (yesOrNo("Is this a  book?")) {
      String author = getToken("Enter author");
      result = library.addBook(title, author, bookID);
    } else {
      result = library.addPeriodical(title, bookID);
    }
    if (result != null) {
      System.out.println(result);
    } else {
      System.out.println("Book could not be added");
    }
    if (!yesOrNo("Add more books?")) {
      break;
    }
  } while (true);
}
```

The method in the UI invokes a different method of `Library` in each case. Accordingly, `Library` provides two methods, one to add periodicals and one to add books.

```
public Book addBook(String title, String author, String id) {
  Book book = new Book(title, author, id);
  if (catalog.insertBook(book)) {
    return (book);
  }
  return null;
}

//new method added for periodical
public Book addPeriodical(String title,  String id) {
  Book book = new Book(title,  id);
  if (catalog.insertBook(book)) {
    return (book);
  }
  return null;
}
```

Let us examine some other methods in `Book`. The process of issuing a book is different from that of a periodical, and that is reflected in the new `issue()` method. The `cutoffDate` is computed and compared against `dateAcquired` to decide if the periodical can be issued.

```
public boolean issue(Member member) {
  borrowedBy = member;
  dueDate = new GregorianCalendar();
  switch (bookType) {
    case PERIODICAL:
      Calendar cutoffDate = new GregorianCalendar();
      cutoffDate.setTimeInMillis(System.currentTimeMillis());
      cutoffDate.add(Calendar.MONTH, -3);
      if (cutoffDate.after(dateAcquired)) {
        dueDate.add(Calendar.WEEK_OF_MONTH, 1);
      } else {
        return false;
      }
      break;
    case BOOK:
      dueDate.add(Calendar.MONTH, 1);
      break;
  }
  return true;
}
```

The getAuthor and toString methods also differ because of the absence of a specific author for periodicals.

```
public String getAuthor() {
  if (bookType == PERIODICAL) {
    return "";
  }
  return author;
}

public String toString() {
  if (bookType == BOOK) {
    return "title " + title + " author " + author + " id " + id
        + " borrowed by " + borrowedBy;
  } else {
    return "title " + title + " id " + id + " borrowed by " +
        borrowedBy + " Acquired  on "
        + dateAcquired.getTime().toString();
  }
}
```

Likewise, all methods that have different behavior for books and periodicals will be modified, and this behavior will be decided based on the value stored in bookType. The above enhancement is exactly how a procedural design would be modified. The process varies slightly for each type of data, and this variation is accounted for within the same procedural unit by switching on the kind of data.

#### 7.3.1.1 Drawbacks of this Approach

We have two fundamental goals:

- The system should be easy to build and test.
- The system should be easily reusable.

It is clear that such an approach involves storing more of the complexity of the system in one class (that is, `Book`) and its methods. This makes the system difficult to build and test. A combinatorial explosion occurs when program segments use a lot of branch statements. Consider, for instance, a method with two `switch` statements, one following the other, each of which has five possible cases. We now have a total of 25 possible computational paths when this method executes. This complexity behooves upon the programmer to put in assertions to catch all exceptional behaviors or, in critical systems, employ some form of formal verification. Our focus should therefore be to produce simpler methods.

A second set of problems arises when we apply the reusability requirement. For a system to be considered highly reusable, changes to the requirements should be incorporated with minimal changes to components that have already been implemented. Changes to business processes, as we well know, are inevitable. In our system, these changes can take two forms: (i) the procedures for performing library operations may change and (ii) we may add new categories of items to the library. The kind of structure that we have affects our ability to modify the code in both these situations. When a procedure changes, say we have some new rules for issuing books, we want to ensure that in re-writing the `issue()` method, we are not ruining the procedure for periodicals. This also means that when testing the system after the changes, we need to test for both books and periodicals. A similar situation develops when we add new categories of items. The existing methods are changed to accommodate one more case, and once again, we need assurance of system behavior for the new items added as well as for the ones that were already in place.

### 7.3.2 Using Inheritance to Improve the Design

As we saw earlier, the existing implementation had to be modified when new items were added. What we shall see now, by contrast, is that inheritance allows us to reuse the existing implementation when new classes are added.

In our example, we are introducing new kinds of items to the library and would like to shield the system by encapsulating the new items in separate classes. In this context, it is useful to ask: Is there a set of guiding principles that can be employed when we introduce inheritance to incorporate the new items? Such principles can then be used to guide the design of our inheritance hierarchy. In practice, software designers are often confronted with situations where changes not anticipated during design need to be incorporated. A closely related question, therefore, would be: Is there a systematic procedure that we can employ when introducing inheritance? We shall now discuss answers to the above questions as we revisit the process of adding periodicals to the library.

#### 7.3.2.1 Designing the Hierarchy

As discussed above, we now have two classes, `Book` and `Periodical`. The original design did not have the `Periodical` class and therefore we need to decide how it will be related to `Book`. Two obvious choices present themselves (see Figure 7.1).

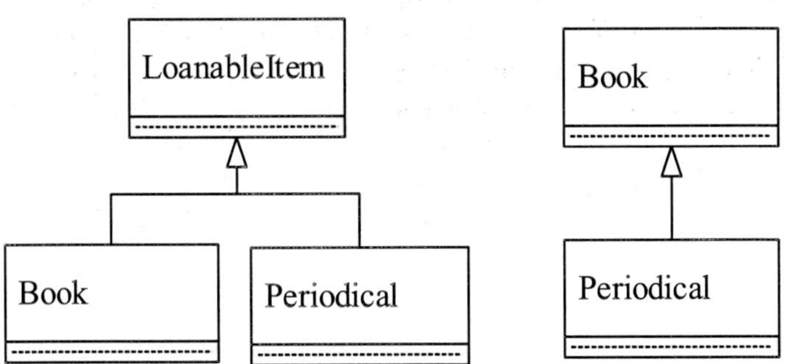


**Fig. 7.1** Two hierarchies for library items.

- **Option 1:** *One class inherits from the other.* Since a `Book` class is already present, `Periodical` simply extends `Book` and overrides the necessary attributes. None of the other classes need to be changed.
- **Option 2:** *Both classes share a common ancestor.* In this hierarchy, we have an ancestor class `LoanableItem` with two descendants, `Book` and `Periodical`. The common ancestor is an abstract class that contains the shared attributes. `Catalog` is defined as a collection of `LoanableItem` and the the other classes in the system (`Library`, `Member`, etc.) will be redefined to deal with `LoanableItem` (instead of `Book`).

**The open–closed principle**

An important (some would argue the most important) guiding tenet of object-oriented design can be summed up in what is referred to as the open–closed principle (OCP):

*A module must be Open for Extension but Closed for Implementation.*

*Extension* is the process by which new features are added to existing software, and *Implementation* is the process that converts an abstract design into concrete code. What this statement implies is that our classes and modules must be written in such a manner that they can be extended, that is, new features can be added, without re-opening the completed implementation, that is, without need for modification of the existing code.

It is obvious that OCP is highly desirable, but a deeper understanding is needed when we apply it. Adding new features to software often requires changes to existing classes. This is a non-trivial task, but the propagation of the effects of change can be contained by proper encapsulation. Sometimes changes can mostly be handled by defining a separate class that incorporates the new features and have only a minimal effect on other classes. This new class, however, needs to be related in some way with the existing classes, *without changing their implementation.* The primary mechanism for enabling this is to define the abstraction in a superclass and place the variations in concrete subclasses. Without an inheritance hierarchy, such a feat would be impossible to accomplish; inheritance allows us to extend software by adding features through new implementations of the same abstraction, even though the abstract ancestor class and the existing concrete implementations remain closed. A naive application of inheritance will not satisfy OCP; a thorough understanding of how the implementation will be extended is essential.

When we have a system with an existing `Book` class, Option 1 can be attractive because the system can be modified and tested more easily. However, there are two significant disadvantages:

- *Dependency on a concrete class.* Since `Periodical` inherits from `Book`, the correct implementation of `Periodical` depends on another concrete implementation.
- *Type conformance.* Inheritance represents an "is a" relationship. Depending on how the two kinds of item are defined, this relationship may not hold. In other words, the type of `Periodical` may not be a true subtype of `Book`.

Let is turn our attention to Option 2. We can make two simple observations about books and periodicals.

- There are many commonalities among them. For example, both have titles, due dates if issued, and methods for getting attributes such as titles and IDs.
- There are also differences: while books and periodicals can both be issued, the process of issuing is different.

**The dependency inversion principle**

Any system that needs to be up and running for a long time needs stability. Simply put, the stability of a system is the amount of work that needs to be put in to disturb the existing equilibrium. If left undisturbed, an unstable system may remain stable for a long time, but with very little effort the equilibrium can be disturbed. Extending the notion to a situation where we have several subsystems within a system, consider something like a house, which has several components: a foundation, a wall structure, a roof, and a dish antenna. The roof depends upon the wall structure, which in turn depends on the foundation. The dish antenna is clearly the least stable of all the parts, and therefore it is very undesirable to depend on it. On the other hand, we want the foundation to be very stable, since all the other components are dependent on it. Since the roof depends on the wall structure, we want to ensure that the wall structure is at least as stable as the roof. To summarize, we want to *depend in the direction of stability.* This rule is often referred to as the **stable dependencies principle (SDP)**. In our case study with the library, we want to ensure that `LoanableItem` is very stable, since the hierarchy depends on it.

In the realm of software, this has some interesting consequences. In general, implementations are concrete and therefore inherently unstable. Abstractions do not specify details and thus remain flexible, which makes them more stable when changes need to be incorporated. Thus we can state the following simple thumb rule, often called the dependency inversion principle:

*Depend upon abstractions; avoid depending upon concrete implementations.*

Intuitively, we can have a superclass that captures the commonalities and subclasses to encapsulate the differences. Hence it is worthwhile to explore the second design choice, which leads us to have an abstract class `LoanableItem` on which all the concrete implementations depend. The inheritance structure is translated into code as follows:

```
public abstract class LoanableItem {
  // code common to all types of items that the library lends
}
public class Book extends LoanableItem {
  // code specific to books
```

```
}
public class Periodical extends LoanableItem {
  // code specific to periodicals
}
```

In the process of filling in the details for these classes, we will decide how these items are created and added to the collection, what attributes are placed in each class, and how the common code is factored out.

**The Liskov substitution principle**

The Liskov substitution principle, named after Barbara Liskov, can be informally stated as follows:
*Any superclass object should be substitutable by a subclass object.*
The seeds of this originated with Bertrand Meyer, who first proposed the idea in his 1988 book[5]. Meyer, and later on, Pierre America[1], made attempts to formalize the notion of subtype, but the issue was finally settled by Liskov and Wing in 1994[3].
Polymorphic assignments can result in methods being invoked on a subclass object. Certifying substitutatbility is complicated, because we cannot think of all possible contexts in which the subclass object may substitute a superclass object. It is therefore useful to formalize the notion. If we view the superclass object's expected behavior as a contract, the subclass object must uphold this contract. We shall discuss the implications of this in a later chapter.
From a practical point of view, what we understand is extending an existing class to accommodate new requirements can be dangerous. It is therefore preferable to define an abstract supertype and extend this to define any number of concrete subtypes. In all contexts, the code is dependent only on the abstract supertype, and therefore we do not face the problem of a concrete subclass extending another concrete superclass. In situations where an existing concrete implementation needs to be reused by another concrete class, we prefer to use composition, that is, the composite reuse principle, often summarized by the phrase *"Favor composition over inheritance"*[2]. This principle advocates that designers should achieve code reuse through composition (by containing instances of other classes that implement the desired functionality) rather than inheritance from a base or parent class.

#### 7.3.2.2 Changes to Other Classes

The main purpose of creating such a hierarchy is to protect all the client classes from changes that occur within the hierarchy. The client classes would now depend on the stable abstraction provided by `LoanableItem` to perform operations common to all types of loanable items. Such code in Library will now invoke methods through references of type LoanableItem, and Catalog is defined as a collection of LoanableItem.

### 7.3.3 Invoking the Constructors

Let us examine the process for adding new items to the library collection. Since the UI knows about the different kinds of items, the method for adding items can query the user about the kind of item, collect the necessary parameters, and invoke the method in Library. In our earlier implementation, we had separate methods for books and periodicals; this makes the implementation unstable since adding new kinds of items requires adding methods to Library. Let us say we can do this with a single method, addLoanableItem. The code in the UI would be something like this:

```
private static final int BOOK = 1;     // declaring the constants
private static final int PERIODICAL = 2;
public void addLoanableItems() {
  LoanableItem result;
  do {
    String typeString = getToken("Enter type: "
                                 + BOOK + " for books\n"
                                 + PERIODICAL +
                                 " for periodicals\n");
    int type = Integer.parseInt(typeString);
    String title = getToken("Enter title");
    String author = null;
    if (type == BOOK) {
      author = getToken("Enter author");
    }
    String id = getToken("Enter id");
    result = library.addLoanableItem(type, title, author, id);
    if (result != null) {
      System.out.println(result);
    } else {
      System.out.println("Item could not be added");
    }
    if (!yesOrNo("Add more Items?")) {
      break;
    }
  } while (true);
}
```

### Things to remember when creating an inheritance hierarchy

**Do not rush in too soon.** Remember that inheritance is a relationship between well-understood abstractions and the hierarchy usually emerges "naturally" in our process. This takes time, except in situations where our data has a pre-existing taxonomy. This implies that we should have a *clear data abstraction in mind before constructing the hierarchy.*

**Allow for future expansion.** Keep in mind that we cannot guess how our system might be used; the best way to plan for that is to be generous when allowing for variations. The rules for this are:

- *Define methods to be as general as possible at each level of an inheritance hierarchy.* When writing methods, avoid details that are too specifically tailored for the current set of subclasses; the methods should abstract out common functionality so that subclasses can invoke the superclass method to perform some of the tasks.
- *Be generous in defining data types and storage to avoid difficult changes later on.* For example, you might consider using a variable of type `double` even though your current data may only require a `float` variable.

**Make sure the construction is secure.** Since we do not know how our system will be used, it is imperative that we do not allow any legal usage to compromise its integrity.

- *Choose the right access modifiers for your attributes.* Applying the optimal access levels to members of a class hierarchy makes the hierarchy easier to maintain by allowing you to control how such members will be used. Declare class members with access modifiers that provide the least amount of access feasible.
- *Only expose items that are needed by derived classes.* Keeping fields `private` helps descendants and clients by reducing naming conflicts and protects them from using items that may need to be changed at a later stage. Members that are only needed by descendants should be marked as `protected`. This ensures that only the derived classes are dependent on these members and makes it easier to update these members during development.
- *The functionality provided by the methods of the base class should not depend on features that can be overridden.* Make sure that base class methods do not depend on features that can be changed by inheriting classes.

The method in `Library` must now decide what kind of item to create. This goes against our philosophy of making the facade as independent as possible of the different types of loanable items. The code becomes less cohesive, so we should be looking for a different approach.

Before proposing solutions, let us take another look at why an inheritance hierarchy is a good idea. We wanted to avoid too much complexity in one class and its methods, so we tried to get rid of conditionals that switched on the type of item by creating a separate subclass for each type, with a common abstract superclass. When invoking the methods on items from this hierarchy, we only refer to the type of the abstract superclass and let dynamic binding take care of the rest. Effectively, we have moved the complexity of the conditional out of the application code and into the interpreter. Dynamic binding works because the system keeps track of the actual concrete subclass of the object, even though the reference is stored in a variable declared to have the type of the superclass. When we are invoking constructors, we are yet to create the object, and so we cannot rely on dynamic binding to make the choice for us. What this implies is that *the conditionals in the constructor invocation cannot be eliminated.* In other words, conditionals that switch on the input cannot be eliminated using dynamic binding, unlike conditionals that switch on stored values. (In a sense, creating new objects is like getting new input, and conditionals on the input are essential for any non-trivial program.) The consequence of all this for our design is that the class that chooses the appropriate constructor will undergo change. Our goal is to protect `Library` from these changes, and some brainstorming gives us three possibilities:

- **Option 1:** One possibility is to extend `Library` and redefine `addLoanableItem()` whenever new types of items are added.
- **Option 2:** A second option is to move the constructor logic into the abstract superclass `LoanableItem`.
- **Option 3:** Third, we could develop a new class that takes care of creating the items.

The first choice is easily dismissed; when we extend `Library`, all the classes that depend on it must change. `Library` is a facade and we can therefore expect several other modules to depend on it, which implies that the stability of this module is critical. The other two options share a common underlying principle of designing for change:

*To protect the stability of a module, move the aspects that are likely to change to a different module.*

Option 2 suggests that we move this to the class `LoanableItem`. This might seem like a logical assignment of responsibilities, since the constructor invocation is in some way related to the inheritance hierarchy. A closer scrutiny reveals, however, that this would essentially defeat the purpose of introducing inheritance. The abstract superclass is designed to be a *stable abstraction* that protects the client classes from changes in the hierarchy. It follows that `LoanableItem` should be designed to be unaware of the structure of the hierarchy that lies under it. This leaves us with Option 3, requiring that we create a new module to encapsulate the changes that occur to the logic for invoking constructors. Not surprisingly, this is a commonly occurring problem, and this is, in fact, the standard approach for dealing with this.

A **factory** is typically employed when we want to make a system independent of how its products are created, composed, and represented. In this case, we would like to make `Library` independent of the process of creating the items. The factory provides a method that can be invoked for creating a new object and thus encapsulates the logic for invocation of constructors. The code for `LoanableItemFactory` is shown below.

```
public class LoanableItemFactory {
  private static final int BOOK = 1;
  private static final int PERIODICAL = 2;
  private static LoanableItemFactory loanableItemFactory;
  private LoanableItemFactory() {
  }
  public static LoanableItemFactory instance() {
    if (loanableItemFactory == null) {
      loanableItemFactory = new LoanableItemFactory());
    }
    return loanableItemFactory;
  }
  public LoanableItem createLoanableItem(Request request) {
    switch (request.getItemType()) {
      case BOOK:
        return new Book(title, author, id);
      case PERIODICAL:
        return new Periodical(title, id);
      default:
        return null;
    }
  }
}
```

The above code defines `LoanableItemFactory` as a singleton that creates objects of type `LoanableItem`. The method `addLoanableItem()` in `Library` is modified as follows:

```
public Result addLoanableItem(Request request) {
  Result result = new Result();
  LoanableItemFactory factory =  LoanableItemFactory.instance();
  LoanableItem item = factory.createLoanableItem(request);
  if (catalog.insertBook(item)) {
    result.setResultCode(Result.OPERATION_COMPLETED);
    result.setLoanableItemFields(item);
    return result;
  }
```

```
  result.setResultCode(Result.OPERATION_FAILED);
  return result;
}
```

### 7.3.4 Distributing the Responsibilities

Next we turn to the task of distributing the attributes and responsibilities across the hierarchy. This is perhaps the most difficult part of designing the hierarchy and requires considerable experience on the part of the software designers. It is useful to keep in mind that we are implementing in a manner that allows the classes in the business logic subsystem to be unaware of the structure of the hierarchy itself. This means that any method that is invoked by code in these classes must be a method of `LoanableItem`. We may also have to store the fields and assign access modifiers based on these considerations. With all this in mind, we start with the following minimum set of attributes for our abstract class.

```
public abstract class LoanableItem implements Serializable,
                                              Matchable<String> {
  private String title;
  private String id;
  protected Member borrowedBy;
  protected Calendar dueDate;
  public boolean matches(String other) {
    return (this.id.equals(id));
  }
  public String getTitle() {
    return title;
  }
  public String getId() {
    return id;
  }
  public Member getBorrower() {
    return borrowedBy;
  }
  public String getDueDate() {
    return (dueDate.getTime().toString());
  }
  // other fields and methods
}
```

The fields `title` and `id` are to be immutable and are therefore defined as `private`. The other fields have been declared `protected` so that they may be accessed by the descendants.

Next, consider a method like getAuthor(). We have the following options which can be justified:

- **Option 1:** Make author a field of the Book class. This is justified by the fact that books have authors, and periodicals do not.
- **Option 2:** Make author a field of the LoanableItem class. We may eventually add other kinds of items, most of which will have authors. We can take care of periodicals by making the author an empty string.

Before resolving this, it is important to understand the difference between the abstraction that a class represents and its implementation. The abstraction defines how the objects of the class interact with other elements of the software system. The abstraction has an associated contract that specifes this behavior; the implementation is obliged to conform to this specification. This brings us to the question: What should the implementation contain? Clearly all the elements essential to the abstraction must be present to satisfy the contract; if we include elements not essential to the abstraction, we are venturing outside the specification of the contract. If we apply this understanding to the Periodical class, the author field does not belong to the specification, and hence should not be present in the implementation. If we place the author field in LoanableItem, the implementation of all the subclasses contains this field, and therefore so will the implementation of Periodical. This idea is also embodied in the **interface segregation principle (ISP)** which states that a client should not be forced to depend on methods it does not use, which implies that the interface of a class should not contain unused methods. In our case, a client of Periodical has no use for getAuthor(), which means that author should not be part of the interface for Periodical, that is, it cannot be part of the interface f LoanableItem.

The above argument seems to have resolved the issue, but unfortunately, things are sometimes more complicated. Say that we are not building a system from scratch, but are adding features to an existing system. Our system may already contain a class Book; we now have to refactor the system to replace Book with the LoanableItem hierarchy. When we do this, we also replace all occurrences of Book with LoanableItem, which in turn requires that the interface for LoanableItem should honor all the requirements in the interface of Book. This will place author and getauthor() in LoanableItem.

### The interface segregation principle

The interface segregation principle (ISP) states that no client should be forced to depend on methods it does not use. ISP was first formulated by Robert C Martin while consulting for Xerox. A new printer system capable of performing a variety of tasks (stapling, faxing, etc.) had been created. The software for this system had one large `Job` class, which was being called whenever any task had to be performed. As the software grew, methods specific to several clients were added, which resulted in a "fat" class. Making modifications became very difficult, which in turn slowed down the development process. Martin applied the dependency inversion principle and added an interface between the tasks and the `Job` class. There were specific interfaces for stapling, faxing, etc., each of which was very lean. The `Job` class implemented all the interfaces. A staple job would only work through the stapling interface, and would be segregated from any changes to the methods for a faxing job.
If this principle is fully implemented, we see "role interfaces" which can be mixed and matched as needed. This avoids the unwanted coupling caused by fat interfaces. Applying ISP can result in a hierarchy of interfaces which give us layers of abstraction. Without layers of abstraction, systems become so coupled at multiple levels that it is no longer possible to make a change in one place without necessitating many additional changes.

We expect that the methods for processing holds will be similar for all items; these are therefore fully implemented in the abstract class to facilitate reuse. We would like to allow descendants to override them as necessary, which means that the list `holds` must be a protected attribute. All these additions to `LoanableItem` are shown below.

```
protected HoldList holds = new HoldList();
public Iterator<Hold> getHolds() {
    return holds.iterator();
}
public void placeHold(Hold hold) {
    holds.addHold(hold);
}
public void removeHold(String memberId) {
   holds.removeHoldOnMember(memberId);
}
public Hold getNextHold() {
    return holds.getNextValidHold();
}
public boolean hasHold(){
```

```
        return !holds.isEmpty();
    }
```

### 7.3.5 Factoring Responsibilities across the Hierarchy

The attributes listed above are the ones we selected for the common ancestor. As noted earlier, descendants can override these as needed. Next we examine the responsibilities that are handled in a shared manner between the ancestor and the descendants. Typically, these methods have some common code that can be factored out and placed in the common ancestor and other code specific to each type that is implemented in the descendants.

The first one we examine is the constructor. This is relatively simple in Java, since a constructor for any subclass must first invoke the superclass constructor. The constructor for `LoanableItem` is `protected` and stores the values of the common fields `title` and `id`.

```
protected LoanableItem(String title, String id) {
  this.title = title;
  this.id = id;
}
```

The constructor for `Book` must set the value for `author`.

```
public Book(String title, String author, String id) {
  super(title, id);
  this.author = author;
}
```

The constructor for `Periodical` needs to store the date of acquisition, and a private field is defined for that. The date itself can be generated using the system clock.

```
private Calendar dateAcquired;
public Periodical(String title, String id) {
  super(title, id);
  this.dateAcquired = new GregorianCalendar(); // sets current
  date and time
}
```

Next we consider methods like `toString()`. Part of this responsibility can be handled by the superclass methods, and the subclass methods simply append the additional information. In the code shown below, the method `LoanableItem` concatenates the fields `title`, `id`, and `borrowedBy`.

```
public String toString() {
  return " title " + title +  " id " + id + " borrowed by "
```

```
  + borrowedBy;
}
```

Both subclasses append their types to the string returned by the superclass method. In addition, `Book` appends the `author` field and `Periodical` appends `dateAcquired`.

```
public String toString() {
  return "Book " +  " author " + author + super.toString();
}

public String toString() {
  return "Periodical " + super.toString() + "\n  Acquired On "
         + dateAcquired.getTime().toString();
}
```

Some methods can have more involved cooperation across the hierarchy. Let us examine the method for issuing an item, which involves checking issuability, assigning the item to a `Member` object, and generating and storing the due date. Both checking of issuability and generation of due date involve rules specific to the items. The only common activity is that of assigning the item to a `Member`, which can be factored out. In Java, the process of due date generation can be simplified if we assign the current date as due date (Step 1) and then add the period of loan (Step 2). Step 1 can also be factored out, giving us the following `issue` method for `LoanableItem`.

```
public boolean issue(Member member){
  if (borrowedBy != null) {
    return false;
  }
  dueDate = new GregorianCalendar();
  borrowedBy = member;
  return true;
}
```

`Book` does not have any additional rules for issuability, so it simply invokes the superclass method and adds the loan period, that is, one month, if the superclass method returns `true`.

```
public boolean issue(Member member) {
  if (super.issue(member)) {
    dueDate.add(Calendar.MONTH, 1); //add loan period
    return true;
  } else {
    return false;
  }
}
```

The method in `Periodical` must first ensure that the periodical is at least three months old before it invokes the superclass method. The loan period of one week is added if the periodical can be issued.

```
public boolean issue(Member member) {
  Calendar cutoffDate = new GregorianCalendar();
  cutoffDate.add(Calendar.MONTH, -3);
  if (cutoffDate.after(dateAcquired)) {
    if (super.issue(member)){
      dueDate.add(Calendar.WEEK_OF_MONTH, 1);
      return true;
    }
  }
  return false;
}
```

## 7.4 Combining Inheritance and Composition

There are two aspects to any concrete class: the abstraction (type) that it represents and the implementation it provides. The abstraction can be captured in an interface, and if a programmer wishes to create a new class that shares the abstraction, we can define the new class to implement that interface. On the other hand, when the implementation needs to be reused, the new class contains a reference to an object of the existing class, that is, we employ object composition. Sometimes we have situations where both the type and implementation have to be inherited, but directly extending the existing class is not an option. We discuss two such examples here.

### 7.4.1 The Java `Thread` Class

Software systems often have to employ run-time structures called concurrent sequential processes (CSPs). A simple example of a CSP can be found in the implementation of a bank account. The customer (owner of the account) could be using an ATM to withdraw cash at the same time when a transaction for depositing a check is being processed. Both these actions represent concurrent processes which access a piece of shared data (the account information). In this situation, it is vital to ensure that both processes do not try to simultaneously modify the `balance` field in the account; in such simultaneous access, depending on the order in which the methods for deposit and withdrawal are executed, we could end up with an error.

Java provides a class called `Thread` that can be used for implementing CSPs. In our example, we would have a separate thread for every process that accesses the account object; that is, if a withdrawal and deposit were to be simultaneously carried out, there would be a thread for the withdrawal process and another thread for the deposit. We can then employ mutual exclusion on the account object, which will ensure that the account is not simultaneously accessed by the two processes. Threads can be suspended, made to sleep for a specified period of time, assigned priorities, share resources, etc.

For any particular threaded application, we have a specific set of tasks that need to be performed on the thread. These tasks are specified through the `run()` method. Since `Thread` is a class, we can create a new class that has all the features of `Thread` through inheritance, and redefine the `run()` method to suit our application. The thread is activated by invoking the `start()` method, which invokes `run()`. However, since Java does not support multiple inheritance, this approach does not allow the user to create a class that extends another existing class and also has all the properties of `Thread`.
As with all reuse, there are two adaptations required (Figure 7.2):

- *Structure the implementation to enable reuse.* This is done by allowing the creation of a `Thread` object, which can use the `run()` method of the application. Java provides a `Thread` constructor that accepts a reference to a `Runnable` target; in this case, `start()` is defined to invoke the `run()` method on the `Runnable` target.
- *Create applications that enable reuse.* Since all the variations across multiple applications are captured in the `run()` method, we encapsulate this method in a separate interface, called `Runnable`. Therefore we create applications that implement `Runnable`, and place the application-specific tasks in the `run()` method.

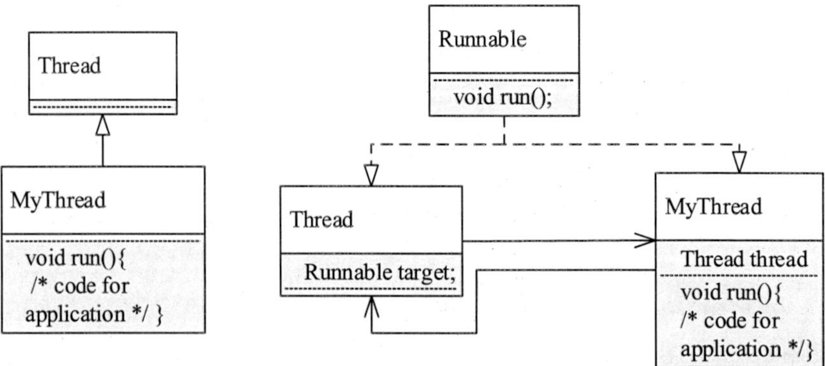


**Fig. 7.2** Two ways of reusing the `Thread` class. The application class can directly inherit from `Thread`, or composition can be employed to connect the reusable part of `Thread` with the `run()` method of the application.

#### 7.4.1.1 A Simple Example

The following example creates a simple "clock" that prints "tic" and "toc" at regular intervals.

```
public class Clock implements Runnable {
  Thread thread = new Thread(this);
  String sound = "tic";
  public void run() {
    try {
      while (true) {
        System.out.println(sound);
        sound = "toc";
        Thread.sleep(1000);
        System.out.println(sound);
        sound = "tic";
        Thread.sleep(1000);
      }
    } catch (InterruptedException ie){
    }
  }
  public Clock() {
    thread.start();
  }
  public static void main (String[] args) {
    new Clock();
  }
}
```

The `run()` method contains an infinite loop that alternately prints the words "tic" and "toc" with a 1000-millisecond delay between consecutive words. This process continues until interrupted by the user.

The `Runnable` interface requires that `Clock` implement the `run()` method. Inside `Clock`, we create a `Thread`, storing this reference in `thread`. A reference to the `Clock` object, that is, our application, is passed to `thread`. (The parameter being supplied here is required to be of type `Runnable`.) The `start()` method of `Thread` is invoked in the `Clock` constructor, and this method in turn invokes the `run()` method of the `Clock` object. In this interface, a `Thread` object is encapsulated along with the class to provide "thread-like" properties to the objects of the class. In essence, what we have done here is to achieve the benefits of inheritance using object composition.

### 7.4.2 Reusing the `Person` Class in `Faculty` and `Student`

A question that confronts object-oriented designers is: In what situations is it appropriate to introduce an inheritance heirarchy? A common mistake beginners make is to extract commonalities and define a superclass, in the mistaken idea that they have facilitated reuse.

Consider the example of a simple university system. We have two classes, `Faculty` and `Student`, both of which have fields like name, address, date of birth, etc. It is tempting to extract these fields into a common superclass `Person`. How should we decide if this is the right thing to do?

To answer this, we go back to our analysis and design phases, where we identified the conceptual and software classes, and ask the following questions:

1. Does the abstraction `Person` correspond to a concept in the specification?
2. Does the need for defining the abstraction `Person` arise as a result of applying established class design principles during the design?
3. Is a class `Person` required to accomodate issues arising during implementation?

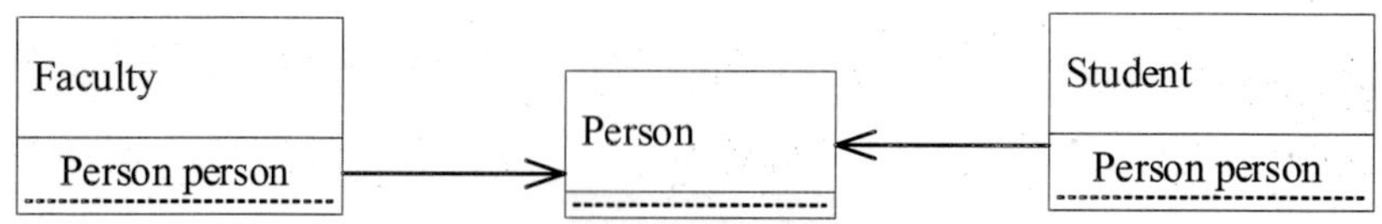


**Fig. 7.3** Reusing `Person` in `Faculty` and `Student` through composition.

If none of these answers is in the affirmative, we are most likely adding an unwanted layer to our class hierarchy. However, this does not address the issue of avoiding duplication of code. In order to avoid duplication, we can use object composition. This solution is represented in Figure 7.3. Both `Faculty` and `Student` hold a reference to a `Person` object and invoke its methods.

On the other hand, a reference to an abstraction for `Person` in the specifications does not automatically justify a `Person` superclass for `Faculty` and `Student`. It may be preferable to have a `Person` interface which is implemented by `Faculty` and `Student`. To avoid re-implementing the code, we could define a class `ConcretePerson` that implements the `Person` interface and store references to a `ConcretePerson` object in `Faculty` and `Student` (Figure 7.4).

Creation of a heirarchy is justified when we see the need for a `Person` hierarchy, and a potential need to introduce variations of `Person` during the lifetime of the software.

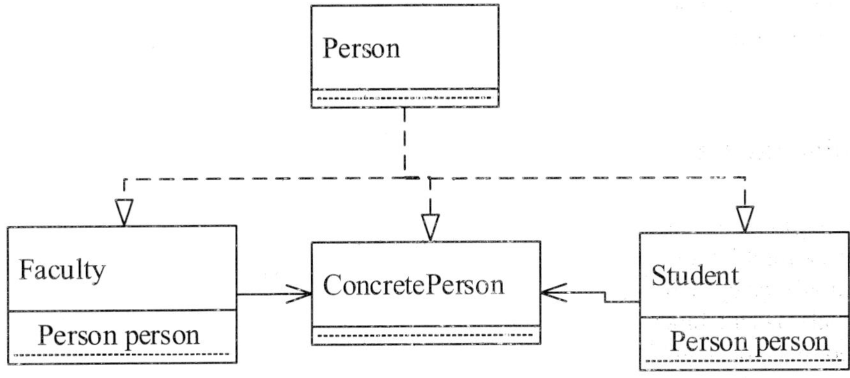


**Fig. 7.4** Defining a `Person` hierarchy through an interface.

## 7.5 The Importance of Substitutability for Reuse

Earlier in this chapter, we introduced the Liskov substitution principle (LSP). The difficulty of ensuring substitutability was one of the justifications for preferring a hierarchy with an abstract superclass over a solution where a concrete class was extended using inheritance. This approach is, however, not applicable in all situations, and sometimes, we have to extend concrete classes. It follows that a proper understanding of substitutability is essential for reusable software.

### 7.5.1 Extending a Simple Counter

Let us start with a simple example that shows us what can go wrong when we extend an existing class. Consider the class `Counter` shown below:

```
public class Counter {
  protected int index;
  public void up() {
     index++;
  }
  public void reset(){
    index = 0;
  }
  public int getValue(){
    return index;
```

```
  }
}
```

Say, we have class Tester with the method doSomething() that uses a Counter object to print the numbers zero through nine.

```
public  class Tester {
 public  void doSomething(Counter counter) {
  for (counter.reset(); counter.getValue() < 10; counter.up()){
     System.out.println(counter.getValue());
    }
  }
}
```

This would be invoked from the main program as shown below:

```
counter = new  Counter();
Tester tester = new Tester();
tester.doSomething(counter);
```

A key concept that underpins the notion of substitutability is the notion of **expected behavior.** Whenever a software system responds to any situation, it is expected to behave in a certain way. This expected behavior is predicated on the requirements. In keeping with this, let us define the expected behavior of doSomething(), as follows:
*The program outputs the numbers 0 through 9, one per line.*
A strictly enforced notion of substitutability will require that this expectation is met whenever this code is executed.
Say, we define a subclass of Counter, namely CounterSub, that allows us to increment the index by any fixed amount. This would be as follows:

```
public class CounterSub extends Counter {
  private int increment;
  public CounterSub(int value) {
    increment = value;
  }
  public void up() {
    index += increment;
  }
}
```

Suppose we tried to use CounterSub instead of Counter as shown below:

```
Counter counterSub = new CounterSub(2);
Tester tester = new Tester();
tester.doSomething(counterSub);
```

Since the value of index increases by 2 each time, the output we see are the numbers 0, 2, 4, 6 and 8, written one per line. This clearly does not meet our expectations.

### 7.5.2 Inheriting from an Abstract Superclass

The same situation can occur when we inherit from an abstract class. Say we have the following abstract class:

```
public abstract class AbstractCounter {
  protected int index;
  public void up() {
    index++;
  }
  public void reset() {
    index = 0;
  }
  public int getValue() {
    return index;
  }
}
```

The class `Tester` could be designed to accept any object that extends `AbstractCounter`, as shown below.

```
public class Tester {
  public void doSomething(AbstractCounter counter) {
    for (counter.reset(); counter.getValue() < 10; counter.up()) {
      System.out.println(counter.getValue());
    }
  }
}
```

When an object of type `Counter1`, shown below, is passed to `doSomething()`, the behavior would be as expected.

```
public class Counter1 extends AbstractCounter {
  public Counter1() {
    index = 0;
  }
}
```

An object of class `Counter2`, shown below, when passed as a parameter in `doSomething(new Counter2(2))` would result in a different output.

```
public class Counter2 extends AbstractCounter {
  private int value;
  public Counter2(int val) {
    value = val;
  }
  public void up() {
    index += value;
```

```
  }
}
```

### 7.5.3 Upgrading to a Generalized Counter

The kind of problem that we saw above is not restricted to defining subclasses. When software is upgraded, it is often accompanied by new versions of classes. The existing applications that were running the old versions of the classes must continue to be fully operational. To the inexperienced software developer, the following generalized version of `Counter` may seem like a good idea. It allows us to create objects that behave like the old `Counter` as well as objects that behave like `CounterSub`.

```
public class Counter {
  private int index;
  private int increment;
  public Counter() {
    increment = 1;
  }
  public Counter(int value) {
    increment = value;
  }
  public void up() {
    index += increment;
  }
  public void reset() {
    index = 0;
  }
  public int getValue() {
    return index;
  }
}
```

However, the following code will produce an unexpected output:

```
counter = new Counter(2);
Tester tester = new Tester();
tester.doSomething(counter);
```

### 7.5.4 Defining, Protecting, and Programming to an Abstraction

Clearly none of the approaches described in the previous subsections can ensure strict substitutability. To understand how we can alleviate such problems, let us start by asking ourselves: Why do we expect that the code for `doSomething()` will produce the expected behavior?
The answer we get is: because we expect that `counter.reset()` will cause `counter.getValue()` to return zero, and `counter.up()` will cause an increase of one in the value returned by `counter.getValue()`.

Thus we see that the expected behavior is, in fact, dependent on the behavior of the class `Counter`. We can now turn our attention to the abstraction associated with the original `Counter` class. The field `index` stores an integer value; this value is set to zero by the method `reset()`, and increased by one by the method `up()`. A client method like `doSomething()` behaves in a reasonable way as long as these properties are respected by the object that is passed as a parameter. In order to facilitate reuse, these properties have to be clearly spelt out when we *define* this abstraction.

We can use some language features to *protect* the abstraction. For instance, the field `index` can be declared to be `private`, and the methods `reset()`, `up()`, and `getValue()` can be declared as `final`. In this situation, regardless of how it is extended, the client method `doSomething()` behaves in a reasonable way.

Such protections can sometimes be too restrictive, and not always possible to enforce. Hence there is a need for software developers to properly document the necessary properties of the abstraction, and write extension code in a manner that respects these properties, that is, *program to the abstraction*. The Liskov substitution principle provides a framework that speaks to all these issues, as we shall see in a later chapter.

## 7.6 Discussion and Further Reading

The mechanism of reuse is often a justification for preferring the object-oriented approach over the procedural one. Reuse obviously allows us to reduce the cost of software development, since we need to develop fewer lines of code. What is also interesting is that designing for reuse also results in controlling the complexity of the system. Some preparation is required to design the software in a manner that enables reuse; in most situations, it also reduces the "description complexity" of the resulting system. In addition, commonly recurring situations have been cataloged as design patterns, decreasing the cost of development. In today's world, it is therefore imperative that all

### Introducing an inheritance hierarchy through refactoring

We sometimes encounter situations in legacy systems where an inheritance hierarchy needs to be introduced in order to clean up the existing code. One has to be especially careful when attempting such an exercise since the dependencies involved can be quite complex. A well-designed, systematic procedure can significantly reduce the chances of errors. The following steps can serve as a guide.

**Replace Conditional with Polymorphism** If you have a conditional that chooses different behavior depending on some feature of the object, move each leg of the conditional to an overriding method in a (possibly newly defined) subclass and make the original method abstract. The steps involved in applying this rule are as follows:

1. Identify a conditional statement in a method that changes its behavior based on the value stored in a particular field. In a large class, it is quite likely that there will be several methods where variation in behavior is obtained by switching on the same field.
2. If the conditional statement is part of a larger method, the conditional may have to be extracted using the Extract Method rule (Chapter 5). If such extraction is not easily done, the class may have to be re-examined more closely.
3. Define an inheritance hierarchy where the subclasses reflect the variations in the field on which we are switching.
4. Create a subclass method that overrides the conditional statement method. Copy one leg of the conditional into each of the subclass methods and adjust the code so that it fits.
5. Remove the conditional from the superclass method and make it abstract. If appropriate, remove the field on which the switching was done.

Note that once the switching is removed, we may no longer need the field to track the variation in the type of the object.

developers learn the language used to describe systems and become familiar with standard design patterns.

### 7.6.1 Language Mechanisms for Reuse

Object composition and inheritance are the two most common mechanisms for reuse in object-oriented design. In both these mechanisms, the implementation of the new class is defined in terms of the functionality of the existing classes. In case of inheritance, since the internal details of the ancestor class are often visible to the descendant, the resulting scenario is referred to as "white-box reuse." On the other hand, object composition requires that the component classes have well-defined interfaces, so that they can be used as "black-boxes."

Object composition has the obvious advantage of keeping the inheritance hierarchies small, thus reducing the complexity of the system. Also, properties that are not naturally tied to one another are kept separate, so that each class is kept encapsulated and focused on one task. A less obvious advantage is that composition allows us to define the object dynamically at run-time. In our example, `Clock` has been defined *statically,* since `thread` will always hold a reference to a `Thread` object. The following example shows how composition can be used to define an object *dynamically*:

```
public class Catalog {
  private List catalogList;
  public Catalog (List list) {
    catalogList = list;
    //other constructor code
  }
  // other fields and methods
}
```

In this case, any object belonging to any class that satisfies the `List` interface can be sent as a parameter to the constructor. For instance, we could do the following:

```
catalog = new Catalog(new ArrayList());
```

This would create a catalog that uses an `ArrayList` to store the collection of books. Note that such a dynamic definition is possible because `Catalog` is defined by composition; if it had been defined as an extension of, say, `LinkedList`, this would not be possible.

### 7.6.2 Programming to an Abstraction

A theme that underlies reuse is that we are programming to an abstraction, and not to an implementation, as can be seen in the examples in this chapter. What this also means is that we are enabling reuse by separating the abstraction from the implementation. In the first example, we looked at Java's implementation of a sorting algorithm. Java provides implementations of two sorting algorithms. The class `Arrays` provides a `sort()` method which implements a Dual-Pivot Quicksort. The array object is passed as a parameter. The `sort()` method in the class `Collections` provides a different implementation, based on a stable, adaptive, iterative Mergesort algorithm. The collection object is passed as a parameter. Both algorithms are programmed to work with the abstraction represented by the `Comparable` interface, and are therefore available to any object that implements this interface. The implementation of the interface is provided by the class whose objects belong to the collection.

The second example showed us how Java provides a fully reusable `Thread` class, by defining the `Runnable` interface and programming the `Thread` class to work with this abstraction. Any class that implements `Runnable` can reuse `Thread`. Likewise, when we created a searchable collection class, we depended on the abstraction contained in the `Matchable` interface and the associated key. The implementation of `Matchable` can be provided by any class; if a class implements this interface, we can reuse our code to create a searchable collection of objects of that class.

In the last example, when we created an inheritance hierarchy, we defined the abstraction for `LoanableItem`. All the other classes in the library system are programmed to work with this abstraction. Each subclass of `LoanableItem` provides its own (distinct) implementation.

### 7.6.3 Dealing with Variability

Systems have to be built for reuse because their requirements and uses are likely to vary. Therefore to choose the manner in which we design for reuse, we should ask ourselves: How should we deal with potential variability? A fundamental principle of object-oriented design states: *encapsulate what varies*. Hence we see that good encapsulation is, in fact, a foundation for reusability.

During the construction of the `LoanableItem` hierarchy, we saw this principle in action. Even though the hierarchy allowed us to add new subtypes of `LoanableItem`, the constructor invocation had to be encapsulated separately in order to make the hierarchy fully reusable. Conditionals that switch on a subtype can be replaced by polymorphism, but this does not apply when we are dealing with constructors, since the concrete object does not exist yet. As we saw in this chapter, reuse also occurs when we build a library that can be used by a variety of applications. In these situations, we built the system such that the parts that varied across applications would be encapsulated entirely within the application. To ensure this, we used interfaces (`Comparable, Runnable, Matchable`) that encapsulated all the necessary methods. The individual applications were required to implement these in order to access the reusable code. A related concept is the principle of **delegation**; in all these examples, we can see that some responsibility was delegated to a different module to enable reusability.

### 7.6.4 Principles of Class Design

In a previous chapter, we presented the single responsibility principle. In this chapter, we have introduced four other principles. These five principles have been cited in the literature as the SOLID principles of class design[4].

These principles are interconnected in interesting ways. The open–closed principle is perhaps the most applicable design rule to justify introducing inheritance. In the early years, this was misconstrued as the flexibility that inheritance provides, that is, we can keep extending classes as requirements change. This misunderstanding was removed through the notion of substitutability, which was eventually formalized as the Liskov substitution principle, and the understanding that we should favor composition over inheritance. Note that the words "open" and "closed" apply to different objectives. The modules should be open for further extension, and closed for clients that are depending on it. The client modules are thus assured that any changes introduced into the system later will not necessitate any modifications.

The dependency inversion principle represents the essence of the difference between the top-down functional approach and the object-oriented approach. This connects to the concept of programming to an abstraction, but can also be seen as the bedrock for the open–closed principle. Without skillful use of abstractions, we cannot ensure that a class is closed for implementation.

The single responsibility principle is closely tied to the interface segregation principle and it is easy to find examples where ISP violations cause SRP violations. Both principles can be seen as a refinement of encapsulating the variability; they help us identify encapsulations that are too broad, and provide thumb rules for defining finer abstractions. In addition to these five principles, six other principles of package design were identified in [4]. In all these principles, we find the themes of reuse, abstraction, stable dependency, and cohesion.

## Projects

1. Complete the implementation of the library system to incorporate the following:

   a. Have the common superclass `ItemList` for `Catalog` and `MemberList`.
   b. Support for loaning out CDs, DVDs, books, and periodicals.

## Exercises

1. Define the appropriate interfaces and create a fully reusable implementation for the `FindMax` algorithm.
2. Consider an algorithm like Radix sort. How can we implement a fully reusable Radix sort algorithm for arrays?
3. Extend the `LoanableItem` hierarchy to create new classes for CDs, DVDs, and books on tape. CDs and DVDs have several common characteristics. Would it be appropriate for these two classes to inherit from a common superclass? Why?
4. (Case studies) Examine the projects presented at the end of Chapter 6 and identify possible situations where we could get variability in the behavior of an object. Which variabilities will you model using inheritance? Defend your choices based on object-oriented design principles.
5. Try to implement `ItemList<T extends Matchable<K>, K>` as a singleton. What are the difficulties you encounter?
6. Suppose that we do not specify `Matchable` as a generic interface. What changes will you make? What drawbacks do you foresee?
7. Compile the source files for the classes given for the generic implementation. Make modifications so that all compiler warning messages disappear.
8. Consider a situation where our `Library` system has to keep track of the rooms that can be rented out to members. Should this be added to the `LoanableItem` hierarchy or considered as an independent class? Explain what factors you would take into consideration when making this decision.
9. Consider a university registration that needs to track graduate and undergraduate students, which have a lot of commonalities, but also some differences. What are the possible ways in which these implementations could reuse code? Explain.
10. A university has special categories of students. For example, students who have completed 90 or more credits get priority for registration; students with a GPA below 2.0 are placed on probation. How should we accommodate these variations? Would it be appropriate to create separate classes for them within the `Student` hierarchy?
11. An airline has several passenger categories, based on the number of frequent flier miles and purchases made on their credit cards. These passenger categories are charged differential baggage fees and have different priorities for seating. What would be an appropriate way to capture these variations?
12. A warehouse deals with both perishable and non-perishable items. Perishable items are priced based on the number of days from the expiry date and are subject to different shipping rules. How would you choose to model these variations?

## References

1. America, P. 1990. Designing an object-oriented programming language with behavioural subtyping. In: *Proceedings of the REX School/Workshop on Foundations of Object-Oriented Languages, J. W. de Bakker, Willem P. de Roever, and Grzegorz Rozenberg (Eds.),* pp. 60–90.
2. Gamma, E, Helm, R, Johnson, R and Vlissides, J. 1994. *Design Patterns: Elements of Reusable Object-oriented Software.* Addison-Wesley.
3. Liskov, BH and Wing, JM. 2001. Behavioural subtyping using invariants and constraints. *Formal methods for distributed processing: A survey of object-oriented approaches,* pp. 254–280.
4. Martin, RC. 2005. *The Principles of OOD.* http://butunclebob.com/ArticleS.UncleBob.PrinciplesOfOod
5. Meyer, B. 1998. *Object-Oriented Software Construction, First Edition.* Prentice Hall.

# Chapter 8
# Modeling with Finite State Machines

Our discussion thus far of the object-oriented software construction process has focused on the use case model. While this is a comprehensive technique that has found widespread application, it is inadequate for handling situations where the operations cannot be modeled by end-to-end use cases. This is typically the case with dynamic systems that respond to external input in real-time.

In this chapter, we present a case study of a system where the use case model does not suffice: a controller for a microwave. (This analysis could be extended to most devices that interact with external entities.) The behavior of the microwave in response to a user's action depends on what state the microwave is in. For instance, if a cook/start button is pressed, the power tube that provides the heat does not always start operating. The case study starts by presenting a model for dealing with this kind of conditional behavior, and then goes on to discuss issues arising in the design and implementation of such systems.

Another commonly occurring situation is the creation of a graphical user interface (GUI). The program that implements the GUI typically presents different screens at different stages of the interaction. Which screen gets displayed depends on the kind of input the application is requesting at that instant. While the underlying application itself may be designed using the use case model, the GUI is modeled as a system that changes its "appearance" in response to the interaction. It turns out that a similar model is useful for analyzing such systems. We will outline an approach to handle such programs in this chapter.

The term **embedded system** is used to refer to a system with a dedicated function, as opposed to a general purpose system. An example of an embedded system is a CD player. It includes mechanical devices to rotate a CD, electrical devices to supply power, sense CDs, etc., and software to support the reading of the music in the CDs. The software that controls hardware devices is termed **embedded software**. The system as a whole needs to behave in a prescribed manner, turning components on or off depending on the input and other environmental variables. In this chapter, we discuss the analysis, design, and implementation of a similar system.

## 8.1 A Simple Example

**Problem** Consider a simple microwave oven whose behavior is governed by the following specifications:

1. The microwave has a door, a light, a power tube, a button, a timer, and a display.
2. When the oven is not in use and the door is closed, the light and the power tube are turned off and the display shows 0 for the cooking time left.
3. When the door is open, the light stays on.
4. If the button is pushed when the door is closed and the oven is not operating, then the oven is activated for one minute. When the oven is activated, the light and the power tube are turned on.
5. If the button is pushed when the oven is operating, one minute is added to the timer.
6. The timer ticks every second. When the oven is operating, the display shows the number of seconds of cooking time remaining.
7. If the door is opened when the oven is operating, the cooking is interrupted and ends (the power tube is turned off and the cook time remaining is now zero.)
8. When the cooking time is completed, the power tube and light are turned off.
9. Pushing the button when the door is open has no effect.

### 8.1.1 How to Approach this Problem

It is useful to contrast this problem with that of the library system. The library requirements (that is, business processes) were what the end user needed to manage the library. We then employed a use case model to define the system. There can be a large number of processes that need to be handled with fairly complex details; but each time a process is executed, the steps are performed in the exact same manner.

In contrast, what the end user wants from the microwave is very simple: to be able to cook/warm food in the microwave. The user could, however, use it in many ways. If we attempt to model all these variations with use cases, we will run into some difficulties. Consider the following sets of scenarios:

**Scenario 1:** *open door → place food in oven → close door → push button → wait for cooking to finish → open door → remove food → close door*

**Scenario 2:** *open door → place food in oven → close door → push button → wait for cooking to finish → open door → remove food and stir → place food in oven → close door → push button → wait for cooking to finish → open door → remove food → close door*

**Scenario 3:** *open door → place food in oven → close door → push button → wait for 30 seconds → open door → remove food and stir → place food in oven → close door → push button → wait for 45 seconds → open door → remove food → close door → stir food → open door → place food in oven → close door → push button → wait for cooking to finish → open door → remove food → close door*

Clearly, there is no set of standard "business processes" that can characterize all the ways in which an actor interacts with the system. What we observe instead is that we are dealing with a continuous sequence of events, and the manner in which these events are processed depends on the current situation. The situation also changes with user actions; for instance, when the user opens the microwave door, we have a different situation, and a user action, like pressing the cook button, needs to be processed differently. What this suggests is that in order to model the system behavior accurately, we should take a different approach.

This discussion tells us that use cases are not the best way to characterize this behavior. Before we propose a better way, it is useful to understand the concept of a finite state model. A **finite state model** is an abstraction that can be in exactly one of a finite number of states at any given time and can change its state in response to some external inputs; the change from one state to another is called a **transition**. The model is defined by a list of its states, its initial state, and the conditions for each transition.

Such a model is not appropriate for something like the library system. If we were to talk about the "current state of the library," it would involve the books, members, and the relationships between them. It is easily seen that we can have an infinite number of states. The microwave system on the other hand remembers at most a small, fixed set of rules and numbers in order to operate. It is also easy to see that the microwave can only be in a limited number of states. We can thus decide that the best approach to this problem is to build a finite state model.

The finite state model is typically formalized as a **finite state machine (FSM)**; an FSM is defined by a set of states, a set of input symbols, and a set of transitions. Each transition is defined by a 4-tuple $(s_i, s_f, I, O)$, where $s_i$ is the initial state, $s_f$ is the final state, $I$ is the input that triggers the transition, and $O$ is the associated output, if any. Two different formulations for FSMs can be found in the literature on automata theory. These are the **Mealy machine** and the **Moore machine**. In a Mealy machine, the output depends on the event and the current state; a Moore machine is a simplification in which the output depends only on the state. The two are equivalent as far as their power is concerned, that is, any system that can be defined in one kind of machine can also be defined in the other, but the number of states and the transitions vary.

### Use case modeling versus finite state modeling

One question we need to address is: *Under what conditions should we use FSMs and under what conditions do we employ use cases?*

To help answer this question, let us examine how the library system designed in the previous chapters changes with each transaction. At the start of each use case (that is, transaction), some pre-conditions hold. The final output of the transaction depends on the pre-conditions that were true at the start of the transaction. The state of the system defines (and is defined by) which pre-conditions are true. These pre-conditions, in turn, are determined by the values held by all of the objects in the system.

Whenever a transaction is completed, such as when a book is issued, the state changes because several objects, including the `Book` and `Member` objects, get updated. (Note that this notion of state is somewhat different from the states of the FSM.) Each transaction has one "most-common" outcome (which we call the **main flow**) and other secondary outcomes, and the set of pre-conditions that hold decides the outcome of the transaction.

If one were to model such a system by listing all the states and how we can switch between them through transactions, we would have a very complex structure with an unmanageable and possibly unbounded set of states because one could imagine books and members being added and deleted and updated throughout the life of the library system. We do not even know what the states are in such cases. On the other hand, the set of interactions that an actor can have with the library system is bounded. This indicates that we should prefer the simple functional specification provided by a use case model.

Contrast this situation with the microwave example. Here we have a possibly unbounded number of ways in which the actor can interact with the system. However, from the specifications, it is clear that we are only interested in how the system reacts to a given input (sometimes referred to as "reactive" systems). The nature of the reaction depends on the state the system is in (the word "state" being used to describe a behavioral response). Also, we typically have a relatively small set of states in which the system could be at any point, and a clear set of transitions between them, which are triggered by events. This indicates that use case modeling is inappropriate and that using an FSM to model the system behavior would be the best choice.

## 8.2 Requirements Analysis using Finite State Modeling

In the previous chapters, we modeled our applications as a set of use cases to determine the user requirements. Here, we model the microwave as an FSM to derive the system specifications. In both cases, our objective is to ensure that all requirements are captured in the resulting model. In use case modeling, we must ensure that every complete operation is represented by a use case, and that all the sub-operations are captured in the detailed use case. Note that we had to carefully list the business processes at the beginning; with these, it was easy to spot the use cases, and write the details of the sub-operations.

In finite state modeling, we must ensure that we have the correct set of states, and that all the system actions in the requirements have been identified with responses to user actions (or other external inputs) in the appropriate state. Such an endeavor is not always easy; if the requirements are not well-written, there is no clear process we can follow, and additional analysis will be required. A well-written set of requirements, however, follows a pattern, which makes it convenient to identify the states and the responses. Consider the statement in Specification 2:

> When the oven is not in use and the door is closed, the light and the power tube are turned off and the display shows 0 for the cooking time left.

The phrase "When the oven is not in use and the door is closed" is a description of the situation of the microwave. The rest of the statement, "the light and the power tube are turned off and the display shows 0 for the cooking time left" describes the characteristics that the system displays (that is, the properties of the system) in that situation.

Next, consider the statement in Specification 4:

> If the button is pushed when the door is closed and the oven is not operating, then the oven is activated for one minute.

The phrase "the button is pushed" describes an action by the user, and the phrase "the door is closed and the oven is not operating" describes the situation in which the microwave is when the user action occurs. The phrase "the oven is activated" defines the new situation with the characteristics "the light and the power tube are turned on." The phrase "for one minute" implies that a timer is being employed in this situation.

The above two statements are parsed in different ways. For the statement in Specification 2, we can create a table with two columns: one column with the situation and the second column with the characteristics (Table 8.1).

We can identify other statements in the requirements that fit this pattern. These are: "when the door is open, the light stays on", "when the oven is activated, the light and the power tube are turned on" and "when the cooking time is completed, the power tube and light are turned off." All of these can be parsed using the above table, resulting in Table 8.2.

| Situation | Characteristic |
|---|---|
| Oven is not in use and the door is closed | The light and the power tube are turned off and the display shows 0 for the cooking time left |

**Table 8.1** Capturing the characteristics in Specification 2

| Situation | Characteristic |
|---|---|
| Oven is not in use and the door is closed | The light and the power tube are turned off and the display shows 0 for the cooking time left |
| Door is open | The light stays on |
| Oven is activated | The light and the power tube are turned on |
| Cooking time is completed | The power tube and the light are turned off |

**Table 8.2** Capturing the characteristics in other specifications

The situations in Table 8.2 suggest a set of potentially different states that the system could be in. Ideally, we would like to minimize the size of this set; as we shall see later, the characteristics help us eliminate redundant states.

The statement in Specification 4 talks about situations changing in response to an action. The situation can change because the system needs to respond to an action by the user. For parsing such statements, we can create a table with four columns, as shown in Table 8.3.

| Situation | User action | System response | New situation |
|---|---|---|---|
| Door is closed and the oven is not operating | The button is pushed | The light and the power tube are turned on; the one-minute timer is started | Oven is activated |

**Table 8.3** Capturing the change in situation characteristics in Specification 4

We can identify other statements that fit this pattern:
"The Button is pushed when the oven is operating (activated), one minute is added to the timer"
"If the door is opened when the oven is operating, the cooking is interrupted and ends (the power tube is turned off and the cook time remaining is now zero.)"
"Pushing the button when the door is open has no effect"
Putting these in the table, we now have Table 8.4.

This appears to give us another situation, that is, cooking is interrupted. Since the door is open when this situation occurs, we find the following characteristics for this situation from Specification 7:

The door is open, the power tube is turned off and the cook time remaining is zero

These characteristics look very similar to the "door is open" situation. However, we cannot be sure if these are identical in all respects, since a cooking

| Situation | User action | System response | New situation |
|---|---|---|---|
| Door is closed and the oven is not operating | The button is pushed | The light and the power tube are turned on; the one-minute timer is started | Oven is activated |
| Oven is activated | The button is pushed | One minute is added to the timer | Oven is activated |
| Oven is activated | The door is opened | The power tube is turned off and the cook time remaining is zero | Cooking is interrupted |
| Door is open | The button is pushed | No response | Door is open |

**Table 8.4** Capturing the change in situation characteristics in other specifications

process has been interrupted. We can include this as a different situation for now and deal with it later.

### Extracting the finite state machine from the requirements

As we parse the requirements for the microwave example, we can see that identifying the states and transitions is very dependent on how the requirements are expressed. In our example, the requirements are written in a manner that is easy to parse. In real-life situations, the requirements often start off as *user stories*, which are informal explanations of a system written from the perspective of the end user. Their purpose is to exemplify how a software feature will provide value to the customer. From user stories it may not even be clear that using an FSM to model the system behavior would be the best choice.

Once we have identified the need for an FSM, we have to decide on the kind of state machine: a general state machine, which is continually moving from one state to another, or a protocol state machine, which captures the protocol for a communication. For a general state machine, we will need to identify system behaviors that can enable all the user stories to be fulfilled. These behaviors, if written in the style described in our example, can be parsed to yield the FSM.

Protocol state machine requirements are better captured as a sequence of steps with multiple options at each event. This machine is active only until the communication is completed.

Not all statements fit neatly into one of these patterns; the following statements do not seem to have a user action:

“The timer ticks every second. When the oven is operating, the display shows the number of seconds of cook time remaining”

"When the cooking time is completed, the power tube and light are turned off"

Looking at these statements, we find other events that our system needs to respond to, but these are not user actions. When the clock ticks a second, the microwave must update the display time. For this to take place, the information about the elapsed second must be sent to the microwave; we assume that the clock sends this as an event. Likewise, when the timer runs out, the microwave must be informed so that it can stop the cooking. To incorporate these, we modify Table 8.4 by labeling the second column as "User action/Clock event." We now have Table 8.5.

| **Situation** | **User action/Clock event** | **System response** | **New situation** |
|---|---|---|---|
| Door is closed and the oven is not operating | The button is pushed | The light and the power tube are turned on; the one-minute timer is started | Oven is activated |
| Oven is activated | The button is pushed | One minute is added to the timer | Oven is activated |
| Oven is activated | The door is opened | The power tube is turned off and the cook time remaining is zero | Cooking is interrupted |
| Door is open | The button is pushed | No response | Door is open |
| Oven is activated | The clock ticks a second | Update the display time | Oven is activated |
| Oven is activated | The timer signals completion | The power tube and the light are turned off | Cooking is completed |

**Table 8.5** Modified table showing all the system responses to user actions and clock events

Once again, we see a new situation, "cooking is interrupted," with characteristics very similar to "door is open and the oven is not operating." For the time being, we will list this as a different situation. Adding in this situation, we get Table 8.6.

| **Situation** | **Characteristic** |
|---|---|
| Oven is not in use and the door is closed | The light and the power tube are turned off and the display shows 0 for the cooking time left |
| Door is open | The light stays on |
| Oven is activated | The light and the power tube are turned on |
| Cooking time is completed | The power tube and the light are turned off |
| Cooking is interrupted | The power tube is turned off, the light stays on |

**Table 8.6** Modified table showing all the situations and their characteristics

In the language of finite state machines, we refer to the different situations as the possible states that the system can be in. The user actions and timer events are the events that the system responds to. For each event, depending on the current state (that is, the existing situation), the system responds by taking some action that results in transitioning to the next state (that is, the new situation). We can now formalize all this by defining our FSM in terms of two components: a set of states and a set of transitions between states.

### 8.2.1 Defining the FSM for the Microwave

The states identified are:

1. IDLE; DOOR CLOSED: The microwave is idle and the door is closed.
2. IDLE; DOOR OPEN: The microwave is idle and the door is open.
3. COOKING: The semantics are obvious from the name of the state.
4. INTERRUPTED: Cooking is interrupted by the door being opened.
5. COMPLETED: The microwave has completed cooking.

We have the following events that cause the microwave to change state:

1. OPEN DOOR: The door is opened.
2. CLOSE DOOR: The door is closed.
3. COOK: The button is pushed.
4. CLOCK TICKS: The clock sends a signal every second.
5. TIMER RUNS OUT: Cooking is completed.

The first three are external events, the result of the actions of an external user. The other two are internal events triggered by the operation of the microwave.

We can now construct Table 8.7, which describes all the actions that correspond to each (*state, event*) pair. The rows in the first column list the possible states of the microwave, while the columns in the first row show the possible events. The other non-blank cells show the state transitions. This table is called a **state transition table**. An example will make clear how we can use this table. When the microwave is in the Cooking state (see row 4, column 1), if the door is opened (row 1, column 2), the cell formed by row 4 and column 2 shows that the microwave enters the Interrupted state.

The information in Table 8.7 can also be represented pictorially using what is called the **UML state transition diagram** as shown in Figure 8.1. Each rectangle with rounded corners corresponds to a microwave state. The directed arcs tell us what the new microwave state will be when a certain event occurs in a given state. For instance, if the microwave is in the Idle; Door Closed state (the rectangle at the top left of the diagram), one of the arcs leading from the rectangle shows that if the cook button is pressed, the microwave enters the Cooking state.

| | Open Door | Close Door | Cook | Clock Ticks | Timer Runs Out |
|---|---|---|---|---|---|
| Idle; Door Closed | Idle; Door Open | Idle; Door Closed | Cooking | Idle; Door Closed | Idle; Door Closed |
| Idle; Door Open | Idle; Door Open | Idle; Door Closed | Idle; Door Open | Idle; Door Open | Idle; Door Open |
| Cooking | Interrupted | Cooking | Cooking | Cooking | Completed |
| Interrupted | Interrupted | Idle; Door Closed | Interrupted | Interrupted | Interrupted |
| Completed | Idle; Door Open | Completed | Cooking | Completed | Completed |

**Table 8.7** Transition table for the microwave. The cells in the first column (other than the blank cell in the top row) list the states. The column headers name the events. The remaining cells represent state transitions in response to events. For example, if the current state is Idle; Door Closed (the left-most column in the second row) and the event is Cook (the fourth column), the state changes to Cooking. Also note that in some states, for certain events, the next state is the same as the current state.

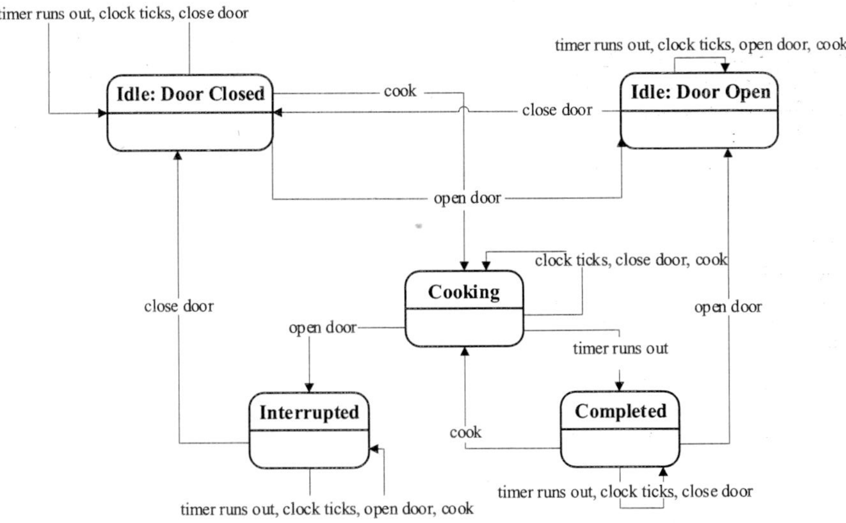


**Fig. 8.1** State transition diagram for the microwave. Each rounded rectangle represents a state. The name of the state is written in the rectangle. The arrows represent state transitions in response to events and the direction of the transition is indicated by the arcs.

### 8.2.2 State Minimization

One observation we make here is that the behavior of our finite state machine is identical in the states Idle; Door Closed and Completed. This tells that we do not need separate states to distinguish the behavior of the system when it is idle with door closed from the behavior when it has completed cooking. Likewise, states Idle; Door Open and Interrupted are indistinguishable; we can therefore combine these two states into a single state Door Open, and merge states Idle; Door Closed and Completed into a single state, Door Closed. In effect, we have simply dropped states Interrupted and Completed from our model. The reduced FSM is described in Table 8.8.

| | Open Door | Close Door | Cook | Clock Ticks | Timer Runs Out |
|---|---|---|---|---|---|
| Door Closed | Door Open | Door Closed | Cooking | Door Closed | Door Closed |
| Door Open | Door Open | Door Closed | Door Open | Door Open | Door Open |
| Cooking | Door Open | Cooking | Cooking | Cooking | Door Closed |

**Table 8.8** Minimized transition table for the microwave. We have collapsed the original table by combining two pairs of states: Idle; Door Open is equivalent to Interrupted, so they form the state Door Open. Idle; Door Closed is equivalent to Completed and they form the state Door Closed.

In general, it is important to find an FSM with a small number of states and there are exact algorithms for state minimization[1]. Usually, fewer states implies a simpler system that is easier to maintain, but in some situations, it may be helpful to add a few redundant states to improve the readability of the design as a whole.

## 8.3 A First Solution to the Microwave Problem

We now proceed to complete the analysis of the microwave system to come up with a set of conceptual classes. As we did in the case of the library system, we then identify and design the physical classes and implement the system.

### 8.3.1 Completing the Analysis

Having created a model, the next step in our analysis is to identify the conceptual classes. As before, we start by constructing the list of nouns: microwave, power tube, light, display, door, cook button, etc. The display and cook button will be part of the user interface (GUI). Since this is only a "software simulation," we cannot have a real power tube or light, and so we simply have to model these by displaying some message on the GUI. Likewise, the opening and closing of the door are simulated by some GUI component(s). This leaves us with a class for the microwave and one for the GUI. The noun "timer" suggests that we need some mechanism to monitor the passage of time. The microwave can keep track of the time remaining with a field, but

[1] Many textbooks on *digital logic design* or *automata theory* would have descriptions of state minimization algorithms.

**Constructing state transition diagrams (tables)**

A beginner may often find it somewhat difficult to construct state transition diagrams (or tables). The discussion in this box gives some more insight into developing these diagrams. As you gain experience, you will find the process a lot easier.

To develop state transition diagrams, we have to identify the states and events and determine the transitions. As you follow the procedure mentioned above, ensure that the states you identify have the following characteristics:

- *States are mutually exclusive.* If $S_1$ and $S_2$ are two states, it should be impossible for the system to be in both of them at the same time. For example, it is impossible for the microwave to be in the states IDLE; DOOR OPEN and IDLE; DOOR CLOSED at the same time. In contrast, we cannot have two states COOKING and DOOR CLOSED (assuming the obvious semantics) because the microwave could have the door closed and still be cooking, which violates the mutual exclusion property. But just because two things are mutually exclusive, there is no implication that they qualify to be states. For example, again assuming the obvious meanings DOOR OPEN and LIGHT OFF are mutually exclusive, we do not think of LIGHT OFF as a state.
- *If two situations' results show different system characteristics, they should be considered as different states.* For example, IDLE; DOOR CLOSED and IDLE; DOOR OPEN are different states because in the former, the light is off and in the latter, the light is on.
- *A system remains in a state unless an event occurs; when the event occurs, there is no ambiguity about the state to which the system transitions.* We are talking of deterministic FSMs, where a given state and event uniquely determine the next state.

Just because "something stays the same way" for a while does not necessarily mean that it is a state. That "something" might even change in response to an event. For example, the light being on remains that way until an event occurs, but it is not a state because it is not fundamental to the behavior of the microwave; rather, it is a consequence of the microwave being in certain states. The light-on phenomenon is an output of the microwave, not a state.

The basic characteristics of an event are:

- *It affects the FSM in some way in the context of the problem.* For example, pressing the cook button would have an effect, unless the door is open. As a result, the system may transition to a different state.
- *It is instantaneous in nature.* Even though we may visualize the action taking place over a period of time, there is a specific instant when we say the event occurs. For example, a user may close the door in a leisurely fashion, but there has to be a specific instant (perhaps based on some sensor being triggered) when the event is deemed to have occurred.

Just as in use case modeling, in FSM modeling as well, requirements may be incompletely specified in the analysis stage. In our example, the existence of the timer was not made explicit, but could be inferred. Once you get a correct set of states and events and fully understand what they mean, the state transition diagram becomes easier to construct.

will have to be informed about the events that mark each unit of time. This can be done by a clock that generates ticks at regular (one second) intervals. The conceptual classes are as follows:

- **Microwave:** This has the responsibility of keeping track of what state the oven is in, and for turning the power tube and light on/off. The oven must listen for the following events: *opening/closing of the door, pushing of the button,* and *the timer running out.* (In a more realistic situation, one would have real devices with software drivers to manipulate them, and these drivers would be invoked from this class.)
- **GUI Display:** As described above, the GUI has components for user input and will display some information to simulate operations. This suggests the following four separate components:
  - One of the components tells us whether the unit is cooking or not cooking.
  - A second component informs us whether the door is open or closed.
  - The third component shows the time remaining for cooking. If the microwave is idle, the display shows 0.
  - The fourth component gives the status of the light: whether it is on or off.
- **Clock:** This is a class that generates clock tick events at regular intervals.

### 8.3.2 Designing the System

The first step in the design is to identify the software classes. This is an easy task here since the conceptual classes could very well be the physical classes. The next step is to figure out how the software classes will distribute the responsibilities to achieve the behavior specified in the model. In our case, this amounts to specifying how the events will be processed. We have two kinds of events:

- *User inputs:* These are recognized by the GUI.
- *Clock ticks:* These originate in `Clock.`

To describe the manner in which the entities of the system handle these, we use sequence diagrams. Figure 8.2 shows how the system handles the user input corresponding to the opening of the door. The diagram suggests that we have a separate method in the `Microwave` class for each kind of event that occurs in the GUI. The actor can see the result of the action through the updates on the display.

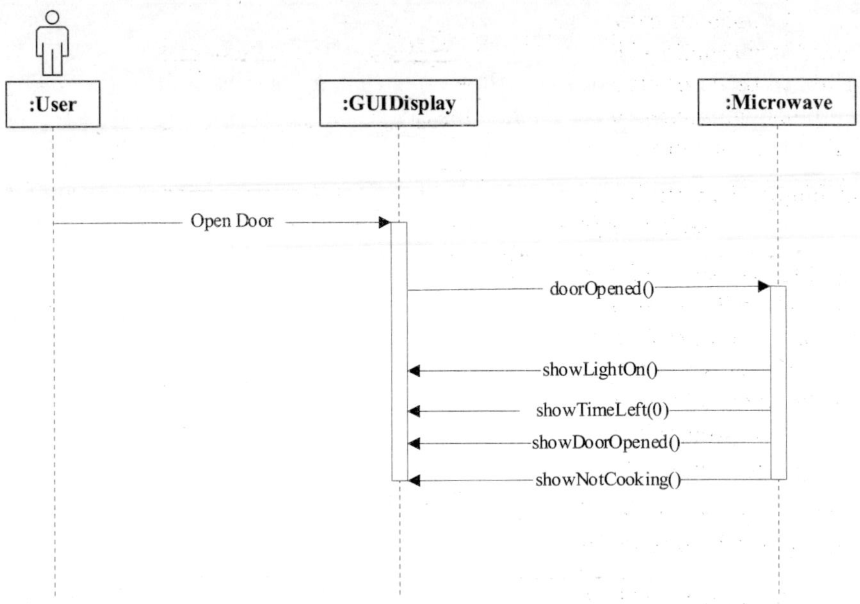


**Fig. 8.2** Sequence diagram for the Door Open event. When the user pushes the button to open the door, the `GUIDisplay` object calls the `doorOpened()` method of the `Microwave` class, which issues a sequence of calls to the `GUIDisplay` object.

The sequence diagram for the other inputs from the user look similar. In each case, `Microwave` does some processing and updates the display. There are several methods to update the different components constituting the display and the appropriate ones will be invoked with the necessary parameters.

Figure 8.3 describes how the system handles a clock tick. Note that unlike the sequence diagrams we have seen earlier, this interaction is not initiated by the actor.

The sequence diagrams for the other events are similar, and they give us enough information to specify the responsibilities of the individual classes. `Microwave` is a singleton class with methods to process the events (door opening, clock tick, etc.) To mimic the FSM, we keep a variable `currentState` that keeps track of the state the microwave is in. We also need a variable that keeps track of the time remaining for cooking. The class diagram is shown in Figure 8.4.

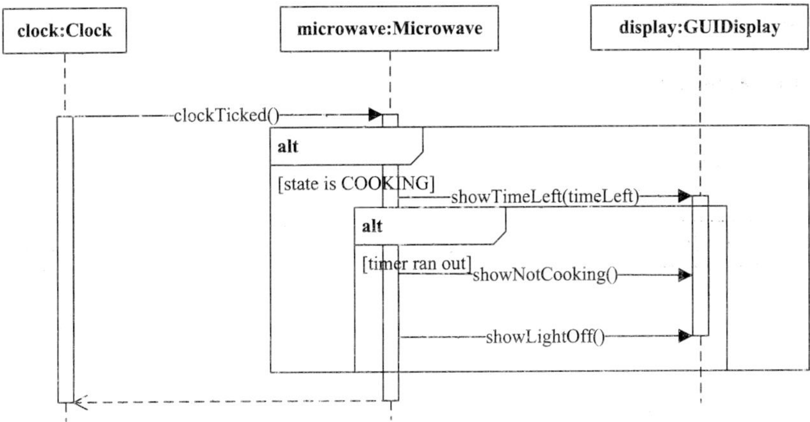


**Fig. 8.3** Sequence diagram for processing a clock tick. The event is generated within the clock. The event is sent to the `Microwave` object, which ignores it unless the current state is the `Cooking` state. If it is the `Cooking` state, the remaining `Cooking` time is updated by calling `showTimeLeft()` in the `GUIDisplay` object. If the time remaining is 0, the light is turned off and the status is shown as `Not Cooking`.

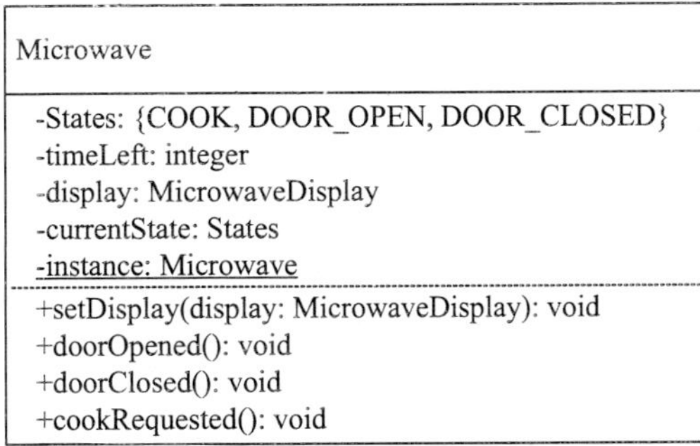


**Fig. 8.4** `Microwave` class diagram. The class is a singleton (see the static field and method) and contains one instance method for each event. When the clock ticks, however, the microwave system itself generates the `Timer Runs out` event.

Although a text-based interface is difficult, if not impossible (no buttons), any number of graphical interfaces are possible. As shown in the sequence diagram for opening the door, the `MicrowaveDisplay` class must provide two kinds of methods:

- Methods that process the input provided by the user.
- Methods that can be invoked by `Microwave` to display output. The reader is invited to draw the sequence diagrams for door closing and the push of the cook button and compile the set of methods in this category.

Methods of the first kind are largely defined by the look and feel desired for the user interface. Methods of the second kind represent the functionality required by `Microwave`. When the door is opened, for instance, `Microwave` requests the display to indicate that the light is on. One way we could do this is to have `Microwave` get a reference to the appropriate object within the GUI and set it; such an approach results in `Microwave` being tied to one kind of look and feel and any attempt to change the look and feel will require changes to `Microwave`. To avoid such tight coupling between the GUI and `Microwave`, the essential functionality is abstracted out in the interface `MicrowaveDisplay` shown in Figure 8.5.

The class `GUIDisplay` implements this interface.

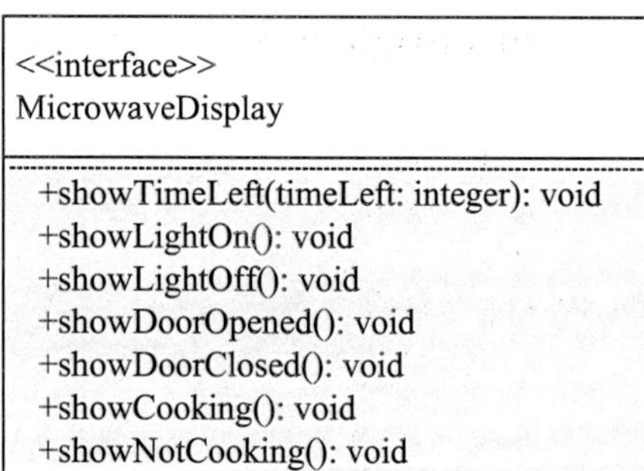


**Fig. 8.5** `MicrowaveDisplay` is an interface that specifies the functionality of any user interface for the microwave application. We expect the user interface to be a simple GUI or one that resembles a real microwave or anything in between.

The `Clock` class needs to initiate an event at regular intervals, so we model it as a thread. As shown in Figure 8.6, it implements the `Runnable` interface.

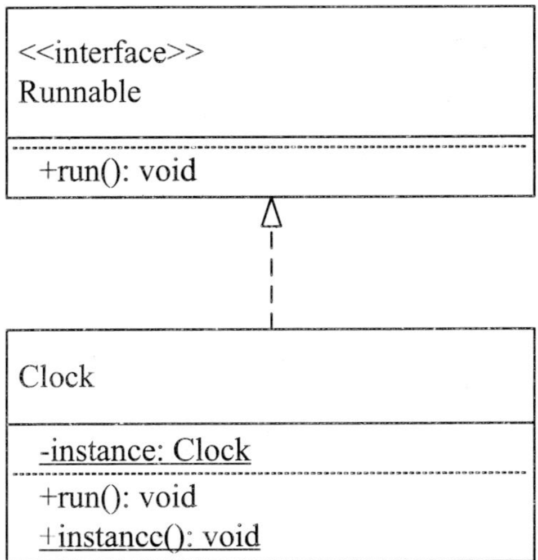


**Fig. 8.6** The `Clock` class is a thread that is an infinite loop, sending notifications to the `Microwave` object every second. It is a singleton, which accounts for the static members.

### 8.3.3 The Implementation Classes

We are now ready to work out the implementation details. The `Clock` class is the simplest and is therefore a good place to start. The `run` method is an infinite loop waking up every second and invoking the `clockTicked` method on the `Microwave` object. The code is given below.

```
public class Clock implements Runnable {
    private static Clock instance;
    private Clock() {
        new Thread(this).start();
    }
    public static Clock instance() {
        if (instance == null) {
            instance = new Clock();
        }
        return instance;
    }
    public void run() {
        try {
            while (true) {
                Thread.sleep(1000);
```

```
                    Microwave.instance().clockTicked();
                }
            } catch (InterruptedException ie) {
            }
    }
}
```

#### 8.3.3.1 The Display Class

GUIDisplay is the concrete class that implements MicrowaveDisplay. To handle user input, it creates a window with a Button for each kind of operation: open door, close door, and cook.

When it is run, the program displays the interface given in Figure 8.7. It has fields for displaying the status.

**Fig. 8.7** Microwave interface: Note that the door is "simulated" by two buttons: one to open and the other to close the door.

### 8.3.4 Display Implementations

We present two implementations: one in Swing and the other in JavaFX. The two implementations are very similar. We have given brief explanations of both implementations. The code omits a few lines that deal with the spacing of widgets. A number of methods to set the displays are straightforward in both implementations.

#### Display Implementation in Swing

The Swing implementation extends JFrame and creates JButton objects (for cook, door close, and door open) and JLabel objects (for the various outputs) in the declarations and constructors and adds them to the content pane.

The buttons are listened to in the class itself using the `actionPerformed()` method.

```
public class GUIDisplay extends JFrame implements
              MicrowaveDisplay, ActionListener {
  private JButton doorCloser;
  private JButton doorOpener;
  private JButton cookJButton;
  private JLabel doorStatus = new JLabel("Door Closed");
  private JLabel timerValue = new JLabel("            ");
  private JLabel lightStatus = new JLabel("Light Off");
  private JLabel cookingStatus = new JLabel("Not cooking");
  private Microwave microwave;
  public GUIDisplay() {
    doorCloser = new JButton("close door");
    doorOpener = new JButton("open door");
    cookJButton = new JButton("cook");
    FlowLayout flowLayout = new FlowLayout();
    flowLayout.setHgap(10);
    flowLayout.setVgap(10);
    setLayout(flowLayout);
    getContentPane().add(doorStatus);
    getContentPane().add(lightStatus);
    getContentPane().add(timerValue);
    getContentPane().add(cookingStatus);
    getContentPane().add(doorCloser);
    getContentPane().add(doorOpener);
    getContentPane().add(cookJButton);
    showDoorClosed();
    showLightOff();
    showTimeLeft(0);
    doorCloser.addActionListener(this);
    doorOpener.addActionListener(this);
    cookJButton.addActionListener(this);
    setTitle("Microwave Version 1");
    microwave = Microwave.instance();
    microwave.setDisplay(this);
    pack();
    setVisible(true);
    addWindowListener(new WindowAdapter() {
      @Override
      public void windowClosing(WindowEvent window) {
        System.exit(0);
      }
    });
```

```
  }
  @Override
  public void showLightOn() {
    lightStatus.setText("Light On");
  }
  @Override
  public void showLightOff() {
    lightStatus.setText("Light Off");
  }
  @Override
  public void showDoorClosed() {
    doorStatus.setText("Door Closed");
  }
  @Override
  public void showDoorOpened() {
    doorStatus.setText("Door Opened");
  }
  @Override
  public void showTimeLeft(int value) {
    timerValue.setText(" " + value);
  }
  @Override
  public void showCooking() {
    cookingStatus.setText("Cooking");
  }
  @Override
  public void showNotCooking() {
     cookingStatus.setText("Not cooking");
  }
  @Override
  public void actionPerformed(ActionEvent event) {
    if (event.getSource().equals(doorCloser)) {
      microwave.doorClosed();
    } else if (event.getSource().equals(doorOpener)) {
      microwave.doorOpened();
    } else if (event.getSource().equals(cookJButton)) {
      microwave.cookRequested();
    }
  }
}
```

### Display Implementation in JavaFX

The JavaFX implementation extends `Application` and creates `Button` objects (for cook, door close, and door open) and `Text` objects (for the various outputs) in the declarations and constructors and adds them to `HBox` (horizontal box). The buttons are listened to in the class itself using the `handle()` method.

```
public class GUIDisplay extends Application implements
         MicrowaveDisplay, EventHandler<ActionEvent> {
    private Button doorCloser;
    private Button doorOpener;
    private Button cookButton;
    private Text doorStatus = new Text("Door Closed");
    private Text timerValue = new Text("            ");
    private Text lightStatus = new Text("Light Off");
    private Text cookingStatus = new Text("Not cooking");
    private Microwave microwave;
    public void start(Stage primaryStage) {
        doorCloser = new Button("close door");
        doorOpener = new Button("open door");
        cookButton = new Button("cook");
        GridPane pane = new GridPane();
        pane.setHgap(10);
        pane.setVgap(10);
        pane.setPadding(new Insets(10, 10, 10, 10));
        pane.add(doorStatus, 0, 0);
        pane.add(lightStatus, 1, 0);
        pane.add(timerValue, 2, 0);
        pane.add(cookingStatus, 3, 0);
        pane.add(doorCloser, 4, 0);
        pane.add(doorOpener, 5, 0);
        pane.add(cookButton, 6, 0);
        showDoorClosed();
        showLightOff();
        showTimeLeft(0);
        doorCloser.setOnAction(this);
        doorOpener.setOnAction(this);
        cookButton.setOnAction(this);
        Scene scene = new Scene(pane);
        primaryStage.setScene(scene);
        primaryStage.setTitle("Microwave Version 1");
        microwave = Microwave.instance();
        microwave.setDisplay(this);
        primaryStage.show();
```

```
        primaryStage.addEventHandler(WindowEvent.
                                WINDOW_CLOSE_REQUEST,
                                     new EventHandler<WindowEvent>() {
            @Override
            public void handle(WindowEvent window) {
                System.exit(0);
            }
        });
    }
    public void showLightOn() {
        lightStatus.setText("Light On");
    }
    public void showLightOff() {
        lightStatus.setText("Light Off");
    }
    public void showDoorClosed() {
        doorStatus.setText("Door Closed");
    }
    public void showDoorOpened() {
        doorStatus.setText("Door Opened");
    }
    public void showTimeLeft(int value) {
        timerValue.setText(" " + value);
    }
    public void showCooking() {
        cookingStatus.setText("Cooking");
    }
    public void showNotCooking() {
        cookingStatus.setText("Not cooking");
    }
    @Override
    public void handle(ActionEvent event) {
        if (event.getSource().equals(doorCloser)) {
            microwave.doorClosed();
        } else if (event.getSource().equals(doorOpener)) {
            microwave.doorOpened();
        } else if (event.getSource().equals(cookButton)) {
            microwave.cookRequested();
        }
    }
}
```

Turning our attention to event processing, we note that the general strategy in each case is to check the current state and take the appropriate action. If the action results in a change of state, some transitional work also needs to be performed. As an example, consider the `cookRequested()` method. The cooking request is processed only if the system is cooking (`COOKING_STATE`) or if the door is closed (`DOOR_CLOSED_STATE`). In the latter, `currentState` is first changed to `COOKING_STATE` and the necessary transitional operations are performed. In the former, 60 seconds are added to the time remaining and the display is updated.

```
public void cookRequested() {
    if (currentState == States.DOOR_CLOSED_STATE) {
        currentState = States.COOKING_STATE;
        display.showCooking();
        display.showLightOn();
        timeLeft = 60;
        display.showTimeLeft(timeLeft);
    } else if (currentState == States.COOKING_STATE) {
        timeLeft += 60;
        display.showTimeLeft(timeLeft);
    }
}
```

The methods for processing the opening and closing of the door are similar and we leave those as exercises.

## 8.4 Critiquing the Simple Solution

The above solution is our first attempt at solving this problem. We have correctly analyzed the problem and proposed an "object-oriented" solution. Our next task is to critically examine our solution to see how well it conforms to the principles of good object-oriented design. With this end in mind, we present two flaws in the above design. As it turns out, these flaws can be corrected by recognizing and applying the appropriate design patterns.

### 8.4.1 Complexity in `Microwave`

`Microwave` has been designed as a large class that takes care of handling all states and events. Although the methods in our class do not seem too complex, it is easy to see that in a larger system, things could easily get out of hand. In previous chapters, we have seen that complexity is caused by having a large number of conditionals in our methods. In `Microwave`, each method that processes an event has conditionals that switch on the value stored in `currentState`. In the previous chapter, we created an inheritance hierarchy to subclass the variant behavior and succeeded in reducing the complexity of the individual methods and also in facilitating reuse. Such subclassing is, indeed, possible here as well, but since a state is a common theme in any application modeled as an FSM, the idea is expressed as a design pattern called the **State pattern.**

### 8.4.2 Communication among Objects

In our design, objects communicate in two contexts:

- Events specific to the operation of the microwave, for example, closing the door.
- Events of a more general nature that could find relevance in any application. The only such event in this application is the ticking of the clock; this is clearly something that would be relevant in any time-dependent operation.

In both these cases, the `Microwave` object is the interested listener. The application-specific events are caught in the GUI and sent to `Microwave` by invoking the appropriate method. There is some coupling involved here, but since the GUI has been developed specifically for this application, this is not a serious concern. As the system operates, one should expect that changes will be needed and these will require new kinds of events to be added. In our current solution, this will mean adding new methods to `Microwave`.

Consider now the more general events, which, in our example, are limited to clock ticks. We have written a class, `Clock`, that is specifically tailored for `Microwave`. Since the clock serves the same purpose in any application, we would like to have a general `Clock` class that can be instantiated wherever it is needed.

In both these cases above, what we see is that our system employs a form of communication where the entire responsibility for the communication rests with the sender, which is not desirable. In the first case, it appears to be less harmful, but as we shall see, reuse is facilitated when the responsibility is moved to the listener. In the second case, moving the responsibility to the listener helps us to define a class that can be used across many applications. In general, designs like the one we had in this section make it the responsibility of the *event generator* to get hold of all the listeners and explicitly maintain a reference to each one of them. When the event occurs, every listener must be notified. This is a poor assignment of responsibilities for three reasons:

- The event generator needs to keep track of all the different classes of objects that are interested in listening, and the various ways in which they must be notified. This makes the sender vulnerable to changes in the listener classes, which can be avoided if we have one standard format that all listeners must adhere to.
- Responsibility for registering interest rests with the sender. This implies that when interested listeners join the system, the sender must somehow

detect them and add them. Instead, if the listeners had this responsibility, they could simply invoke the appropriate method on the sender.

- The set of listeners cannot change dynamically. We would like to have the flexibility that a listener object can shut off all incoming messages from a particular sender. (This would be preferable to a situation where the listener hears all the messages but does not act on those from some sources.) Such a change in listener preference cannot be detected by the sender alone. If the listeners could register and de-register themselves, this would be easily accomplished.

The above drawbacks point to the fact that in a situation where the responsibility rests with the sender, we have **tightly coupled communication.** A standard solution framework for loosely coupled communication is the **Observer pattern**, which we will use for listening to clock ticks.

## 8.5 Using the State Pattern

Using the State pattern is closely connected to the idea of modeling with FSMs. Typical situations that employ the State pattern have the following characteristic elements:

- A collection of states, with each state being defined by distinct behavior.
- A set of external inputs to which the system must respond.
- A **context** in which the FSM operates.

The necessity of the first two is obvious. The third must exist simply because the states are ephemeral and we need some "temporal glue" that provides continuity to the system. In our example, the context does not serve any purpose beyond that; in general, the context may be a class that plays a much broader role and the FSM may be used to model only a small portion of the system responsibilities. The context must therefore have the following:

- A field to track the current state of the FSM.
- A mechanism to record the change of state.

In addition, the context may provide other mechanisms depending on the particular details of our implementation. These include, but are not limited to, the following:

- Provide a mechanism to effect state transitions.
- Provide methods for entities outside the system to communicate with the FSM.
- Keep track of external entities that may need to be notified in response to internal changes.

### 8.5.1 Creating the State Hierarchy

In the solution given earlier, the `Microwave` class had a variable `currentState` on which the behavior was conditionally executed. This is reminiscent of the use of `bookType` in the library system in Chapter 7. Since the design in that case was improved by replacing conditionals with subclasses, we should expect to do something similar here as well with an abstract superclass subclassed by several concrete ones. The natural thing here would be to have an abstract superclass that denotes the microwave state and one concrete subclass for each of the possible actual states.

There is, however, an important difference. The library system would have numerous `LoanableItem` objects, each of which would assume the type of one of the subclasses. In the microwave, however, there is just one microwave and rather than belong to one of the state subclasses, the microwave actually moves from state to state. As a consequence, it is more appropriate to divide the `Microwave` class into two:

- The first part, which deals with state information. This forms a hierarchy with an abstract superclass to denote the general idea of a microwave state and one subclass for each of the actual states. This structure is shown in Figure 8.8.
- The second part, which deals with contextual information. We could view the original `Microwave` class as now simply holding the contextual information required for the operation of the FSM. It is therefore aptly renamed `MicrowaveContext`.

`MicrowaveContext` will be a singleton, and so will each of the concrete state subclasses. The specific state that the microwave is currently in will have to be remembered by the `MicrowaveContext` object, and accordingly, we will need to provide a mechanism to update this information whenever a state transition occurs. To enable this, let us examine a couple of options for managing the state transitions.

### 8.5.2 Transitioning between States

Transitioning to a new state is an operation that involves knowledge of the other states. Before we decide how to implement this, it is important that we examine how information about the states and transitions is stored. We have seen that the FSM can be represented either by a transition table or in a pictorial fashion, with boxes showing the states and arrows showing the transitions between them. These two representations are somewhat like, but not the same as, the two standard methods for storing directed graphs: adjacency matrices and adjacency lists. In an **adjacency matrix**, we have a centralized storage structure. Each vertex has an associated index, and we use

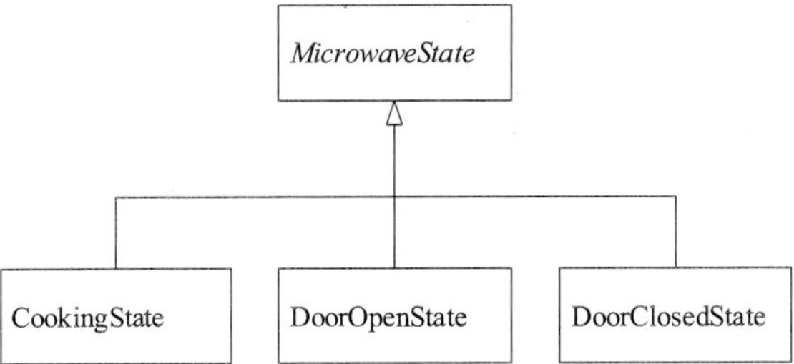


**Fig. 8.8** Microwave state hierarchy: The three states in which the microwave can be are represented by three classes. Since we need to refer to the current state without actually knowing what it is, we relate them through the superclass `MicrowaveState`.

these indices to access the vertices and determine the connectivity between vertices. In an **adjacency list**, we have a more distributed storage; each vertex contains a list of the vertices which are its immediate neighbors. These two representations lead to two possible implementations for handling transitions between states.

### 8.5.2.1 Centralized Representation

In this approach, we first associate an index with each state. Let us assign index 0 to the Door Closed state (the initial state), index 1 to the Door Open state, and index 2 to the Cooking state. To keep track of this mapping, we create an array; thus the context has an array of `MicrowaveState` named `states` such that `states[0]` would store a reference to the Door Closed state, `states[1]` would store a reference to the Door Open state, and `states[2]` would store a reference to the Cooking state. Some applications may designate an error state to handle unexpected conditions; in our case we might use index 3 for that.

Next, we work on the transitions. We know from the state transition table (Table 8.8) that transitions may occur only when one of the events occurs. We may assign numeric values 0, 1, 2, 3, and 4 to Open Door, Close Door, Press Cook, Clock Ticks, and Timer Runs Out, respectively. Thus, the transition table can be represented as below.

| | | | | |
|---|---|---|---|---|
| 1 | 0 | 2 | 0 | 0 |
| 1 | 0 | 1 | 1 | 1 |
| 1 | 2 | 2 | 2 | 0 |

This table is interpreted as follows. The rows correspond to transitions from a given state and the columns represent transitions when a certain input event occurs. For example, entries in the first row (indexed 0) correspond to transitions from the Door Closed state. Similarly, entries in the first column (indexed 0) show the transitions when the Open Door event occurs. We can interpret the other rows and columns in a similar way. For example, the entry at (2,4) holds the index of the state that the system transitions to when the Timer Runs Out event occurs in the Cooking state.
The Java code for setting up the table is given below:

```
int[][] transitions = {{1, 0 , 2 , 0 , 0},
                       {1, 0 , 1 , 1 , 1},
                       {1, 2 , 2 , 2 , 0}};
```

That was simple enough, but then the implementation would be cleaner if the event Timer Runs Out (corresponding to the last column) can be externally generated. If we intend to keep `Clock` as general as possible, we need an extra class, say, `Timer`, which can be set to some value initially, then receive clock signals, and eventually send the Timer Runs Out event to `Microwave`. In addition, we might want the `Timer` object to be capable of pausing and resuming whenever cooking is interrupted and resumed.

An alternative to generating the Timer Runs Out event externally would be to have the `Microwave` itself keep track of the remaining cook time. In such an arrangement, we can treat the transition table as still valid, provided that we simulate the Timer Runs Out event internally and then use it to index the table as before.

The variable `currentState` now stores an `int`, which is the index of the current state. When a state wants to relinquish control, it invokes the `changeState()` method on the context, passing the index of the event in question. The code for `changeState()` would be

```
public void changeState(int event) {
  currentState = transitions[currentState][event];
}
```

The parameter `event` would be a number that represents one of the five events and hence would be between 0 and 4.

The method determines the index of the next state by looking up the transition table. The reference to the actual state object is determined by indexing into the array `states`.

#### 8.5.2.2 Localized Representation

In this representation, each state directly provides a reference to the next state when it has to relinquish control. The context, of course, needs to be informed of the change of state, and this is done once again using the `changeState()` method.

```
public void changeState(MicrowaveState state) {
  currentState = state;
}
```

The context stores a reference to the current state, as before.

**Using the State pattern**

The intent of the State pattern is *to allow an object to change behavior when its internal state changes.* The intent of this pattern (as with several other patterns) is fully understood only when we see the entire process of analysis, design, and implementation involved in incorporating this pattern.
The first step is to recognize the need for the finite state model in the analysis. This is easy to do in a lot of situations, but it is possible that this recognition occurs only later in the process. In our example, we recognize the applicability of the finite state model; the naive approach implements this by keeping a field in the microwave, such that the value of the field represents the current state. In the method for each response, we end up switching on the value of this field. Applying the standard refactoring rule, we recognize that the conditional can be replaced by polymorphism.
However, unlike with `LoanableItem` in the library example, this cannot be a simple hierarchy, since there is only one microwave. The State pattern handles this by creating a separate class that takes care of the event responses and encapsulating within the microwave; to keep the nomenclature straight, we call this new class `MicrowaveState` and rename the encapsulating class as `MicrowaveContext`. `MicrowaveState` is now an abstract class with concrete subclasses for each state the microwave can be in.

#### 8.5.2.3 Comparison of the Approaches

Both approaches have their pros and cons. In the centralized approach, each state can be written independently of the others. The approach has the advantage that the code for a state does not have to be modified unless we want to change its behavior. The transitions can be changed and new states linked to existing ones in code external to the states. This allows a kind of reuse where we can create a library of states for a particular application domain and use these repeatedly for several applications.

In the localized approach, each state is aware of all the other states and therefore the author of each state is required to be aware of how it connects to the FSM. This approach has the advantage of simplicity in that the additional work of decoding all the exit conditions and "assembling" the FSM is not required. In situations where an FSM is being used to model something specific, like an algorithm for a specialized communication protocol, it is unlikely that a library of states can be reused across the domain. In that case, it may be beneficial to use the localized approach and embed the transition information within each state. We implement the transitions for our case study using the localized approach.

### 8.5.3 The State Classes

We now elaborate on the state classes. The abstract class, `MicrowaveState`, contains methods to handle the various events and its class diagram is shown in Figure 8.9. The meaning of most of the methods should be obvious. When the microwave changes state, some actions may need to be carried out such as variable initializations and communication with external agents. It is convenient to have all of these actions executed in a method, which we term `enter()`. Similarly, while leaving a state, some clean-up might be necessary, which calls for the `leave()` method. These two are declared `abstract`. The other five methods specify the actions for the five possible events.

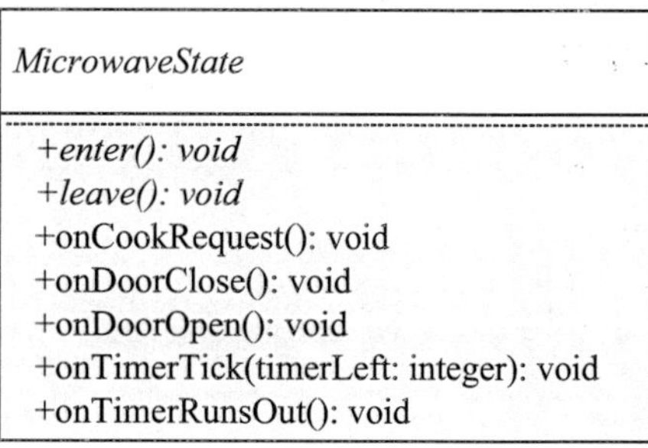


**Fig. 8.9** Class diagram for `MicrowaveState`. The `enter()` method is a placeholder for carrying out the necessary processing while entering this state. The `leave()` method specifies what is to be done while leaving the state. The other five methods specify the actions for the five possible events and will do nothing as the default action.

The display needs to be updated as state transitions occur. We need to determine what actions should be carried out as the microwave enters and leaves the different states. While there is more than one way of assigning responsibilities to the `enter()` and `leave()` methods, a close examination of the states shows that the following would work:

1. When the DoorOpenState is entered, the status of the door should be shown as open and when leaving the state, the door status should be set as closed.
2. At the time of entering the DoorClosed state, the light status should be displayed as turned off and while leaving the state, the light status should be shown as turned on.
3. As the state transitions to the Cooking state, the timer should be activated, the time left for cooking should be shown as 60 seconds, and the microwave status should be shown as cooking. While leaving the state, the timer should be turned off, the time left should be displayed as 0, and the microwave status should be shown as not cooking.

Next, we develop the class diagrams for the individual states. When the door is open, the microwave does not respond to anything other than the Door Close event. Therefore, in the class diagram for `DoorOpenState` (Figure 8.10), we only show the methods `doorClosed()`, `enter()`, and `leave()`. Similar interpretations can be made for `DoorClosedState` and `CookingState`, which are shown in Figures 8.11 and 8.12 respectively.

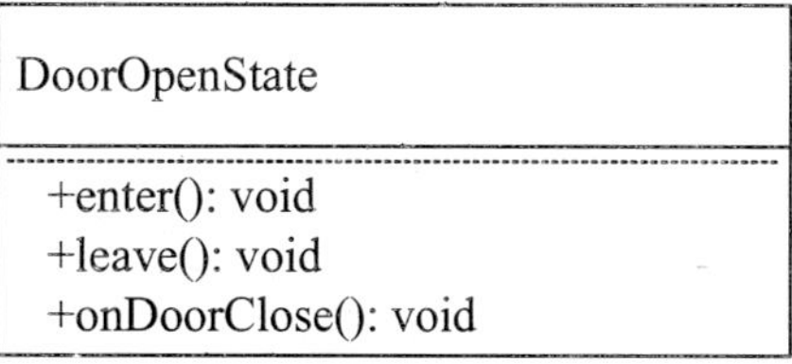


**Fig. 8.10** Class diagram for `DoorOpenState`. Only the methods that override the superclass's methods are shown here. The `enter()` method would make the display show that the door is open. The `leave()` method would make the display show that the door is closed. The only event this state reacts to is the Door Close event.

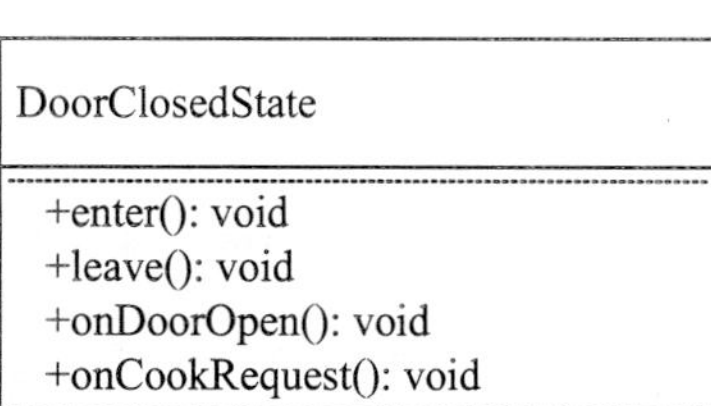


**Fig. 8.11** Class diagram for `DoorClosedState`. Only the methods that override the superclass's methods are shown here. The `enter()` method would make the display show that the light is turned off. The `leave()` method would make the display show that the light is turned on. The only events this state reacts to are the Door Open and Cook Request events.

| CookingState |
|---|
| +enter(): void<br>+leave(): void<br>+onDoorOpen(): void<br>+onCookRequest(): void<br>+onTimerTick(timeLeft: integer): void<br>+onTimerRunsOut(): void |

**Fig. 8.12** Class diagram for `CookingState`. This class overrides all methods of the superclass except `doorClosed()`. The `enter()` method would initialize the cooking process by setting up the timer. It would also display the time remaining for cooking as 60 seconds and display that the microwave is cooking. The `leave()` method would make the display show that the microwave is no longer cooking and that the remaining cook time is 0.

## 8.6 Communicating the Timing Events

In our initial implementation, the `Microwave` object kept track of the cooking time. This simple approach overlooked the fact that a timer is an object in its own right. Creating a separate `Timer` class abstracts out the functionality needed to set a timer value and be notified when the timer runs out. This simplifies the construction of the FSM and helps with the construction of more complicated systems should we wish to employ multiple timers, perhaps one for cooking, and others for setting alarms. (Some real-life microwaves do have more than one timer.)

An obvious consequence of the decision to introduce a timer is that the `Timer` object, and not `MicrowaveContext`, would now become the client of `Clock`. The `Clock` is a utility that is required in a wide range of applications, and must therefore notify the `Timer` in a loosely coupled manner.
Loosely coupled communication must have three properties:

- The listener is responsible for registering interest.
- All interested listeners share some common interface so that the sender need not distinguish between listeners.
- The sender has a mechanism for maintaining a collection of interested listeners.

The Observer pattern gives us a mechanism that makes this possible.

### 8.6.1 The Observer Pattern

There are two categories of players in the Observer pattern:

- The **observable**, which is usually a single object, and
- The **observer**, of which there may be several. It is the responsibility of the observable to provide a method by which the observer can register interest. Once an observer has been registered, it is the responsibility of the observable to notify that observer of any state changes. In order to accomplish this without causing tight coupling, every observer must have a method with a signature that has been agreed upon.

To implement the Observer pattern, we employ a Java class named `PropertyChangeSupport` and an interface called `PropertyChangeListener`. We extend `PropertyChangeSupport` to create an observable and implement the `PropertyChangeListener` interface to develop an observer.
`PropertyChangeSupport` has two main categories of methods:

- *Methods for adding and deleting observers.* The method `addPropertyChangeListener (PropertyChangeListener listener)` adds the given listener to this list. An observer can be deleted by using the method
`removePropertyChangeListener(PropertyChangeListener listener)`.
- *Methods for notifying observers.* A method named `firePropertyChange()` and its variants enable notification of the `PropertyChangeListener` objects of "noteworthy" events occurring within the observer. One specific signature is

  ```
  firePropertyChange(String propertyName, Object oldValue,
  Object newValue)
  ```

  which informs registered observers of a change to a property identified by `propertyName` within an observable. The old and new values are to be passed as well. The caller can indicate there is no specific property by passing `null` values for all three parameters.

Every class that wishes to be an observer implements the `PropertyChangeListener` interface, which has the method `propertyChange()` with the following signature:

```
public abstract void propertyChange(PropertyChangeEvent event);
```

When `firePropertyChange()` is invoked on the `PropertyChangeSupport` object, the `propertyChange()` method is invoked once for each observer in the list of "interested observers." The `PropertyChangeEvent` object has methods that can be used by the listener to determine the property name and the old and new values of the property.

The interaction between PropertyChangeSupport and two PropertyChangeListener objects is depicted in the sequence diagram in Figure 8.13. The figure shows an event occurring in PropertyChangeSupport, which calls the firePropertyChange() method. In response to the firePropertyChange() method call, the PropertyChangeSupport object calls the propertyChange() methods of the two observers supplying them with information about the event (event).

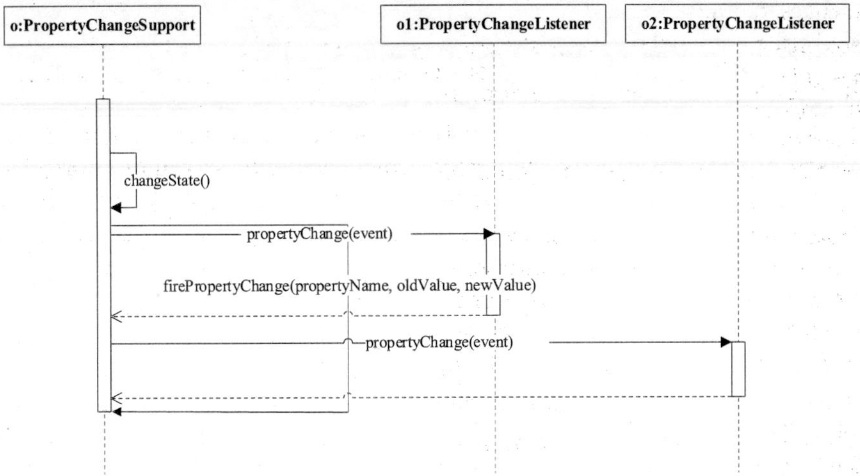


**Fig. 8.13** Sequence diagram for notifying observers. When an event occurs, say, due to the execution of the changeState() method in the observable, the observable invokes the firePropertyChange() method, which calls the propertyChange(event) method on each of the observers registered with the PropertyChangeSupport object.

## 8.6.2 Generating and Handling Timing Events

Note that we now have a timer that keeps track of when the microwave needs to stop cooking. The timer must therefore watch the time, that is, observe the clock; whenever the clock ticks, the timer takes the necessary action.

It is useful to understand the interplay between all of these. The clock is a general purpose utility that can be used in a variety of situations. To enable this versatility, it should not be coupled closely with any other class and is therefore modeled as an observable entity. The timer is an application that uses the clock; it must then be modeled as an observer of the clock. The timer handles the task of notifying the microwave when a timing event occurs. Let us look at how this relationship can be designed.

#### 8.6.2.1 Using the Timer with the Microwave

The `Timer` class must have the following functionality:

- The timer must have a client. The purpose of a `Timer` object is to inform a client object about timing signals. The `Timer` object is dedicated to working with its client.
- The timer must have a time period set at construction time. We should be able to create a timer that counts down to 0 from an initial value given at construction time.
- At the end of the time period, the timer must notify its client.

In addition, it would be desirable to have the following functionality in a `Timer` class:

- The timer should should notify its client whenever a certain period has elapsed. For the microwave, we need notifications every second, but in general, one could have this value specified by the creator at construction time or even changed periodically.
- It should be possible to pause and resume the timer. If we wish to modify the microwave application so that we could resume cooking after opening the door, this feature would be very convenient.

An issue that remains is how the communication between `Timer` and its client should take place. We have at least two options:

- They communicate using the Observer pattern, with `Timer` being the observable and the client being the observer.
- `Timer` calls specifically named methods of the client to notify it of the timer running out.

The advantage of using the Observer pattern is that it uses a well-known paradigm and is readily understood. If we make the assumption that a timer can have multiple clients, then this approach is justified.

In this problem, though, we make the assumption that a single timer will have only one client. If that is the case, the Observer pattern would be an overkill: we do not wish to incur the overhead of maintaining `PropertyChangeSupport` and its apparent overhead of maintaining a list of observers and a loop to notify the observers.

Even if we assume that a timer may only have one client, it is quite possible that there could be multiple timers, each having its own client. In that case, it is, however, not desirable to use specifically named methods in the client for notifications. For the `Timer` class to be more widely useful, we should have potential clients implement a common interface, which we term `Notifiable`. The functionality is given in Figure 8.14.

The `Timer` class diagram is shown in Figure 8.15. While instantiating, the creator must supply the client object and the initial time value. The time could be added to or the timer could be stopped using the appropriately

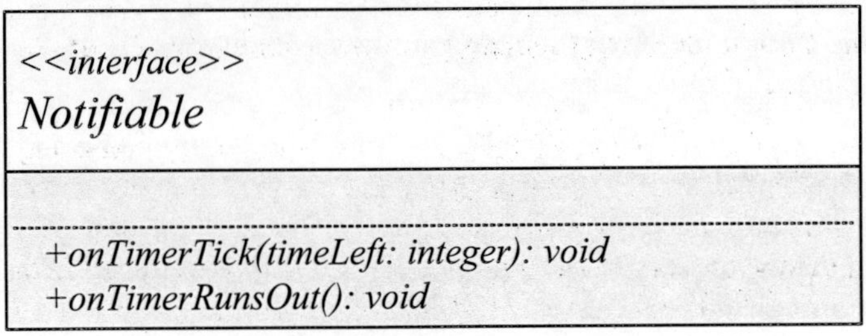

*<<interface>>*
*Notifiable*

*+onTimerTick(timeLeft: integer): void*
*+onTimerRunsOut(): void*

**Fig. 8.14** Interface `Notifiable`. Generally speaking, any object may need to create a timer. For a timer to report back to its creator, it then becomes necessary to have an interface the timer's creator can implement, so it can be appropriately notified.

named methods. Additionally, one could add to the functionality with obvious choices including methods to pause and resume the timer.

Timer

-timeLeft: integer
-client: Notifiable

+Timer(client: Notifiable, timeValue: integer)
+addTimeValue(value: integer): void
+stop(): void

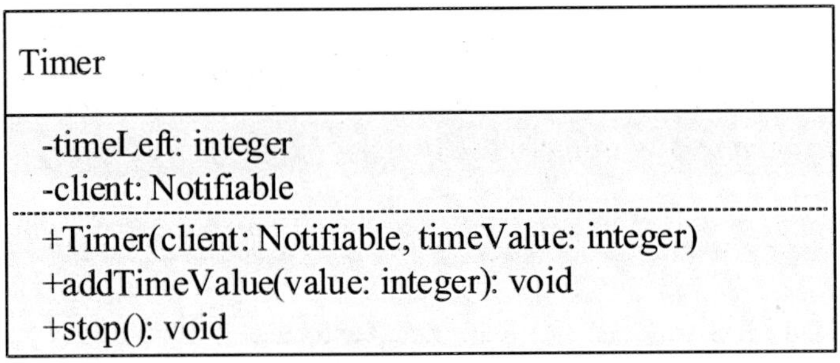

**Fig. 8.15** The `Timer` class. The class is instantiated by a client, which implements the `Notifiable` interface. The client's ID is maintained by the timer, so it can notify the client. One could add more methods, for example, to pause and resume the timer.

### Creating the `Timer` Object

We now need to address the question of who should assume the responsibility of creating and managing the `Timer` object. Two options come to mind:

- **Option 1:** The `MicrowaveContext` instance can create a `Timer` object. The notifications would be sent to `MicrowaveContext`. `MicrowaveContext` fowards these notifications to the current state, which can process or ignore the messages.

- **Option 2:** The `CookingState` class itself creates the `Timer` and receives the signals directly.

The first approach has the advantage that it provides a uniform approach to handling events. As discussed earlier, all communication between the FSM and external entities goes through the context. With this approach, notifications from `MicrowaveDisplay` and `Timer` are all sent to `MicrowaveContext`, which delivers them to the currently active state. On the flip side, we are loading the context with information that is not central to its role, thus violating the single responsibility principle, and perhaps the interface segregation principle. This drawback is significant, since the lifetime of any `timer` object does not extend across state transitions. Sending timer messages through the context only results in exposing the context to details of how the state is implemented.

The second approach, however, recognizes the fact that `Timer` is needed by the `CookingState` class, and makes `CookingState` responsible for managing its needs. This avoids the unnecessary coupling between `CookingState` and `MicrowaveContext` that would otherwise result, and also avoids some difficulties that might occur in system enhancements, as explained below.

A problem with having the context as the `Timer`'s client is that it makes the design not very extensible in certain situations. Assume that in the future, we want to provide several pre-determined cooking schemes: for example, we might have a specific scheme for boiling a cup of water and another for reheating frozen pasta. Perhaps the former might involve using the power tube for 100 seconds at 100% power and the second cooking scheme might cook for two minutes at 50% of the maximum power level followed by one minute at 100% power. Since such schemes have different behaviors, we would have multiple state classes as well. `MicrowaveContext` would then be the client of the timers for all such new classes as well, and would ultimately have more complicated data structures to keep track of these timers and significantly more complicated interactions with the state classes. It would certainly be simpler if each state class managed all the timers it needs.

#### 8.6.2.2 Interactions between the Context and the State Classes

The context manages the states and hence must be coupled to the state classes. The interactions between state classes and the context are designed taking into account the way the concrete state classes perform the necessary computations.

Obviously, there are things each state performs that only have local effects (for example, managing a `Timer` object), and they can be handled in fairly obvious ways. But there are actions the states perform that have an effect outside the state:

- Actions that require a change of state.
- Actions that require making changes to an entity outside the FSM.

In a typical FSM, each state has some impact on the environment in which it is operating. In our case, these are actions that change the display. For instance, when the cook button is pressed while in the cooking state, the number of seconds remaining should be increased by 60. The question here is how to implement the communication from the cooking state to the display object. It should be no surprise that we have more than one option for handling these:

- **Option 1:** All communication goes through the context.
- **Option 2:** Each state communicates independently with the external entities.

The first option is appropriate in situations where we want the entire FSM subsystem to be a unit that can inter-operate with several environments; in such situations, the context can act as a facade and shield the states from external changes. For instance, we may decide that we will no longer have a simple display to show what is going on, but want to manipulate device drivers that actually turn the light and power tube on and off. Such a change could be accomplished by changing only the context; if we had chosen the second option, every state would have to be changed to communicate with the new external environment. The downside is that Option 1 requires that the context provide methods for communication that can be invoked by the states. This would result in the additional overhead of a method call.

In the second option, each state must keep track of the concrete entities that it wishes to communicate with and has to be tailored to that interface. This clearly makes the state dependent on these interfaces and thus introduces some additional coupling. This seems to suggest that Option 1 is always preferable, which would not be correct for the following reason. Consider a situation where each state has some distinct external entities which it communicates with; *if all the communication went through the context, the context would have to provide methods for each kind of entity, making it a very unwieldy class.* In such a situation it is preferable that each state communicate directly with its external clients. The coupling that may result can be significantly reduced if all the external entities were to be implementations of stable abstractions.

The class diagram for `MicrowaveContext` is shown in Figure 8.16. In this design, we have chosen Option 1, that is, all communication between the states and the UI goes through the context. It is convenient to have in the context a method `setDisplay()` to set the reference to the display object. The current state can be changed by executing the method `changeState()`. Figure 8.17 shows the sequence of calls that takes place when the clock ticks.

| MicrowaveContext |
|---|
| -currentState: MicrowaveState<br>-display: MicrowaveDisplay |
| +setDisplay(display: MicrowaveDisplay): void<br>+onDoorClose(): void<br>+onDoorOpen(): void<br>+onCookRequest(): void<br>+changeState(state: MicrowaveState): void<br>+showTimeLeft(timeLeft: integer): void<br>+showCooking(): void<br>+showNotCooking(): void<br>+showDoorOpened(): void<br>+showDoorClosed(): void<br>+showLightOn(): void<br>+showLightOff(): void |

**Fig. 8.16** Class diagram for `MicrowaveContext`. There are three event methods, one for each event that comes from the GUI. Then there are the methods called by the state classes to change the display. The `changeState()` method is called to change the state of the FSM.

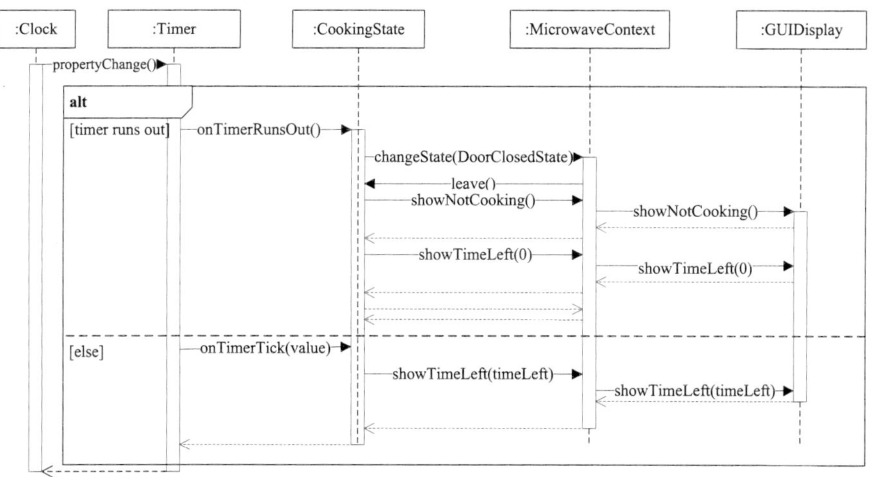


**Fig. 8.17** The sequence of actions that takes place when the clock ticks. The `Clock` object notifies the `Timer` object. Depending on whether the timer runs out or not, the `CookingState` class issues different messages to `MicrowaveContext`. Notice a sequence of dotted lines that show the replies to the `leave()` and `changeState()` method calls.

#### 8.6.2.3 Implementation Using the State and Observer Patterns

We begin showing salient portions of our implementation with the major changes in `Clock`. The class maintains a `PropertyChangeSupport` object to keep track of the observers, and delegates calls to add the observers to this object. After each clock tick, the `firePropertyChange()` method is called to inform the observers of a clock tick. Note that there is no real property involved, so we follow the recommendation of the JDK and pass `null` values for the property name and the new and old values.

```
public class Clock implements Runnable {
 // several fields and methods not shown
 private final PropertyChangeSupport propertyChangeSupport
                               = new PropertyChangeSupport(this);
 public void addPropertyChangeListener(PropertyChangeListener
 listener) {
 this.propertyChangeSupport.addPropertyChangeListener(listener);
 }

  public void run() {
    try {
     while (true) {
       Thread.sleep(1000);
       this.propertyChangeSupport.firePropertyChange(null, null,
       true);
     }
   } catch (InterruptedException ie) {
 }
}
```

The `Timer` class maintains fields to keep track of the time and the client and these values are given at creation time, so every timer is set up for a certain client with an initial time value. The timer then adds itself as an observer of the clock.

For the methods, `addTimeValue()`, which changes the timer value, is quite straightforward. Each clock tick results in a call to the `propertyChange()` method. The timer decrements the time counter and checks if it has reached 0. Depending on this, one of the two methods, `onTimerTick()` or `onTimerRunsOut()`, is called. Once the timer has run out, the timer takes itself out as an observer of the clock.

```
public class Timer implements PropertyChangeListener {
  private int timeValue;
  private Notifiable client;
  public Timer(Notifiable client, int timeValue) {
```

```
    this.client = client;
    this.timeValue = timeValue;
    Clock.getInstance().addPropertyChangeListener(this);
  }
  public void addTimeValue(int value) {
    timeValue += value;
  }
  public void stop() {
    Clock.getInstance().removePropertyChangeListener(this);
  }
  public int getTimeValue() {
    return timeValue;
  }
  @Override
  public void propertyChange(PropertyChangeEvent arg0) {
    if (--timeValue <= 0) {
      client.onTimerRunsOut();
      Clock.getInstance().removePropertyChangeListener(this);
    } else {
      client.onTimerTick();
    }
  }
}
```

Moving onto the `MicrowaveContext` class, we note that the `changeState()` method calls the `leave()` method of the current state before switching to the new state and initializing it.

```
public void changeState(MicrowaveState nextState) {
     currentState.leave();
     currentState = nextState;
     currentState.enter();
}
```

Some representative methods of `MicrowaveContext` are given below. These are fairly straightforward methods.

```
public void doorClosed() {
   currentState.doorClosed();
}

public void showTimeLeft(int time) {
   display.showTimeLeft(time);
}
```

The `enter()` and `leave()` methods of `CookingState` are given below. The `enter()` method creates a timer and modifies the display, whereas the `leave()` method sets the reference to the `Timer` to `null`, so it can be garbage-collected.

```
public void enter() {
 timer = new Timer(this, 60);
 MicrowaveContext.instance().showCooking();
 MicrowaveContext.instance().showTimeLeft(timer.getTimeValue());
 }

public void leave() {
 timer.stop();
 timer = null;
 MicrowaveContext.instance().showNotCooking();
 MicrowaveContext.instance().showTimeLeft(0);
 }
```

`MicrowaveState` has default methods for processing each of the events, and the concrete state classes are supposed to override the appropriate ones to implement the required functionality.

```
public abstract class MicrowaveState {
  public abstract void enter();
  public abstract void leave();
  public void onCookRequest() {
  }
  public void onDoorOpen() {
  }
  public void onDoorClose() {
  }
  public void onTimerTick() {
  }
  public void onTimerRunsOut() {
  }
}
```

**The Observer pattern**

*Where do we employ this?* An abstraction has several parts, which have to be encapsulated separately, but there is a need to maintain communication between them.
*What problem are we facing?* Communicating with an object essentially requires that some method of the object be invoked. This implies that the object initiating the communication must know which method of the recipient(s) is to be invoked. If the sender must keep track of the methods of all recipients, we get tight coupling between the various parts of the abstraction.
*How have we solved it?* We place the responsibility for communication on the receiver instead of the sender. The sender (also known as the subject or the observable) has a method that allows recipients (observers) to register their interest with the sender. All the recipients of the message implement a common method (or an interface) for receiving messages. When there is a need for communication, the sender invokes the common method on all the receivers that have registered their interest with the sender.

## 8.7 Replacing Event Conditionals with Polymorphism

In the design presented above, the `handle` method in `GUIDisplay` handles clicks on the buttons. This conditional switches on the kind of event, which in turn is decided by the external input.

```
public void handle(ActionEvent event) {
    if (event.getSource().equals(doorCloser)) {
        microwaveContext.onDoorClose();
    } else if (event.getSource().equals(doorOpener)) {
        microwaveContext.onDoorOpen();
    } else if (event.getSource().equals(cookButton)) {
        microwaveContext.onCookRequest();
    }
}
```

The other source of events is the `Timer` class.

In a more complicated system, the number of events and states could be quite large and there could be numerous sources of events. Having the events correctly delivered to the correct state could be quite an error-prone process. In this section, we describe a design strategy that practically eliminates these issues. The approach has the following characteristics:

- It eliminates most of the conditionals in the system. This is based on the refactoring rule of replacing conditionals by polymorphism.
- The process is simple and easy to follow.
- The approach increases the number of classes. While this is a drawback, the classes are quite simple and small and the code is quite obvious.

The major conditionals in the previous solution to the system appear in the `handle()` method, which switches to different method calls based on the button that was clicked. This method has conditionals to determine the method to be called. We can eliminate the conditionals by replacing the conditionals by polymorphism.

As we know, replacing conditionals by polymorphism requires the creation of a subtype for each leg of the conditional. Here it translates into the creation of a hierarchy of `Button` classes.

This hierarchy is shown in Figure 8.18. The common superclass `GUIButton` is abstract and should help us treat all buttons in a uniform way, should that be necessary. In its constructor, it also makes every subclass listen to its own clicks.

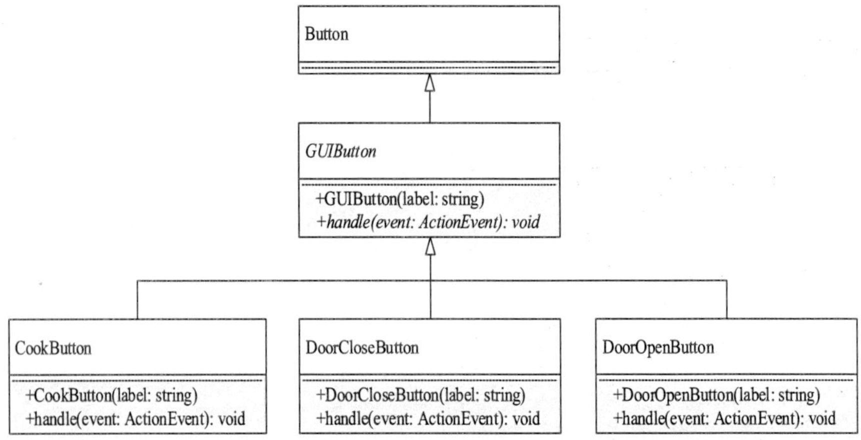


**Fig. 8.18** `Button` hierarchy: The three concrete `Button` classes represent the three buttons in the interface. Each button handles its own clicks by calling an appropriate method of the context.

As a representative piece of code, let us take a look at the `CookButton` class's code.

```
public class CookButton extends GUIButton implements
                          EventHandler<ActionEvent> {
    public CookButton(String string) {
        super(string);
```

```
    }
    public void handle(ActionEvent event) {
        MicrowaveContext.instance().onCookRequest();
    }
}
```

To see the interaction among the classes in the hierarchy, let us assume that the current state is DoorClosedState and that the button to open the door is clicked. The sequence of actions that takes place is as follows:

1. The user clicks the cook button. This generates an instance of ActionEvent and control goes to the handle() method of CookButton.
2. The handle() method calls the onCookRequest() method of MicrowaveContext.
3. The onCookRequest() method of MicrowaveContext calls the onCookRequest() method of DoorClosedState. This is a polymorphic call.
4. The onCookRequest() method of DoorClosedState changes the current state by calling the changeState() method of MicrowaveContext, which in turn modifies the display through calls to the leave() method of DoorClosedState and the enter() method of CookingState.

### 8.7.1 Code Organization

As the reader might expect, the code is organized into several packages:

- states: This package contains the three concrete states, the abstract superclass MicrowaveState, and the context class.
- timer: The thread class Clock, the Timer class, and the Notifiable interface are in this package.
- buttons: There is one Button subclass for each button in the GUI. They are subclasses of GUIButton, which is in the same package. Obviously, the implementation is different in the JavaFX and Swing versions.
- display: The interface MicrowaveDisplay, which is in this package, is the same as in the first version of the microwave. Its implementation is different in the JavaFX and Swing versions.
- start: It starts the program.

Finally, the state classes are the same as before, except for the fact that the names of the event-handling methods have been changed.

**Concrete versus abstract entities in design patterns**

Often in design patterns, we find both an abstract and a concrete version of an entity. Sometimes the abstract entity is present just as a type (interface) and at other times, it is an abstract class. In the Iterator pattern, we encountered the use of interfaces. Interfaces suffice in situations where all the required properties of the entity can be expressed without any implementation.

In the State pattern, the abstract state class allows us to capture default behavior and also store references to other entities. In our microwave implementation, we do not have an abstract context. However, in an implementation where the state transitions are stored as a table, an abstract context helps with reuse.

In the Observer pattern, the observable is an abstract class. The mechanism used to enforce the pattern requires that the observable store references to the observers, and notify them as needed. If no implementation is provided, we may end up in a situation where the correctness of the pattern is compromised. Since the observer entity on the other hand needs just the `update` method with no restrictions on its behavior, it is left as an interface.

Another important benefit of abstract entities is that they enable some form of type checking. The abstract `Observer` class maintains a polymorphic container to keep track of all observers and the abstract entity helps ensure that all these objects have implemented the `update` method. In the absence of this, observable would be storing a collection of objects and strong typing would not be possible.

## 8.8 Employing the FSM Model for Other Types of Applications

The discussion so far in this chapter clearly makes a strong case for the FSM model. By employing the model, we are not only able to characterize all the behavior accurately, but also compartmentalize the different behaviors and reduce coupling. One aspect of this case study is that all the variation in behavior occurs in the back end. In other words, when the system transitions across states, the structure of the GUI display panel remains unchanged. We shall now see some examples of situations where the visible aspect of the GUI changes when we transition to another state.

Consider an e-commerce website. On connecting to the site, the user typically sees some sort of login request – they can log in as a registered user with a userID and password or continue as a guest. Depending on the option chosen, the user sees different options on the screen: unlike the guest, the registered user may see different promotions, and any special coupons issued to them. Both screens connect to the same back end and database, but the list of possible user actions is different. We can model this GUI using an FSM, by considering the registered user screen and guest screen as two different states that the front end can be in.

Another situation arises when we implement something like a communication protocol with an associated GUI. As we saw in Chapter 3, protocol state machines can capture the behaviors of one of the parties in the transaction. This can be combined with a GUI, when different user input(s) are needed in each stage; the GUI prompts the user for the kind of input needed.

### 8.8.1 Graphical User Interfaces (GUIs)

A GUI application typically involves many screens, each having multiple widgets such as textboxes, scrollbars, buttons, etc. Using some of these widgets (for example, clicking on a button), we can transition to a different screen.

For a little more specificity, consider the following scenario (also depicted in Figure 8.19). The GUI has three screens (Screen 1, Screen 2, and Screen 3) and shows exactly one of the three screens at any given time:

- Screen 1 has two buttons, B1 and B2. Clicking on B1 causes the GUI to display Screen 2 and clicking on B2 closes the program itself.
- Screen 2 has a single button, B3. Clicking on it results in Screen 3 being displayed.
- Screen 3 has a single button, B4. Clicking on it results in Screen 1 being displayed.

We can think of each of the three screens as one of the states of an FSM and the clicking of the buttons as events. We can model the application as an FSM and come up with a state transition diagram as shown in Figure 8.20. Note the following aspects:

- To avoid complexity, we have not shown events that cannot occur: for example, in the state `Screen1`, button B3 cannot be pressed; we could complete the diagram by a transition to the same state for such impossible events.
- The terminated state does not correspond to an actual software class. It is inserted only to show that when button B2 is pressed, the system should exit.

It is fairly straightforward to design and implement the system from the state transition diagram.

An argument can certainly be made that the above scenario is extremely simplistic, but the point here is that there is a way to apply the FSM modeling

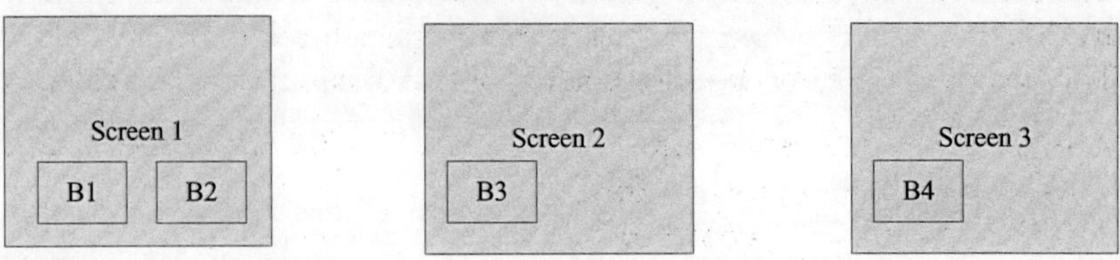


**Fig. 8.19** A simple GUI application with three screens. Screen 1 has two buttons, and the other two have one button each. Clicking on B1 causes the GUI to switch to Screen 2, clicking on B3 causes a switch to Screen 3, and clicking on B4 makes the GUI show Screen 1. A click on B2 closes the program. The point is that this can be analyzed and solved using the FSM approach.

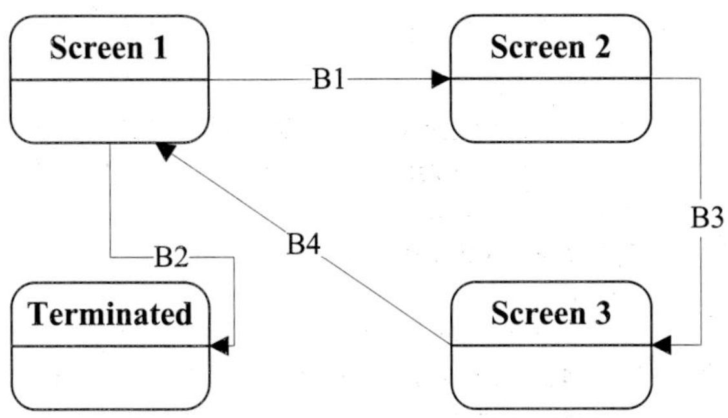


**Fig. 8.20** The state transition diagram for the GUI application. We have added a fourth state to take care of the program's termination. To avoid complexity, we have not shown events that cannot occur: for example, in the state `Screen1`, button B3 cannot be pressed; we could complete the diagram by a transition to the same state for such impossible events.

approach to construct GUI programs. In the project assignments at the end of this chapter, we shall see how this concept can be used to build a sophisticated GUI for the Library system we designed earlier.

## 8.8.2 Modeling a Network Protocol

As another example of an application, consider a file transfer program, which allows the download (upload) of files from (to) a remote computer. A simplified version of the file transfer protocol can be captured in the following steps:

1. The system asks the user to provide the ID and password for the remote machine.
2. The system connects with the remote machine and checks the credentials.
   - If the ID and password provided are invalid, the system goes back to asking for ID and password
   - If the ID and password provided are valid, the system requests the path name of the local file and the remote file, and whether the transfer is an upload or a download
3. The system checks the validity of the two path names.
   - If the path names are invalid, the system goes back to asking for path names
   - If the path names are valid, the system completes the file transfer and goes back to asking for path names

Such a program could be thought of as consisting of a set of states as outlined below:

- *The start state.* A user may may supply the user ID and password of an account he/she holds on a remote machine and the IP address of that machine to log in. Assuming these are valid and a connection can be established, the program moves into the logged-in state. The program allows a command to exit.
- *The logged-in state.* The user may supply the name of a remote file $F_r$, the name of a local file $F_l$, and choose either upload or download. The program goes into the file transfer state. The program allows a command to log out, which moves it to the start state.
- *The file transfer state.* The program uploads or downloads the file. Once the file transfer is complete, the program goes back to the logged-in state.

When we model this as an FSM, clearly we need to respect the protocol and also provide additional options; for instance, a logout button to disconnect from the remote machine needs to be provided in all stages.

This is a simplified version of the file transfer protocol. A real file transfer program would be much more versatile, allowing transfers of files from multiple directories, handling errors, and so on. But those can be handled by adding more events and states to the analysis (see Projects).

## 8.9 Discussion and Further Reading

### 8.9.1 Implementing the State Pattern

The State pattern can be implemented in different ways, and the particular implementation that we choose depends on the role played by the context and the kind of relationship we have between the states. At one end of the spectrum, we have an implementation where the context is nothing but a repository for shared information. This is the approach recommended in [2]. When a state has completed all of its actions, it passes control to the next state along with a reference to the context object. We have two choices as to how this can be realized. One approach is to create a new instance of a state whenever a state terminates. Another approach is where each state is a singleton and the current state invokes a method to obtain a reference to the next state. In such an implementation, there is some coupling between the individual states and this requires that each state be fully responsible for listening and responding to external events.

At the other end of the spectrum, we have a situation where each state is completely unaware of the existence of other states. This is accomplished by the current state terminating with a call to the context, which looks up a transition table to decide what the next state should be [1]. The context in this implementation provides methods to add states and transitions, which populate the transition table. These methods are accessible from code outside, which allows the context to be reused in other applications. Such an approach is particularly suitable for designing multi-panel interactive systems, such as a GUI for an application [5]. The approach that we have taken in the design of the microwave lies somewhere in the middle of this range.

### 8.9.2 Features of the State Pattern

The examples in the chapter should be illustrative enough that the following salient aspects of the State pattern can be appreciated:

- An application can be in one of many states, and its behavior depends on the state it is in. In our example, the `microwave` object can be in one of three possible states: Cooking, Door Open, and Door Closed.
- We create one class per state. We may choose to put their common functionality in an abstract superclass or make all of these states implement a common interface, so they all conform to some common type.
- One instance of each state class is created. In the case of the microwave, the three classes corresponding to the three states are all singletons. This way, unnecessary object creation and deletion are avoided.
- There is a context that orchestrates the whole show. This object remembers the current state and any shared data.
- Exactly one state is active at any given time. The context delegates the input event to the state that is currently active and therefore only the active state responds to events.
- When an event that requires a change of state occurs, we determine the next state, which then becomes active. For example, this transfer of control

occurs for the microwave application by having each state determine the next state and then calling the `changeState()` method of the context. The mechanism for deciding the next state can be done in one of two ways:

1. One approach would be to have a centralized controller that uses the matrix (see Section 8.5.2.1) to decide what the next state is. In this technique, after responding to an event, the state can return the input event to the controller, which can use the current state and the input event to determine the next state.
2. The second approach is to have the current state determine the next state. We used this approach in our microwave example.

The advantages of using the pattern are as follows:

- There is no longer a need to switch on the state in order to decide what action needs to be taken. Instead, we polymorphically choose a method to be executed.
- New states can be added and old states reused without changing the implementation. For example, in the microwave example, we can resume cooking after an interruption by simply having a new version of the class `CookingState`. (The reader is encouraged to make this modification.)
- The code is more cohesive. Each state contains code relevant to it and nothing else. Only events that are of interest in this state are processed.

### 8.9.3 Consequences of Observer

The simplicity of the Observer pattern belies the power it conceals. In essence, we have allowed an arbitrary object to be registered as a listener, and the actions of the observable result in a method (`propertyChange()` in Java) provided by the observer. Likewise, an object can become a listener to an arbitrary number of classes. As one should expect, such power brings with it a lot of caveats and consequences.

For a start, we have the problem of memory leaks. In a system that provides automatic garbage collection, objects for which no references are maintained can be cleaned up during garbage collection. If an observable stores a reference to an object, it is tricky to decide when an object is no longer needed and some explicit mechanism may be needed to signal the end of an object's lifetime. Next we have the problem of the order in which observers are notified. The pattern itself does not specify any order, and if any temporal ordering is desired, explicit mechanisms, such as introduction of intermediaries, may be needed.

Since any arbitrary object can become a listener, we may end up in situations where an update method invoked by the observable has unsafe code, say for instance, an unhandled exception or a delay. The standard approach to avoid this is for the observable to have every observer on a separate thread. This solution in turn leads to other caveats for programmers, such as not registering listeners from within constructors and not adding new listeners when existing ones are being notified.

A class that listens to several observables can end up with a `propertyChange()` method that is quite complex. The order in which an observer deals with notifications from observables can change the result of the computation. Two such problems, *Cyclic Dependencies* and *Update Causality* are discussed in [3].

Computations involving threads have its own share of pitfalls, and these have to be understood in the context of the Observer pattern. Several questions arise, such as: *How do you handle simultaneous notifications on multiple threads? What about modifying the listener list from one thread while notifications are in progress on another?* and *What happens when the notification is sent from one thread to an object that is being used by a second thread?* These and other issues are discussed in [4].

### 8.9.4 Recognizing and Processing External Events

The entire process for receiving and processing input involves the following steps: (i) providing a mechanism for input on the UI; (ii) listening to user actions on the input mechanism; (iii) generating appropriate internal events; (iv) processing the events.

The reader should observe the division of responsibilities among the states and the UI. Generally speaking, the UI is responsible for the "look and feel" and the back end handles the processing. Reuse is most benefited if the back end is "UI-agnostic," and that would be impossible if variations in the user interface affected the logic in the back end. A UI may provide a user with multiple mechanisms for the same operation (using a menu, a key sequence, etc.) and the back end should be able to handle all of these uniformly.

Next we deal with the issue of communicating the event to the back end. At first glance, the Observer pattern seems suitable for this, but a closer examination tells us that this may lead to a situation where the observer must use a conditional to distinguish between several observables. It is therefore preferable to use one of other mechanisms discussed in the chapter.

## Projects

1. **Creating a controller for a Digital Camera.** A digital camera has several possible modes of operation. Each mode has its own interface, and the user can switch between modes. One mode, for instance, is the *Viewing*

mode, in which stored pictures can be viewed, deleted, etc. In the *Setting* mode, other parameters, such as the kind of pictures to be taken, can be modified.

- Study models of digital cameras on the market, and define a set of requirements for the UI.
- Design a software controller that meets these specifications.

Note that in such a system, both the view and the behavior will change when the state changes. Also, in a typical camera, the control buttons remain the same regardless of the mode of operation, but the effect of activating them changes. How will you model such functionality?

2. **A user interface for a warehouse management system.** In Chapter 6, a case study for a warehouse database was presented. Create a complete GUI for such a system.

- The UI has an initial login panel that allows the user to log in. The user could be a *client*, a *salesclerk*, or a *manager*. Each type of user has a different set of access privileges. This will involve having some kind of password protection and can be accomplished using a separate subsystem that tracks the registered users and their passwords. The GUI will directly communicate with this system.
- When a user logs in, the appropriate menu is revealed. A salesclerk, for instance, performs operations like processing purchase orders from clients, receiving shipments, etc. However, a salesclerk can become a particular client and carry out those operations too. The salesclerk menu should provide an option like "become a client". Likewise, a manager can become a salesclerk.
- The GUI should have a "back" button to go back to the previous state.
- Each menu panel should have a "logout" option.

When a salesclerk becomes a client, this will require that we go through a panel that collects the particular client's ID. When the logout option is chosen, the state should go back to the salesclerk menu, whereas if the user was a client, the user will be logged out. Can this state be shared by the client and the salesclerk? How will you accomplish this? If the final choice of next state depends on stored information, where should this information be stored and in which class should the next state be computed? How is this impacted by the manner in which we are implementing the State pattern?

3. Following the previous project, define and implement a more sophisticated GUI for the library system.
4. Implement a simple CD player. The player has the following buttons:

a. Insert/Eject: If a CD is inside the player, pressing this button causes the CD to be stopped and ejected. Otherwise, a CD is inserted and played.

b. Play: Causes the player to resume playing a CD (if a CD is inside) from the position it was paused or from the beginning. If there is no CD, pressing this button has no effect.
c. Stop: Causes the player to pause playing/fast forwarding/rewinding, so pressing the Play button later causes the player to resume from this position. If this button is pressed when the player is paused, the CD is stopped, so a further push of the Play button plays the CD from the start. If there is no CD, pressing this button has no effect.
d. Fast Forward: If a CD is inside, the player plays the CD forward at double speed. Pressing this button while fast forwarding causes the player to resume playing again. If there is no CD, pressing this button has no effect.
e. Rewind: If a CD is inside, the player plays the CD backward at double speed. Pressing this button while rewinding causes the player to resume playing again. If there is no CD, pressing this button has no effect.

All CDs play for exactly one hour. When the player reaches the end of the CD while playing or fast forwarding, it stops (so it reverts to the start). The user interface must be a GUI with the above five buttons and two displays: one showing the number of minutes and seconds elapsed if playing a CD and the other showing the state: "playing," "paused," etc.

5. A room has the following options for climate control: blow a fan, use an air-conditioner, employ a heater, or do nothing. A temperature regulator for the room can be set in one of four different modes to choose the desired option. (Imagine a slider control that can be set to one of the four positions.)

   a. Do nothing: None of the three devices (fan, air-conditioner, and heater) is active.
   b. Fan: The fan blows for 10 minutes and then stays inactive for another 10 minutes; the cycle repeats.
   c. Air-conditioner: The air-conditioner immediately turns on. If the room temperature is too high, it operates until the room temperature hits the set temperature.
   d. Heater: The heater immediately turns on. If the room is too cold, it operates until the room temperature hits the set temperature.

   Apart from the four manual controls, assume that the regulator gets three other signals: room is too hot, room is too cold, and the temperature is just right.
   Develop the state transition table and diagram. Implement the system.
6. Research the various elements and options of file transfer programs. Define an appropriate FSM, and build a GUI for the complete protocol. How might such a GUI be converted into a functional file transfer application?

## Exercises

1. (Defining a Protocol State Machine). Consider a system that beeps to remind an automobile driver to wear a seat belt. It can be captured by the following requirements:
   If the engine is turned on and the seat belt is not buckled, a six-second timer is initiated
   If the seat belt is buckled or the engine is turned off, the timer is stopped; if the timer runs out, the beeper is activated.
   The beeper stops if the seat belt is buckled or the engine is switched off or the beeper has sounded for six seconds.

   (a) Write the sequence of steps in this communication between the system and the driver. These would start as follows:
   1. Driver turns on the engine
   2. If the seat belt is buckled, the process is complete; otherwise a six-second timer is initiated
   3. (i) Driver buckles seat belt, or (ii) driver turns off engine, or (iii) six seconds elapse.
   Note that (i), (ii) and (iii) are all possible events in Step 3. The protocol must specify what happens in each case.

   (b) Convert the steps from (a) into a protocol state machine, using the format described in Chapter 3.

2. Modify the implementation of the microwave controller so that individual states register with event sources. What changes will have to be made to the state classes? How will the states access the object with which they have to register/de-register themselves?
3. In the implementation of the State pattern for the microwave, the context keeps track of the current state, but the next state is decided by the current state. Suggest at least two other implementations of the State pattern for the microwave. Compare and contrast all three implementations in the context of performance, simplicity of design, and ease of reuse.
4. Modify the design of the microwave system to add each of the following requirements:

   a. An "extend cooking" button is added to the display; if this button is pressed when cooking is in progress, 30 seconds are added to the cooking time.
   b. The system has a "clear" button, that sets the remaining cooking time to zero. The system also stores the remaining time if the cooking is interrupted by the opening of the door. When the system enters the cooking state again, this stored value is used as the cooking time; however, if the clear button has been pressed in the meantime, it runs for 60 seconds.

c. The system displays an "error" message if an inappropriate action is performed. For instance, if the cook button is pressed when the door is open, the message "Please close the door" is displayed.

## References


1. Cargill, T. 1992. *C++ Programming Style.* Addison-Wesley Professional Computing Series.
2. Gamma, E, Helm, R, Johnson, R and Vlissides, J. 1994. *Design Patterns: Elements of Reusable Object-oriented Software.* Addison-Wesley Professional Computing Series.
3. Gruntz, D. 2004. Java Design: On the Observer Pattern. *Technical report, University of Applied Sciences, Aargau.*
4. Lee, EA. 2006. The Problem with Threads. *Computer* 39(5): 33–42, IEEE.
5. Meyer, B. 1997. *Object-Oriented Software Construction.* Prentice Hall.

# Chapter 9
# Interactive Systems and the Model–View–Controller Architecture

So far we have seen examples and case studies involving relatively simple software systems. This simplicity enabled us to use a fairly general step-by-step approach, namely, specify the requirements, model the behavior, find the classes, assign responsibilities, capture class interactions, and so on. In larger systems, such an approach may not lead to an efficient design, and it would be wise to rely on the experience of software designers who have worked on the problem and devised strategies to tackle the problem.

This is somewhat akin to planning our strategy for a game of chess. A chess game has three stages – an opening, a middle game, and an endgame. At the opening, the field is undisturbed and the number of possibilities is immense; towards the end, there are fewer pieces and fewer options. If we are in an endgame situation, we can solve the problem using a fairly direct approach using first principles; to decide how to open is a much more complicated operation and requires knowledge of "standard openings." These standard openings have been developed and have evolved along with the game, and provide a framework for the player. Likewise, when we have a complex problem, we need a framework or structure within which to operate. For the problem of creating software systems, such a structure is provided by choosing a **software architecture** (sometimes referred to as an **architectural pattern**).

In this chapter, we start by describing a well-known software architecture called the **Model–View–Controller** or **MVC** pattern. Next, we analyze, design, and build a small interactive system using such an architecture. The purpose behind this exercise is twofold:

- *To demonstrate how to design with an architecture in mind.* In our earlier case studies, there was no specific architecture. We "started from scratch," looked through nouns and tried to find classes. As we shall see, when an architecture has been chosen, this is no longer the case.
- *To understand how the MVC architecture is employed.* There are some principles to follow and some typical problems that we encounter when

we employ MVC. Through our example, we can demonstrate how these principles are adhered to and what solutions are available for these problems.

Finally, we discuss pattern-based solutions in software development and some other frequently employed architectural patterns.

## 9.1 The Model–View–Controller Architectural Pattern

MVC is a relatively old pattern, with its origin going back to the early days of the Smalltalk programming language. As one might suspect from its name, the pattern divides the application into three subsystems: Model, View, and Controller. The pattern separates the application object or the data, which is termed the Model, from the manner in which it is rendered to the end user (View) and from the way in which the end user manipulates it (Controller). In contrast to a system where all of these three functionalities are lumped together (and thus has a low degree of cohesion), the MVC pattern helps produce highly cohesive modules with a low degree of coupling. This facilitates greater flexibility and reuse. MVC also provides a powerful way to organize systems that support multiple presentations of the same information.

The structure is shown in Figure 9.1. The Model stores the data and any object can play the role of Model. To a great extent, the Model is unaware of the existence of either the View or the Controller and does not explicitly participate in the proceedings. The View displays the data stored in the application in a format suitable for the end user. Moreover, the data may be displayed at an appropriate level of abstraction. For instance, if the Model stores information about bank accounts, a certain View may choose to display only the number of accounts and the total of the account balances. The Controller captures the user inputs. In contrast to its relationship with the Model, a View is fairly closely connected to a Controller and vice-versa.

In a typical application, the Model changes only when user input causes the Controller to inform the Model of the changes. The View must be notified when the Model changes, so these two entities must have a communication mechanism, one that is preferably loosely coupled. The Controller maintains references to keep track of the Model and the View.

The MVC model provides a broad division of responsibilities, but the design and implementation phases require a mapping of each of these three subsystems to a set of one or more physical classes. Also, a graphical user interface (GUI) provides a way for users to input, view, search, and update data stored in the model.

For example, consider an application familiar to most people using the Internet these days. An online store maintains in its database information about a (possibly large) set of items. From the store customer's point of view,

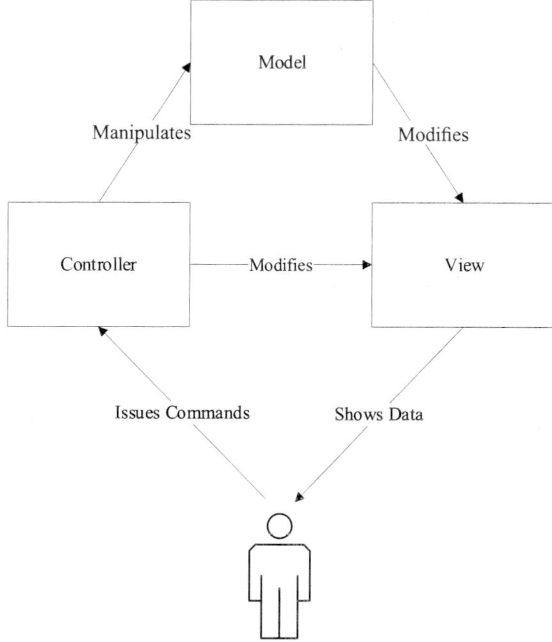


**Fig. 9.1** The Model–View–Controller architecture. The Model stores the data related to some application. The data is displayed to the user by the View. The user issues commands to manipulate the data through the Controller. In practice, the Controller may issue commands to the View to modify the display, without an actual modification of the data stored in the Model.

the web pages displayed by the system provide a mechanism for viewing, selecting, purchasing, and a host of other operations on this information. The GUI not only displays the information stored in the Model, but also provides controls to allow the user to manipulate the data stored in the Model. Some of the operations like clicking on an item to select it for purchase can be viewed as an input operation, whereas the display of a product is clearly an output operation.

Much of the processing in the online store would be performed by code located on the server maintained for the application. When a user clicks on a product on the screen, the code on the server would receive the input, retrieve information from the database, and provide the appropriate displays. The code on the server that handles the input would be part of the Controller subsystem and the code on the server to display the information would be a part of the View.

The code to display the GUI usually involves an intricate arrangement of a host of classes and interfaces and is highly technology dependent. The framework used for GUI design and development changes over time, and for the sake of modifiability, it would be preferable to isolate the code related to the GUI itself (based on Swing and JavaFX in this book) from the modules that deal with commands and data at a more "logical" level. For example, a command to create a rectangle shape in a drawing program may be physically issued through the push of a JavaFX `Button` object and must necessarily be received through JavaFX code, but the code needed to create a rectangle object is independent of the GUI technology and is more stable. Such a division of responsibilities permits modifiability; for example, if and when a new technology replaces JavaFX, it would be easier to replace just the JavaFX modules. Once we adopt this design approach, we can see that at the software level, we have four subsystems: the Model, View, Controller, and GUI. The GUI, as we just mentioned, contains the essential code for interacting with the user. All user input would be received by the GUI and sent to the Controller. The data from the Model to be shown to the user goes through the View to the GUI. (The data may be condensed, analyzed, reformatted, etc. within the View, so displaying it is not necessarily a trivial process.)

User-generated events may cause a Controller to change a Model, or View, or both. For example, suppose that the Model stored the text that is being edited by the end user. When the user deletes or adds text, the Controller captures the changes and notifies the Model. The View, which observes the Model, then refreshes its display, with the result that the end user sees the changes he/she made to the data. In this case, user input caused a change to both the Model and the View.

On the other hand, the Controller may also send messages to the user through the GUI. Consider, for instance, a user scrolling the data. Since no changes are made to the data itself, the Model does not change and need not be notified. But the View now needs to display previously hidden data, which makes it necessary for the View to contact the Model and retrieve information.

More than one View–Controller pair may be associated with a Model. Whenever user input causes one of the Controllers to notify changes to the Model, all associated Views are automatically updated.

It could also be the case that the Model is changed not through one of the Controllers, but through some other mechanism. In this case, the Model must notify all associated Views of the changes.

### 9.1.1 Examples

The MVC concept finds application in many situations. The examples here demonstrate the versatility of the concept.

A library system could have a View that shows information about a book: the title, ID, number of copies, and whether a copy is available for checkout. This View could be connected to a GUI screen, which is connected to a Controller. A library staff member uses this screen to add copies of books.

At the same time, there could be a second View displayed on a second screen where a customer checks whether the same book is available for checkout. As the library staff member changes the book information, the Model is updated, and the second View is notified, resulting in an update of the second GUI screen, which informs the customer about changes to the book's status.

A second example is that of a mail sever. A user logs into the server and looks at the messages in the mailbox. In a second window, the user logs in again to the same mail server and composes a message. The two screens form two separate Views of the same Model.

Suppose that we have a graph-plot of pairs of $(x, y)$ values. The collection of data points constitutes the Model. The graph View software provides the user with several output formats – bar graphs, line graphs, pie charts, etc. When the user changes formats, the View changes without any change to the Model.

### 9.1.2 Implementation

The View and Model interaction is modeled using the Observer pattern. The Model, as the observable, maintains references to all of the Views (the observers) that are interested in observing it. Whenever an action that changes the Model occurs, the Model automatically notifies all of these Views. The Views then refresh their displays.
The definition for the Model will be as follows:

```
public class Model {
  // code
  private PropertyChangeSupport propertyChangeSupport =
          new PropertyChangeSupport(this);
  public void changeData() {
    // code to update data and construct a PropertyChangeEvent,
       event
    this.propertyChangeSupport.firePropertyChange(event);
  }
}
```

Each of the Views is an observer and implements the `propertyChange()` method.

```
public class View implements PropertyChangeListener {
  // code
  public void propertyChange(PropertyChangeEvent event) {
    // process the event
  }
}
```

If a View is no longer interested in the Model, it can be deleted from the list of observers. Since the Controllers react to user input, they may send messages directly to the Views, asking them to refresh their displays.

### 9.1.3 Benefits

The MVC paradigm provides a natural division of responsibilities and affords the following advantages:

- *Cohesion of modules*: Instead of putting unrelated code (display and data) in the same module, we separate the functionality, so that each module is cohesive.
- *Flexibility*: The Model is unaware of the exact nature of the View–Controller pair(s) it is working with. It is simply an observable. This adds flexibility.
- *Lower coupling*: Modularity of the design improves the chances that components can be swapped in and out as the user or programmer desires. This also promotes parallel development, easier debugging, and maintenance.
- *Adaptability to change*: Components can be changed with less interference to the rest of the system.
- *Applicability to distributed systems*: Since the modules are separated, it is possible to have the View–Controller pair in a system that is geographically separated from the Model.

## 9.2 Analyzing a Simple Drawing Program

We now apply the MVC architectural pattern to the process of designing a simple program that allows us to create and label figures. As always, our analysis begins with the task of defining the requirements. We start with very few requirements, which typify the kind of requests this program will be expected to support. Once these are understood, it will be fairly straightforward to incorporate more features.

### 9.2.1 Specifying the Requirements

Our simple program will allow the user to perform operations like drawing lines and polygons, adding labels, and grouping, ungrouping, moving, and deleting sets of shapes (or figures). In addition, it permits undo and redo of commands, use of the Escape key to cancel an operation, and save (retrieve) a created figure to (from) a file. The system provides a menu to initiate an operation.

Let us examine the requirements and understand each in detail.

#### 9.2.1.1 Drawing Lines and Polygons

To draw a line, the user clicks the first endpoint and moves the mouse and as that movement occurs, the program would show a shifting line between the position of the first click and the current mouse position, enabling the user to preview the line before the second click. In addition, the system will also allow the operation to be cancelled after the first mouse-click.

To draw a polygon, we must accommodate an arbitrary number of mouse-clicks. In this case, the system provides feedback to the user by displaying the polygon formed by the clicked points and the current mouse position. The user indicates the last vertex by right-clicking the mouse.

#### 9.2.1.2 Adding Labels

A label is a string. The left endpoint of the label is specified by a mouse-click. Once this point is specified, the user types in the string using keystrokes. Since the string can be of arbitrary length, the end of the string needs to be specified. We also allow the user to create several labels within one operation, clicking the mouse again for each additional label. Clicking the mouse thus serves as both the start of a label and the end of the previous label (if any). A right-click of the mouse terminates the command.

#### 9.2.1.3 Performing Delete, Move, Group, and Ungroup

All of these operations apply to a set of shapes (or figures); thus each of these must be prefixed by a sub-operation which selects the set of shapes. The delete operation removes all the selected shapes from the figure. Move translates the selected shapes by a specified distance along a specified direction.

Grouping a set of shapes allows us to manipulate (delete and move) them as a single unit; a group itself is a shape that contains multiple component shapes. Grouping is a hierarchical process: two or more shapes, some of which are groups, can be grouped to form another group. Ungrouping splits a group into its components.

### Group and Ungroup Example

Suppose $Line_1$, $Label_1$, and $Polygon_1$ are three shapes, as shown in the first part of Figure 9.2. We can group the shapes $Line_1$ and $Label_1$ to form a group, which we refer to as $G_1$. Deleting (moving) $G_1$ deletes (moves) both $Line_1$ and $Label_1$. We can form a second group $G_2$ using $G_1$ and $Polygon_1$. Deleting or moving $G_2$ causes the corresponding operation to be performed on $Line_1$, $Label_1$, and $Polygon_1$.
If we ungroup $G_2$, we get its constituent parts, which are $G_1$ and $Polygon_1$. $G_1$ can be ungrouped to get its constituents $Line_1$ and $Label_1$.
Save the drawing in a file. We can open a file containing a drawing and edit it.
Undo recent operations of the drawing process. If needed, the operations can be redone as well.

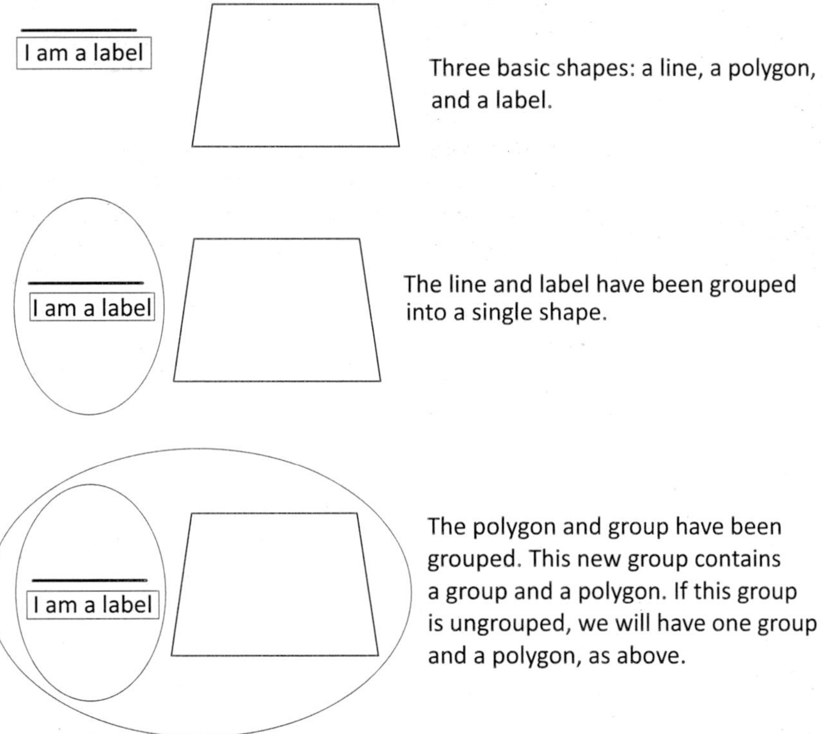


**Fig. 9.2** An example of grouping. We initially have three "basic" shapes: a line, a polygon, and a label. Then, we apply the Group command to place the line and label into a single group. The ellipse denotes a group. Finally, we group this and the polygon to create another group. If we ungroup now, we get the situation shown by the figure in the middle: a group and a polygon.

Compared to the drawing programs available in the market, this looks very trivial. Nonetheless, the functionality is rich enough to show how the responsibilities can be divided so that the MVC pattern can be applied.

## 9.2.2 Defining the User Interface

We now specify exactly how the software interacts with the user. As in earlier examples, non-functional requirements will not be the focus of our attention. Without more ado, let us adopt the following "look and feel:"

- The software will have a single window divided into two panels. The look of the View–Controller pair of the drawing program is shown in Figure 9.3.[1]
  - A button/command panel with a host of buttons, with one button per operation. They will have labels such as Line, Polygon, Undo, and so on.
  - A drawing panel on which the figure will be displayed. The user can left-click the mouse to specify where the vertices associated with the shapes should go.
- The user can abandon the current command by pressing the Escape key.
- When drawing is in progress, the shape of the cursor (called the default cursor shape) when the mouse is on the command panel is different from the shape (called the drawing cursor shape) when the mouse moves to the display panel.
- As a label is entered, a text cursor will be shown to indicate the point at which the next character will be entered.

We will use Swing and JavaFX to implement the GUI.

## 9.2.3 Meta Operations

Meta operations are the non-drawing operations that the system provides. These operations act on other operations or connect the program with the system. The operations cancel, undo, redo, save, and retrieve are meta operations; meta operations are commonly available in interactive systems, regardless of the application. The cancel operation is invoked by pressing the Escape key when one of the drawing operations is being performed; it causes the system to abandon whatever drawing operation is currently being performed. The drawing is restored to what it was before the command was initiated.

[1] The mouse is duplicated to show its possible shapes in the two panels. The actual shapes would depend on the technology.

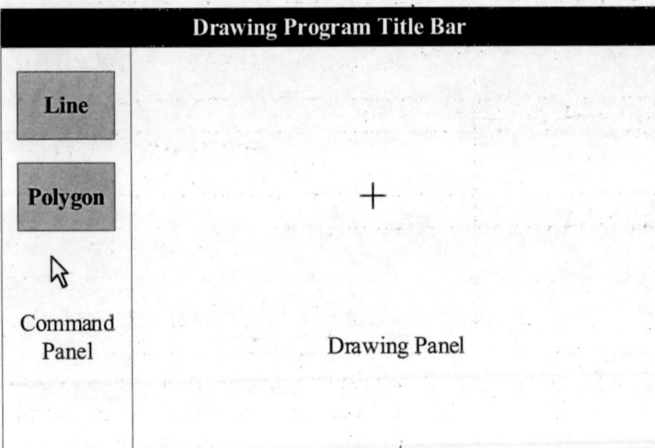


**Fig. 9.3** The basic layout of the drawing program. Note that besides the customary title bar, the screen is divided into two panels: one for the command buttons (such as Line and Polygon) called the command panel and one for the drawing itself, which we term the drawing panel. The drawing panel shows a cross-hair cursor (indicating that drawing is in progress) and the command panel has an arrow cursor (default cursor shape). Obviously, the two cursors cannot coexist, but we draw both to show the reader how the cursors would look in the two panels.

#### 9.2.3.1 Save and Retrieve

The drawing can be saved to disk and retrieved at a later point. The use cases are quite straightforward (Tables 9.1 and 9.2).

| Action performed by the actor | Response from the system |
|---|---|
| 1. The user wants to save the drawing to a file on disk. | |
| 2. The user clicks the Save button. | |
| | 3. The system provides an interface to select a directory and specify the file name. |
| 4. The user selects a directory and file name to save the drawing. | |
| | 5. If the file does not exist, the system saves the drawing and the use case ends. If the file exists on disk, the system asks if the file should be replaced. |
| 6. The user responds in the affirmative or negative. | |
| | 7. If the response is affirmative, the system replaces the file on disk with the content of the drawing. Otherwise, it abandons the save operation. The use case ends. |

**Table 9.1** Use case for saving the drawing on disk. The system provides the user the ability to select the directory and specify the file name.

| Action performed by the actor | Response from the system |
|---|---|
| 1. The user wants to retrieve a drawing from a file on disk. | |
| 2. The user clicks the Open button. | |
| | 3. The system provides an interface to navigate to an existing file. |
| 4. The user selects a file. | |
| | 5. If the file contains a saved drawing, the system replaces the drawing panel with the content from disk. Otherwise, it displays an error message. In either case, the use case ends. |

**Table 9.2** Use case for retrieving the drawing from disk. The system provides the user the ability to select the file from the disk.

### 9.2.3.2 Undo and Redo

As most readers would know, undo and redo are common operations in word processors, drawing programs, spreadsheet programs, etc. As the terms imply, undo undoes the last operation and the following redo executes that operation again.

When we build a system, a more precise understanding of these operations is needed. The undo operation reverts the drawing to the situation it was in immediately prior to the most recent operation. If any item (line, polygon, or label) was added, then that addition is undone. From the user's point of view, the effect is the same as deleting the item; for someone building the system, it should be noted that these are different. Deleting the most recently created item takes the drawing to a new situation; we can restore the item by performing an undo. The undo operation reverts the system to a prior situation; restoring the item will require a redo. Likewise, if some items were grouped (or ungrouped) in the last operation, then the grouping (or ungrouping) is reversed; the drawing is restored to the form it was in prior to the grouping (ungrouping) operation.

It is easy to see that uncontrolled undo and redo can result in meaningless requests. Consider a situation where we have the sequence:

```
select a shape
set the color of the shape to blue
undo
delete the shape
redo
```

A redo means we are trying to undo the last undo operation. In the above example, the last undo operation was to reverse the change of color of `shape` to blue. Therefore, with redo, we are trying to change the color of the deleted object `shape` back to blue. Without undoing the deletion of `shape`, it is logically inconsistent to perform this color change. It may therefore be necessary for a system to disallow all redo operations under certain circumstances.

Undo and redo are requested by the user by clicking on the buttons marked “undo” and “redo” respectively; we skip detailed use cases for these.

## 9.3 Detailed Use Cases for the Drawing Operations

We have already seen use cases for saving and retrieving the drawing. We now write the use cases for drawing each of the three shapes. This will be followed by use cases for selection, move, deletion, and so on. As mentioned earlier, the use cases for undo and redo are fairly trivial, so we will not show them.

### 9.3.1 Drawing the Shapes

We now write the use cases for drawing a line and polygon and for creating labels. In all of the use cases, we assume the following:

- As we have noted earlier, when a command is in progress, if and when the mouse is moved to the drawing panel, the cursor is changed from the default to the drawing cursor shape. With current technology, the default cursor shape is the arrow and the drawing cursor shape is the cross-hair. These may change as GUI technology changes.
- If the mouse is moved to the command panel, the cursor takes the default cursor shape.
- Pressing the Escape key abandons the construction of the current shape.

We can now write the detailed use cases for each shape creation operation.

#### 9.3.1.1 Drawing a Line

The first one, for drawing a line, is shown in Table 9.3. As we discussed earlier, the system displays a shifting line between the first click and the mouse position. This is captured in the detailed use case by indicating that the system goes back to a prior step and sets up a loop.

#### 9.3.1.2 Drawing a Polygon

The use case for drawing a polygon would naturally begin with a click on a button named Polygon. The user would click on multiple points to specify the successive vertices of the polygon. As successive vertices are specified, the program would continue to draw the successive edges. We, however, need a

| Action performed by the actor | Response from the system |
|---|---|
| 1. The user clicks on the Line button in the command panel and moves the cursor to the drawing panel. | |
| | 2. The cursor takes the drawing cursor shape. |
| 3. The user clicks the first endpoint. | |
| | 4. The system displays the line formed by the first endpoint and the current mouse position. |
| 5. The user either moves the mouse or clicks on the second endpoint. | |
| | 6. If the user moves the mouse, the system goes back to Step 4; if the user clicks on the other endpoint of the line, the system displays the line with the two specified endpoints, and the cursor returns to the default. |

**Table 9.3** Use case for drawing a line. In Step 2, we explicitly write the change in shape of the cursor, in order to emphasize the response of the system to the draw line command. Note that the user may move the mouse any number of times between the drawing and command panels and the cursor will change the shape accordingly; this is captured in the loop back from Step 6 to Step 4.

mechanism to specify the "last" vertex that would be connected to the first vertex, to close the polygon. We assume that the user would indicate this by clicking the right mouse button. The use case is shown in Table 9.4.

| Action performed by the actor | Response from the system |
|---|---|
| 1. The user clicks on the Polygon button in the command panel and moves the cursor to the drawing panel. | |
| | 2. The cursor takes the drawing cursor shape. |
| 3. The user clicks on a drawing panel point that would be the first vertex of the polygon to be drawn. | |
| | 4. The system displays the polygon formed by all the clicked points and the mouse location. |
| 5. The user either moves the cursor to the another point or clicks the mouse. | |
| | 6. If the user moves the mouse, the system goes back to Step 4. If the user left-clicks the mouse, the system adds another vertex to the polygon and goes back to Step 4. If the user right-clicks the mouse, the system recognizes the point as the last vertex, displays the complete polygon, and terminates the use case. |

**Table 9.4** Use case for drawing a polygon. We need to have a special way of indicating the $N^{th}$ vertex when drawing an $N$-vertex polygon. This is specified by right-click of the mouse.

### 9.3.1.3 Drawing Labels

To provide an interesting variation, we allow for multiple labels to be added with the same command. To start the process of adding labels, the user clicks on the Label button. This is followed by a mouse-click on the drawing panel, following which the user types in the desired label. After typing in the label, the user can either click on another point to create another label or click the right mouse button, which ends the command. These details are spelled out in the use case in Table 9.5.

| Action performed by the actor | Response from the system |
|---|---|
| 1. The user clicks on the Label button in the command panel and moves the mouse to the drawing panel. | |
| | 2. The cursor takes the drawing cursor shape. |
| 3. The user clicks on the left endpoint of the intended label. | |
| | 4. The system displays a vertical bar at the location of the mouse-click (that is, where the next character will be placed). |
| | 5. The system waits for user response. |
| 6. The user does one of the following: type a character, press the Backspace key, left-click the mouse at some location, or right-click the mouse. | |
| | 7. If a character is typed, the system replaces the vertical bar with the character followed by a vertical bar, and goes back to Step 5. If the Backspace key is pressed when a label has no characters, the system goes back to Step 5; otherwise the bar and character in the label immediately preceding the bar are replaced by a bar, and the system goes back to Step 5. If the left mouse button is clicked, the system removes the vertical bar from the end of the character sequence and goes back to Step 4. If a right mouse-click is received, the system changes to the default cursor and ends the command. |

**Table 9.5** Use case for adding labels. The system allows the user to create a sequence of labels with this command. After each label, the user clicks at the start point of the next label. After finishing the last label, the user right-clicks the mouse.

The reader would note that this system is very restrictive in some ways: for example, the label fonts and font sizes cannot be selected or changed. This has been done for simplicity and will not in any way detract from the design experience.

## 9.3.2 Shape Manipulation Operations

In this section, we show use cases for moving, deleting, grouping, and ungrouping shapes.

Prior to performing any of these operations, one or more shapes must be selected. Although shape(s) selection is not a use case in its own right, for reducing the size of the use cases for shape manipulation, we show the steps for selection in Table 9.6. While reading the use cases for moving, deleting, grouping, and ungrouping, you will see that the first step is numbered 5; the first four steps will, of course, come from this selection process.

| **Action performed by the actor** | **Response from the system** |
|---|---|
| 1. The user wants to mark one or more shapes as being selected. | |
| 2. The user presses the Control key and left-clicks the mouse on a vertex in a shape. | |
| | 3. If the click point maps to a shape using rules 1, 2, 3, and 6 in Table 9.8, the system records the shape as selected and modifies the display of the shape. (See Rule 5 in Table 9.8). |
| 4. If the user wants to select more shapes, he/she goes to Step 2. Otherwise, he/she either moves on to a shape manipulation command by right-clicking the mouse or abandons the whole process by pressing the Escape key or left-clicking the mouse. | |

**Table 9.6** The process for selecting shapes. The user can select multiple shapes by left-clicking the mouse with the Control key pressed on or near vertices in the shapes. These are the common initial steps for the move, group, ungroup and delete commands.

After selecting one or more shapes, the user may right-click the mouse to get a pop-up menu from which he/she may choose one of the following operations: delete, move, group, or ungroup. Note that these options perform something tangible only if the user has selected at least one shape. Also, one of these operations has to be chosen by a right-click immediately after the selection steps are complete. Once the chosen operation is completed, or if the user does not choose any operation, there are no longer any selected items.

### 9.3.2.1 Deleting the Selected Shapes

Deletion is the simplest of the shape manipulation operations: all the selected shapes are deleted. The use case for the delete operation is given in Table 9.7.

| Action performed by the actor | Response from the system |
|---|---|
| 5. The user right-clicks the mouse anywhere on the drawing panel. | |
| | 6. The system displays a pop-up menu with four operations: delete, move, group, and ungroup. |
| 7. The user clicks the delete operation in the menu. | |
| | 8. The shapes that have been marked as "selected" are deleted. If no shapes were marked, the system displays a message that no shapes were selected. The use case is terminated. |

**Table 9.7** Use case for deleting shapes. The first four steps are described in the process for selecting shapes. The user then right-clicks the mouse and clicks on the Delete menu item to delete the selected shapes.

| No. | Rule |
|---|---|
| 1 | Selection vertex for a line is either endpoint. |
| 2 | Selection vertex for a label is the vertex that was initially clicked for placing the label in the drawing. |
| 3 | Selection vertex for a polygon is any of the vertices of the polygon. |
| 4 | Unselected shapes are shown in blue. |
| 5 | Selected shapes are shown in red. |
| 6 | A shape is selected if the user left-clicks the mouse with coordinates $x$ and $y$, respectively, such that the following is true. Suppose $x_s$ and $y_s$ are the $x$ and $y$ coordinates, respectively, of some vertex as specified by rules 1, 2, or 3; then $\|x - x_s\| + \|y - y_s\| \leq 10$. |
| 7 | As the mouse is moved when drawing a line or polygon, the appearance of the shape on the screen should be what it would be if the mouse is clicked at its current position. |
| 8 | As characters are typed in creating a label, the next insertion point must be indicated by a vertical bar. After the label is completed, the bar should not appear in the label. |

**Table 9.8** Rules used in use cases

#### 9.3.2.2 Moving the Selected Shapes

The use case for the move operation is given in Table 9.9. As in the case of deletion, the use case is only applicable if the user has selected at least one shape. To move the selected items, the user has to specify a displacement in the X direction and a displacement in the Y direction. This can be done by specifying two points, $(x_1, y_1)$ and $(x_2, y_2)$; the displacement in the X direction is $(x_2 - x_1)$ and the displacement in the Y direction is $(y_2 - y_1)$. After the selection is complete, the user has to click on the screen to choose the move operation; the coordinates of this click are $(x_1, y_1)$. The mouse is clicked again to indicate the point $(x_2, y_2)$.

| Action performed by the actor | Response from the system |
|---|---|
| 5. The user right-clicks the mouse anywhere on the drawing panel. | |
| | 6. The system displays a pop-up menu with four operations: delete, move, group, and ungroup. |
| 7. The user clicks the move operation from the menu. | |
| | 8. The system records the coordinates, $(c_x, c_y)$, of the clicked point. |
| | 9. The system waits for user response. |
| 10. The user moves the mouse or left-clicks the mouse. | |
| | 11. If the mouse is moved to point $(m_x, m_y)$, the system translates all the selected shapes by the vector $(m_x - c_x, m_y - c_y)$, and goes back to Step 9. If the mouse is left-clicked at $(m_x, m_y)$, the system translates all the selected shapes by the vector $(m_x - c_x, m_y - c_y)$, unselects all the shapes, and ends the use case. |

**Table 9.9** Use case for moving shapes. The first four steps are described in the use case for selecting shapes. The user then right-clicks the mouse and clicks on the Move menu item and moves the mouse. The shapes are moved in a corresponding manner. When satisfied with the new position, the user finalizes the location by left-clicking the mouse.

### 9.3.2.3 Grouping and Ungrouping Selected Shapes

The use case for the group and ungroup operations follows a similar pattern and the details are given in Table 9.10 and Table 9.11, respectively. As in the case of move and deletion, the use case is only applicable if the user has selected at least one shape. Also note that no shape is selected after a group or ungroup operation.

| Action performed by the actor | Response from the system |
|---|---|
| 5. The user right-clicks the mouse anywhere on the drawing panel. | |
| | 6. The system displays a pop-up menu with four operations: delete, move, group, and ungroup. |
| 7. The user clicks on the group operation. | |
| | 8. The system groups all of the selected shapes into a single group. The shapes are unselected. The use case ends. |

**Table 9.10** Use case for grouping shapes. The first four steps are described in the process for selecting shapes. The user then right-clicks the mouse and clicks on the Group menu item.

| Action performed by the actor | Response from the system |
|---|---|
| 5. The user right-clicks the mouse anywhere on the drawing panel. | |
| | 6. The system displays a pop-up menu with four operations: delete, move, group, and ungroup. |
| 7. The user clicks the ungroup operation. | |
| | 8. The system ungroups all of the selected shapes that are grouped. The shapes are unselected. The use case ends. |

**Table 9.11** Use case for ungrouping shapes. The first four steps are described in the process for selecting shapes. The user then right-clicks the mouse and clicks on the Ungroup menu item. All shapes that are groups in the selected set are ungrouped.

## 9.4 Designing the Drawing Program

The overall design calls for the creation of four subsystems: the Model, View, Controller, and the GUI. In previous examples and case studies we have encountered some problems, for which we designed solutions by following good design principles. Apart from these, we encounter some problems that arise due to the use of this architecture, and involve new concepts.

- **User Interface Independence:** We should expect that technology to construct the GUI would change. The standard approach to cater to such changes is to isolate what can change, by putting the related code into a separate entity such as a class. This will potentially help us replace the GUI without making any changes to the Model, View, and Controller subsystems. Our design goal is to make the Model, View, and Controller (what we refer to in this chapter as the back end) completely independent of GUI code (the front end).
- **Model–View Separation:** As we have seen in MVC, we have the data and the mechanisms to modify the data integrated in the Model. The View and Controller define the look and feel of the system, and also trigger the mechanisms that modify the data; these subsystems change when a different look and feel is adopted for a later version of the application. Since the data created by the user is stored in the Model, it is important to maintain access to the Model. This requires that we maintain access to files created by older versions of the software, and allow for saving them under the newer version. In MVC, this is accomplished by maintaining Model–View separation. This separation also allows the user to to choose the kind of View that they would like to see.
- **Undo and Redo:** The system should be able to perform undo and redo. There are specific design approaches to build such functionality into the system.

- **Implementing Groups:** As we have seen, a group is a hierarchical collection of shapes that needs to be treated as a shape. To paraphrase, all the functionality required of shapes would be imposed on groups as well. The issue is how to realize the idea of a group, so the code to manipulate shapes (such as delete, move, etc.) would work seamlessly with groups.

It is essential to explore a couple of aspects before we take up the above problems.

### 9.4.1 Shape Representation

A fairly easy aspect to tackle concerns the representation of shapes. Clearly, the various shapes that the drawing program allows the user to draw are likely to have common properties and behavior, and from the object-oriented design principles, we know that it is appropriate to have an abstract superclass for all these shapes, which we will call `Shape`. Thus, we have the class hierarchy shown in Figure 9.4.

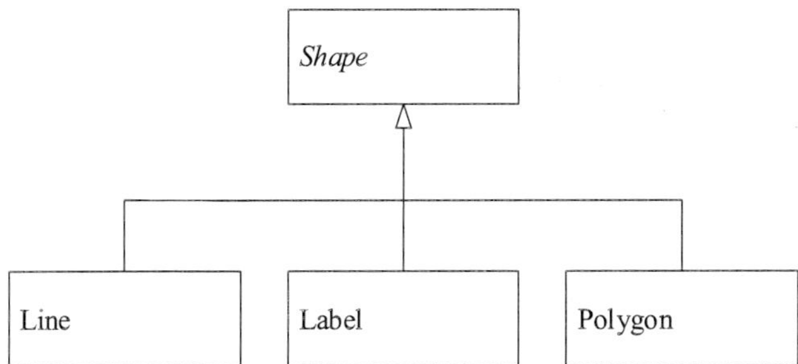


**Fig. 9.4** The `Shape` hierarchy. Since lines, labels, and polygons are shapes that can be drawn by the end user, they naturally fit into a hierarchy.

We expect the individual shapes to have a unique set of fields. For example, the `Line` class will have two fields to store the endpoints. The `Polygon` class could store an array holding the vertices that make up that shape, and so on. The Model keeps a collection of line, polygon, and label objects. The collection is accessed by the View from the Model when the drawing is to be rendered on the screen. The Model also provides mechanisms to access and modify its collection objects.

## 9.4.2 Interaction between Model, View, and Controller

We can get a sense of the broad division of responsibilities among the subsystems by exploring the overall sequence of actions that occur when the Line button is clicked. The sequence diagram is shown in Figure 9.5. Note that many details that would only impede a fundamental understanding are omitted in this diagram. When the user clicks on the button to draw a line, the command is received by the Controller, which creates a `Line` object. At some point, the `Line` object should be added to the Model. It is shown as being

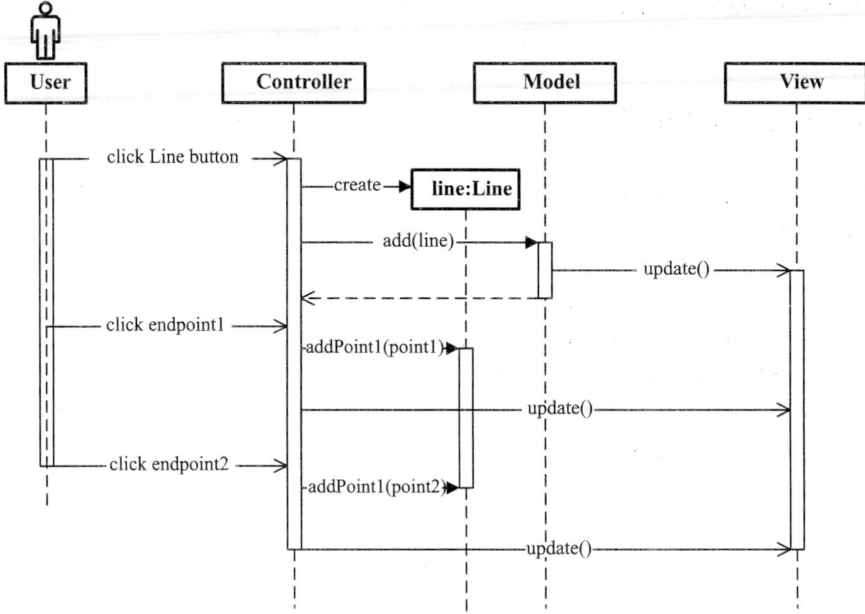


**Fig. 9.5** The interactions between the Model, View, and Controller subsystems. The diagram shows the broad division of responsibilities and interactions. Observe that the Controller receives all input and creates new drawing objects and adds them to the collection; when the Model changes, it notifies the View; occasionally, the Controller notifies the View without going through the Model.

done immediately after creation, but that need not happen exactly at this point, because the user would not notice a line with no endpoints. The user then clicks the first endpoint, which is also received by the Controller, which adds to the `Line` object and notifies the View that a change has occurred. The View once again updates the interface. Subsequently, when the second endpoint is clicked, the Controller receives that endpoint as well, updates the `Line` object, and notifies the View once more. At this time, the drawing of the line is complete, and the new line is visible on the user interface.

What the reader should observe in the diagram are the following:

- The Controller receives all input.
- The Controller creates new shapes and adds to the Model.
- When the Model changes, it notifies the View, which updates the presentation.
- When a change in presentation is required without any change to the Model, the Controller notifies the View.

### 9.4.3 Interface-Independent Controller

The Controller (which must be independent of the interface) needs to respond to user input (the technology provides mechanisms for user input). For each user action, we have a Controller response; we can encapsulate the response in a method. For example, say that the user wants to input a point (data); the Controller has a method, `onPointInput(..)`, that can be invoked to trigger the response. The user interface is free to define/create any mechanism for the user to input the point; all it has to do is ensure that the correct method, `onPointInput(..)`, is invoked.

In addition to choosing the mechanism to interact with the user, we can build the GUI using any available technology, such as Swing or JavaFX. Each has its own specific ways of creating and displaying buttons and responding to clicks on them. It is conceivable that the technology would be replaced sometime in the future by something more attuned to changes in hardware and user interface considerations. If and when that happens, it should be possible to replace the code without too much difficulty.

To design the Controller in anticipation of such changes, we use an approach we have seen before: determine what could change and isolate the related functionality in one or more modules. Our idea is to divide the responsibility of handling the user input into two distinct sets of Java classes. We separate the Controller into two separate layers:

- A set of classes that creates a GUI in a specific technology. This is the GUI shown in Figure 9.1. If we are using Swing (JavaFX), this will use classes and interfaces in the Swing- (JavaFX-) related packages.
- The back end, which is a set of classes that performs the logic to handle the input. This will use standard Java classes that are independent of the GUI technology. This is the Controller shown in Figure 9.1.

We would expect the GUI to be implemented by a set of classes. The division of responsibility among these classes would depend on the application programming interface supported for that technology. For example, a class might be created to receive all text characters, a second class would handle all other keystrokes, a third class could be the receiver of mouse-related events, and so on. The sole responsibility of these classes is receiving user input and delivering them in an interface-independent way to the Controller.

At the back end, the design and implementation of the Controller would also presumably involve multiple classes. The division of responsibility among them would be determined in a manner that is fully independent of the GUI.

Consider the use case for drawing a line, which we list below, ignoring the columns. We highlight phrases that correspond to an action by the user on the GUI or by the system:

1. The user **clicks on the Line button** in the command panel and **moves the cursor to the drawing panel**.
2. The cursor takes the drawing cursor shape.
3. The user **clicks the first endpoint**.
4. The system displays the line formed by the first endpoint and the current mouse position.
5. The user either **moves the mouse** or **clicks on the second endpoint**.
6. If the user **moves the mouse**, the system goes back to Step 4; if the user **clicks on the other endpoint of the line**, the system displays the line with the two specified endpoints, and the cursor returns to the default.

Let us consider the first highlighted action, **clicks on the Line button** in the command panel. This action is initially handled by some object to be specified by the GUI code. Similarly, we can get a list of all user inputs by examining the use cases. The user actions from the use cases and the three general statements we listed at the beginning of Section 9.3.1 can be viewed as events, as in the microwave example in the previous chapter, and are shown in Table 9.12.

The first column in the table lists the events. The first 11 events correspond to button clicks or menu item selection. The next six events correspond to mouse-clicks and movements. The last three are the events for character typing, pressing the Backspace key and the Escape key.

We have removed the context from the actions. The Controller should be the one to decide what the context is and determine what actions should be taken for the input. For example, we simply say that clicking the mouse in the drawing panel is an event; it could be for one of several different purposes: specifying the first endpoint of a line, the leftmost position of a label, and so on.

The GUI classes do not and need not know the organization of the Controller classes that react to the user inputs and vice-versa. The handling of these events is abstracted out using a set of methods in the Controller. These method names are listed in the second column of Table 9.12. The GUI classes will have access to an instance of the Controller class that implements these methods. When the events occur, the GUI will simply delegate responsibility to this Controller class.

| Event | Controller Method |
|---|---|
| Line button pressed | onLineCommand() |
| Polygon button pressed | onPolygonCommand() |
| Label button pressed | onLabelCommand() |
| Undo button pressed | onUndoCommand() |
| Redo button pressed | onRedoCommand() |
| Delete menu item selected | onDeleteCommand() |
| Move menu item selected | onMoveCommand() |
| Group menu item selected | onGroupCommand() |
| Ungroup menu item selected | onUngroupCommand() |
| Save button pressed | onSaveCommand() |
| Retrieve button pressed | onRetrieveCommand() |
| Mouse enters the drawing panel | onMouseEntered() |
| Moves leaves the drawing panel | onMouseExited() |
| Left mouse-click | onPointInput(double x, double y) |
| Control + Left mouse-click | onControlClick(double x, double y) |
| Mouse moved | onCursorMoved(double x, double y) |
| Right-click | onRightClick(double x, double y) |
| Character typed | onCharacterTyped(String character) |
| Backspace key pressed | onBackSpace() |
| Escape key pressed | onAbandonRequest() |

**Table 9.12** List of events

### 9.4.4 Interface-Independent View

As we have seen, the View is an observer of the Model and displays the shapes. For the sake of simplicity, in our design we will have only one View that displays all the shapes. In this section, we address the question of how to make the View interface-independent.

As in the case of making the Controller interface-independent, we can begin by examining the use cases and see what is involved in displaying the drawing. Here is, for example, the use case for drawing a line, without the columns, but this time with the display-related actions highlighted.

1. The user clicks on the Line button in the command panel and moves the cursor to the drawing panel.
2. **The cursor takes the drawing cursor shape.**
3. The user clicks the first endpoint.
4. The system **displays the line formed by the first endpoint and the current mouse position.**
5. The user either moves the mouse or clicks on the second endpoint.
6. If the user moves the mouse, the system goes back to Step 4; if the user clicks on the other endpoint of the line, the system **displays the line with the two specified endpoints**, and **the cursor returns to the default.**

We now pick out the displays made on the GUI, most of which, by definition of the MVC pattern, are done by the View. These are:

1. The cursor takes the drawing cursor shape.
2. The system shows the line formed by the first endpoint and the current mouse position.
3. The system displays the line with the two specified endpoints.
4. The cursor returns to the default.

One could reason that changing the cursor shape is an activity restricted entirely to the Controller, because mouse-clicks are inputs. On the other hand, we could say that all changes to the GUI should be handled by the View. We satisfy both these considerations as follows: the Controller makes the decision that the cursor appearance in the drawing panel be changed because it knows when a shape-drawing command is in progress and instructs the View to make that take place.

Thus, the following are to be included in the functionality of the View:

1. Listen to property changes in the Model.
2. Change the cursor to its default shape.
3. Change the cursor to indicate that drawing is in progress.
4. Draw the shapes in the Model, as specified by the user requirements.

To keep matters relatively simple, we will have a single class called `View` that implements the above functionality of a View. Extensions to multiple Views would be addressed through a programming project at the end of the chapter.

Another consideration in the design of the View is that it should be able to render all shapes (even types that may be added in the future). This and interface independence are explored further in the next subsection.

### 9.4.5 Model–View Separation

One common action that we want to perform on any shape is **rendering**, which is the process by which the data stored in the Model is displayed by the View. Regardless of how we implement this, the actual details of how the drawing is done are dependent on the following two parameters:

- The technology and tools that are used in creating the GUI. For instance, if we use Java's `Swing` package, the drawing could be on a `JPanel` object and the rendering methods will then have to be invoked on the associated `Graphics` object. If we create a JavaFX GUI, we might use that technology's `Canvas` class, and rendering in that case will be done through a `GraphicsContext` object.
- The shape itself. Clearly, the process of drawing a label is different from that of drawing a line. Even for a line, much depends on how that shape is represented. If a line is stored by its equation, the code for drawing it would be very different from the line that is stored as two endpoints.

The technology and tools are known to the author of the GUI, whereas the structure of the shape is known to the author of the shape. Since the information required is in two different classes (or subsets of classes), we need to decide which class will have the responsibility for implementing the rendering. We have the following options:

- **Option 1.** Let us say that the entire rendering is done in the GUI, that is, there is code in the GUI that accesses the fields of each shape and then draws them. Since the Model stores these shapes in a polymorphic container, the GUI would have to query the type of each shape returned by the enumeration in order to choose the appropriate method(s).
- **Option 2.** If the shape were responsible, each shape would have a `render()` method that accesses the fields and draws the shape. The problem with this is that the way an object is to be rendered depends on the rendering technology. The functionality available in the toolkit has to be considered. For instance, suppose we also need to support circles and consider the problem of rendering a circle: a circle is almost always drawn as a sequence of short line segments. If the only method given in the toolkit is that for drawing lines, the circle will have to be decomposed into straight lines.

At this point it appears that we are stuck between two bad choices. However, a closer look at the first option reveals a fairly serious problem, which is somewhat intractable: we are querying each object in the collection to determine its type and decide the appropriate methods to invoke. This is very much at odds with object-oriented philosophy, where we would like methods to be invoked in a polymorphic manner.

This really means that the `render()` method for each shape should be stored in the shape itself, which is, in fact, the approach for the second option. This simplifies our task somewhat, so we can focus on the task of fixing the shortcomings of the second option.

Essentially, what we want is that each shape be customized for each kind of GUI, which boils down to having a different `render()` method for each type of technology.

One way to accomplish this is to use inheritance. Say that we have three kinds of rendering technologies, the AWT (an old Java rendering technology that is now obsolete), Swing (which is still supported) and JavaFX.

What we do is create a separate subclass for each `Shape` type, for each technology. For instance, as shown below, the class `Line` would encapsulate the details of a line, except for rendering, which would be delegated to a separate subclass for each technology.

```
public abstract class Shape {
// some methods that all Shapes in the system must satisfy
  public abstract void render();
}
```

```
public abstract class Line extends Shape {
// some fields and methods
}

public class AWTLine extends Line {
// Line class for AWT rendering
  public void render() {
  // code to draw a circle using  AWT
  }
}

public class SwingLine extends Line {
// Line class for Swing
  public void render(){
  // code to draw a circle using  Swing
  }
}

public class FXLine extends Line {
// Line class for FX
  public void render(){
  // code to draw a circle using  FX
  }
}
```

In each case, the `render()` method will invoke the methods available in the respective GUI technology to render the shape. For instance, in the `SwingLine` class, the `render()` method would have to get hold of the `Graphics` object and invoke the `drawLine()` method. The code for this could look like this:

```
public class SwingLine extends Line {
// Line class for SwingUI
  public void render(){
    Graphics graphics = (View.getInstance()).getGraphics();
    graphics.drawLine(...);
  }
}
```

The system could potentially employ many types of shapes, each of which has a corresponding abstract class. Each abstract class ends up with as many subclasses as the types of rendering technologies we need to accommodate.

This solution has some drawbacks. The number of classes needed to accommodate such a solution is given by:

*Number of Types of Shapes* × *Number of Rendering Technologies* (see Figure 9.6).

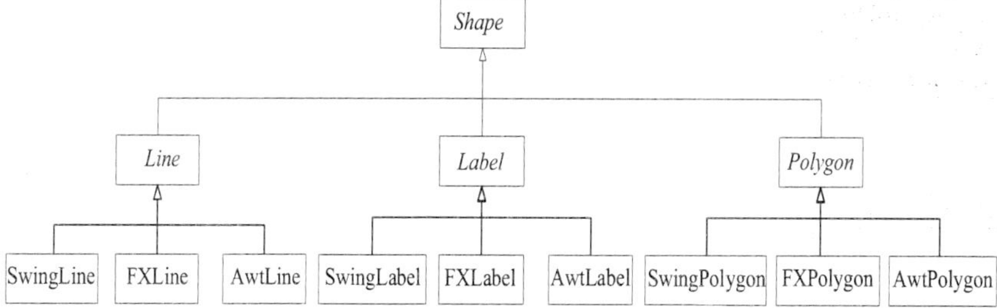


**Fig. 9.6** Class explosion due to multiple GUI implementations. We are creating a new concrete subclass for each type of renderer to be supported. The three shape classes are abstract because rendering depends on the technology being used.

This causes an unacceptable explosion in the number of classes. Next, consider the situation where shapes are being created in the Controller. Some kind of conditional will be needed to decide which concrete class should be instantiated, and this requires the code in the Controller to be aware of the rendering technology in use at that time. A third and more subtle point is that of software upgrades. Suppose we create a version of our drawing program that supports a hypothetical technology named `Past`. All the shapes created in the Model will belong to the `Past` classes, and can be used only with a system where the `Past` package is available. If a later version of the software does not support `Past` (or we move the files to a system that does not support it), we cannot access the old files anymore. If the objects created in the Model were independent of the type of GUI, this problem could be avoided.

We now describe an approach that does not result in class explosion. In this approach, we have exactly one class for each shape `Line`, `Polygon`, etc.) and one class for each type of renderer. To understand the principles, observe the following:

- We have two possible ways in which objects can vary: one of shapes and the other of rendering technologies. The variation in the shapes as well as the rendering technologies can each be represented by a hierarchy. We will use the term **internal variation** to refer to the differences represented by the `Shape` hierarchy and the term **external variation** to refer to the variations in the rendering hierarchy.
- Each `Shape` class has a `render()` method, which is responsible for rendering that shape.
- The `render()` method needs to make use of the rendering technology without committing to any specific technology. In other words, the objects of the internal variation need to make use of the functionality provided by objects in the external variation.

With the two hierarchies in place, we set up a *bridge* between them. The `render()` method needs to make use of the rendering technology without committing to any specific technology. This approach is quite standard in problems of this kind and is called the **Bridge pattern.** Figure 9.7 describes the interaction diagram between the classes and visually represents the bridge between the two hierarchies.

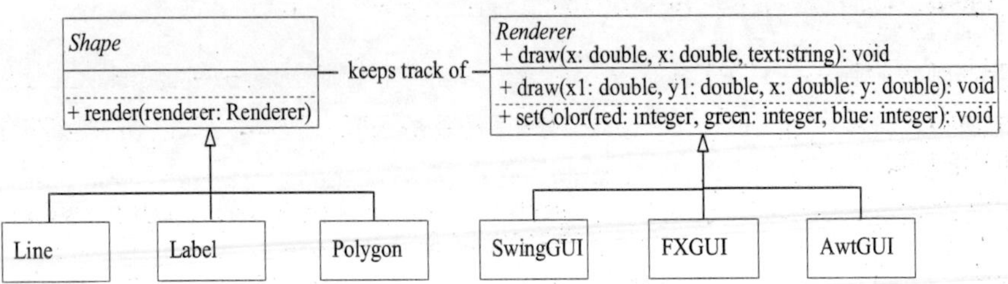


**Fig. 9.7** The Bridge pattern as employed in the drawing program. The basic principle is that we have two independent hierarchies, with both being allowed to vary. As new GUIs are created, we create appropriate subclasses to the `Renderer` class. To allow for dynamically changing the supported GUI, we chose to make the renderer a parameter of the `render()` method. In a more traditional implementation, we would store the renderer as a field of `Shape`.

The `render()` method needs information from both the GUI and the shape. Depending on the nature of shapes we need to support, `Renderer` would have a variety of basic `draw()` methods to render lines, text, arcs, images, etc. The `Shape` classes invoke the appropriate drawing methods on the `Renderer` object, which could be obtained just in time before rendering the shapes. The `Renderer` object stores all technology-related information needed for drawing and its `draw()` methods receive appropriate details of the shape as parameters.

Note that the total number of classes is now reduced to

*Number of Types of Shapes + Number of Renderers*

Since we have only one concrete class for each shape, the creation process is simple. Finally, by factoring out the `render()` method, we are no longer concerned with what kind of GUI is being used or what GUI will be used to edit it at a later stage. Our software for the Model is thus "completely" reusable.

As is often the case in object-oriented design, one price we pay is through loss of performance. In this case, this is seen in the increased number of method calls. Every time we invoke the `render()` method, we have to get the `Renderer` object and invoke its functionality.

What is left in the design of the Bridge pattern is the following:

- The methods of the `Renderer` hierarchy.
- The flow of control to render the shapes.

To see what methods should go into the `Renderer` hierarchy, somewhat arbitrarily, we will make `Renderer` an interface. Clearly, we need to draw lines, polygons, and text. If we assume that any shape with straight lines is stored as a sequence of vertices, drawing it could be facilitated with the use of a method to draw a line as below.

```
public abstract void draw(double x1, double y1, double x2,
double y2);
```

To write a label, we could have the method shown below:

```
public abstract void draw(double x, double y, String text);
```

Since we would like to vary the shape color, we add the following method to the interface:

```
public abstract void setColor(int red, int green, int blue);
```

While colors could be represented differently in different GUI technologies, we could adopt the convention that each of the parameters represents the respective color value on a scale from 0 to 255.
The UML diagram is shown in Figure 9.8.

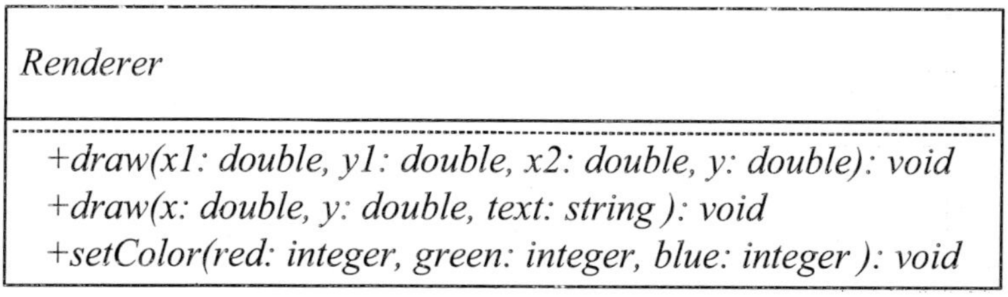

| *Renderer* |
|---|
| *+draw(x1: double, y1: double, x2: double, y: double): void*<br>*+draw(x: double, y: double, text: string ): void*<br>*+setColor(red: integer, green: integer, blue: integer ): void* |

**Fig. 9.8** The `Renderer` interface. The primary methods are to draw a line and write a string. The expectation is that all rendering needs can be met by invoking these methods in some combination. The color can be changed using the `setColor()` method.

### 9.4.6 Design to Support Undo and Redo

Undo and redo are unlike the other operations. If an undo operation is treated the same as any other operation, then two successive undo operations cancel each other out, since the second undo reverses the effect of the first undo and is thus a no-op (no operation). The undo (and redo) operations must therefore have a special status, if several operations must be undone.

Clearly, to implement undo, some kind of a stack would be needed to remember the operations that have been completed. When an undo is requested, an element from the top of the stack is popped, and this element has to be "decoded" to find out what the last operation was. This would require some kind of conditional, and the complexity of this method would increase with the number of different kinds of operations we implement. In

earlier chapters we have seen how such complexity can be reduced by *replacing conditional logic with polymorphism.* We will shortly see how that can help us improve the design of the Controller.
A simple scheme for implementing undo could be something like this:

1. Create a stack for storing the history of the operations.
2. Define a data class that stores the information necessary to undo the operation.
3. Implement code, so that whenever any operation is carried out, the relevant information is packed into the associated data object and pushed onto the stack.
4. Implement an `undo()` method in the Controller that simply pops the stack, decodes the popped data object and invokes the appropriate method to extract the information and perform the task of undoing the operation.

One obvious approach for implementing this is to define a class `StackObject` that stores each object with an identifying `String`.

```
public class StackObject {
  private String commandName;
  private Object info;
  public StackObject(String commandName, Object info) {
    this.commandName = commandName;
    this.info = info;
  }
  public String getCommandName() {
    return commandName;
  }
  public Object getInfo() {
    return info;
  }
}
```

As an example, when the operation for adding a line is completed, the appropriate `StackObject` instance is created and pushed on the stack.
We define a `Stack` object named `history`.

```
Stack history;
```

We could do the following in the course of creating a line:

```
Line line = new Line(x, y);
Model.getInstance().addShape(line);
history.push(new StackObject("line", line));
update the View to display the line;
```

Decoding involves popping the stack, reading the string, and figuring out what the object is all about. We could create a new class `UndoManager` to take care of all undo operations.

```
public class UndoManager {
  public  void undo(){
    StackObject stackObject = history.pop();
    String name = stackObject.getCommandName();
    Object info = stackObject.getInfo();
    switch(name) {
    case "line": undoLine(info); break;
    case "polygon": undoPolygon(info); break;
    // one case for each command
    }
  }
}
```

Finally, undoing line creation is simply a matter of retrieving the reference to the shape and removing it from the Model. The `undoLine()` method would be along the following lines. The method could be in `UndoManager`.

```
public void undoLine(Line line){
  Model.getInstance().removeShape(line);
}
```

There are two obvious drawbacks with this approach:

- The long conditional statement in the `undo()` method of `UndoManager`.
- The task of rewriting the code whenever we make changes like adding or modifying the implementation of an operation.

The object-oriented approach for dealing with the first drawback is to subclass the behavior by creating an inheritance hierarchy and replacing conditional logic with polymorphism. (Recollect that this is accomplished by making the original method abstract and moving each leg of the conditional to an overriding method in the corresponding subclass.) Let us refactor the code to accomplish this. Before replacing the conditional, however, we see that the `undo()` method is mostly using the data stored in `StackObject`. We can rewrite `UndoManager` as follows:

```
public class UndoManager {
  private Stack history;
  public  void undo() {
    StackObject stackObject = history.pop();
    stackObject.undo();
  }
  // other fields and methods
}

public abstract class StackObject {
  public abstract boolean undo();
```

```
}

public class LineObject extends StackObject {
  public boolean undo() {
    Shape line = (Line) this.getInfo();
  }
// other fields and methods
}
```

This code is a lot simpler and cleaner. Note that we no longer "decode" the stored objects and therefore the name field is not required. The code to create a line now creates a `LineObject` and pushes it onto the stack.

### Employing the Command Pattern

We have thus associated an object with each operation. For instance, whenever we execute an operation to create a line, a `LineObject` is created and pushed onto the stack. This object need not merely be a repository of associated data but can also encapsulate the routines that manipulate this data. Such an approach is built into the Command pattern, the intent of which is as follows [1]:

> Encapsulate a request as an object, thereby letting you parameterize clients with different requests, queue or log requests, and support undoable operations.

The abstract `Command` class has abstract methods to `execute()`, `undo()`, and `redo()`. The concrete command classes (such as `LineCommand`) implement these methods and store the associated data needed to undo and redo these operations.

```
public abstract class Command {
  public abstract boolean undo();
  public abstract boolean redo();
  public abstract void execute();
}

public class LineCommand extends Command {
    private Line line;
    public LineCommand(Point point1) {
        line = new Line(point1);
        execute();
    }
    public void execute() {
        Model.instance().addShape(line);
    }
    public boolean undo() {
```

```
        Model.instance().removeShape(line);
        return true;
    }
    public boolean redo() {
        execute();
        return true;
    }
    public void setPoint2(Point point) {
        line.setPoint2(point);
    }
}
```

As we saw, the class `UndoManager` manages undo and redo. The `history` stack stores a list of the commands that have been executed. As a result, the `undo()` method simply gets the command from the stack and invokes its `undo()` method.

The class is a singleton, but below, we only show the code for performing undo and redo:

```
public class UndoManager {
  private Stack<Command> history;
  private Stack<Command> redoStack;
  public void undo() {
    if (!(history.empty())) {
      Command command = history.peek();
      if (command.undo()) {
        history.pop();
        redoStack.push(command);
      }
    }
  }
  public void redo() {
    if (!(redoStack.empty())) {
      Command command = (redoStack.peek());
      if (command.redo()) {
        redoStack.pop();
        history.push(command);
      }
    }
  }
```

## 9.4.7 Grouping, Ungrouping, and Shape Collections

A group imposes a hierarchy on a set of shapes. As we have seen, multiple shapes may be put together to form a Group object. This Group object may be used in conjunction with shapes such as lines and polygons or other groups to form another Group object. A Group object may be ungrouped to obtain the children that formed the group.

As we have seen, the drawing program has a superclass called `Shape`. The different subsystems create, manipulate, and render `Shape` objects. For example, we could have the View execute code as below.

```
for (Shape shape : shapeCollection) {
   shape.render(renderer);
}
```

A fundamental question to address in this regard is how this code can work when a shape is not an "elementary" shape such as a line or label, but is composed of multiple shapes which is the case when we have a group. Such issues come up fairly frequently in problem solving, and as one might expect, there is a specific design pattern named **Composite** to solve this problem. Once again, quoting the Gang of Four [1], the intent of the Composite pattern is the following:

> Compose objects into tree structures to represent part–whole hierarchies. Composite lets clients treat individual objects and compositions of objects uniformly.

To see how the Composite pattern works, examine the code above. If a group of shapes has to be treated like a `Shape`, we need to have a class named `Group` that extends `Shape`. This way, every `Group` object is an instance of `Shape` and the above code will compile error free.

Let us revisit the example in Figure 9.2, where we have created three `Shape` objects: `line1`, `label1`, and `polygon1`, of type `Line`, `Label`, and `Polygon`, respectively. At this time, the Model will store the three `Shape` objects. The rendering loop iterates three times to render the three shapes.

Now suppose that we group `line1` and `label1` to form a `Group` object, say, `group1`. Now, the Model will store just two objects: `polygon1` and `group1`. That is, we delete the objects `line1` and `label1` and insert `group1` into the collection. After this, the rendering loop will iterate twice, once calling `render()` in `Polygon` and then calling `render()` in `Group`. When `render()` in `Group` is invoked, we should get `line1` and `label1` rendered. This can be accomplished by having `Group` store the collection of `Shape` objects it is composed of and have its `render()` method invoke the `render()` on every shape.

The `Group` class will have code to add shapes. The code would be along the following lines:

```
public class Group extends Shape {
```

```
    private List<Shape> shapes = new LinkedList<>();
    public void add(Shape shape) {
      shapes.add(shape);
    }
    public void render(Renderer renderer) {
      for (Shape shape : shapes) {
        shape.render(renderer);
      }
    }
  }
```

Note that even when the Group object has a deep hierarchy, every "elementary" shape will get rendered because render() will follow the hierarchy.

The structure of the Shape hierarchy is now as given in Figure 9.9. Besides the original methods, the Shape class has methods to maintain a collection of Shape objects. The default implementation of the add() method in Shape does nothing and getChildren() returns an empty list. Group maintains a list of Shape objects and implements the add() and getChildren() methods of Shape in the obvious manner.

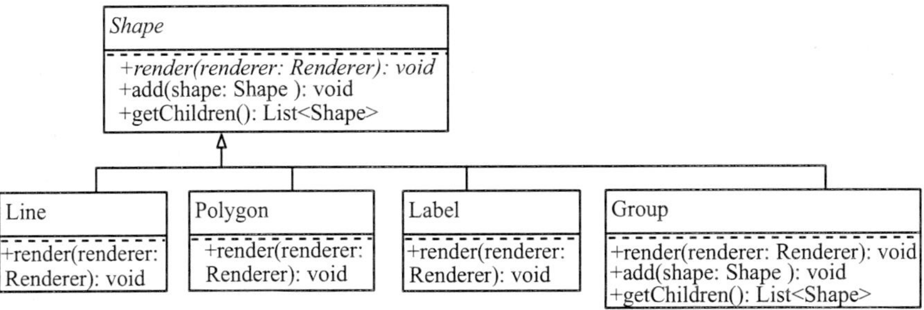


**Fig. 9.9** The Shape hierarchy with Group as a subclass. The Shape class has methods to add a Shape object and return the children of the shape; the add() method in Shape does nothing and getChildren() returns an empty list. Group maintains a list of Shape objects and implements the add() and getChildren() methods of Shape.

### 9.4.8 Selecting, Deletion, and Moving

The user left-clicks the mouse with the Control key pressed to select one or more shapes. These shapes can then be deleted, moved, grouped, or ungrouped. The Controller needs to keep track of the selected shapes, so it can know what to delete, move, group, or ungroup. Obviously, this needs a collection.

A basic question that arises in this regard is where this collection should be stored. Two options arise:

- **Option 1:** The Model is responsible for maintaining the collection of shapes, so it could possibly store the collection of selected shapes.
- **Option 2:** The Controller subsystem manipulates the selected shapes, so it should maintain the shapes.

Maintaining the list of selected shapes in the Model implies that the Model is aware of shape selection, which makes it less cohesive. On the other hand, Controller cohesiveness would be affected if it has to deal with details of maintaining a collection. We can take a more reasonable approach by creating a base class that is just a collection class for shapes and extend this twice: once as a class adapter to create the Model and then as a singleton subclass to have the selected shape class. The organization would be as follows:

- `ShapeList` A collection class for `Shape` objects.
- `Model` A singleton subclass of `ShapeList`. This would also have functionality to add and remove Views, so the class is an observable.
- `SelectedShapes` A singleton subclass of `ShapeList`. This would be used by Controller to maintain the list of selected shapes.

### 9.4.9 Controller Structure

Every command (create line, save, retrieve, etc.) is represented by a separate `Command` class. A class called `Controller` receives all requests issued through the GUI:

- If the request is to create a new shape or retrieve a saved drawing or save the current drawing, the `Controller` object checks that there is no shape creation in progress. If that is the case, it creates a new `Command` object. If a shape is already being created, the request is ignored.
- If the request is anything other than what is specified above, it could be a mouse-click, character input, etc. If a command is in progress, the Controller dispatches the request to that command. If no command is in progress, the request is ignored.

Thus a `Command` object such as `LineCommand` needs to handle two sets of operations:

- Operations related to the Command pattern: execute, undo, and redo
- Inputs such as mouse-clicks, key presses, etc.

### 9.4.10 Sequence Diagrams for Shape Manipulation

To arrive at the design details of the subsystems, we need to consider how we will realize the functionality for shape selection, deletion, move, grouping, and ungrouping.

#### Selecting Shapes

The essence of what occurs in the selection process is shown in Figure 9.10. When the user clicks the mouse with the Control key pressed, the GUI calls the `onControlClick()` method of `Controller` with the x and y coordinates. The very first selection of an object creates the selection command. The user is in a loop selecting multiple shapes. Each control-click would either select an unselected shape or unselect a selected shape, although any unselection is not shown in the diagram to avoid clutter. `Controller` checks whether the clicked point is close to any of the shapes by calling the `isCloseTo()` method of `Model`. Details of this step are not shown in the sequence diagram. The Model will need to iterate over the collection and determine for each shape whether any of the vertices is close to the clicked point. This check is best done by the appropriate subclass of `Shape`, because that subclass encapsulates the details. But since Model is using polymorphic reference, the `Shape` class must define an abstract method `isCloseTo(double x, double y)` to facilitate the search for a shape. The selected shape is marked as selected and added to the `SelectedShapes` collection. The process continues as long as user input is a mouse-click with the Control key pressed.

#### Deleting Shapes

The sequence diagram is shown in Figure 9.11. Pushing the `Delete` menu item in the pop-up menu results in the GUI calling the `onDelete()` method of `Controller`, which creates a `DeleteCommand` object. Recall that deletion is only permitted when at least one shape is selected, so `SelectedShapes` will be a non-empty collection. These shapes are retrieved using the method `getShapes()` in `SelectedShapes`. This `DeleteCommand` object then deletes all of the selected shapes in `Model` as well as `SelectedShapes`.

#### Moving Shapes

The sequence diagram is shown in Figure 9.12. Similar to the case of deletion, the process begins with pushing the `Move` menu item in the pop-up menu. The GUI calls the `onMoveCommand()` method of `Controller`, which creates a

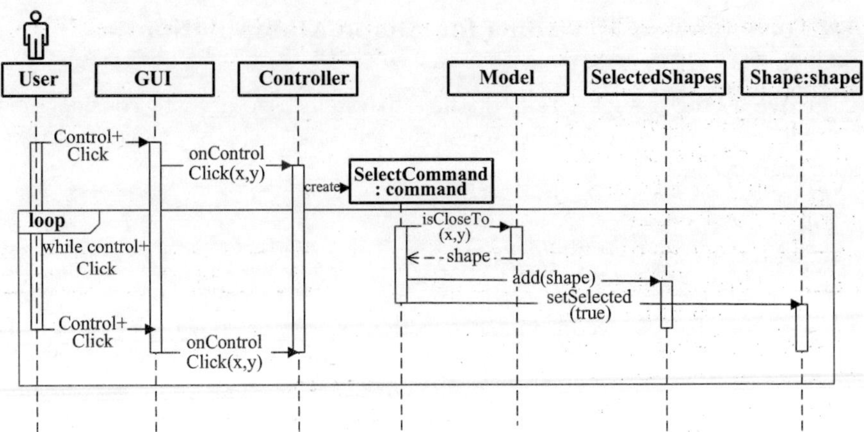


**Fig. 9.10** Sequence diagram for selecting shapes. When the mouse is left-clicked with the Control key pressed, the GUI sends a message to `Controller`, which checks whether the clicked point is close to any of the shapes. If it is, the shape is added to a collection and marked as selected. Notice that we do not show the details of the GUI class. The central idea here is the collection class for selected shapes and the marking of selected shapes.

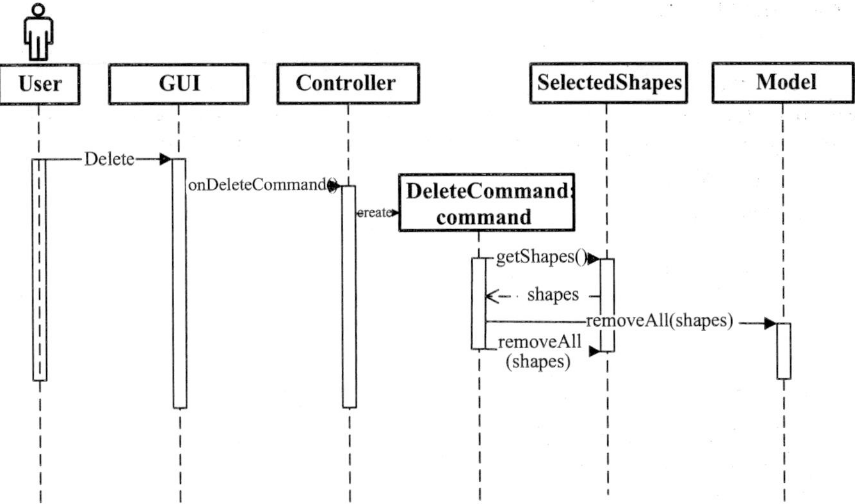


**Fig. 9.11** Sequence diagram for deleting shapes. Pushing the `Delete` menu item in the pop-up menu results in the GUI calling the `onDelete()` method of `Controller`, which creates a `DeleteCommand` object. This object deletes all of the selected shapes in `Model` as well as `SelectedShapes`.

MoveCommand object. The selected shapes are retrieved from SelectedShapes. As long as the user moves the mouse, the shapes are moved using the move() method of Shape. The selected shapes are cleared from SelectedShapes, so they are unselected at the end of the commmand.

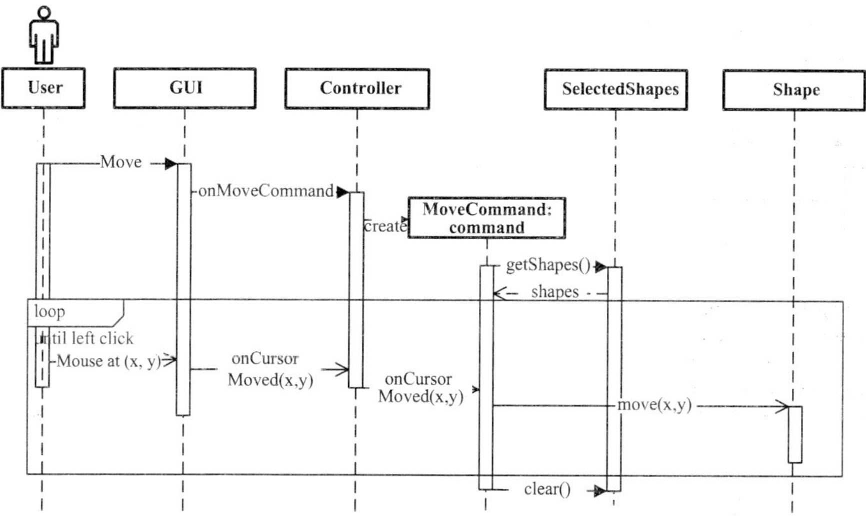


**Fig. 9.12** Sequence diagram for moving shapes. Pushing the Move menu item in the pop-up menu results in the GUI calling the onMove() method of Controller, which creates a MoveCommand object. This object moves all of the selected shapes.

## Grouping Shapes

The sequence diagram is shown in Figure 9.13. When the Group menu item is clicked, the GUI calls the onGroupCommand() method of Controller, which creates a GroupCommand object. As in the previous cases, the selected shapes are retrieved from SelectedShapes. The command creates a Group object and adds all the selected shapes to it. The Group object is added to the model and the selected shapes are removed from Model and SelectedShapes.

## Ungrouping Shapes

The sequence diagram is shown in Figure 9.14. Overall, the process is similar to the previous three. Selecting the Ungroup menu item results in the GUI calling the onUngroupCommand() method of Controller, which creates an UngroupCommand object. The selected shapes are retrieved from SelectedShapes. A slightly tricky point here is that some of the selected

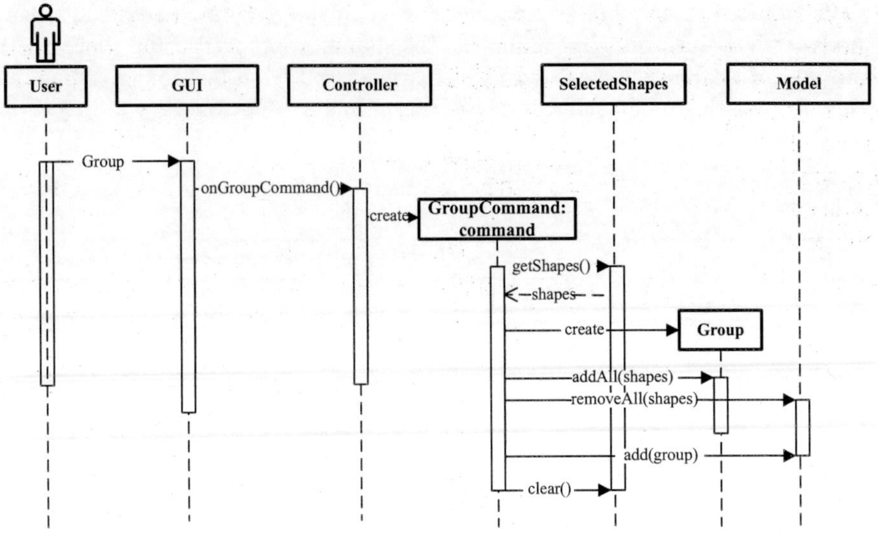


**Fig. 9.13** Class diagram for grouping shapes. Pushing the `Group` menu item in the pop-up menu results in the GUI calling the `onGroupCommand()` method of `Controller`, which creates a `GroupCommand` object. This object creates a `Group` shape and adds all the selected shapes to it. The selected shapes are removed from the Model and the collection of selected shapes. The new `Group` object is added to the Model.

shapes may be group objects and others may be more basic shapes like labels and lines. All the `Group` objects are ungrouped by calling the `getChildren()` method of every selected shape: a `Group` object returns the list of shapes it is composed of, whereas elementary shapes return empty. The selected shapes are removed from `Model` and `SelectedShapes` and the shapes after ungrouping are added to `Model`.

### 9.4.11 Details of Classes

The last step in the design process is defining the details of the classes. We have already defined the methods for the `Controller` class and the `Command` class. Moving on to the Model subsystem, we need to get the details of the following classes: `Model`, `Shape`, `SelectedShapes`, and `ShapeList`. Examining the sequence diagrams (Figures 9.5, 9.10, 9.11, 9.12, 9.13, 9.14), we can see the following methods: `add(Shape shape)`, `isCloseTo(double x, double y)`, and `removeAll(List shapes)`. Considering `SelectedShapes`, we can see the following methods: `getShapes()`, `clear()`, and `addShape(Shape shape)`. It is convenient to put all these collection methods into the superclass `ShapeList`; see the class diagram in Figure 9.15.

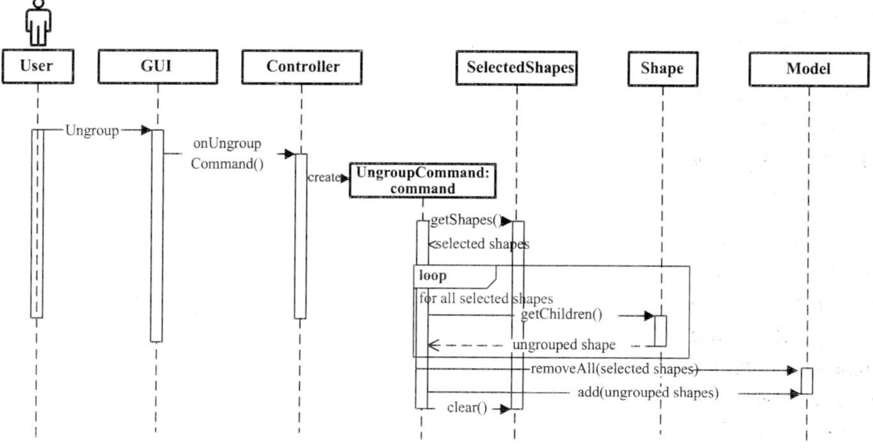


**Fig. 9.14** Sequence diagram for ungrouping shapes. Some of the selected shapes may not be groups. The `Ungroup` command calls the `getChildren()` method of every selected shape and assembles the set of shapes after ungrouping. These shapes are added to the Model, while the selected shapes are removed from the Model and the collection of selected shapes.

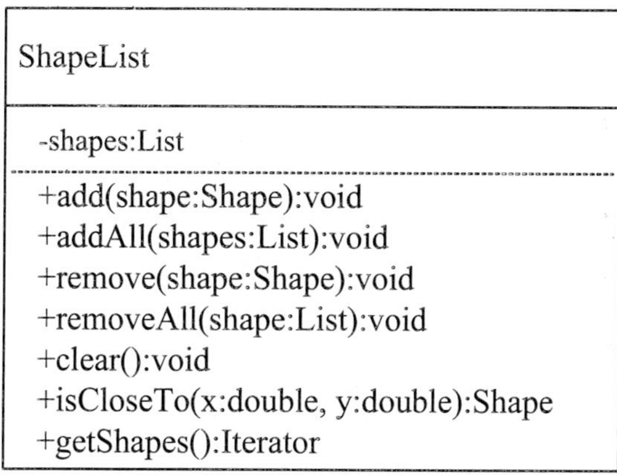


**Fig. 9.15** Class diagram for `ShapeList`. This class has methods to manage a collection of shapes.

The class `ShapeList` has two subclasses: `SelectedShapes`, which is a singleton, but has no extra instance methods, and `Model`, which adds methods to make the Model an observable. Since we know how to make a class observable, we do not show the class diagram here.

The only major class we need to finalize in the Model subsystem is the `Shape` class. We know from earlier discussions that it must have the following methods: `render()`, `addChild()`. `getChildren()`, `isCloseTo()`, and `move()`.

It should have fields for remembering the color of the shape and whether it is selected. See the class diagram in Figure 9.16.

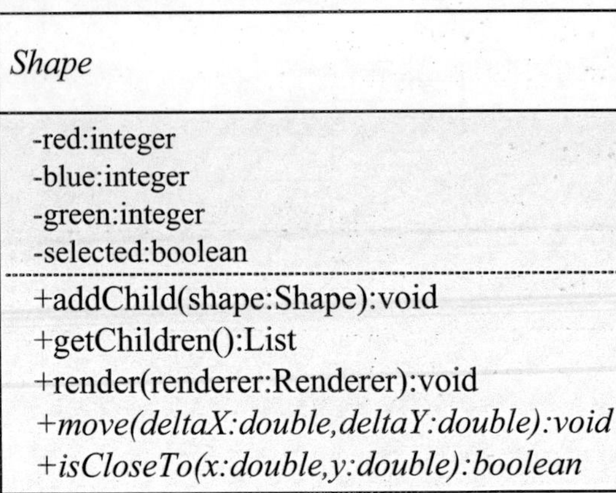


**Fig. 9.16** Class diagram for `Shape`. Implementation of `move()` and `isCloseTo()` would be dependent on the subclasses. The `render()` method would set the rendering color, but the rest of the functionality would depend on the individual subclasses.

### 9.4.12 Final Details of View Design

The View is an observer of the Model and its primary function is to display the drawing. For simplicity, we have one singleton class named `View`, which, as we have seen, uses the Bridge pattern to display the shapes in a GUI-technology–independent manner.

Two other functionalities required of the drawing program are the ability to display and dismiss the context menu and modify the appearance of the cursor. Ultimately, this must be accomplished by the GUI and to accomplish interface-independence, we need to have the GUI functionality represented by an interface, which we call `GuiDisplay`, shown in Figure 9.17.

To manage the context menu, we need a couple of methods in the GUI: one to show the context menu at a specific point and another to dismiss the menu when it is no longer needed: we name these methods `showContextMenu()` and `dismissContextMenu()`. The former will have two parameters specifying the x aand y coordinates where the menu should be displayed. Similarly, we also have methods named `setCursorToDefault()` and `setCursorToDrawing()` with the obvious semantics.

Two other methods in `GuiDisplay` are to set up the drawing, which we call `draw()`, and to get a reference to the renderer, which is named `getRenderer()`.

To determine how the View would interact with the GUI, we note that in a centralized system, there is little point in having multiple GUI windows concurrently rendering data displayed by a single view. To support multiple technologies for the same view, note that the View can refer to the GUI using the interface `GuiDisplay`.

| *GUIDisplay* |
|---|
| *+draw():void*<br>*+setCursorToDefault():void*<br>*+setCursorToDrawing():void*<br>*+showContextMenu(x:double,y:double):void*<br>*+dismissContextMenu();void*<br>*+getRenderer():Renderer* |

**Fig. 9.17** Interface to be implemented by the GUI. We could make the GUI an observable of the View or use a dedicated communication mechanism between the two. Some of these methods will also be in the View.

To get a fuller picture of how the shapes are drawn, assume for some reason – perhaps, we are drawing a new shape – the GUI needs to be updated. The sequence of actions is as follows:

1. The Controller or Model notifies notifies the View. The notification mechanism is different in the two cases. `Model` fires a property change and classes in the Controller subsystem calls the `update()` method in `View`.
2. In response to this notification, `View` calls the `draw()` method of `GuiDisplay`. Whichever GUI is attached to the `View` object receives this call.
3. The `GUI` object prepares to draw the shapes: it could perform actions like erasing the screen, setting up a `Renderer` object, drawing an outline on the screen, etc.
4. After readying the screen, the `GuiDisplay` object calls a method in `View`, so the View subsystem can render the shapes. This method in `View` is named `draw()`.
5. The `draw()` method of `View` calls the `getRenderer()` method of `GuiDisplay` to obtain a renderer.
6. The `draw()` method of `View` enters a loop, issuing a call to the `render()` method of `Shape`, so every shape gets rendered.

The process is shown pictorially in the sequence diagram given in Figure 9.18.

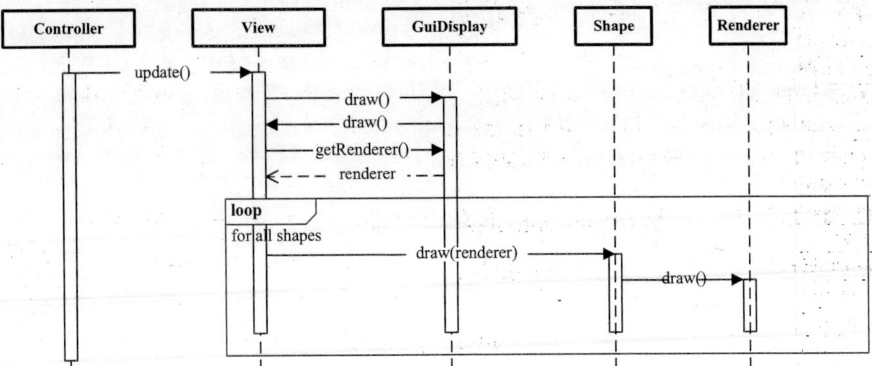


**Fig. 9.18** The sequence of steps for updating the screen. Notice that the `View` and `GuiDisplay` classes have the similarly-named method `draw()`, but have different roles. In particular, the `draw()` in `GuiDisplay` prepares the screen for drawing, but does not draw the shapes themselves; that takes place when the `Renderer` object's `draw()` methods are called. Also, we have not shown the specific `renderer` object's `draw()` methods that are called; that depends on the shape.

Finally, we need to see how the context menu and cursor shape are managed. Obviously, the `View` class needs to have a reference to the `GuiDisplay` object. There is little point in having the Controller classes keep a reference to the `GuiDisplay` object as well, because it adds to the complexity. Instead, the Controller classes call methods in the `View` class (for example, we have methods named `showContextMenu()` in `View`, to show the context menu) at appropriate times.

### 9.4.13 GUI Design

Although GUI design is not a central theme for us in this book, we touch upon the main aspects of how the GUI is structured, to give the reader a better understanding of the program. While we have separate implementations for JavaFX and Swing, the approach is the same for both technologies. There are fine differences in the implementation, but they are not all that important. There are three major groups of classes. The first group has three classes. They provide the visual interface:

- `ButtonPanel`. It holds all the buttons.
- `DrawingPanel`. All drawing takes place in an area defined by this class. This class also implements `GuiDisplay`.

- DrawingProgram. This is the window holding a ButtonPanel object and a DrawingPanel object. This class has the main() method.

The second set of classes forms the controller at the GUI level. They are as given below:

- There is a set of button objects with a superclass named GUIButton and one subclass for each button in the button panel.
- A class named MouseClickHandler to handle mouse-clicks on the drawing panel.
- A class named KeyPressedHandler to listen to keystrokes.

There is only one class in the third set. It implements the Renderer interface.

## 9.5 Implementation

Much of the implementation can be understood by following the way the program gets started and then following the implementation of the use cases given below:

- Drawing a line
- Selecting shapes
- Grouping shapes
- Moving shapes

It should be noted that selecting shapes is not a separate operation, but a precursor to other operations like grouping and moving. Since selection is performed in the same manner for all these other operations, we list it separately.

### 9.5.1 Starting the Program

The main() method resides in DrawingProgram. When the program is started, this class creates an instance each of ButtonPanel and DrawingPanel and puts them in a window. ButtonPanel creates each button and puts them in a container. Each GUIButton is responsible for handling the clicks on itself. DrawingProgram sets up the listeners for keystrokes and mouse-clicks on the drawing panel.

### 9.5.2 Drawing a Line

The class that implements the Line button is named LineButton. The event handling method of this class (actionPerformed() in Swing and handle() in JavaFX) issues a call to the Controller as given below.

```
Controller.getInstance().onLineCommand();
```

The Controller class has a field to store the current command in progress.

```
private Command currentCommand;
```

When currentCommand has a non-null value, it means no command is in progress. Thus, the code for onLineCommand() is

```
public void onLineCommand() {
  if (currentCommand == null) {
    setCommand(new LineCommand());
  }
}
```

The method setCommand() sets currentCommand to the value in the parameter. The method given below can be used to end the current command.

```
public void commandEnded() {
   currentCommand = null;
}
```

LineCommand, similiar to all other Command classes, encapsulates the process of creating a line. The structure is given below.

```
public class LineCommand extends Command {
  private Line line;
  private int numberOfPoints;
  // methods
}
```

The class uses the default constructor. No Line object is created at the time LineCommand is instantiated.
Assume that the mouse enters the drawing panel. The GUI recognizes this cursor movement and issues the call

```
Controller.getInstance().onMouseEntered();
```

Controller instructs the View to modify the cursor shape. Since line drawing is in progress, currentCommand is not null, so the View gets the call to modify the cursor shape.

```
public void onMouseEntered() {
  if (currentCommand != null) {
    View.getInstance().setCursorToDrawing();
  }
}
```

View issues a call to the GUI to modify the cursor shape.

```
public void setCursorToDrawing() {
  guiDisplay.setCursorToDrawing();
}
```

Assume that the user now clicks the mouse to specify a point. The code in both Swing and JavaFX is very similar. Here is the code for Swing.

```
if (mouseEvent.isControlDown()) {
  Controller.getInstance().onControlClick(mouseEvent.getX(),
  mouseEvent.getY());
} else if (mouseEvent.getButton() == MouseEvent.BUTTON1) {
  Controller.getInstance().onPointInput(mouseEvent.getX(),
  mouseEvent.getY());
} else if (mouseEvent.getButton() == MouseEvent.BUTTON3) {
  Controller.getInstance().onRightClick(mouseEvent.getX(),
  mouseEvent.getY());
}
```

The JavaFX code is as follows:

```
if (mouseEvent.isControlDown()) {
  Controller.getInstance().onControlClick(mouseEvent.getX(),
  mouseEvent.getY());
} else if (mouseEvent.getButton() == MouseButton.PRIMARY) {
  Controller.getInstance().onPointInput(mouseEvent.getX(),
  mouseEvent.getY());
} else if (mouseEvent.getButton() == MouseButton.SECONDARY) {
  Controller.getInstance().onRightClick(mouseEvent.getX(),
  mouseEvent.getY());
}
```

The reader might recall that when events such as mouse-clicks are delivered, Controller simply sends them to the current command to handle them, if a command is in progress. Otherwise, the event is ignored. Here is the code in Controller.

```
public void onPointInput(double x, double y) {
  if (currentCommand != null) {
    currentCommand.onPointInput(x, y);
  }
}
```

Since line drawing has already been initiated, we need to see what happens in LineCommand.

```
public void onPointInput(double x, double y) {
  if (numberOfPoints == 0) {
```

```
      line = new Line(x, y);
      numberOfPoints++;
      UndoManager.getInstance().beginCommand(this);
      execute();
    } else {
      line.setPoint2(x, y);
      Controller.getInstance().commandEnded();
    }
    View.getInstance().update();
  }
```

When the first point is specified, numberOfPoints is zero, so the code creates a Line object and gets the LineCommand object pushed onto the history stack. The execute() method simply stores the Line object in the Model.

```
  public void execute() {
    Model.instance().add(line);
  }
```

The Line class stores the two endpoints as CanvasPoint objects. The non-trivial methods (that is, methods other than getters and setters) are given in the code below. The method distanceMeasure() returns a measure of the distance between this point and another point whose coordinates are given as parameters. Note that this is not the actual distance, but a measure that depends on the distance (see Table 9.8). The move() method supports moving a point.

```
public class CanvasPoint implements Serializable {
  private double x;
  private double y;
  public CanvasPoint(double x, double y) {
    this.x = x;
    this.y = y;
  }

  public double distanceMeasure(double otherPointX,
  double otherPointY) {
    return Math.abs(x - otherPointX) + Math.abs(y - otherPointY);
  }

  public void move(double deltaX, double deltaY) {
    x = x + deltaX;
    y = y + deltaY;
  }
}
```

Model extends the collection class ShapeList. Much of the code in the class is typical for a collection class, so we do not show that code.

```
public class ShapeList implements Serializable {
  private List<Shape> shapeList = new LinkedList<Shape>();
  // methods
}
```

As shape drawing progresses, the Command classes issue the call to update the View. Here is the code for updating the View.

```
  public void update() {
    guiDisplay.draw();
  }
```

The draw() method in the GUI is highly dependent on the technology. But here is the pseudocode for that.

```
    set up the Renderer object
    clear the screen
    View.getInstance().draw(this);
```

The draw() method of View has a loop to render each shape.

```
  public void draw(GUIDisplay view) {
    List<Shape> shapes = Model.instance().getShapeList();
    for (Shape shape : shapes) {
      shape.render(view.getRenderer());
    }
  }
```

The render() method in Line is given below.

```
  public void render(Renderer renderer) {
    super.render(renderer);
    renderer.draw(point1.getX(), point1.getY(), point2.getX(),
    point2.getY());
  }
```

The superclass's draw() method sets the color.

```
  public void render(Renderer renderer) {
    if (selected) {
      renderer.setColor(255, 0, 0);
    } else {
      renderer.setColor(0, 0, 255);
    }
  }
```

Thus, when the first point of a line is clicked, the Line object is created and added to the Model, and the shape is rendered on the screen (as a single pixel). When the user clicks the second point of the line, the reader can check that the onPointInput() method in LineCommand sets the second vertex in the Line object and ends the command.

### 9.5.3 Selecting Shapes

Suppose the user clicks the mouse with the Control key pressed. As we have seen in the code for mouse-clicks, the method onControlClick() is called with the x and y coordinates.

Selection is slightly different from other commands in the sense that there is no button for the command. The click begins the command and, at the same time, selects a shape (if clicked sufficiently close to one). The code in Controller creates the Command object and passes the clicked position to it.

```
public void onControlClick(double x, double y) {
  if (currentCommand == null) {
    setCommand(new SelectCommand());
  }
  currentCommand.onControlClick(x, y);
}
```

The SelectCommand class checks whether the clicked position is close to any shape. If the shape is not yet selected, it is marked so and added to the SelectedShapes collection. Otherwise, the shape is marked as not selected and removed from the collection.

```
public void onControlClick(double x, double y) {
  Shape shape = Model.instance().isCloseTo(x, y);
  if (shape != null) {
    if (shape.isSelected()) {
      SelectedShapes.getInstance().remove(shape);
      shape.setSelected(false);
    } else {
      SelectedShapes.getInstance().add(shape);
      shape.setSelected(true);
    }
  }
  View.getInstance().update();
}
```

The code for checking whether a shape is close to a given point has a loop. It is in the collection class ShapeList.

```
public Shape isCloseTo(double x, double y) {
  for (Shape shape : shapeList) {
    if (shape.isCloseTo(x, y)) {
```

```
        return shape;
      }
    }
    return null;
  }
```

In Line, the code for checking whether one of the vertices is close to the point is as follows:

```
public boolean isCloseTo(double x, double y) {
  return point1.distanceMeasure(x, y) < 10 ||
         point2.distanceMeasure(x, y) < 10;
}
```

### 9.5.4 Grouping Shapes

When the user right-clicks the mouse after selecting a set of shapes, the SelectCommand's onRightClick() method is called. As the following code shows, this method invokes the showContextMenu() method of View.

```
  public void onRightClick(double x, double y) {
    if (SelectedShapes.getInstance().size() != 0) {
      View.getInstance().showContextMenu(x, y);
      Controller.getInstance().commandEnded();
    }
  }
```

Suppose the user clicks the Group menu item. In Swing, the following code snippet is invoked:

```
    groupShapes.addActionListener(event -> {
      Controller.getInstance().onGroupCommand();
    });
```

The corresponding JavaFX code is as follows:

```
    groupShapes.setOnAction(event -> {
      Controller.getInstance().onGroupCommand();
    });
```

Controller instantiates a GroupCommand object, which has the following structure. The field group is the Group object created from the selected shapes. The shapes involved in the group are in the collection object shapes.

```
public class GroupCommand extends Command {
  private Group group;
  private List<Shape> shapes;
  // constructor and methods not shown
}
```

The constructor of `GroupCommand` copies all the selected shapes into the `Group` object and to the `shapes` field.

```
public GroupCommand() {
 UndoManager.getInstance().beginCommand(this);
 shapes = new LinkedList<>();
 group = new Group();
 this.shapes.addAll(SelectedShapes.getInstance().getShapeList());
 group.addAll(shapes);
 group.setSelected(false);
 SelectedShapes.getInstance().clear();
}
```

The `Group` class extends `Shape`. The following methods essentially implement the concepts we discussed in the Composite pattern:

```
  public void addAll(List<Shape> shapes) {
    this.children.addAll(shapes);
  }
  public void render(Renderer renderer) {
    super.render(renderer);
    for (Shape shape : children) {
      shape.render(renderer);
    }
  }
  public boolean isCloseTo(double x, double y) {
    for (Shape shape : children) {
      if (shape.isCloseTo(x, y)) {
        return true;
      }
    }
    return false;
  }
  public void move(double deltaX, double deltaY) {
    for (Shape shape : children) {
      shape.move(deltaX, deltaY);
    }
  }
```

After creating the `GroupCommand` object, `Controller` invokes its `execute()` method to replace the shapes with the `Group` object. The code for `execute()` is given below.

```
  public void execute() {
    Model.instance().removeAll(shapes);
    Model.instance().add(group);
    View.getInstance().update();
  }
```

### 9.5.5 Moving Shapes

The first couple of steps of moving a set of shapes closely follow grouping of shapes: some shapes are selected and the context menu shown. When the user selects the Move menu item, Controller eventually creates a MoveCommand object.

```
public class MoveCommand extends Command {
  private List<Shape> shapes;
  private double originalPointX;
  private double originalPointY;
  private double deltaX;
  private double deltaY;
  // constructor aned methods not shown
}
```

The fields warrant some explanation. The shapes field is the collection of shapes to be moved. We remember the original location of the shapes in originalPointX and originalPointY for the purpose of undoing the command, if needed. As the shapes are moved and continuously occupy new positions, it is necessary to track the progress and render the shapes at their new locations. The code for doing this is in the following method. In general, we move a set of shapes. To help us move each shape by the same x and y offsets, we adopt the following approach. We have SelectedShapes select a specific location of a specific shape in its collection. We call the x and y coordinates of this location the reference coordinates. The idea is that we will make these reference coordinates equal to the the current x and y coordinates of the mouse position. All other locations of all the shapes in SelectedShapes will be moved by the same x and y offsets (deltaX and deltaY in the code), so the whole collection moves together, uniformly.

```
public void onCursorMoved(double x, double y) {
  if (SelectedShapes.getInstance().getShapeList().size() != 0) {
    deltaX = x - SelectedShapes.getInstance().getReferenceX();
    deltaY = y - SelectedShapes.getInstance().getReferenceY();
    for (Shape shape :
     SelectedShapes.getInstance().getShapeList()) {
      shape.move(deltaX, deltaY);
    }
  }
  View.getInstance().update();
}
```

When the user left-clicks the mouse, the command ends. The fields deltaX and deltaY end up having the x and y offsets of the shapes from the original location.

```
public void onPointInput(double x, double y) {
 this.shapes.addAll(SelectedShapes.getInstance().getShapeList());
 if (shapes.size() != 0) {
   deltaX = x - SelectedShapes.getInstance().getReferenceX();
   deltaY = y - SelectedShapes.getInstance().getReferenceY();
   execute();
  }
  Controller.getInstance().commandEnded();
  SelectedShapes.getInstance().clear();
  View.getInstance().update();
}
public void execute() {
  if (shapes.size() != 0) {
    for (Shape shape : shapes) {
      shape.move(deltaX, deltaY);
    }
  }
}
```

## 9.6 Pattern-based Solutions

As explained earlier, a pattern is a solution template that addresses a recurring problem in specific situations. In a general sense, these could apply to any domain. (A standard opening in chess, for instance, can be looked at as a "chess pattern.") In the context of creating software, three kinds of patterns have been identified. At the highest level, we have **architectural patterns.** These typically partition a system into subsystems and broadly define the role that each subsystem plays and how they all fit together. Architectural patterns have the following characteristics:

- They have evolved over time. In the early years of software development, it was not very clear to the designers how systems should be laid out. Over time, some categorization emerged, of the kinds software systems that are needed. In due course, it became clearer as to how these systems and the demands on them change over their lifetime. This enabled practitioners to figure out what kind of layout could alleviate some of the commonly encountered problems.
- A given pattern is usually applicable for a certain class of software system. The MVC pattern for instance, is well-suited for interactive systems, but would be a poor fit for designing an operating system.
- The need for these is not obvious to the untrained eye. When a designer first encounters a new class of software, it is not very obvious what the architecture should be. One reason for this is that the designer is not

aware of how the requirements might change over time, or what kind of modifications are likely to be needed. It is therefore prudent to follow the dictates of the wisdom of past practitioners. This is somewhat different from design patterns, which we are able to "derive" by applying some of the well-established "axioms" of object-oriented analysis and design. (In the case of our MVC example, we did justify the choice of the architecture, but this was done by demonstrating that it would be easier to add new operations to the system. Such an understanding is usually something that is acquired over the lifetime of a system.)

At the next level, we have the **design patterns**. These solve problems that could appear in many kinds of software systems. Once the principles of object-oriented analysis and design have been established, it is easier to derive these. Examples of these can be found throughout this text.

At the lowest level we have the patterns that are called **idioms**. Idioms are the patterns of programming and are usually associated with specific languages. They typically refer to the use of certain syntactic elements of the language. As programmers, we often find ourselves using the same code snippet every time we have to accomplish a certain task. Sometimes, we may save these as "macros" to be copied and pasted as needed, thus enabling us to be more productive in terms of code generation. Idioms are something like these, but they are usually carefully designed to take the language features (and quirks) into account to make sure that the code is safe and efficient. The following code, for instance, is commonly used to swap:

```
temp = a;
a = b;
b = temp;
```

In Perl, a commonly used scripting language, the list assignment syntax allows us to employ a more succinct expression:

```
($a, $b) = ($b, $a);
```

This would be an example of an idiom in Perl. In addition to safety and efficiency, the familiarity of the code snippet makes the code more readable and reduces the need for comments. Typical Perl programmers might be more comfortable with the second whereas a Java programmer would prefer the first.

Not all idioms are without conflict. There are two possible idioms for an infinite loop:

```
for (; ;) { /* some code */ }
while (true) { /* some code */ }
```

It has been argued that the first should be preferred for efficiency, since no expression evaluation is involved at the end of each iteration. However, with the hardware capacity available nowadays, some programmers are making a case for the second based on readability and elegance.

Familiarity with and acceptance of established patterns is clearly a must for success in any domain of activity. Most of our focus in our case studies has therefore been to convince the student of their usefulness by showing how they provide elegant solutions to naturally arising design problems. However, as mentioned earlier, it is much more difficult for a beginner to grasp the significance of architectural patterns in this manner.

### 9.6.1 Examples of Architectural Patterns

In this subsection, we summarize some of the most important architectural patterns.

#### 9.6.1.1 The Repository

This architecture is characterized by the presence of a single data structure called the **central repository**. Subsystems access and modify the data stored in this. An example of such a system could be software used for managing an airline. The subsystems in this case could be for managing reservations, scheduling staff, and scheduling aircraft. All of these would access a central data repository that holds information about the aircraft, staff, and passengers. These would be inter-related, since the choice of an aircraft could likely influence the choice of staff and be influenced by the volume of passenger traffic. In such systems, the control flow can be dictated by the central repository (changes in the data characteristics could trigger some operations), or from one of the subsystems.

Another application of such a system could be for managing a large bank. The account information would have to be centrally located and could be accessed and modified from several peripheral locations. A software development system or a compiler could also employ such an architecture by having a centralized parse tree or symbol table.

#### 9.6.1.2 The Client–Server

In such a layout, there is a central subsystem known as a **server** and several smaller subsystems known as **clients**. There is a fair amount of independence in the control flow, and each subsystem may be using a different thread. Synchronization techniques are often employed to manage requests and transmit results.

The World Wide Web (WWW) is probably the best example of such an architecture. The browsers running on PCs are like clients and the sites they access play the role of servers. The server could also be housing a database and the clients could be processes that are querying and updating the database. A variant/generalization of this is **peer-to-peer** architecture where the the individual sites have the same role.

#### 9.6.1.3 The Pipe and Filter

The system in this case is made up of **filters**, that is, subsystems that process data, and **pipes** which can be used to interconnect the filters. The filters are completely mutually independent and are aware only of the input data that comes through a pipe, that is, the filter knows the form and content of the data that comes in, and not how it was generated. This kind of architecture produces a system that is very flexible and can be dynamically reconfigured. In their simplest form, the pipes could all be identical, and each filter could perform a fixed task on data input stream. An example of this would be that of processing incoming/outgoing data packets over a computer network. Each "layer" would be like a filter that adds to, subtracts from, or modifies the packet and sends it forward.

Several operating systems allow users to create more complex operations by linking together simpler ones. In its most general form, one could have pipes that "reformat" the data, so that any sequence of filters could be used.

## 9.7 Discussion and Conclusion

Software architectures and design patterns bear some similarity in that they both present efficient solutions to commonly occurring problems. The process of learning how to apply these is, however, very different. It is possible (and perhaps pedagogically preferable) to "discover" design patterns by critically examining our designs and refactoring them. Such a process does not lend itself well to the task of learning about architectures due to the complexity of the problem we are encountering. The software designer's best bet is to learn about commonly used architectures in the given problem domain and adapt them to the current needs.

We introduced design patterns by coming up with some "reasonable" design and then critically examining it using our knowledge of the principles of object-oriented analysis and design. This process is not very different from that of refactoring to introduce patterns into existing code. The process for refactoring to introduce patterns has been well-studied and cataloged.

### 9.7.1 Adapting to Distributed Systems

As we noted at the beginning of the chapter, the MVC pattern works quite well in distributed applications such as a web application. The Controller would then consist of Java **servlets** and the View would be a collection of Java Server Pages (JSP). The Model would be a database implemented on a server.

The servlets have methods to get requests from the user and process them. Here is the broad outline. All requests are received in the `doPost()` method, which calls the `processRequest()` method. The latter invokes methods in the Model to process the request and then sends the response through what is called a JSP page.

```
public class OrderServlet extends HttpServlet {
  private void processRequest(HttpServletRequest request,
                              HttpServletResponse response)
      throws ServletException, IOException {
      // process the order request
      // send the response as a JSP file
      RequestDispatcher dispatcher =
      request.getRequestDispatcher("/WEB-INF/jsp/
       order_response.jsp");
      dispatcher.forward(request, response);
  }

  @Override
  public void doPost(HttpServletRequest request,
   HttpServletResponse response)
    throws IOException, ServletException {
    processRequest(request, response);
  }
}
```

Stated somewhat simplistically, a JSP page consists of HTML markup embedded with JSP tags. The file is processed on the server and results in a web page being displayed on the client side.

### 9.7.2 Interaction between the GUI and the MVC Subsystems

When a Java GUI is created, the JVM sets up a GUI thread on which all actions on the GUI take place. It is easy to see that in both Swing and JavaFX implementations, all execution in the Controller, Model, and View also take place on the GUI thread. For example, when we click on the mouse, the event results in some code in the GUI being executed, which calls methods in the Controller, which might call methods in the Model, and View as well.

This arrangement works quite well in the drawing program, but if the code at the back end (that is, the MVC subsystems) is time consuming, the GUI response will be sluggish. Depending on the nature of the GUI, it may be expected to respond to other events, and executing the back end code on the GUI thread is not always feasible. For a real situation, assume that the GUI is created on a smart phone. The primary function of a phone is communication. If the GUI response takes more than a few milliseconds, the phone will not respond to events such as accepting a phone call. The operating system may end up aborting applications that are not nimble.

To overcome this issue, we can restrict the GUI to purely user interface-related work. Back end code is executed on a separate thread. For example, on the Android operating system, the back end code can be a subclass of an Android Java class called `ViewModel`, which can store data (usually, not for the whole application, but related to a specific computation) and when the data becomes ready, the GUI can be alerted.

### 9.7.3 GUI Frameworks

As we have mentioned several times, technology changes could potentially result in new GUI frameworks. It is challenging for a software engineer to master the details of new frameworks as they are released, but understanding some fundamental design approaches and learning one framework well can provide a sufficient footing with which new frameworks can be learned more easily.

In both Swing and JavaFX, we construct windows with multiple widgets that have considerable dependencies among them. For example, in the drawing program, once the `Line` button is clicked, we have the cursor take a drawing shape when moved to the drawing panel; this behavior lasts for as long as line drawing is in effect. We could also, if we chose to, have all other buttons disabled when the `Line` button is clicked.

The dependencies among the widgets are dependent on the application. The multitude of behaviors that a certain widget (for example, a button) can exhibit make them rather laborious to customize through subclassing. Instead, in these two frameworks, we have widgets that come with sufficient functionality that can be invoked from an intermediary to realize the required behavior.

For instance, suppose we want all other buttons to be disabled when the `Line` button is clicked. A painful and unrealistic way to accomplish this would be for every button to be subclassed into two: disabled and enabled; when the `Line` button is clicked, we replace all buttons with their disabled versions.

Instead, what we have is a class called `JButton` in Swing or `Button` in JavaFX with methods to enable or disable. In Swing, we have the method

```
public void setEnabled(boolean b)
```

while JavaFX has the method

```
public final void setDisable(boolean value)
```

Actually, these methods are not defined in the button classes, but in superclasses.

Thus, these frameworks provide a multitude of widget classes with rich functionalities. As events occur on them, an intermediary, which might be any designated object in these two frameworks, gets notified and it invokes the necessary methods to accomplish the required behavior. Such an intermediary is called a **mediator** and forms the central "character" in the **Mediator pattern**.

The mediator in this case coordinates the actions of the widgets. For example, when a button is clicked, the notification comes to the mediator, which could issue the appropriate method call on all other buttons to disable them. This helps prevent every button from knowing about the others. Without using a mediator, every widget may need to know about every other widget, with $n(n-1)/2$ possible interactions; with a mediator, the number of interconnections drops significantly to $n$ (one between each widget and the mediator).

### 9.7.4 The Space Overhead for the Command Pattern

One of the drawbacks of the Command pattern is that it places a large demand on the memory resources, which in turn could have a serious effect on performance. The reason for this is that all the code for executing, undoing, redoing, etc., is being stored with each `Command` object. We could restrict the number of levels of undo and redo to some manageable number to avoid this problem, but this solution may not always be acceptable.

### 9.7.5 Building the Back End Using the State Pattern

The reader might have noted that some of the `Command` objects go through several states before completing their respective commands. For example, when label creation is initiated, the `LabelCommand` class goes through several phases.

1. Initially, the command has just started. There is no label. The Command is waiting for a mouse-click (in the main flow).

2. After a left mouse-click, the first label's location is known. In the typical case, a character will be typed.
3. As characters are typed, they are assembled to form the label.
4. If the user clicks the left mouse button, we are back in the second phase. If the user clicks the right mouse button, the command ends.

Clearly, mouse-clicks and characters are not the only inputs the Command entertains. Pressing the Escape key ends the command. When the user presses the Backspace key, the last character (if one exists) is deleted.

Thus capturing label creation as a use case is a bit tedious because of the number of different inputs the command receives at any time. We had multiple conditionals in `LabelCommand`. All of that can be avoided by implementing this command using the State pattern. Such a design would have the following states:

- INITIAL: The state immediately after the LABEL button is pushed.
- LABEL: The state in which one or more labels are created.

The events the states must react to at least in one state are as follows.

- LEFT MOUSE BUTTON CLICK
- RIGHT MOUSE BUTTON CLICK
- CHARACTER TYPING
- BACKSPACE
- ESCAPE

The state transition table would be along the following lines (Table 9.13). Note that there is a host of events (for example, mouse-click with the Control key pressed) that are ignored. The events corresponding to these are ignored in the table. To fit the table, we have abbreviated the state and event names. We assume the existence of a state called QUIESCENT in which no command is in progress.

| | LEFT MOUSE | RIGHT MOUSE | CHAR | BACKSPACE | ESCAPE |
|---|---|---|---|---|---|
| QUIESCENT | INITIAL | QUIESCENT | QUIESCENT | QUIESCENT | QUIESCENT |
| INITIAL | LABEL | QUIESCENT | INITIAL | INITIAL | QUIESCENT |
| LABEL | LABEL | QUIESCENT | LABEL | LABEL | QUIESCENT |

**Table 9.13** State transition table

This approach gets rid of all conditionals in the code for `LabelCommand` at the expense of an increase of one extra class. The conditionals are fairly simple in nature, so one might question the value of using the State pattern. In a more complicated shape, the trade-offs might be more pronounced, and to some extent at least, the decision is subjective.

In any case, the reader is invited to refactor the entire project using the FSM approach.

### 9.7.6 How to Store the Shapes

The manner in which shapes are stored in the Model can affect the time it takes to render the shapes and thus affect performance. Consider the problem of rendering a curve, that is specified by the user as a collection of "control points." If the constructor decomposed the curve into a collection of line segments, then the process of rendering would be to simply draw each line segment. On the other hand, if the Model stored only the control points, rendering (that is, the corresponding `render()` method) would have to compute all the line segments and then draw them. In the first case, we are creating a large number of objects and storing these in the Model. The rendering could be slowed down because of the large number of objects that have to be accessed. In the second, rendering may be delayed by the amount of computation.

### 9.7.7 Exercising Caution When Allowing Undo

Implementing the undo operation can be quite tricky. The process of executing a command could involve the methods of several classes and care must be taken to ensure that these are correctly reversible. A full treatment of this is beyond the scope of this text, but we can highlight a few of these issues.

#### 9.7.7.1 What should be Saved to Undo an Operation?

We must keep in mind that what we are undoing is the consequences of the operation on the entire system. Consider the process of undoing the creation of a line. The only inputs to the operation are the two endpoints, and elementary mathematics tells us that we do not need any other information to define a line. However, this information is not sufficient for us to undo the effects of this operation. The consequence to the system is that the line object is added to the Model, and what we need to store is a reference to this object. The Model also must allow for a specified shape to be removed; if this were not possible, the operation of removing a line would not be undoable.

#### 9.7.7.2 Designing and Implementing with Undo in Mind

The manner in which responsibilities are divided between the Model and the Controller and the public methods that are implemented can affect the ease of undo operations. Since our `Line` object is created in the Controller, it is easy to store this in the `Command` object and then use the reference to remove the object when undoing. If the Model took the endpoints and invoked the constructor, we would need some additional machinery to implement undo. Likewise, our Model has a method to remove a specified shape, which is effectively an "undo" of the operation that adds an item. If the methods invoked by the `Command` object on other subsystems cannot be easily reversed, it may not be feasible to undo the operation.

## Projects

1. *Creating a simple spreadsheet.* The sheet will display a simple grid and allow for data and formulae to be entered into the boxes. The following features will be available:

   - Allow for a column to be widened. This will be done by the user selecting a column and activating the operation from the menu.
   - Automatic evaluation and re-evaluation of formulae.
   - Drawing a graph using data from two columns.

2. Implement the drawing program described in this chapter using a *Document–View* architecture. Implement each command as a singleton that keeps its own stack. What pros and cons do you see for this approach?
3. Implement the drawing program to support multiple View–Controller pairs.
4. Implement the drawing program, so the Controller uses the FSM approach.
5. Create a simple graphical toy that consists of a circle, triangles, and rectangles. All these shapes will be filled, and represent a two-dimensional ball and two-dimensional triangular and rectangular blocks. A menu will allow the user to create new blocks, change the color of an existing shape, move the shapes, increase the size of the ball, rotate the blocks, or drop the ball. When the ball is dropped, it will fall vertically and thereafter behave in accordance with the idealized laws of physics, with a co-efficient of restitution of 0.5 (half the kinetic energy is lost whenever the ball collides with a block or a boundary). The blocks do not move when hit by the ball. There will be a designated threshold so that when the ball's velocity drops below this threshold, it will be assumed to have stopped.

## Exercises

1. Consider the following requirement: "Whenever a delete operation is invoked, a request is made by the system asking the user to confirm the deletion." How should such a requirement be incorporated?
2. During the rendering process, the View invokes the `render()` method on the shape, which then invokes the `draw()` method on the `Renderer`. We can modify the implementation to have the View directly invoke `draw()`. What changes would be needed to do this? What are the pros and cons of this approach?
3. Modify the line drawing operation so that multiple lines can be created with one request.
4. Some drawing systems allow for lines of varying thickness. How would such a feature be implemented?
5. Implement a circle drawing operation so that the first click specifies the center. After that a "circle of variable radius" is drawn such that center is on the first click and the current cursor position lies on the boundary. When the second point is clicked, a circle is drawn with the first mouse-click as the center and the second mouse-click on the circle boundary.
6. A line can be specified by two points or by an equation. Consider a system where an "origin" can be specified by a mouse-click. After this is done, a line is specified by an equation of the form $ax + by + c = 0$ (the input would specify $a, b$ and $c$). The line specified by this equation is drawn with reference to the current location of the origin. Note that this line would span the entire drawing panel. How would you implement such an operation?
7. Add an operation for drawing a triangle that allows for undoing individual mouse-clicks. The triangle will be specified by mouse-clicks on the three vertices.
8. Drawing a closed cubic curve. The B-spline is a popular cubic curve, since it makes it very easy to draw a smooth curve consisting of many segments. Implement this feature as follows: (i) the user clicks on a succession of points, terminating by clicking on the first point again; (ii) after 4 clicks, the first piece of the curve appears; (iii) an additional piece is rendered at each subsequent click. The curve is drawn using the mouse-click locations as "control points". Four control points are used to generate each section of the curve, with the first four generating the first section, clicks 2, 3, 4 and 5 generating the next section, and so on. For any four control points $P_0, P_1, P_2$, and $P_3$, the curve can be generated by the parametric equation:

$$B(t) = \frac{1}{6}(-P_0 + 3P_1 - 3P_2 + P_3)t^3 + \frac{1}{2}(P_0 - 2P_1 + P_2)t^2 + \frac{1}{2}(-P_0 + P_2)t + \frac{1}{6}(P_0 + 4P_1 + P_2) \qquad (9.1)$$

The parameter $t$ varies between 0 and 1, and is incremented in small steps, with one intermediate curve point being generated at each step. The curve itself is drawn as a series of line segments, each segment connecting the curve points generated by successive increments.

9. Suppose we wish to add the ability to display images (PNG, JPG, etc.) to the drawing program. What new classes and interfaces would the system need? What existing classes and interfaces would have additional/modified methods?

## References

1. Gamma, E, Helm, R, Johnson, R and Vlissides, J. 1994. *Design Patterns: Elements of Reusable Object-oriented Software.* Addison-Wesley Professional Computing Series.

# Chapter 10
# A Deeper Look into Inheritance

In the previous chapters, we have seen how the object-oriented methodology leads to software that is easier to build and test, and can be be reused. In applying these principles, we have understood how established design patterns help us recognize the solutions for frequently occurring problems.

To enable all this, object-oriented languages provide us with two tools: composition and inheritance. Although we favor composition over inheritance, we have seen situations where the power of inheritance is essential; it is vital, therefore, to have a good understanding of inheritance. In this chapter, we explore the tool of inheritance in greater detail, learning how to use it, and how to avoid the pitfalls. We start by looking at some of the situations in which inheritance may be applicable. Although an extensive discussion of these situations is beyond our scope, we will see that the notion of subtype can be very broad.

In the next section, we discuss some of the problems that can result when inheritance is used carelessly. These are unintended consequences, and being aware of them can be helpful in avoiding some problems that arise later in the software lifecycle. In tandem with these problems, it is also important to learn of ways in which we can employ inheritance and avoid the negative consequences. When we employ inheritance, it is sometimes necessary to put additional structures in place to ensure that the reusability is not adversely affected. Examples of these are discussed in the section that follows.

In situations where a property cannot be described by a set of methods, it can be tricky to ensure that the property is inherited correctly. We discuss two examples that illustrate this: the *singleton* property and the *clonability* property. In both these cases, additional machinery has to be put in place to ensure the subtypes satisfy the property.

The last two topics in this chapter have a more theoretical flavor. The notion of substitutability of subtypes is a complex one that requires a formal definition of subtype. We look more closely at a theoretical framework for the subtype relationship, and how it can be used in practice for recognizing situations where inheritance cannot be employed. In a more generalized setting, a class can inherit from more than one parent class. In the the final section, we introduce the concept of multiple inheritance and discuss its power, which, as we shall see, comes with some associated difficulties.

## 10.1 Applications of Inheritance

This section presents varied applications of inheritance, illustrating the different circumstances in which this powerful technique can be used. Although the programming language rules concerning inheritance are not overly complicated as long as a class inherits from at most one other class, the design process can sometimes be tricky. It is therefore useful to see various situations in which inheritance can be employed.

A word of caution is in order before we proceed. The examples presented here make perfect sense when we view the classes as simple abstractions, but a complete analysis of all the properties is required to complete the implementation. In later sections of this chapter, we learn why this is required, and view examples of how such an analysis could be performed.

### 10.1.1 Restricting Behaviors and Properties

One circumstance in which inheritance can be applied is when a class has characteristics that are a restriction of the characteristics of some other class. Suppose we have two classes `Rectangle` and `Square` to represent rectangles and squares. Every square is a rectangle in which length is equal to breadth, that is, *the property that length be equal to breadth restricts the number of rectangles that qualify to be classified as squares.* Thus, `Square` is obtained from `Rectangle` by restricting a property; note that we are not attaching any more functionality to squares than rectangles.

As a second example, suppose that we create a graphical user interface with many types of widgets, including labels. Suppose we have the requirement that the text in all the labels be colored blue. In this case, it is convenient to have a subclass that simply sets the color to blue. In Swing, the class `JLabel` can be subclassed as given below.

```
import java.awt.Color;
import javax.swing.JLabel;
public class SpecialLabel extends JLabel {
  public SpecialLabel(String text) {
    super(text);
    setForeground(Color.blue);
  }
```

```
}
```

The equivaent code in JavaFX is as follows:

```
import javafx.scene.control.Label;
import javafx.scene.paint.Color;
public class SpecialLabel extends Label {
  public SpecialLabel(String text) {
    super(text);
    this.setTextFill(Color.BLUE);
  }
}
```

In this case, the behavior of `SpecialLabel` is restricted in that it always displays a blue foreground.

### 10.1.2 Abstract Superclass

Sometimes the only purpose of having a superclass is to extract the common attributes and methods of potential subclasses, thus maximizing reuse. No objects of the superclass itself are allowed, thus necessitating that the superclass be abstract. In such cases, we have a set of subclasses that partition the universe of objects in the superclass.

As an example, consider accounts in a bank. An account is a general concept, and, perhaps, in some banks, all accounts are checking accounts or savings accounts. The bank allows opening of only checking or savings accounts. Therefore, `Account` is a class that helps us build software more quickly, by providing some of the functionality that is common to all types of accounts. The partitioning is indicated in the Venn diagram in Figure 10.1, which shows that the set of all accounts is partitioned into savings and checking accounts.

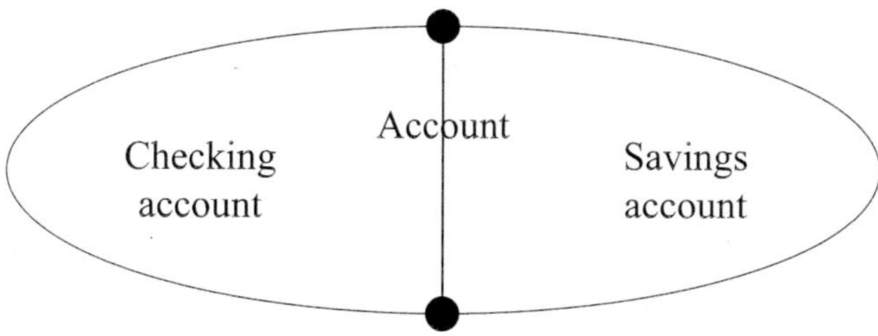


**Fig. 10.1** Partitioning a set of objects

### 10.1.3 Adding Features

In an earlier section, we saw that sometimes classes are extended to restrict the behavior of the superclass. Sometimes, we may do the opposite: we may extend an ancestor class, by adding new features, to obtain a descendant. Consider a class named `DataStream` that serves as a reader of data. Imagine a situation where we need a class that has the added property of "re-readability," that is, reading some input again. To achieve this, we add new functionality, namely, the ability of "unreading" so that a character read from the stream can be pushed back. This is shown in Figure 10.2. Another example of this would be a class for "Vehicle" that can be defined by extending an existing "Entity" class and adding the attribute "speed."

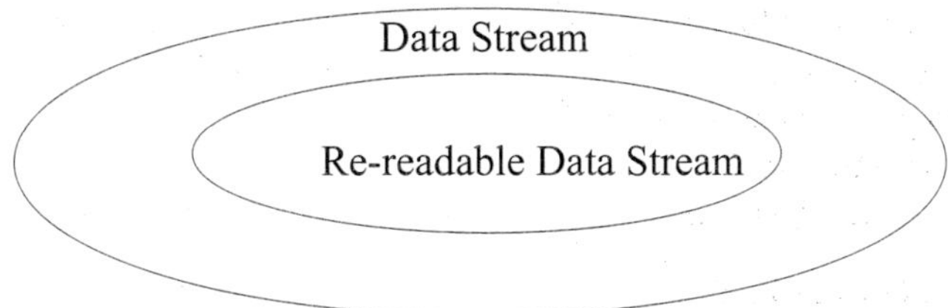


**Fig. 10.2** Adding more features

### 10.1.4 Hiding Features of the Superclass

Sometimes we want to restrict behavior by suppressing some functionality of the superclass. Such a kind of restriction is discussed in the following example, where some of the features are eliminated in the subclass.

Let `List` be a class that allows the creation of a list in which objects can be added anywhere: at the front, at the tail, or at any position in between. It is easy to get a class `Queue` that allows adding only at the tail and removing from the front. All other add and remove methods, which allow for adding at or removing from other positions, should be disallowed. This can be accomplished in C++ using private[1] inheritance, as shown below:

```
#include <iostream.h>
#include <stdlib.h>

class List {
```

[1] In private inheritance, all the non-private superclass attributes become private attributes of the subclass.

```
  private:
    // data structures
  public:
    List() {
      // initialize data structures
    }
    bool add(int index, int value) {
    // code to add at the specified position and return true or
       false
    }
    bool add(int value) {
    // code to add at the end and return true or false
    }
    int remove(int index) {
    // code to delete the object at the specified position and
    // return true or false
    }
    int remove() {
    // code to delete the object at the front and return true or
       false
    }
};
class Queue: private List {
  public:
    int dequeue() {
      return List::remove();
    }
    bool enqueue(int value) {
      return List::add(value);
   }
};
```

Such an application has also been referred to in the literature as **structural inheritance** because the features inherited from the superclass (`List`) provide the structure needed for implementing the subclass (`Queue`). This kind of an application does have its critics due to the fact that the "is-a" relationship between the ancestor and the descendant is not preserved.

### 10.1.5 Combining Structural and Type Inheritance

We can also have situations where two kinds of inheritance are applied to define a class that suits our application. The most common case is one where one superclass provides the necessary structure and another, usually an interface, defines the function. A *binary search tree*, for instance, can be seen as a class that extends *binary tree* (structure inheritance) and implements the `OrderedList` interface (which defines the function of the binary search tree). The `OrderedList` operations are *implemented* using the methods provided by the class representing the binary tree, giving the name **implementation inheritance** to this usage.

## 10.2 Inheritance: Some Limitations and Caveats

Although it facilitates reuse, inheritance by subclassing is not always the best strategy to construct new classes, even if there is justification for doing so on the surface. Among the reasons:

- Subclassing could result in deep hierarchies, which usually makes the code quite difficult to understand.
- In systems that do not support multiple inheritance, subclassing is not always feasible.
- Exposing all the superclass methods to the subclass may compromise integrity.
- Sometimes a superclass may have to be changed, causing subclass code to become illegal.
- The derived class's type may not be a true subtype of the superclass's type.

We elaborate on each of the above aspects in the following subsections.

### 10.2.1 Deep Hierarchies

When subclassing, we obviously add one more to the length of the hierarchy. The fields and methods available for use in the derived class include all of the inherited fields and methods and the ones added to the class itself. For example, the class `JFrame` in the package `javax.swing` has a hierarchy of depth 6, assuming that `java.lang.Object` is at depth 1. The data in Table 10.1 (for JDK 15), shows the number of declared fields and methods in each class; it is easy to see that the cumulative numbers will make it a challenging task to remember the interactions between the methods. Choosing the right field/method can be critical for good software development; thus the number of fields and methods can be viewed as a measure of the effort involved in developing and maintaining the source code. Clearly, it is advisable to keep the hierarchy to a reasonable depth.

| Class name | Number of declared fields | Number of declared methods |
|---|---|---|
| `java.awt.Component` | 98 | 335 |
| `java.awt.Container` | 28 | 155 |
| `java.awt.Window` | 41 | 146 |
| `java.awt.Frame` | 31 | 34 |
| `javax.swing.JFrame` | 6 | 30 |

**Table 10.1** Class size increases with hierarchy depth. The table shows how large classes can become with subclassing.

### 10.2.2 Lack of Multiple Inheritance

In certain situations, it may be desirable to create a subclass from multiple classes. However, some languages such as Java allow subclassing of at most one class. In such circumstances, we cannot limit ourselves to subclassing, but adopt other approaches in conjunction with it, or abandon subclassing altogether.

### 10.2.3 Exposed Superclass Features

It may be necessary to hide selected features of the superclass. For example, if we extend the class `java.util.LinkedList` to implement a queue, all of the methods of the superclass will be exposed, which may compromise its integrity. Facilities such as the `renames` clause in the language Eiffel enable this. Explicitly hiding a superclass's field/method is also possible in C++.

### 10.2.4 Changes in the Superclass

While it is not desirable to change the set of methods supported by a class, such changes are sometimes inevitable. (As an example, in the Java class system, the class `java.awt.Component` added the public method `setEnabled(boolean)` in JDK 1.1.) Imagine an application system $A_1$, some classes of which extend a set of classes from some other system $A_2$. Suppose $A_2$ is modified to include a number of useful features. To exploit these enhancements, assume that the corresponding subclasses of $A_1$ use the new versions.

Although $A_1$ can now exploit all of the new functionality incorporated into the classes of $A_2$, there are potential problems as well. To see one possible problem, consider the two classes `B` and `D` given below, where `D` extends `B`.

```
public class B {
  public void m1() {
```

```
  }
}

public class D extends B {
  public void m2() {
  }
}
```

Suppose that the following method is now added to B.

```
public int m2() {
  return 1;
}
```

Now class D is illegal because method m2's return type is inconsistent with that of the correspondingly named method in B.

### 10.2.5 Creating False Subtypes

Perhaps the most insidious consequence of freely extending classes is the creation of false subtypes. In Chapter 7, we introduced the concept of substitutability. As an example, we demonstrated that extending the class Counter by CounterSub, we caused some unexpected behavior. Such extensions can also produce more harmful behaviors; for instance, if the method doSomething() were to be written as follows, we would end up with an infinite loop when an instance of CounterSub is passed as a parameter:

```
public void doSomething(Counter counter) {
 for (counter.reset(); counter.getValue() != 11; counter.up()) {
    System.out.println(counter.getValue());
  }
}
```

The need for preventing false subtypes led to the formalization of the notion of **behavioral subtyping.** Looking back at the history of this idea, Barbara Liskov recounted in a 2016 interview [4]:

> This led me to start thinking about "What does it really mean to have a supertype and subtype?" And I came up with a rule, an informal rule which I presented in my keynote at OOPSLA which simply said that a subtype should behave like a supertype as far as you can tell by using the supertype methods. So it wasn't that it couldn't behave differently. It's just that as long as you limited your interaction with its objects to the supertype methods, you would get the behavior you expected.

Requiring every subclass instance to pass as a superclass instance is the essence of *substitutability.* One of the rules that is implicit in the use of inheritance is the **Liskov substitution principle (LSP)** which can be summarized as follows:

*Subclasses should be substitutable for their baseclasses.*

A natural question one might ask is: "Isn't this what the is-a relationship is all about?" When we seek an is-a relationship between `CounterSub` and `Counter`, we are in effect arguing that a counter that increments by two is-a counter that that increments by one. Thus the flaw in this extension is rather obvious, and one can easily argue that such an extension violates the purpose of the superclass and should not be attempted. To understand the difficulty of the problem, it is necessary to examine other examples that are more complicated. In the less obvious violations, we usually see a (somewhat simplistic) justification for the is-a relationship.

#### 10.2.5.1 Can `Set` be a Subclass of `Bag`?

Consider the container classes, `Bag` and `Set`. Let us have `Bag` and `Set` provide the following methods:

- `void add(Item item)`, which causes the specified item to be added to the container.
- `Object remove()`, which removes an arbitrary item from the container; returns `null` if the container is empty.
- `boolean isEmpty()`, which checks if the container has any items and returns true (false) if and only if the container is empty (not empty).
- `boolean belongsTo(item)`, which checks if the specified item is in the container and returns true (false) if and only if the item is (is not) in the container.

We can say that "`Set` is a `Bag` that does not allow duplicates," which can be seen as an "is-a" relationship with restrictions, and therefore acceptable. `Set` needs a method `Object remove(item)`, which removes a specified item if it is present in the set, doing nothing otherwise. `Set` has two kinds of `remove()` methods now; since these methods have different signatures, this is acceptable. If we are substituting a `Bag` object with a `Set` object, only `remove()` without parameters will be used by the client object.

Let us address the question: Is `Set` substitutable for `Bag`? The method that is significantly different is `add()`: In `Bag`, the number of items always increases, assuming that the size is unbounded; in `Set`, the number of items increases only if `item` does not already exist in the `Set`. Using this, we can construct a client method scenario where the substitution fails.

Consider the following client method written to take a `Bag` reference as the input parameter:

```
void clientMethod(Bag b) {
    // some code
```

```
    count = 0;
    while (not done) {
      b.add(item1);
      count++;
      //some code without add or remove
    }
    while (count > 0) {
      item2 = b.remove();
      count--;
      item2.print();
      //some code without add or remove
    }
}
```

This method has a loop that performs an `add()` operation in each iteration, followed by a loop that performs an equal number of `remove()` operations. A null pointer exception will never be thrown on `print()` since the bag will contain enough items after the first loop. If `b` is a set, however, some of the `add()` operations may not increase the number of items in the set, which opens up the possibility of `item2` being `null` after a `remove()` operation.

At every step of this process, our choices seemed logical, but we ended up with an undesirable state of affairs. So it is natural to ask: what went wrong? The answer lies in a precise definition of the is-a relationship: A `Set` object is substitutable for a `Bag` object if and only if the behavior of `Set` objects conforms to the behavior of `Bag` objects in *all* situations. It is important to keep in mind that we are inheriting from the existing class `Set` and we must ensure substitutability in all situations. What we have shown here is that for the method `clientMethod()`, the outcome changes when such a substitution is made.

### 10.2.6 How to Verify Substitutability

In our discussion on substitutability in Chapter 7, we looked at three different situations and discussed how superclass abstraction is violated. Inheritance is one of the three, but we can take a broader view of this subject, by examining what kinds of changes can be made to a class without disrupting the functionality of the software. Changes can occur in a class due to changes in the specification. Say that a class `C` is modified due to new specifications. Let the original class be denoted by $C_{orig}$ and the new class denoted by $C_{repl}$. We can say that $C_{repl}$ is not disruptive if it does not "break the contract" between $C_{orig}$ and the rest of the modules in the software.

The question then arises: What is the nature of the contract between a class (like $C_{orig}$) and the clients that interact with it? The *syntactic* aspect of this contract is in the interface of $C_{orig}$, that is, the signature of the public methods of $C_{orig}$. Adhering to this contract would imply that $C_{repl}$ uses the same method names. The corresponding methods of $C_{repl}$ accept all the input parameters that the methods of $C_{orig}$ do and the methods of $C_{repl}$ do not return an object of any class other than those returned by the methods of $C_{orig}$; in addition, the methods of $C_{repl}$ do not throw any exceptions not thrown by the corresponding methods of $C_{orig}$. It follows then that the input parameters of the methods of $C_{repl}$ be superclasses of the input parameters of the corresponding methods of $C_{orig}$, and the return types and exceptions of $C_{repl}$'s methods be subclasses of the corresponding elements of $C_{orig}$. This, as we have seen, can be checked by a compiler. We will discuss later in this chapter how subclasses can introduce variations in these without violating language rules.

The *semantic* aspect of the contract, on the other hand, is not automatically explicit and is not verifiable using a compiler. This is captured by how each of the methods of $C_{orig}$ acts on the input parameters and how they change the internal state of the $C_{orig}$ object. The semantics of the method will also determine the properties of the result object that is generated. In Chapter 7, we observed that the output of `doSomething()` was predicated on the following properties:

- `counter.reset()` will cause `counter.getValue()` to return zero
- `counter.up()` will cause an increase of one in the value returned by `counter.getValue()`

These properties are captured in the postconditions for the methods. It follows then that if a subclass method does not satisfy the postcondition of the corresponding superclass method, we cannot guarantee substitutability. A natural question that follows is whether we can define rules to check when an inheritance is valid, without having to look at all the situations in which it can be used, and whether we can check these conditions to guarantee complete substitutability. Later in this chapter, we will look at how the formalism associated with behavioral subtyping helps us answer this question.

## 10.3 Working with Inheritance

When we employ inheritance, a single class, say `C1`, is replaced by a hierarchy. This affects all the other classes that would interact with `C1`. We look at some examples of these situations, and the kinds of adaptations that mitigate the problems that arise.

The first situation deals with instantiating objects corresponding to the classes in the hierarchy. If we had only one class, `C1`, client classes can directly invoke the constructor; with inheritance, client classes have to make a choice, and this can result in coupling.

The next situation deals with creating a subclass, say `C2`, that derives from `C1`. Say that `C1` has a method `m1()` that returns (using normal exit or by throwing an exception) an object of the class `some other class`. It is conceivable that `C2` may redefine `m1()` to return an object of a class other than `some other class`. Once again, we need to be cognizant of the adaptation needed to facilitate this.

The third situation we consider is one where we add some external functionality to a hierarchy. Since the external functionality resides in a method in a separate class, `C1` is passed as a parameter to this method. If we replace `C1` with a hierarchy, we will likely need separate methods for each subclass. Therefore, when invoking the method for an object from the hierarchy, we either need specific information about the subclass of the object (which requires the external class to keep track of all details of the hierarchy) or have a language that supports double dispatch (most languages, like Java, do not support double dispatch due to high overhead costs). Anticipating such a situation, we can employ a pattern to design a hierarchy that facilitates the addition of external functionality.

### 10.3.1 Employing Creational Patterns

Factories are creational patterns that are generally employed for creating objects without specifying the exact class of the object. In Chapter 7, we defined a class `LoanableItemFactory` that encapsulated the creation process for `LoanableItem` objects. A simple factory like that is sufficient when we are creating items that belong to a single hierarchy; more sophisticated patterns are needed when the use of inheritance becomes more complex.

The **Factory Method** pattern is employed in situations where we have two independent hierarchies, and the concrete classes in the first hierarchy create objects belonging to classes in the second hierarchy. However, the exact kind of object of the second hierarchy to be created is determined using the input provided at run-time. In such a situation, the logic for invocation of the constructor is encapsulated in a separate method in the abstract superclass of the first hierarchy. The **Abstract Factory** pattern is used in situations where we have several parallel concrete hierarchies, and the system has to be configurable with any one of them. For instance, we could have a hierarchy of paint objects for generating paint objects of several colors. The same colors are used for several situations, namely, interior, exterior, furniture, etc. However, the paint object that must be used has a different implementation for each situation. In such a case, we would have an `AbstractColorFactory` that would have descendants like `InteriorColorFactory`, `ExteriorColorFactory`, etc. The `AbstractColorFactory` would specify the methods (such as `makeRedPaint()`) for creating abstract paint objects, and the concrete descendants would implement these methods to provide concrete paint objects for the given situation (the `makeRedPaint()` method in `ExteriorColorFactory` would create `ExteriorRedPaint`). The client class could then be adapted for any painting situation (interior, furniture, etc.) by configuring it with the appropriate concrete factory. The methods in the chosen factory would then be used to generate the concrete paint objects needed for the situation.

### 10.3.2 Introducing a Parallel Hierarchy

Parallel hierarchies are useful when we want to provide specialized features in the descendants. A simple example of this can be found in the kinds of exceptions that can be thrown by the methods of a class. The following is the standard rule for throwing exceptions when we employ inheritance:

*A subclass method that overrides a method of a superclass may not throw an exception that is not thrown by the superclass method.*

This may seem puzzling at first glance – after all a subclass can add new features – but a closer look reveals that this rule is really a consequence of the LSP (see exercises). Of course, such a violation could never be achieved in Java, since it can be detected statically at compile time.

There are several situations, however, where we would like to create a subclass and obtain more specific information in the case of exceptional behavior. As an example, consider a class that processes a stream of data.

```
public class StreamProcessor {
  // fields and constructors not shown
  public void processStream() throws StreamException {
  // code not shown
  }
  // other methods not shown
}

public class StreamException extends Exception {
// fields and methods as needed
}
```

The method `processStream()` opens a stream and does some elementary processing of the data and creates an output stream. In the course of writing the data, exceptions may arise, which cause the method to throw `StreamException`. A subclass is expected to override this method.

Now consider a subclass of the above, `FileProcessor`, which uses data from a file. Since a file is a specific kind of data stream, this would be a valid use of inheritance. An exceptional situation arises when the file does not exist,

and it is advantageous for users of the subclass to clearly know the reason for the exception.
The subclass with the overriding method is given below.

```
public class FileProcessor extends StreamProcessor {
  String fileName;
  // other fields and constructors not shown
  public void processStream() throws InvalidStreamException {
    BufferedReader reader =
     new BufferedReader(new FileReader(fileName));
    // process the file
  }
  // other methods not shown
}
public class InvalidStreamException extends Exception {
// fields and methods as needed
}
```

Since `InvalidStreamException` is not a subclass of `StreamException`, the above code will not compile. The way to get around this is to create an **exception hierarchy**.

```
public class InvalidStreamException extends StreamException {
// fields and methods as needed
}
```

Now our client class can be written to deal with `InvalidStreamException` as needed.

### 10.3.3 Adding New Functionality to a Hierarchy

Replacing a class with a hierarchy can pose additional problems when new functionality has to be added. Consider the following situation: a client (or end user) wants to print a list of items in the library, with a specific format for each kind of `LoanableItem`. Such a feature is typically provided by asking the client to encapsulate the `print()` method(s) within an object, and invoking these methods with the `LoanableItem` as a parameter. In a situation where we have only one `Book` class, `Library` may accomplish this with a method like the one shown below.

```
public void processBooks(BookFormat format) {
  for (Iterator<Book> iterator = Catalog.instance().iterator();
                                           iterator.hasNext();) {
    Book book = iterator.next();
    format.print(book);
```

```
  }
}
```

BookFormat is the class that encapsulates the the print() method. We can generalize this to accept any operation by defining an interface and having the encapsulating object implement this interface. The interface could be as follows:

```
public interface BookOperation {
  public void apply(Book book);
}
```

The printing problem would then be solved as follows:

```
public class BookFormat implements BookOperation {
    ...
}
```

The method processBooks() would be rewritten as:

```
public void processBooks(BookOperation operation) {
  for (Iterator<Book> iterator = Catalog.instance().iterator();
                                          iterator.hasNext();) {
    Book book = iterator.next();
    operation.apply(book);
  }
}
```

Such a method could be provided as part of Library. The client wishing to print would define the BookFormat class to invoke it (through an interface) as:

```
   BookOperation bookOperation = new BookFormat();
   Library.instance().processBooks(bookOperation);
```

When we examine the above solution in the context of the LoanableItem hierarchy, it is found to be wanting. The method processBooks() works only if iterator.next() returns a Book object. If the catalog stores different types of LoanableItem objects, the code would be more like the following:

```
public void processBooks(BookOperation operation) {
  for (Iterator<LoanableItem> iterator = Catalog.instance().
                                     iterator();
                                       iterator.hasNext();) {
    LoanableItem loanableItem = iterator.next();
    if (loanableItem instanceof Book) {
       operation.apply((Book) loanableItem);
    }
  }
}
```

We determine the type of `LoanableItem` using RTTI, and if it is a `Book` object, call the `apply()` method. We could have a class, say, `LoanableItemOperation`, which has a separate method for processing objects of each subclass of `LoanableItem`. This would need a long conditional statement in `processBooks()`, which defeats the purpose of having a hierarchy.

Despite the above issue, the approach can be tweaked to obtain a much cleaner and therefore satisfactory solution. The solution is in the **Visitor** pattern. Visitor allows us define a new operation on all the types of objects within a structure, such that the operation can be performed without knowing the specific kind of object we are operating on.

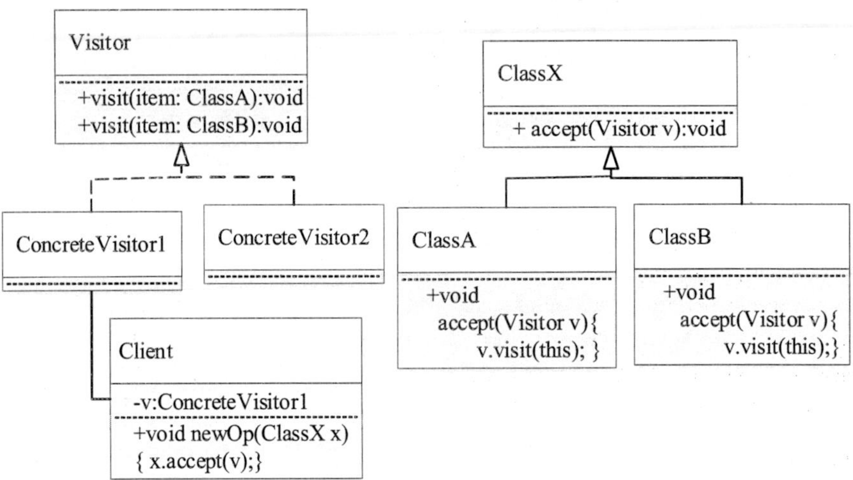


**Fig. 10.3** Class diagram for the Visitor pattern

### The Visitor pattern

The Visitor pattern allows us to define a new operation that has to be performed on the objects inside an existing object structure. It is a behavioral pattern, that is, it realizes a communication pattern between objects. The communication pattern in this case is a sequence of messages that realize *double dispatch*; if the language (or run-time environment) supports double dispatch, there is no need for this pattern.

The problem is as follows: We have an object structure that contains objects of two classes, `ClassA` and `ClassB`, both of which are subclasses of `ClassX`. A client would like to define a new operation to be performed on these objects. The operation has to be performed on a given object, without knowing its type. (Since we cannot add a new method to these classes, dynamic binding cannot be relied on.)

The class diagram in Figure 10.3 represents the solution. The object structure defines the `Visitor` interface with `visit()` methods for each class. The client defines the class `ConcreteVisitor1` that implements `Visitor`; the `visit()` methods implement the new operation desired by the client. Both `ClassA` and `ClassB` have a method `accept()` that (1) takes a `Visitor` object as parameter, and (2) invokes `visit()` on the `Visitor` object, passing `this` as a parameter. Thus the correct `visit()` method is invoked without the client knowing whether the object belongs to `ClassA` or `ClassB`. This control flow is captured in the sequence diagram in Figure 10.4.

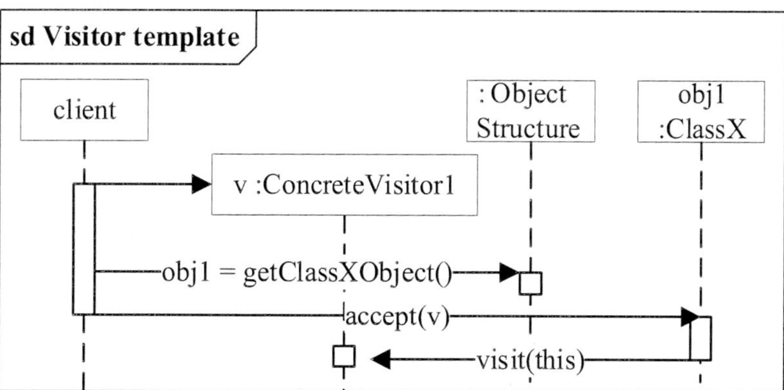


**Fig. 10.4** Sequence diagram for the Visitor pattern

To apply the Visitor pattern for such problems, we perform the following:

1. Define the interface that visitors must implement. This interface will contain a `visit()` method for each class on which the new operation has to be performed. In our example, we define `LoanableItemVisitor` as follows:

   ```
   public interface LoanableItemVisitor {
     public void visit(LoanableItem loanableItem);
     public void visit(Book book);
     public void visit(Periodical periodical);
   }
   ```

   The method `visit(LoanableItem)` can be used to handle any subclass of `LoanableItem` for which no operation is needed.
2. Add an `accept()` method to all the classes in the object structure. For our example, this method is as follows:

   ```
   public void accept(LoanableItemVisitor visitor) {
    visitor.visit(this);
   }
   ```

   This method will be a part of `LoanableItem`, `Book` and `Periodical`.
3. Define a class that implements the visitors' interface and performs the required operation. This class will contain all the `visit()` methods. These methods are invoked from the `accept()` methods in each of the classes. Our class, `PrintLoanableItem`, has `visit()` methods to print the required kinds of `LoanableItem`.

   ```
   class PrintLoanableItem implements LoanableItemVisitor {
     public void visit (Book book) {
       // code to print a book
     }
     public void visit (Periodical periodical) {
       // code to print a periodical
     }
     public void visit (LoanableItem item){
       System.out.println("Unspecified item");
     }
   }
   ```

   This is set up to treat anything other than `Book` and `Periodical` as "unspecified."
4. The object structure is set up to allow access to individual objects. This mechanism is used by the client to get references to the objects, without knowing exactly what kind of object it is dealing with. In our example, `Library` has a method `getLoanableItems()` that returns all the catalog items as an `Iterator`.
5. Write the code to apply any new operation. The client will contain the code that instantiates the visitor, gets references to the objects, and invokes the `accept()` method. For our example, we do the following:

```
public void printCatalogItems() {
  // instantiate visitor
  LoanableItemVisitor printer = new PrintLoanableItem();
  for (Iterator<LoanableItem> items = Library.instance().
   getLoanableItems();
                                        items.hasNext();) {
    LoanableItem item = items.next(); // get reference to
     object
    item.accept(printer); // the item will call visit()
  }
}
```

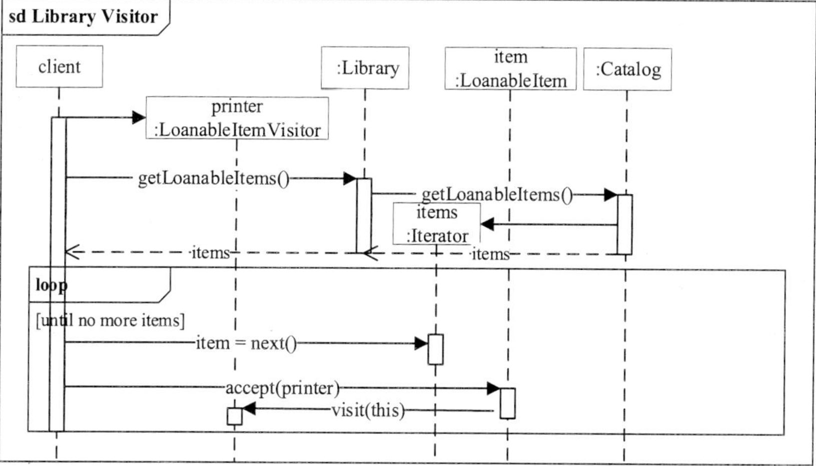


**Fig. 10.5** Visitor pattern applied for printing all the items in `Catalog`. `Library` provides a general method to apply a new operation to all loanable items; the client (which could be part of the UI) defines the specific methods for printing each kind of item.

The control flow for our example is captured in Figure 10.5. There are three issues that arise when we apply Visitor, which we address below.

### 10.3.3.1 Passing Parameters and Returning Results

The `accept()` method can be viewed as a general purpose method provided by a hierarchy to add new features. This makes the scope of the method very broad; however, this also means that we cannot pass any parameters through this method. Likewise the return type has to be something that can accommodate all possible uses; the way we do this is to have the return type as `void`.

From these choices, it appears that we have severely restricted what can be accomplished. If we had chosen `Object` to be passed as an additional parameter and returned an `Object`, one could argue that we would get a high degree of reusability. The downside to this approach is that we would add a lot of code to pack and unpack the objects involved. Fortunately, it turns out that there is a very simple way of sending additional data in and out. If we look at the sequence diagram, we see that the sequence of calls originates in the client object. This object has complete access to the `Visitor` object within which the `visit()` method resides. The code in the client class can place the necessary parameters in the `Visitor` object itself. Likewise any values that may be returned from the `visit()` method are needed only by the client object; these values can be placed in the `Visitor` object by the `visit()` method.

## 10.4 Transmitting Complex Properties Using Inheritance

So far we have addressed inheritance in situations where the subclass behavior is achieved by modifying or adding to the attributes and methods of the superclass. There are situations where we have properties that are not characterized in this simple way. Ensuring that these properties are correctly inherited can be a challenge. Fortunately, such situations are not common; we provide a couple of examples that illustrate the difficulties involved.

### 10.4.1 Creating a Singleton Hierarchy

The singleton property is maintained in a class through two attributes: a private constructor and a method to supply an instance. Ensuring that such a property is passed from a superclass to a subclass requires careful construction. The difficulty we face here is that we are dealing with a property of the entire class (that is, it has only one instance), and not just the properties of the individual objects.

In some applications, it is necessary to develop subclasses of a singleton class where the subclasses themselves are singletons. For an example of such a system, consider a distributed system with one or more server machines and many client sites. A server machine runs several server processes. In our example, we have exactly four processes:

- A general-purpose server that provides many services, including time, directory, file, replication, and name services. However, some of these services are somewhat primitive in nature.
- A directory server that provides sophisticated directory services.

- A file server that allows reading and updating of data.
- A file server that allows only reading; only new files can be written.

Since the general-purpose server already provides basic support for directory and file management, it seems reasonable to assume that the specialized classes for instantiating the directory and file servers are subclasses of the class for the general-purpose server. All of the classes are singletons.

For a second example, consider a large corporation with offices all around the globe. The corporate headquarters is located in, say, New York. Every country in which the corporation operates has its own separate national headquarters to control operations within that country. For instance, the company may operate in France and have its headquarters in Paris. A sample hierarchy is given in Figure 10.6.

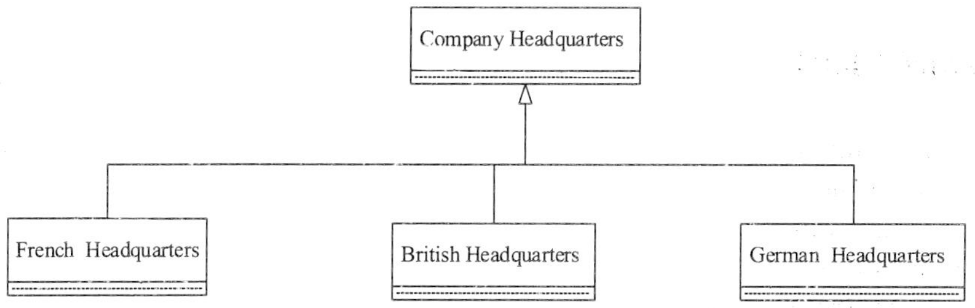


**Fig. 10.6** Singleton hierarchy

Let us further assume that the functionality of each of the national headquarters is quite similar to the functionality of the corporate headquarters. However, there are differences between the corporate headquarters and between the individual national headquarters (in matters such as labor and other laws, currency, etc.)

Thus, we implement the above system using a singleton class for the corporate headquarters and a separate singleton subclass for each of the national headquarters.

In general, the problem of interest in this context can be boiled down to the following: We need to implement two classes `B` and `D`, where `B` is the superclass of `D`, and both of the classes are singletons.
Suppose we attempt to implement `D` as below.

```
public class D extends B {
  private static D singleton;
  private D() {
  }
  public static D instance() {
    if (singleton == null) {
```

```
      singleton = new D();
    }
    return singleton;
  }
  // application code
}
```

This code has a problem. Since B has a private constructor, it is impossible for D to be instantiated. The constructor of D makes an implicit call to the no-argument constructor of the superclass, B, and the compiler blocks this because the superclass's constructor is private.

The solution developed below recognizes the fact that the instantiation of B has to be performed differently when we have a singleton heirarchy.

1. B is instantiated through the `instance` method. The class does not have any public constructors.
2. For D to be instantiated, it is necessary that some constructor of B be accessible from code within D. Since this constructor cannot be public, it follows that the constructor be `protected`. Therefore, we have

```
public class B {
  private static B singleton;
  protected B() {
  }
  public static B instance() {
    if (singleton == null) {
      singleton = new B();
    }
    return singleton;
  }
  // more application code
}
public class D extends B {
  private static D singleton;
  protected D() {
  }
  public static D instance() {
    if (singleton == null) {
      singleton = new D();
    }
    return singleton;
  }
  // more application code
}
```

3. The code has the flaw that within class D, it is possible to instantiate multiple instances of B, violating the fundamental property of a singleton class.
   Therefore, we must control the behavior when B's constructor is invoked from D. This can achieved by using the Java reflection mechanism, which, as we saw earlier, allows Java code to discover the properties and behaviors of an object at execution time. In particular, this mechanism allows, at run-time, the discovery of the name of the class to which an object belongs, the names of the supported interfaces, field names, methods, and constructors. Let C be a class and p be a reference created as below.

   ```
   C p = new C();
   ```

   Since the expression p.getClass().getName() returns "C", we can modify the class B as below.

   ```
   import java.lang.reflect.*;
   public class B {
     private static B singleton;
     protected B() throws Exception {
       if (getClass().getName().equals("B")) {
         throw new Exception();
       }
     }
     public static B instance() {
       if (singleton == null) {
         singleton = new B();
       }
       return singleton;
     }
     // more application code
   }
   ```

   Any attempt to instantiate B directly will now fail because the invocation will have to go through the protected method, which throws an exception whenever B is instantiated. Our solution requires that the constructor knows what kind of object is being created at execution time, calling for RTTI, which, in this case, is obtained through reflection. In this situation, the instanceof operator does not suffice; every instance of D is an instance of B and the resulting constructor would not allow the creation of any object whatsoever.
4. The above modification introduces the problem that instances of B cannot be created at all! (When the instance() method of B invokes the constructor, an exception is thrown.) This is corrected by introducing a private constructor. Since constructors must have differing signatures, we introduce an artificial parameter to this constructor. This step thus yields

```
import java.lang.reflect.*;
public class B {
  private static B singleton;
  protected B() throws Exception {
    if (getClass().getName().equals("B")) {
      throw new Exception();
    }
  }
  private B(int i) {
  }
  public static B instance() {
    if (singleton == null) {
      singleton = new B(1);
    }
    return singleton;
  }
  // more application code
}
```

The descendants of B use the protected constructor, but only to create instances of B that are embedded in instances of the descendants, which cannot be independently accessed. Only one explicitly constructed instance of B exists, which is done using the private constructor.

### 10.4.2 Inheriting the Property of Self-replication

In this section, we highlight a common protocol in object-oriented programming in the context of inheritance. While the reader has had occasions to see examples of this, the example used to demonstrate this is perhaps more illuminating than some others.

From time to time, situations arise that require replicating objects, a process known as **cloning**. As an example, suppose in a drawing program – like the one we studied earlier in the book – we wish to support copying and pasting shapes. Let us say the shape is a line with attributes including the two endpoints, color, and so on. The attributes would be fields such as the following:

```
private MyPoint point1;
private MyPoint point2;
private int color;
```

The semantics should be obvious. We assume MyPoint encapsulates the functionality of an endpoint of a line.

One approach to implementing the paste operation would be to make a copy of every bit of the line object in memory, with the copy of the bits representing the line pasted in the drawing.

Suppose the following is the pattern of bits representing the line object before copy and paste. The pattern is quite simplistic; integers in Java are 32 bits long and object references could be 32 or even 64 bits in length, but to get the central ideas across, we assume the color and the two endpoints take just 8 bits each. The sequence of bits with dashes are the references to the two endpoints and the color field.
We have

```
1001101110001110010000110000101010110000000
     ---------    ---------     ---------

     point1       color         point2
```

Recall that the two references `point1` and `point2` are addresses of some locations in memory storing the values of the endpoints. The color field stores the color value directly.

If we copy the entire object, the replicated version would be identical to the original.

```
1001101110001110010000110000101010110000000
     ---------    ---------     ---------

     point1       color         point2
```

Since the coordinates of the endpoints of the pasted version are different from those of the original line, suppose we modify the values stored in the target of the references, but not change the references themselves.

Since the original line and its copy (the pasted version) refer to the same objects storing the endpoints, both versions of the line coincide, which is not what we intended. Instead, it is fairly obvious that we should have new references in the copy.

So a simple copy of the bits is not always a satisfactory strategy for cloning, but it could be a fundamental feature that serves as the basis for something more useful. Pseudocode for simple cloning using bit-copy written in Java-like syntax would be along the following lines:

```
public Object clone() {
   Object target;
   for every bit b in this object {
      copy b to target;
   }
   return target;
}
```

The process of cloning could be thought of as a two-step process:

1. Perform a bit-by-bit copy of the entire object.

2. After Step (1) is completed, modify some or all of the mutable objects within the class as appropriate.

Creating a copy therefore requires some knowledge about the object being copied, and this knowledge is available only within the object being copied.

The `Object` class in Java has a method named `clone()`, which does a bit-by-bit copy of the object. To see how to implement the above two-step approach, consider the example below.

```
public class Shape implements Cloneable {
  private int color;

  public Shape(int color) {
    this.color = color;
  }
  @Override
  public Shape clone() {
    Shape shape = null;
    try {
      shape = (Shape) super.clone();
    } catch (CloneNotSupportedException cnse) {
      cnse.printStackTrace();
    } finally {
      return shape;
    }
  }
}
```

The code could be slightly misleading in the sense that one might suspect that `clone()` is a method in the `Cloneable` interface. Not so. The method `clone()` is defined in the `Object` class. `Cloneable` has no methods in it and a class implements it to announce to the `clone()` method in `Object` that that method may make the bit-by-bit copy.

The `clone()` method calls the superclass's (`Object`'s) `clone()` method, which does a bit-by-bit copy. Since the only field in the `Shape` class is of the primitive type `int`, there is no risk of sharing any references. Java ensures that the resulting type of the object created using the bit-by-bit copy is `Shape`. The superclass's `clone()` throws the exception `CloneNotSupportedException`, which is handled in the `try-catch` block.

This is the protocol we wish to emphasize. The superclass method (in this case, `clone()` in `Object`) does something fundamental and the override of that method in the subclass must call the superclass's implementation before proceeding. Programming manuals on some platforms may emphasize this in multiple contexts and violating the requirements could be flagged as a compilation error, or worse, perhaps result in untraceable bugs.

Now suppose we have two more classes: `MyPoint` to represent a point on a plane and `Line` to encapsulate a line. The classes with their `clone()` methods are shown below.

```
public class MyPoint implements Cloneable {
  private int x;
  private int y;

  public MyPoint(int x, int y) {
    super();
    this.x = x;
    this.y = y;
  }

  public MyPoint clone() {
    MyPoint myPoint = null;
    try {
      myPoint = (MyPoint) super.clone();
    } catch (CloneNotSupportedException cnse) {
      cnse.printStackTrace();
    } finally {
      return myPoint;
    }
  }
}

public class Line extends Shape {
  private MyPoint point1;
  private MyPoint point2;

  public Line(MyPoint point1, MyPoint point2, int color) {
    super(color);
    this.point1 = point1;
    this.point2 = point2;
  }

  public Line clone() {
    Line line = (Line) super.clone();
    line.point1 = point1.clone();
    line.point2 = point2.clone();
    return line;
  }

}
```

Notice the cloning of the two `MyPoint` objects in `Line`. After the `clone()` method of `Object` makes a bit-by-bit copy, the references to the two `MyPoint` objects are modified by cloning them.

## 10.5 Using LSP to Verify Substitutability*

Earlier in this chapter, we saw an example where objects of a seemingly naturally derived subclass were not substitutable for objects of the superclass. These problems occurred because the author of the subclass did not correctly anticipate all the ways in which a client class's methods might access and modify these objects. The original statement of LSP expressed this requirement as follows:

> If for each object $O_1$ of type $S$ there is an object $O_2$ of type $T$ such that for all programs $P$ defined in terms of $T$ the behavior of $P$ is unchanged when $O_1$ is substituted for $O_2$, then $S$ is a subtype of $T$.

The question then arises: Is it possible to anticipate all the behaviors of client classes? Fortunately, we do not need to address this question; instead, we look at how the behaviors of a subclass object and a superclass object compare, when a client invokes a superclass method.

Liskov and Wing [2] were able to get a handle on a set of rules that allow us to verify (or refute) substitutability of subclass objects. These rules capture three aspects of substitutability:

- Any invariant that holds for supertype objects should be respected by subtype objects.
- Any method that is redefined in the subtype must preserve the behavior of the corresponding supertype method.
- The subtype should preserve the history properties of the supertype.

The reader will note that there are terms like "preserve the behavior" that need clarification. Unfortunately, a complete explanation of these is beyond the scope of this text. In this section, we look at a few examples of how these rules are applied.

### 10.5.1 The Relationship between `Bag`, `Set`, and `Queue`

Let us take a look at three container classes, `Bag`, `Set`, and `Queue`. All of them provide methods similar to the following:

- `void add(Item item)`, which allows the specified item to be added to the container.

- `Object remove()`, which removes an arbitrary item from the container; returns `null` if the container is empty.
- `boolean isEmpty()`, which checks if the container has any items and returns true (false) if and only if the container is empty (not empty).
- `boolean belongsTo(item)`, which checks if the specified item is in the container and returns true (false) if and only if the item is (is not) in the container.

Let us assume that we can redefine them as needed; for instance, in `Queue`, the `add()` method would be refined to perform an `enqueue()` operation.

#### 10.5.1.1 `Bag` and `Set`

Earlier in the chapter, using a somewhat contrived example, we made the case that `Set` cannot substitute for `Bag`. This approach of guessing at possible situations where substitutability is violated is not very reliable. Using the formalization provided by the LSP, we can reach the same conclusion by examining the postconditions associated with two `add()` methods.

In `Bag`, we have: The number of items in the container equals one plus the number of items that existed before we called `add()`

In `Set`, we have: The number of items in the container equals one of the following:

(a) one plus the number of items that existed before we called `add()`, if `item` was not already present in the bag
(b) the number of items that existed before we called `add()`, if `item` was already present in the bag

Therefore, the postcondition of the subclass method does not always imply the postcondition of the superclass method, which is a violation of the LSP.

#### 10.5.1.2 `Bag` and `Queue`

We can say that "`Queue` is a bag in which `remove()` returns the least recently added item." Note that we do not have to worry about any details of the data structure or queue implementation, since all we need is to guarantee the FIFO property. However, the data structure will be different, since `remove()` has to ensure the FIFO property.

The `Bag` methods `add()`, `remove()`, `isEmpty()`, and `belongsTo()` will be redefined to work with the data structure chosen for `Queue`. The methods `enqueue()` and `dequeue()` invoke the modified `add()` and modified `remove()`, respectively. The only postcondition that changes is the one for `remove()`. The postcondition for `Bag` is:

- If the container is not empty, an arbitrary item is returned, and the number of items decreases by one.
- If the container is empty, a `null` pointer is returned.

The postcondition for `Queue` is:

- If the container is not empty, the least recently added item is returned, and the number of items decreases by one. If the container is empty, a `null` pointer is returned.

Since the postcondition of `remove()` for `Queue` implies the postcondition of `remove()` for `Bag`, this extension does not suffer from these issues and appears to be a valid extension. However, in order to complete this "proof," we also need to satisfy the **history constraint**, which prevents the subtype from going through state changes that cannot occur in the supertype. Addressing all the aspects of this is beyond our scope, but in our example, we are satisfying this constraint, since the only methods we add, `enqueue()` and `dequeue()`, invoke the modified `add ()` and modified `remove()`.

### 10.5.2 Generic Subclassing: Queue of String and Queue of Object

Similar arguments can be applied to decide substitutability when we have generic parameters. Although generally, it appears that inheritance is acceptable when we go from more general to more specific types, establishing that we have a true subtype is non-trivial.

#### 10.5.2.1 Queue of String Subclassing Queue of Object

As a justification, we can say that "A queue of `String` is a queue of `Object` in which we add strings only." Say, we have defined a class `QueueOfObject` and a class `QueueOfString` that extends `QueueOfObject`. Let us consider the following scenario:

```
public class Client1 {
    public void cm1(QueueOfObject queueOfObject) {
        Object object = new Object();
        queueOfObject.enqueue(object);
    }
}
```

Say that we try to replace a `QueueOfObject` instance with a `QueueOfString` instance, as follows:

```
    Client1 client1 = new Client1();
```

```
client1.cm1(new QueueOfString());
```

We can see that there is a problem with the invocation of `enqueue()`, since the `enqueue()` method in the `QueueOfString` instance expects a `String` object as a parameter. In the language of the LSP, we say that:

> The parameter in the subclass method must be a supertype of the parameter in the superclass method

What this requires of the code is that the subclass accept any parameter that the superclass method will accept.

#### 10.5.2.2 Queue of `Object` Subclassing Queue of `String`

Note that the essential objection to defining queue of `String` as a subclass of queue of `Object` arose from the fact that `Object` cannot be a subclass of `String`. To complete the discussion, it is therefore natural to ask: Can a queue of `Object` subclass a queue of `String`?. Say that the class `Client2` has a method `cm2` as shown below.

```
public class Client2 {
    public void cm2(QueueOfString queueOfString) {
        String s1 = queueOfString.dequeue();
    }
}
```

Consider the following code that invokes `cm2()`:

```
Client2 client2 = new Client2();
QueueOfObject queueOfObject = new QueueOfObject();
queueOfObject.enqueue(new Object());
client2.cm2(queueOfObject);
```

When the `dequeue()` method is invoked in `cm2()`, an object of type `Object` is returned, which may not conform to `String`. In the language of the LSP, we say that:

> The return type of the subclass method must be a subtype of the return type of the superclass method

What this implies is that the subclass method should not return an object whose class does not conform to the class of the object that the client is expecting.This implies that a queue of `Object` cannot subclass a queue of `String`.

### 10.5.3 Using Queue of `Object` in lieu of Queue of `String`

The result from the previous subsection suggests that a general purpose data structure (like a queue of objects) cannot be used in a situation where we want something more specific (like a queue of strings). It should be pointed out that such a conclusion is not warranted. Within a subsystem where all objects respect the requirement that only strings be added to the queue, it is completely safe to use a queue of objects. In a situation where type safety is important, one may employ a generic version of the class, or create an adapter.

The important thing to note is that we are not seeking substitutability in such a situation. The queue of objects is only used as a building block for implementing a queue of strings. Substitutability comes into the picture only when an existing object within a system has to be replaced by another one.

### 10.5.4 Why is a `Pixel` Object not a `SolidRectangle`?

Say that a package provides a class `SolidRectangle` that creates a solid (that is, all the pixels in the rectangle are filled), axis-parallel (or *isothetic*) rectangle. Each `SolidRectangle` object is defined by two points, which are the ends of one of the diagonals. A simple version of this class could look like this:

```
class SolidRectangle {
  private Point corner1;
  private Point corner2;
  public SolidRectangle(Point point1, Point point2) {
    corner1 = point1;
    corner2 = point2;
  }
  public void setCorner1(Point point) {
    corner1 = point;
  }
  public void setCorner2(Point point) {
    corner2 = point;
  }
  public Point getCorner1() {
    return corner1;
  }
  public Point getCorner2() {
    return corner2;
  }
}
```

In some situations, it could conceivably be convenient to have a separate class for dealing with an individual pixel, which is just a $1 \times 1$ rectangle. This suggests that we could simply extend `SolidRectangle`.

```
class Pixel extends SolidRectangle {
  public Pixel(Point point) {
    super(point, point);
  }
}
```

Note that the set of `Pixel` objects is just a subset of the `SolidRectangle` objects, with the restriction `corner1 = corner2`. Accordingly, the methods for setting these corners should be redefined in the subclass, so that this invariant property is preserved.

```
public void setCorner1(Point point) {
  super.setCorner1(point);
  super.setCorner2(point);
}
public void setCorner2(Point point) {
  super.setCorner1(point);
  super.setCorner2(point);
}
```

Consider the following method in a client class that takes as input parameter a `SolidRectangle` object:

```
public void clientMethod(SolidRectangle rectangle,
                                            Point point) {
  Triangle triangle1;
  //... some code
  rectangle.setCorner1(new Point(1, 1));
  rectangle.setCorner2(new Point(4, 4));
  float x = 1 / (distance(rectangle.getCorner1(), rectangle.
   getCorner2()));
  //... some code
}
```

This code was written by a client using `SolidRectangle`, but unaware of `Pixel`. Since the client has ensured that the two corners are set to two distinct points, the distance between them is not zero, and things will be fine. Now if this method is invoked and a reference to a `Pixel` object is passed as the actual parameter, both the corners will end up being assigned the same point, and the distance between them will be zero, leading to an exception.

In order to understand this in the context of the LSP, let us look at how the `Pixel` class was derived from `SolidRect`. The only change that we made was to redefine the `setCorner1()` and `setCorner2()` methods. In `SolidRectangle` these were:

```
  public void setCorner1(Point point) {
    corner1 = point;
  }
  public void setCorner2(Point point) {
    corner2 = point;
  }
```

In Pixel, we had to enforce the condition that corner1 is always equal to corner2. Accordingly, the methods were redefined as:

```
public void setCorner1(Point point) {
  super.setCorner1(point);
  super.setCorner2(point);
}
public void setCorner2(Point point) {
  super.setCorner1(point);
  super.setCorner2(point);
}
```

Clearly the setCorner1() and setCorner2() methods do not "preserve the behavior;" we need to understand how this anomaly can be detected. The second aspect of substitutability states that:

> Any method that is redefined in the subtype must preserve the behavior of the corresponding supertype method

One of the ways we characterize the behavior of a method is through the postcondition, and this relationship must conform to the following:

> The postcondition of the method in the superclass must be implied by the postcondition of the method in the subclass

The postcondition for setCorner1() in SolidRectangle is straightforward and can be informally stated as: The value of corner1 is set to the value of the parameter point.
Likewise, the postcondition for setCorner1() in pixel is: The value of corner1 and corner2 are set to the value of the parameter point.

At first glance, it appears that setting the values of corner1 and corner2 to point implies the condition that the value of corner1 is set to point. A more careful scrutiny tells us that our postcondition for SolidRectangle is incomplete; in all setter methods, the implicit postcondition is that the values of all other fields are left unchanged. With this stronger requirement, it is now clear that the postcondition of setCorner1() in SolidRectangle is not implied by the postcondition of the setCorner1() in Pixel when corner2 had a stored value that is different from the value passed through point.

### 10.5.5 LSP in Programming Languages

The syntactic aspect of the LSP, that is, what can be checked by a compiler, requires that:

- Return types of the subclass methods be subtypes of the return types of the overridden superclass methods, that is, *return types are covariant*
- Parameter types of the subclass methods be supertypes of the corresponding parameter types of the overridden superclass methods, that is, *parameter types are contravariant*

In the early versions of Java, the syntactic aspects of the LSP were enforced by checking that the return types and parameter types of the subclass were exactly the same as those of the superclass, that is, *invariant*. In Version 5, Java relaxed the rule for return types and allowed the return type of the subclass method to be any subtype (covariant) of the return type of the overridden superclass method. C++ required both return types and parameters to be invariant until 1998, when they started allowing covariance of return types. Scala and Sather are two examples of languages that support both covariance of return types and contravariance of parameter types. It should be noted that while contravariance of parameter types is needed for type safety, covariance of parameter types does provide more flexibility. Type safety can be ensured if we have an overloaded method in which at least one option is type safe.

## 10.6 Multiple Inheritance*

So far, we have seen situations where a class inherits from only one other class. The term **multiple inheritance** is used to describe the ability of a class to subclass multiple classes. Let us consider two examples:

- An amphibious vehicle can run on both land and water. It will, therefore, have properties of both an automobile and a boat. With classes `Automobile` and `Boat` available, we can create a class that subclasses both.
- A mobile home serves as a home, but could also be driven from location to location. Therefore, it has properties of both a home (it will have bedrooms, kitchen, etc.) and a car (the unit has an engine and can be driven like a car). If we have classes `Car` and `House`, then the class `MobileHome` can be constructed by utilizing the implementations of both of these existing classes.

Figure 10.7 illustrates these examples using UML diagrams.

In both these examples, the descendant inherits properties from both the ancestors. A `Mobilehome` inherits features such as `maximumSpeed` and `gasMileage` from `Car` and features like `totalLivingArea` and

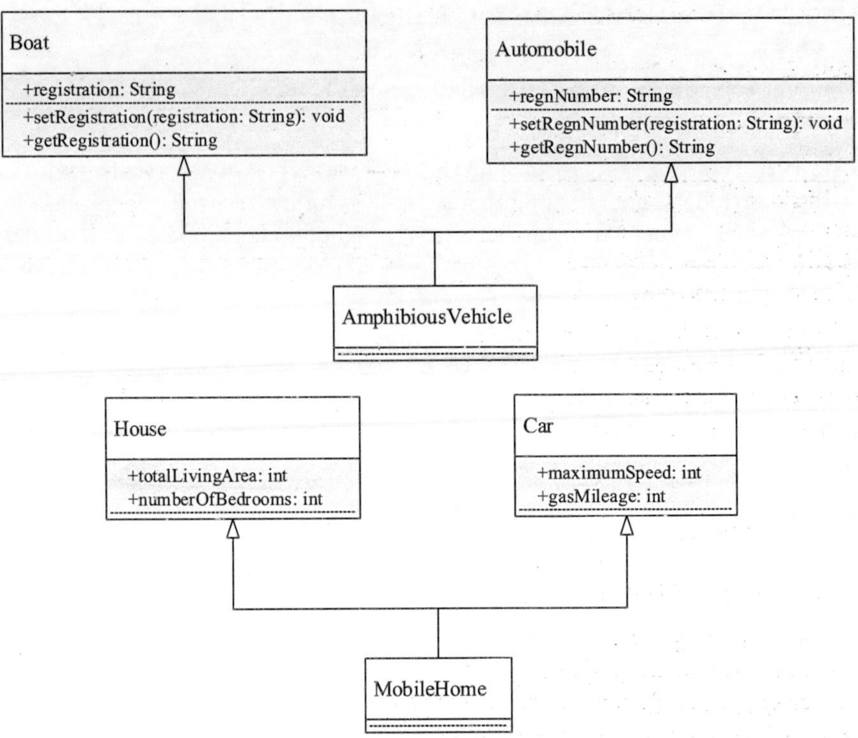


**Fig. 10.7** Examples of multiple inheritance

`numberOfBedrooms` from `House`. Programming languages typically allow for multiple inheritance by allowing a class to extend more than one class. This ability does pose some new challenges as we shall see later in this section.

Since the class `AmphibiousVehicle` extends `Automobile` and `Boat`, an instance of an `AmphibiousVehicle` can be viewed as containing both an instance of `Boat` and an instance of `Automobile` (Figure 10.8).

Consider the following code:[2]

```
public class Boat {
   private String registration;
   public Boat(String registration) {
     this.registration = registration;
   }
   public void setRegistration(String registration) {
     this.registration = registration;
```

[2] Since Java does not support multiple inheritance in this form, this code does not conform to Java syntax.

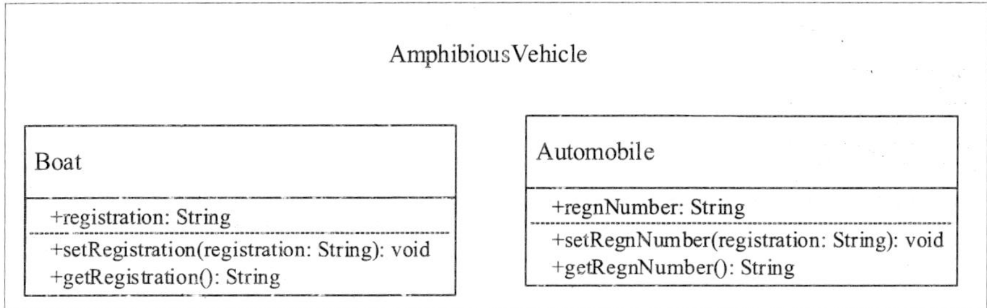


**Fig. 10.8** Conceptual view of `AmphibiousVehicle`

```
   }
   public String getRegistration() {
     return registration;
   }
}

public class Automobile {
   private String regnNumber;
   public Boat(String registration) {
      this.regnNumber = registration;
   }
   public void setRegnNumber(String registration) {
     this.regnNumber = registration;
   }
   public String getRegnNumber() {
     return regnNumber;
   }
}

public class AmphibiousVehicle extends Boat, Automobile {
   public AmphibiousVehicle(String registration) {
      Boat(registration);
      Automobile(registration);
   }
}
```

Both `Automobile` and `Boat` have a field to store the registration number and `AmphibiousVehicle` inherits the field from both these classes, as shown in Figure 10.8. Since these different names essentially capture the same attribute, we have some ambiguity. Consider the following situation:

```
Automobile automobile;
```

```
Boat boat;
AmphibiousVehicle amphibiousVehicle;
```

An `AmphibiousVehicle` object can be stored in an `Automobile` reference or a `Boat` reference.

```
amphibiousVehicle =  new AmphibiousVehicle("001");
automobile = amphibiousVehicle;
boat = amphibiousVehicle;
```

There appear to be several ways in which the registration number of this object can be accessed: `amphibiousVehicle.registration`, `amphibiousVehicle.regnNumber`, `automobile.regnNumber`, or `boat.registration`. This multiplicity of field names can make the code hard to read. In addition, we now have a possible polymorphic assignment of the kind:

```
boat = (Amphibiousvehicle) automobile;
```

This would not be possible under single inheritance, since `Car` and `Boat` belong to different hierarchies.

In creating such a hierarchy, it is therefore important to keep the semantics of the attributes in mind. The public methods present a more serious problem. Consider the code

```
amphibiousVehicle.setRegistration("xyz");
// some code
amphibiousVehicle.setRegnNumber("abc");
```

This results in the situation shown in Figure 10.9.

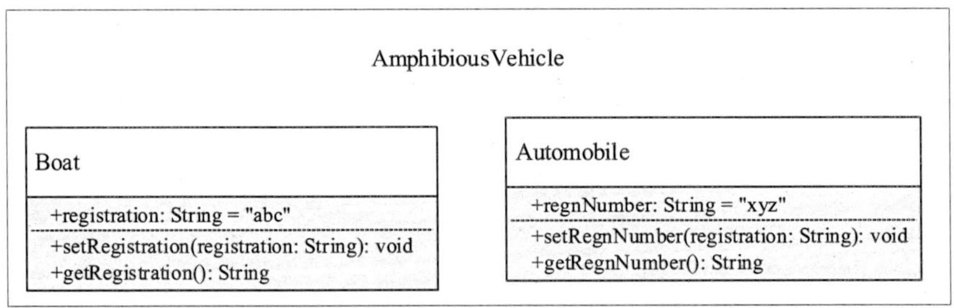


**Fig. 10.9** `AmphibiousVehicle` showing assignments

The entities `amphibiousVehicle.registration` and `amphibiousVehicle.regnNumber` will now contain different values, causing inconsistencies.

### 10.6.1 Mechanisms for Resolving Conflicts

Any language that provides a mechanism for multiple inheritance must also provide the means for resolving these conflicts. For the example above, let us assume that the designer chooses to store the registration of AmphibiousVehicle in the Automobile object, but would like to use the method names setRegistration and getRegistration. The methods setRegnNumber() and getRegnNumber() inherited from Automobile must now be "un-inherited" so that there is no ambiguity. One option is to declare the unwanted methods and fields as abstract in the descendant class. The class AmphibiousVehicle would now be something like this:[3]

```
public class AmphibiousVehicle extends Boat, Automobile {
  public AmphibiousVehicle(String string) {
    Automobile(string);
  }
  public abstract setRegnNumber(String string);
  public abstract getRegnNumber(String string);
  public void setRegistration(String string) {
    Automobile.setRegnNumber(string);
  }
  public String getRegistration() {
    return Automobile.getRegnNumber();
  }
}
```

Note that we are not explicitly invoking the constructor for Boat. The default constructor is invoked and consequently, there is no copy of the registration being stored in the Boat object. The methods setRegistration() and getRegistration() have been suitably redefined to access the fields of the Automobile object.

### 10.6.2 Repeated Inheritance

Since multiple inheritance could generate a hierarchy that is not a simple tree, we could end up with a situation where a descendant could be reached from an ancestor by following two different paths, giving rise to what is referred to as the "diamond of repeated inheritance" (Figure 10.10). Such a structure results when we have a class Vehicle which serves as an ancestor for both Automobile and Boat.

[3] We would like to remind the reader that the Java-like code we have given is not valid in the Java language.

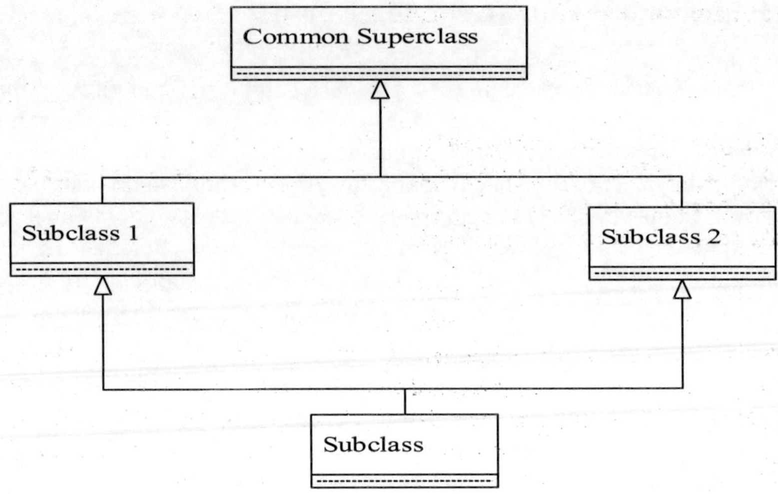


**Fig. 10.10** Diamond of repeated inheritance

```
public class Vehicle {
  private String registration;
  public Vehicle(String string) {
    registration = string;
  }
  public void setRegistration(String string) {
    registration = string;
  }
  public string getRegistration() {
    return registration;
  }
}

public class Automobile extends Vehicle {
  private int maximumSpeed;
  public Automobile(String string, int speed) {
    Vehicle(string);
    maximumSpeed = speed;
  }
}

public class Boat extends Vehicle {
  private int maximumKnots;
  public Boat(String string, int knots) {
    Vehicle(string);
```

```
    maximumKnots = knots;
  }
}

class AmphibiousVehicle extends Boat, Automobile {
  public AmphibiousVehicle(String string, int speed, int knots) {
    Boat(string, knots);
    Automobile(string, speed);
  }
}
```

This is a more serious problem than what we faced when a field was duplicated. The constructor for `AmphibiousVehicle` must invoke constructors `Automobile` and `Boat`, both of which invoke the constructor for `Vehicle`. As a result, we have a situation where there are two copies of `registration`. Note that the registration information is actually being stored in a private field of `Vehicle` and the only way to access it is through the methods of `Vehicle`. If the accessor or modifier of `AmphibiousVehicle` is invoked, it is not clear which copy is being modified. The author of `AmphibiousVehicle` has to be aware of these issues and should override these methods to ensure that both copies are updated.

When we are dealing with large hierarchies, it is not always possible for the author of the subclass (such as `AmphibiousVehicle`) to detect the problem. In such a situation, the programming language must ensure that the repeated ancestor is not created twice. C++, for instance, uses the following solution: The inheritance relationship between `Vehicle` and its immediate descendants should be declared as **virtual** (or "shareable"). This means that the space occupied by the two `Vehicle` objects must be shared and as a result the compiler flags an error when the constructor is invoked twice. The constructor in `AmphibiousVehicle` is then required to explicitly invoke all three constructors. In our "Java-like" syntax, the constructor for `AmphibiousVehicle` is as follows:

```
public AmphibiousVehicle(String string, int speed, int knots) {
  Vehicle(string);
  Boat(string, knots);
  Automobile(string, speed);
}
```

When the `Vehicle` constructor is invoked, a `Vehicle` object is created, and the same space is shared by the `Automobile` and `Boat` objects. Since only one copy of the `Vehicle` attributes is maintained, we have no inconsistency.

When the calls to constructors propagate up the hierarchy, calls to "virtual ancestors" are ignored. In our example, when the constructor for `Boat` (or `Automobile`) is invoked, the call to the `Vehicle` constructor is ignored because `Boat` (or `Automobile`) is defined a *virtual* descendant of `Vehicle` and the

Vehicle object has already been created. Since the inheritance hierarchy is statically determined, such an approach is feasible.
The above code suffers from two problems:

- It requires that AmphibiousVehicle be cognizant of the entire hierarchy. If that class's constructor misses any one of the superclass constructor calls and the corresponding class does not have a default constructor, the compiler flags an error.
  On the other hand, if any default constructors exist, the code may end up being buggy. For instance the code

  ```
  public AmphibiousVehicle(String string, int speed, int knots)
     {
      Boat(string, knots);
      Automobile(string, speed);
  }
  ```

  would not generate any compiler errors if Vehicle had a default constructor. In this situation, the registration field in Vehicle will be initialized to the default value instead of the specified parameter, string.
- This approach is not general enough since it cannot work in situations where there is an existing hierarchy and the inheritances are not virtual.

In the example with AmphibiousVehicle, we saw that repeated inheritance can cause a constructor to be invoked twice. We were able to resolve the consistency problem by redefining the methods and attributes. In situations where invoking the constructor has a more "visible" effect, however, this could pose a more serious problem.

Consider the following example where Window has two descendants: MenuWindow, which is a window with a menu, and BorderWindow, which is a window with a border. A fourth class, MenuAndBorderWindow, completes the diamond by inheriting from both MenuWindow and BorderWindow.

Consider a situation where we have a method display() for Window that displays the window. The display() method in BorderWindow first invokes the ancestor's display() method (which displays the window) and then invokes its own method that displays the border. Likewise, the display() method in MenuWindow first invokes the ancestor's display() method (which displays the window) and then invokes its own method that displays the menu. How should we deal with the display() method of MenuAndBorderWindow? If we invoke the display() methods of both the immediate superclasses, we end up in a situation where the window will be displayed twice. Even worse, when the window is drawn the second time in the sequence, it might clobber the border drawn by BorderWindow.

```
public class MenuAndBorderWindow extends MenuWindow,
 BorderWindow {
// fields and other methods not shown
```

```
  public void display() {
    MenuWindow.display();
    BorderWindow.display();
  }
}

public class MenuWindow extends Window {
// fields and other methods not shown
  public void display() {
    Window.display();
    // code for displaying menu goes here
  }
}

public class BorderWindow extends Window {
// fields and other methods not shown
  public void display() {
    Window.display();
    // code for displaying border goes here
  }
}
```

In general, there is no simple solution to such problems. The software designer has to be aware of these issues and exercise the necessary caution. The above problem, for instance, could be resolved by having `MenuAndBorderWindow` inherit from all three superclasses. Its `display` would then first invoke the method in `Window` and then invoke methods from `MenuWindow` and `BorderWindow` that display the menu and the border, respectively. (We are assuming here that we can invoke the methods for displaying these; this would be another example of a situation where the protected access mode would come in handy.)

```
public class MenuAndBorderWindow extends MenuWindow,
 BorderWindow, Window {
  // fields and other methods not shown
  public void display() {
    Window.display();
    BorderWindow.showBorder();
    MenuWindow.showMenu();
  }
}

public class MenuWindow extends Window {
  // fields and other methods not shown
  public void display() {
    Window.display();
```

```
    this.showMenu();
  }
  protected void showMenu() {
    // code for displaying the menu
  }
}

public class BorderWindow extends Window {
  // fields and other methods not shown
  public void display() {
    Window.display();
    this.showBorder();
  }
  protected void showBorder() {
    // code for displaying the border
  }
}
```

### 10.6.3 Multiple Inheritance in Java

Java does not support real multiple inheritance, in the sense that a class can inherit an implementation from one other class only. To deal with the situation where a class has to inherit attributes from more than one class, the only option is to create the class as a subclass of one of the classes and implement the rest. For example, assume that we would like to create a class `C` that ideally extends classes `C1` and `C2` that implement interfaces `I1` and `I2`, respectively. Then, the code for `C` would be

```
public class C extends C1 implements I1, I2 {
  // code
}
```

Since an interface can be viewed as a type, a class that extends another class and implements an interface can be viewed as a subtype of both the ancestor class and the interface. This gives the flavor of multiple inheritance to the language. In the above example, objects of type `C` are also of type `I2`.

## 10.7 Discussion and Further Reading

This chapter has explored some of the consequences of inheritance. Software systems are usually complex, and it is always a difficult task to characterize them completely. Inheritance poses an added challenge since it allows an existing system to change. Attempts have been made by researchers to define taxonomies to understand both the nature of inheritance and to identify changes in object-oriented systems [1, 3].

### 10.7.1 Relating Genericity and Inheritance

Both genericity and inheritance enable reuse; however, the mechanisms are very different. The example with `QueueOfString` and `QueueOfObject` highlights this very nicely. The two classes seem to be closely related, but neither of them subclasses the other. When we define a generic queue, what we are defining is really a template for a class; both `String` and `Object` can be used to complete the template. In UML diagrams, subclasses are typically represented at a lower level that the superclass; if we follow this convention, all different generic instantiations of a class are at the "same level," but each of them belongs to a different hierarchy. Thus `Queue` of `Object` is a subclass of `Bag` of `Object`and `Queue` of `String` is subclass of `Bag` of `String`. Figure 10.11 captures all these relationships.

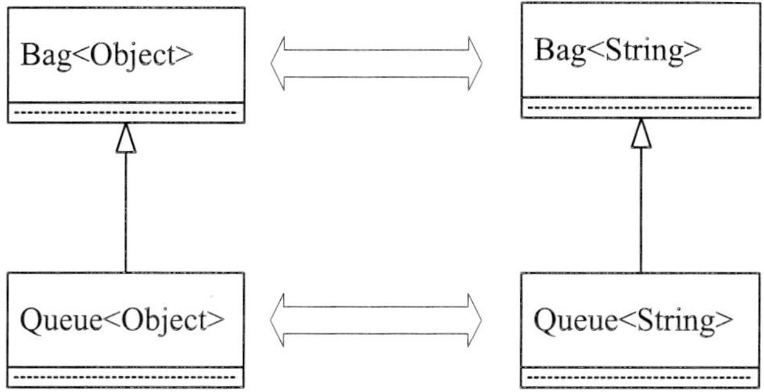


**Fig. 10.11** Relating genericity with subclassing

### 10.7.2 Using the Visitor Pattern

The Visitor pattern can be used for any general collection of objects, not necessarily constituting a hierarchy. All that we need is that there should be a matching signature for the class of every object in the collection. The `Object` class can be used as a "catch-all" to prevent run-time errors. Using this pattern increases the cost of execution due to the additional method call. That can be prevented if the language provided the feature of "double dispatch," that is, the parameter type and the concrete class are both matched when invoking dynamic binding. This feature was provided in Smalltalk, but has not found favor with other language designers due to the high cost of method calls.

### 10.7.3 Performance Issues for Single Versus Double Dispatch

An issue that is often raised with object-oriented systems is that of poor run-time performance. There are several reasons for this and solutions have been proposed, and it would be beyond the scope of this text to go into these in any detail. In the context of inheritance, however, we shall look into one of these issues: **the overhead caused by dynamic binding.**

When we subclass the conditional behavior by introducing an inheritance hierarchy, we rely on dynamic binding to ensure that the correct version of the method is called. This decision has to be made at run-time, as opposed to method calls whose target can be statically determined during compilation. Normally, with every variable in the system, some sort of type information will be stored. In an object-oriented system, due to polymorphism, the actual type of the object whose reference we store in the given variable can change dynamically. The standard way to implement dynamic binding is to have a table of method addresses for each class. Whenever a method is invoked on a variable, the type of object the variable refers to is looked up. The actual type of the reference is used to select the appropriate table and the method name is used to index the table to determine the address of the method to be invoked. Thus dynamic binding introduces a fixed amount of additional overhead for every method invocation. This overhead is usually a small percentage of the overhead associated with any method invocation and hence does not cause a serious degradation of performance. Providing double (or multiple) dispatch is expensive: we then have to choose the most appropriate method within the object, which involves examining the hierarchy. The Visitor pattern allows us to gain the benefits of double dispatch.

### 10.7.4 Ensuring the Safety of Reuse

The Liskov substitution principle is compact reminder of the most basic invariant an inheritance relationship must satisfy. The principle can be formulated succinctly [2] as follows:

Let $q(x)$ be a property provable about objects $x$ of type T. Then $q(y)$ should be true for objects $y$ of type S where S is a subtype of T.

Thus, Liskov and Wing's notion of "subtype" is based on the notion of substitutability; that is, if S is a subtype of T, then objects of type T in a program may be replaced with objects of type S without altering any of the desirable properties of that program. This definition can, in fact, be applied to a range of situations to validate or disprove substitutatbility

As an example of another, perhaps more surprising, example of LSP violation, the reader should look at Exercise 5. To fix the bugs created by LSP violations, the only option we have is to check every piece of client code and put in conditionals that employ run-time type identification. This is clearly not feasible. LSP violations are effective reminders of two of the design principles introduced in this chapter, namely, favor composition over inheritance and depend upon abstractions. If the class `Pixel` had been implemented by *adapting* `SolidRectangle`, we would not face any problem with client methods. Our implementation also violates the dependency rule, since `SolidRectangle` is a concrete implementation.

## Projects

1. Implement the classes `Account`, `CheckingAccount`, and `SavingsAccount` as shown in Figure 10.1.
2. Consider the classes `DataStream` and `ReReadableDataStream` depicted in Figure 10.2. Show how to implement the two classes. Remember that `ReReadableDataStream` must work regardless of the source from which `DataStream` reads.
3. Implement the `Cloneable` interface for the `Book`, `Member`, and `Hold` classes without having to set any fields to the `null` value.

## Exercises

1. Extend the `LoanableItem` hierarchy to create new classes for CDs, DVDs, and books on tape. CDs and DVDs have several common characteristics. Would it be appropriate for these two classes to inherit from a common superclass? Why?
2. As mentioned in the chapter, a subclass method that overrides a method of a superclass may throw subclasses of exceptions that are thrown by the superclass method, but it cannot throw exceptions that are not thrown by the overridden method. Why?
3. A university registration system has a class `Student` that tracks student information. When a student's GPA falls below a certain level, he/she is placed on academic probation. Would you model this by creating a subclass `WeakStudent` that extends `Student`?

4. Keeping in mind that a circle is a special kind of ellipse in which the two foci coincide, create a scenario in which an LSP violation can occur when a class `Ellipse` is extended to define `Circle`.
5. Consider the following classes and explain whether LSP is violated.

```
class Rectangle {
  private int width;
  private int height;
  public Rectangle(int width, int height) {
    this.width = width;
    this.height = height;
  }
  public void setHeight(int height) {
    this.height = height;
  }
  public void setWidth(int width) {
    this.width = width;
  }
  public int getHeight() {
    return height;
  }
  public int getWidth() {
    return width;
  }
}
public class Square extends Rectangle {
  public Square(int side) {
    super(side, side);
  }
  public void setWidth(int side) {
    super.setWidth(side);
    super.setHeight(side);
  }
  public void setHeight(int side) {
    super.setWidth(side);
    super.setHeight(side);
  }
  }
}
```

6. Consider the possibility of defining `Bag` as a subclass of `Set`.

   (a) We explore this possibility by first defining an "is-a" relationship between `Bag` and `Set`. Write a sentence that establishes such a relationship.

(b) Consider the `remove()` method. `Set` specifies the item to be removed, whereas `Bag` also allows for removing an arbitrary item. Does this difference hurt substitutability?
(c) What would be a suitable postcondition for the `remove(item)` method in `Set`?
(d) What would be a suitable postcondition for the `remove(item)` method in `Bag`?
(e) Consider the `add()` method. What would be suitable postconditions for this method in `Set` and `Bag`? Does this conflict in any way with LSP?
(f) Construct a scenario in a client method where substituting `Bag` for `Set` creates a problem.

7. Consider classes `Bag` and `Stack`. Can `Stack` be subclass of `Bag`? Defend your answer, following the examples discussed in the chapter.
8. (Discussion) Can we define `Bag` as a subclass of `Queue` or `Stack`?
9. Can a stack of `String` subclass a stack of `Object`, or vice-versa? Explain.
10. The DigUs mobile service provider has some custom software that deals with many different types of events. They use a proprietary method of prioritizing the events, and a special class called `DigUsQ` is used to store and dispatch them. All the event classes are subtypes of the `DigUsEvent` class. To reuse the prioritzing software, someone suggests creating a `QofDigEvent` class and defining queues for all kinds of events by extending this class. What do you think of this? What alternative can you propose?
11. (Case studies) Examine the projects presented at the end of Chapter 4 and identify possible situations where we could get variability in the behavior of an object. Which variabilities will you model using inheritance? Defend your choices based on object-oriented design principles.

## References


1. Girod, X. 1991. Conception par objects - *MECANO: une methode et un environnement de construction d'application par objects.* PhD thesis, Joseph Fourier University, Grenoble, France.
2. Liskov, BH and Wing, JM. 2001. Behavioural Subtyping using Invariants and Constraints. *Formal Methods for Distributed Processing: A Survey of Object-oriented Approaches,* 254–280 pp.
3. Clarke, BMP and Gibson, P. 2003. Using a Taxonomy Tool to Identify Changes in Object-oriented Software. In: *The 7th European Conference on Software Maintenance and Reengineering,* Benevento, Italy, March 26–28, 2003.
4. Vleck, TV. 2016. *Interview with Barbara Liskov, ACM Turing Award Recipient 2008,* last accessed May 7, 2024. https://amturing.acm.org/pdf/LiskovTuringTranscript.pdf.

# Appendix: Java Essentials

## A.1 Language Basics

Although Java is an object-oriented language, one could broadly divide its features into two parts:

- The non-object-oriented features.
- The object-oriented features.

However, object-orientedness is built into the language such that it is quite difficult to completely avoid the term "object" while discussing even simple programs. However, such discussion can be kept to a minimum.

We do not plan to cover every aspect of the Java language; just the features needed to understand the discussions in the book. We also do not propose to do a formal presentation of the syntax.

## A.2 A Simple Java Program

Here is the standard example of a Hello World program.

```
public class HelloWorld {
  public static void main(String[] args) {
       System.out.println("Hello, World!");
    }
  }
```

### Compilation and Execution

You can type this in any text editor. The program *must* be stored in a file named `HelloWorld.java`. It is compiled by typing

```
javac HelloWorld.java
```

As you might have guessed, `javac` is the Java compiler. The compiler reads `HelloWorld.java` and creates a file called `HelloWorld.class`.

The `HelloWorld.class` file contains what are called byte codes. Normally, compilers convert a high-level language program into a machine language program suitable for execution by the native hardware. In the case of Java, though, the byte codes in the compiler output are instructions for the Java Virtual Machine (JVM), not for the hardware. Java programs run on the JVM and not directly on the hardware.

To execute the program, type

```
java HelloWorld
```

The program prints the single line

```
Hello, World!
```

### Anatomy of the Program

It is not hard to guess that the message `Hello, World!` is printed by the line

```
System.out.println("Hello, World!");
```

in the program.

It is virtually impossible to write any interesting Java program without using classes and objects. So we need a basic understanding of what they are.

Objects are structures that usually relate to some real-life entity. Examples of objects in a program could be a library book, a room in a hotel, or an airline reservation. Objects are created using classes. Thus, we could have classes such as the following

- A class, say, Book, that can be used to create instances of books.
- A class called Room using which we can create all of the rooms in a certain hotel.
- A class for representing the reservation held by a passenger in a certain flight.

Java has an extensive collection of constructs for defining classes. We cover most of those issues in the main part of the book.

The first line

```
public class HelloWorld {
```

declares a class called `HelloWorld`. Class names, like other identifiers, can begin with uppercase letters, the currency symbol, or the underscore. Succeeding characters can be any of these or digits.

The word `public` means that the class is accessible from anywhere in the file system. We will discuss this aspect elsewhere in the book. The left curly bracket essentially begins the description of the class.

Every Java program will contain at least one class. Typically, you will put the code for each class in a separate file. Java requires that the file be named `<class_name>.java`. If you put more than one class in the same file, at most one of these classes can be designated `public`, and the file must be named using that class. If no class is public, pick any one of the class names for naming your file.

Let us proceed to examine the other lines. Consider the second line

```
  public static void main(String[] args) {
```

This defines a method named `main`, which begins the execution of any Java application. Java requires that this method be preceded by the words `public`, `static`, and `void`. The word `void` indicates that the method returns nothing. `static` means that the method can be invoked without any objects.

Methods can accept parameters just as functions and procedures do. `main` accepts any number of `String` arguments when the program is invoked. These are collected into an array of `String` objects and passed to the program: `String` is a class supported by the Java language itself and one that we will use throughout the book.

In our example, the program does not expect any parameters.

The left-curly bracket begins the details of the method, which has just one statement:

```
System.out.println("Hello, World!");
```

Let us examine each part of this statement.

`System` is a class known to the Java language. Among other things, the `System` class captures and supplies an assorted set of features for performing standard input and standard output, and querying system properties and environment variables. `out` is an object that represents the standard output (console). `System.out` is the syntax for accessing the `out` object that is kept track of by the `System` class.

`println` is another example of a method. In object-oriented languages, methods are usually associated with objects. In this case, `println` is a method that can be executed by the object `System.out`.

The method `println` accepts one parameter, which should be a `String`; that is, something between double quotes. The method causes that string to be printed on the standard output.

Finally, the semi-colon terminates the statement.

The first right-curly bracket ends the method and the last right-curly bracket ends the class.

### Comments

There are three types of comments in Java programs. Two forward slashes (//) make everything till the end of line comments. /* begins a comment that ends with a */; such comments may span multiple lines. Multiple line comments may also begin with /** and end with */; files containing such comments may be processed using the `javadoc` utility to produce HTML documentation.

## A.3 Primitive Data Types

Java supports eight *primitive data types* using which we can define variables to denote numbers, characters, and logical values. These types are: int, long, float, double, char, boolean, short, and byte. Among these byte, short, int, and long are numeric types supporting negative and non-negative integers. Float and long are used for floating point numbers.

The length of the corresponding variables are given below:

| **Type** | **Size** |
|---|---|
| byte | 1 |
| short | 2 |
| int | 4 |
| long | 8 |
| float | 4 |
| double | 4 |

Variables are defined by first specifying the type and then a list of variable names. The definition must be terminated by a semi-colon. Although more than one variable may be defined in single declaration, the usual style is to define only one.

Variable names may begin with the currency symbol, an alphabetic character, or the underscore. These and digits may appear in succeeding positions.

We now show examples of defining variables and assigning values.

```
int numberOfClasses;
numberOfClasses = 4;
System.out.println("I am taking " + numberOfClasses
                                        + " classes");
```

In the above, "+" concatenates the arguments after converting them to `String` objects.
Variables may be initialized as they are defined:

```
double balance = 750.00;
double deposit = 200.00;
double $cost = 8.5;
System.out.print("Initial balance " + balance + " Deposit "
                                        + deposit);
```

Character constants begin and end with single quotes.

```
char stop = 's';
char _delimiter = ':';
```

Like many other languages, Java uses the operators +, -, *, and / with their usual meanings. The operator % is used for finding the remainder after division. As in most other languages, multiplication and division have precedence over addition and subtraction. The mod operator has the same precedence as multiplication and division.

```
double balance = balance + deposit;
System.out.println(" New balance " + balance);

double income;
double taxRate;
double tax;
double netIncome;

income = 30000.00;
taxRate = 0.15;
tax = (income - 15000.0) * taxRate;
netIncome = income - tax;

int numberOfCookies = 36;
int numberOfChildren = 8;
int cookiesPerChild;
int cookiesLeftover;
cookiesPerChild = numberOfCookies / numberOfChildren;
cookiesLeftover = numberOfCookies % numberOfChildren;
```

Booleans are used for logical operations. These variables can take one of two values: `true` or `false`.

```
boolean succeeded = true;
```

## A.4 Relational Operators

Java uses the following operators for comparing variables of primitive types. (Only equality and inequality testing is applicable to boolean variables.)

== equals
!= not equal to
> greater than
< less than
>= greater than or equal to
<= less than or equal to

### Strings

We create a `String` object by writing code:

```
String errorMessage = "could not find the file";
```

In the above, `errorMessage` is a variable that refers to a `String` object, which contains the character sequence enclosed between double quotes.

Objects respond to methods, which are like functions and procedures in other languages. For example, the above `String` object can be used to print the number of characters stored in it.

```
System.out.println(errorMessage.length());
```

We are invoking the method `length()` on the object `errorMessage`. It should return 23.

In general, a method is invoked as shown below:

```
<object_reference>.method_name(parameters);
```

Incidentally, objects of type `String` respond to a large collection of methods including the following:

`indexof(char c)` - returns the first location of the character `c` in a string
`charAt(int index)` - what is the character at the given (0-relative) index?

## A.5 A Note on Input and Output

Inputting numeric values through the keyboard has been a problem in Java. We need to read a string and extract a number from it. One way of inputting data is through a graphical user interface (GUI). A class called `JOptionPane` has a method named `showInputDialog`, which can be used for accepting a string. The string can then be parsed to retrieve the proper value.

```
String response;
response = JOptionPane.showInputDialog("Enter a number");
int num = Integer.parseInt(response);
```

The code opens up a dialog box for entering a string. After inputting the data, the user can click "O.K." The string is stored in response, which is parsed by the code

```
Integer.parseInt(response);
```

It returns the integer value stored in the string. (If the string does not have an integer in it, it would cause an "exception.")

Messages can also be displayed in a window using the method `showMessageDialog` in `JOptionPane`. The format is

```
JOptionPane.showMessageDialog(null, message-as-a-string);
```

## A.6 Selection Statements

Java supports `if-else` statements and `switch` statements. Both allow nesting.

The syntax of the `if-else` statement is

```
if <condition>
   <statement>
[else
    <statement>]
```

The `else` part is optional.

Here is a program that accepts the age of a person and prints out whether the person is eligible to vote.

```
import javax.swing.*;
public class VoteEligibility {
  public static void main(String[] s) {
```

```
    int age;
    age = Integer.parseInt(JOptionPane.showInputDialog(
                                 "Please enter your age"));
    if (age >= 18) {
      JOptionPane.showMessageDialog(null, "you are eligible to
                                                         vote");
    } else {
      JOptionPane.showMessageDialog(null, "wait " + (18 - age) +
                                                     " years!");
    }
    System.exit(0);
  }
}
```

The next example selects people younger than 20 and all females over 30.

```
selected = false;
if (age < 20) {
    selected = true;
} else if (age > 30) {
  gender =  JOptionPane.showInputDialog("Enter gender: ").
                                                  charAt(0);
  if (gender == 'f' || gender == 'F') {
    selected = true;
  }
}
```

The logical operators are

| | |
|---|---|
| `&&` | logical and |
| `\|\|` | logical or |
| `!` | logical not |

The `switch` statement allows us to handle the situation when there are numerous cases. Here is an example.

```
int month = Integer.parseInt(JOptionPane.showInputDialog(null,
                             "Enter month 1-12"));
switch (month) {
    case 1:     JOptionPane.showMessageDialog(null, "January");
                break;
    case 2:     JOptionPane.showMessageDialog(null, "February");
                break;
    case 3:     JOptionPane.showMessageDialog(null, "March");
                break;
```

```
        case 4:     JOptionPane.showMessageDialog(null, "April");
                    break;
        case 5:     JOptionPane.showMessageDialog(null, "May");
                    break;
        case 6:     JOptionPane.showMessageDialog(null, "June");
                    break;
        case 7:     JOptionPane.showMessageDialog(null, "July");
                    break;
        case 8:     JOptionPane.showMessageDialog(null, "August");
                    break;
        case 9:     JOptionPane.showMessageDialog(null, "September");
                    break;
        case 10:    JOptionPane.showMessageDialog(null, "October");
                    break;
        case 11:    JOptionPane.showMessageDialog(null, "November");
                    break;
        case 12:    JOptionPane.showMessageDialog(null, "December");
                    break;
}
```

## A.7 Loops

Java, like C and C++, allows three types of loops: `for`, `while`, and `do`.

The `while` loop has a simple syntax.

```
while (condition)
   statement;
```

The statement is executed as long as the condition is true. Before each iteration, the condition is checked. If it is true, the loop is executed once and the condition is checked once again and the process repeats until the condition is false.

Here are some examples of the use of the `while` loop.

```
int number = 10;
while (number <= 25) {
   System.out.println(number);
   number++;
}
```

The second example is a program that reads in a string, counts the number of vowels, and prints each occurrence. The `charAt` method returns the character at the given position (zero-relative) in the string. The method indexOf checks whether a given character appears in a string.

```
import javax.swing.*;
public class CountVowelsWhile {
 public static void main(String[] s) {
  String vowels = "aeiou";
  String string = JOptionPane.showInputDialog("Enter a string");
  int counter = 0;
  int position = 0;
  while (position < string.length()) {
    if (vowels.indexOf(string.charAt(position)) >= 0) {
       counter++;
       System.out.println(string.charAt(position));
  }
       position++;
   }
   System.out.println("There are " + counter + " occurrences of
                                       vowels in " + string);
   System.exit(0);
 }
}
```

The for loop has the following syntax:

```
for (expression1; condition; expression2)
     statement;
```

The code works as follows:

1. Evaluate expression1.
2. Evaluate condition.
3. If the evaluation in (2) returns true, enter the loop and execute the statement, which can be a block. Otherwise, exit the loop.
4. Evaluate expression 2.
5. Go to (2) above.

Here are examples of the use of for loops.

We solve the problems given for while using the for loop. The first example prints all integers from 10 to 25. The code first creates an int variable number and initializes it to 10. It then checks whether number is less than or equal to 25. Since it is not, it enters the loop and prints the current value of number, which is 10. It then increments number by 1 and checks again whether number is less than or equal to 25. The loop continues this way until number is 26 at which time the loop is exited.

```
for (int number = 10; number <= 25; number++) {
    System.out.println(number);
}
```

The program that reads in a string, counts the number of vowels, and prints each occurrence is given below using the `for` loop.

```
import javax.swing.*;
public class CountVowels {
 public static void main(String[] s) {
  String vowels = "aeiou";
  String string = JOptionPane.showInputDialog("Enter a string");
  int counter = 0;
  for (int position = 0; position < string.length();
                                                position++) {
      if (vowels.indexOf(string.charAt(position)) >= 0) {
         counter++;
         System.out.println(string.charAt(position));
     }
   }
   System.out.println("There are " + counter + " occurrences of
                                        vowels in " + string);
   System.exit(0);
  }
}
```

A program that uses both `while` and `for` loops to examine a sequence of strings to check if they are palindromes is given below.

```
import javax.swing.*;
public class Palindrome {
 public static void main(String[] s) {
  String input;
  boolean endOfInput = false;
  while (!endOfInput) {
    input = JOptionPane.showInputDialog(null, "Enter a string");
    if (input.length() == 0) {
       endOfInput = true;
    } else {
       boolean isAPalindrome = true;
       for (int left = 0, right = input.length() - 1; left
                                    < right; left++, right--) {
           if (input.charAt(left) != input.charAt(right)) {
              isAPalindrome = false;
```

```
                }
            }
            if (isAPalindrome) {
                JOptionPane.showMessageDialog(null, input
                                              + " is a palindrome");
            } else {
                JOptionPane.showMessageDialog(null, input
                                              + " is not a palindrome");
            }
        }
    }
    System.exit(0);
  }
}
```

The do loop executes at least once. At the end of the first and succeeding iterations, a condition is checked. If the condition is true, the next iteration is performed. The syntax is

```
do
   statement
while (condition);
```

The following example makes the user enter "Yes", "No", or "cancel" (case-insensitive).

```
String response;
do {
  response = JOptionPane.showInputDialog("Enter yes, no, or
                                                     cancel");
} while (! response.equalsIgnoreCase("yes")
    && ! response.equalsIgnoreCase("no")
    && ! response.equalsIgnoreCase("cancel"));
```

## A.8 Methods

Method are like functions in C. They are always enclosed within a class declaration. A method must return a `void` or a known type. Methods may accept any number of parameters. Each formal argument must be written with the type name followed by the parameter name. Parameters must be separated by a comma.

Parameters are passed by value. Changes to the parameters in the callee do not affect the original. In the following example, although the values of `c` and `d` are swapped, the values in the actual parameters are unchanged.

```
void swap(int c, int d) {
  int temp = c;
  c = d;
  d = temp;
}
...
int a = 1;
int b = 2;
swap(a, b);
```

## A.9 Arrays

Java supports the creation of arrays of any number of dimensions. The process of creating an array can be thought of as consisting of two steps:

1. Declare a variable that refers to the array. This is not the array itself, but eventually contains the address of the array, which has to be dynamically allocated.
2. Allocate the array itself and make the variable declared in (1) above to point to this array.

The following code creates a variable that can serve as a reference to an array of integers.

```
int[] a;
```

An array of five integers is created during execution by the following code.

```
new int[5];
```

The new operator returns the address of the array; this is termed the reference in Java. We make a hold the reference to the array by writing

```
a = new int[5];
```

The first cell of the array is indexed by 0. If the array has n elements, the last cell is indexed n - 1.

Array cells are referred by the notation a[index]. The following code stores 1 in a[0], 2 in a[1], etc. and then prints these values.

```
for (int index = 0; index < 5; index++) {
    a[index] = index + 1;
}
for (int index = 0; index < 5; index++) {
    System.out.println(a[index]);
```

```
}
```

The following program reads in a sequence of numbers and prints them in reverse. The number of numbers is the first number read in. An array large enough to hold the sequence is then allocated.

```
import javax.swing.*;
public class PrintInReverse {
  public static void main(String[] s) {
    int[] numbers;
    int numberOfNumbers = Integer.parseInt(
              JOptionPane.showInputDialog("Enter max. number of
               numbers"));
    numbers = new int[numberOfNumbers];
    boolean lookForAnotherNumber = true;
    int count = 0;
    while (lookForAnotherNumber) {
      if (count >= numbers.length) {
        lookForAnotherNumber = false;
      } else {
        String string = JOptionPane.showInputDialog("Enter a
         number");
        if (string.length() == 0) {
          lookForAnotherNumber = false;
        } else {
          int number = Integer.parseInt(string);
          numbers[count++] = number;
        }
      }
    }
    for (int index = count - 1; index >= 0; index--) {
      System.out.println(numbers[index]);
    }
    System.exit(0);
  }
}
```

### Multi-dimensional Arrays

Let us look at an example of creating multi-dimensional arrays, which will suggest how to allocate arrays of higher dimension.

```
double [][] prices;
prices = new double[5][10];
prices[2][4] = 76.5;
```

# Index